ART,
ALIENATION,
and the
HUMANITIES

SUNY series in the Philosophy
of the Social Sciences
Lenore Langsdorf, editor

and

SUNY series, The Philosophy of Education
Philip L. Smith, editor

ART, ALIENATION, and the HUMANITIES

A Critical Engagement with Herbert Marcuse

Charles Reitz

State University of New York Press

Published by
State University of New York Press, Albany

© 2000 State University of New York

Printed in the United States of America

For information, address State University of New York
Press, State University Plaza, Albany, N.Y., 12246

Production by Diane Ganeles
Marketing by Fran Keneston

Library of Congress Cataloging-in-Publication Data

Reitz, Charles.
    Art, alienation, and the humanities: a critical engagement with
  Herbert Marcuse / Charles Reitz.
        p.   cm. — (SUNY series in the philosophy of the social
  sciences)   (SUNY series, the philosophy of education)
      Includes bibliographical references (p.   ) and index.
      ISBN 0-7914-4461-9 (HC: acid-free paper). — ISBN 0-7914-4462-7
  (PB: acid-free paper)
      1. Marcuse, Herbert, 1898—Aesthetics.   2. Education—Philosophy.
  I. Title.   II. Series: SUNY series in philosophy of social sciences.   III. Series:
  SUNY series in philosophy of education.
  B945.M2984R45   2000
  111'.85'092—dc21   99-38495
                                                                        CIP

10 9 8 7 6 5 4 3 2 1

To talk about education is to talk about politics;
to criticize education is to criticize society.

—Michael L. Simmons Jr.,
to whom this volume is respectfully dedicated.

Contents

Acknowledgments

This book has benefited immensely from the critical commentary on earlier drafts by Douglas Kellner, James Lawler, David Brodsky, Patricia Pollock Brodsky, Morteza Ardebili, Stephen Spartan, and an anonymous SUNY Press reviewer. I sincerely thank each of them for their intellectual interest and for their scholarly efforts to strengthen this publication. SUNY Press editor Jane Bunker has been extremely helpful in every area of the development of this project. I am also particularly appreciative of the efforts of Lenore Langsdorf, Philip L. Smith, Marilyn Silverman, Diane Ganeles, Fran Keneston, and William Eastman. Special thanks to Peter Marcuse for permission to publish excerpts from his father's unpublished papers. Jochen Stollberg of the Frankfurt Marcuse Archive was extraordinarily hospitable during my visits and was a key facilitator of my research into original documents. Guenter Kroll and Gertrud Marx were likewise instrumental in Frankfurt.

Special acknowledgment and thanks must also be extended to the Board of Trustees and the Faculty Association of Kansas City Kansas Community College for the sabbatical semester that supported a key segment of the manuscript revision process.

I also owe long-standing debts of gratitude to the following individuals who have cared for this project and assisted materially in its development: Michael L. Simmons Jr., Jane Cullen, Georg G. Iggers, Roger Woock, Gene Grabiner, Virginia Enquist Grabiner, Stefan Morawski, and James E. and Dorothy McClellan. If I have persisted in certain formulations despite the good advice of informed and talented colleagues, my own obstinacy is to blame. I bear full responsibility for weaknesses that remain.

To my entire family, both forward and back, for having helped me to learn and to care and to do, I extend heartfelt thanks. Without the encouragement of my wife, Roena L. Haynie, this book would never have been undertaken or completed. Prominent among others who have supported my work leading to this effort are Jerome Heckmann, Valdenia Winn, Ken Clark, Fred Whitehead, Melanie Jackson Scott, Tamara Agha-Jaffar, Mehdi Shariati, Alfred Kisubi, Henry Louis, Paul Jewell, Ruth Bridges, Gail James, Charles Wilson, John Ryan, Barbara Morrison, Elizabeth Budd, Frank Baron, Peggy Landsman, Richard Logan, Ken Stone, Nagarajan, Sylvia Dick, John Spritzler, Finley Campbell, Kenneth Urbanski, Theodore Kisiel, Wilma Iggers, James McGoldrick, James M. Demske, Jean Malona, Detlev and Heike Hoffmann, Hans-Ulrich and Regula Werner, Dieter Gersemann, and Wolfgang Herrmann. Special thanks also to Aeron, Deirdre, and Lyda.

I wish to acknowledge the following periodicals for graciously permitting me to utilize in reedited form materials from previously published essays:

"Elements of EduAction: Critical Pedagogy and the Community College," *The Journal of Critical Pedagogy* (www.lib.wmc.edu/pub/jcp/issueI-2/reitz.html), April 1998.

"Liberating *the Critical* in Critical Theory," *Researcher*, Vol. 11, No. 2, December 1996. (Also at www.lib.wmc.edu/pub/researcher/issueXI-2/reitz.html).

Excerpts from the following are published with permission of the Literary Estate of Herbert Marcuse, Peter Marcuse, Executor:

"*Heidegger*, Einführung in das akademische Studium. Sommer 1929," in the Frankfurt Marcuse Archive (*Stadt- und Universitätsbibliothek*), manuscript number 0013.01.

"The New German Mentality: Memorandum on a Study in the Psychological Foundations of National Socialism and the Chances of Their Destruction," (1942) in the Frankfurt Marcuse Archive, manuscript number 0119.00.

"Presentation of the Enemy" (1942) in the Frankfurt Marcuse Archive, manuscript number 0129.01.

"Education and Social Change," outline to a 1968 lecture, in the Frankfurt Marcuse Archive, manuscript number 0343.01

Untitled lecture with a note in Marcuse's hand "Berkeley, Oct 18 '75"; logged under the title "Students, University and Education" in the Frankfurt Marcuse Archive, manuscript number 0503.02.

Supplementary material from previously unpublished works of Herbert Marcuse, much now in the Archives of the Goethe University in Frankfurt/Main, has been and will be published in a six-volume series by Routledge Publishers, England, edited by Douglas Kellner. All rights to further publication are retained by the Estate.

The rights to reproduce excerpts from the following works have been granted by copyright holders:

From *The Aesthetic Dimension, Toward a Critique of Marxist Aesthetics* by Herbert Marcuse. (c) 1977 by Herbert Marcuse. Reprinted by permission of Beacon, Boston.

From *Counterrevolution and Revolt* by Herbert Marcuse. (c) 1972 by Herbert Marcuse. Reprinted by permission of Beacon Press, Boston.

From *One-Dimensional Man, Studies in the Ideology of Advanced Industrial Society* by Herbert Marcuse. (c) 1964 by Herbert Marcuse. Reprinted by permission of Beacon Press, Boston.

From *Eros and Civilization, A Philosophical Inquiry into Freud* by Herbert Marcuse. (c) 1955, 1966 by Beacon Press, Boston. Reprinted by permission of Beacon Press, Boston.

From *Negations, Essays in Critical Theory* by Herbert Marcuse. (c) 1968 by Herbert Marcuse. Reprinted by permission of Beacon Press, Boston.

From *Soviet Marxism: A Critical Analysis* by Herbert Marcuse. (c) 1958 by Columbia University Press. Reprinted with permission of the publisher.

From *Schriften I: Der deutsche Künstlerroman; frühe Aufsätze*, by Herbert Marcuse, 1978, Suhrkamp Verlag, Fankfurt am Main.

From *Hegels Ontologie und die Theorie der Geschichtlichkeit*, by Herbert Marcuse, 1968, Vittorio Klostermann Verlag, Frankfurt am Main.

I thank especially *Telos* Publications for permission to quote from the following:

"Contributions to a Phenomenology of Historical Materialism," *Telos*, No. 4, Fall 1969.

"The Concept of Negation in the Dialectic," *Telos*, No. 8, Summer 1971.

"On the Philosophical Foundation of the Concept of Labor in Economics," *Telos*, No. 16, Summer 1973.

"On the Problem of the Dialectic," *Telos*, No. 27, Spring 1976.

"Theory and Politics: A Discussion with Herbert Marcuse, Jürgen Habermas, Heinz Lubasz, and Tilman Spengler," *Telos*, No. 38, Winter 1978–79.

The altered version of "The Scream" by Edward Munch is reproduced with courtesy of The Munch Estate and ARS, New York. © 1999 The Munch Museum/The Munch-Ellingsen Group/Artists Rights Society (ARS), New York.

Art credit: "Marcuse, Munch, and the Millennium" by Jerome Heckmann. Photo credit: Mychael Kimbrough.

Author's Note

Citations from Marcuse's works are to the specific editions designated in the following list of his titles and abbreviations. Exact source and page references are included in parentheses at the conclusion of each particular Marcuse quotation. English translations from German sources are mine, unless otherwise indicated. A glossary of selected foreign words and phrases is included in the back of this book. Please note that throughout this study, citations referring to the word *esthetic* have been rendered *aesthetic* in the interest of standardization to Marcuse's spellings. So too *eros* is rendered *Eros*, *fantasy* as *phantasy*, and *marxism* as *Marxism*. I avoid using masculine grammatical forms; nonetheless I reproduce occasionally Marcuse's use of the terms *man* or *he* as generic designations of humanity.

MARCUSE'S TEXTS
Abbreviations to Selected Primary References
in Chronological Order
("g" indicates German language text)

1922 KRg *Schriften I: Der deutsche Künstlerroman; frühe Aufsätze* [*Writings* Vol. 1: *The German Artist Novel; Early Essays*] (Frankfurt /M: Suhrkamp, 1978).

1928 PH "Contributions to a Phenomenology of Historical Materialism," *Telos*, No. 4, Fall 1969.

1928 PHg "Beiträge zur Phänomenologie des Historischen Materialismus," *Philosophische Hefte*, No. 1, 1928.

1930   PD   "On the Problem of the Dialectic," *Telos*, No. 27, Spring
              1976.

1930   PDga   "Zum Problem der Dialektik I," *Die Gesellschaft*, Vol. 7, Part
              1, 1930.

1930   TMg   "Transzendentaler Marxismus?" *Die Gesellschaft*, Vol. 7, Part
              2, 1930.

1931   PDgb   "Zum Problem der Dialektik II," *Die Gesellschaft*, Vol. 8, Part
              2, 1931.

1931   GWg   "Das Problem der geschichtlichen Wirklichkeit: Wilhelm
              Dilthey," *Die Gesellschaft*, Vol. 7, 1931.

1932   HM   "The Foundation of Historical Materialism," in *Studies in
              Critical Philosophy* (Boston: Beacon, 1973).

1932   HMg   "Neue Quellen zur Grundlegung des Historischen Materi-
              alismus," *Die Gesellschaft*, Vol. 9, 1932.

1932   HOg   *Hegels Ontologie und die Theorie der Geschichtlichkeit* (Frank-
              furt/M: Vittorio Klostermann Verlag, 1968).

1933   CL   "On the Philosophical Foundation of the Concept of Labor
              in Economics," *Telos*, No. 16, Summer 1973.

1934   LT   "The Struggle Against Liberalism in the Totalitarian View of
              the State," *Negations, Essays in Critical Theory* (Boston: Beacon,
              1968).

1936   CE   "The Concept of Essence," in *Negations, Essays in Critical
              Theory* (Boston: Beacon, 1968).

1937   AC   "The Affirmative Character of Culture," in *Negations, Essays
              in Critical Theory* (Boston: Beacon, 1968).

1937   ACg   "Über die affirmative Charakter der Kultur," in Herbert
              Marcuse, *Kultur und Gesellschaft I* (Frankfurt/M: Suhrkamp,
              1965).

1937   CT   "Philosophy and Critical Theory," in *Negations, Essays in
              Critical Theory* (Boston: Beacon, 1968).

1941   RR   *Reason and Revolution, Hegel and the Rise of Social Theory*
              (Boston: Beacon, 1960).

1948   SE   "Sartre's Existentialism," in *Studies in Critical Philosophy*
              (Boston: Beacon, 1973).

1955   EC   *Eros and Civilization, A Philosophical Inquiry into Freud*
              (Boston: Beacon, 1966).

1958   SM   *Soviet Marxism, A Critical Analysis* (New York: Vintage, 1961).

1960   ND   "A Note on Dialectic," preface to 1960 edition of *Reason and
              Revolution* (Boston: Beacon, 1960).

1964 OD *One-Dimensional Man, Studies in the Ideology of Advanced Industrial Society* (Boston: Beacon, 1964).

1964 MW "Industrialization and Capitalism in the Work of Max Weber," *Negations, Essays in Critical Theory* (Boston: Beacon, 1968).

1965 RC "Remarks on a Redefinition of Culture," *Daedalus*, Vol. 94, No. 1, Winter 1965.

1965 RT "Repressive Tolerance," in Robert Paul Wolff, Barrington Moore Jr., and Herbert Marcuse (eds.) *A Critique of Pure Tolerance* (Boston: Beacon, 1969).

1966 SH "Socialist Humanism?" in Erich Fromm (ed.) *Socialist Humanism* (Garden City, NY: Doubleday, 1966).

1966 PP "Political Preface 1966" to *Eros and Civilization* (Boston: Beacon, 1966).

1967 AO "Art in the One-Dimensional Society," Lee Baxandall (ed.) *Radical Perspectives in the Arts* (Baltimore: Penguin, 1973).

1968 ES "Education and Social Change" outline to a lecture in the Frankfurt Marcuse Archive (*Stadt- und Universitätsbibliothek*), manuscript number 0343.01

1969 EL *An Essay on Liberation* (Boston: Beacon, 1969).

1970 FL *Five Lectures—Psychoanalysis, Politics, Utopia* (Boston: Beacon, 1970).

1970 CN "The Concept of Negation in the Dialectic," *Telos*, No. 8, Summer 1971.

1972 AF "Art as Form of Reality," *New Left Review*, No. 74, July–August 1972.

1972 CR *Counterrevolution and Revolt* (Boston: Beacon, 1972).

1974 HP "Heidegger's Politics: An Interview," by Herbert Marcuse and Frederick Olafson, *Graduate Faculty Philosophy Journal*, Vol. 6, No. 1, Winter 1977.

1975 BK Untitled lecture with a note in Marcuse's hand "Berkeley, Oct 18 '75"; logged under the title "Students, University and Education" in the Frankfurt Marcuse Archive (*Stadt- und Universitätsbibliothek*), manuscript number 0503.02

1978 AD *The Aesthetic Dimension, Toward a Critique of Marxist Aesthetics* (Boston: Beacon, 1978).

1978 TP "Theory and Politics: A Discussion with Herbert Marcuse, Jürgen Habermas, Heinz Lubasz, and Tilman Spengler," *Telos*, No. 38, Winter 1978-79.

1978 TPg "Theorie und Politik," in *Gespräche mit Herbert Marcuse* (Frankfurt/M: Suhrkamp, 1996).

1978 PB "Protosocialism and Late Capitalism: Toward a Theoretical Synthesis Based on Bahro's Analysis," *International Journal of Politics*, Vol. 10, Nos. 2–3, 1978.

1979 RP "The Reification of the Proletariat," *Canadian Journal of Political and Social Theory*, Vol. 3, No. 1, Winter 1979.

1979 EM "Ecology and the Critique of Modern Society," *Capitalism, Nature, Socialism*, Vol. 3, No. 3, September 1992.

1998 WF *Technology, War and Fascism: Collected Papers of Herbert Marcuse*, edited by Douglas Kellner (London and New York: Routledge, 1998).

1998 FAg *Feindanalysen: Über die Deutschen*, edited by Peter-Erwin Jansen (Lüneburg, Germany: Verlag Dietrich zu Klampen, 1998).

CHAPTER ONE

—⁓—

Recalling Marcuse: Art, Alienation, and the Humanities

Truth is ugly. We possess *art* lest *we perish of the truth*.

—Friedrich Nietzsche,
Will to Power, number 822

What are the intellectual, moral, and political qualities of life and thought that can make theory *critical*, society *democratic*, and education *liberating*? These questions continue as the central philosophical issues of our time. They challenge every one of us concerned with the increasing dehumanization of the civic, occupational, and personal spheres of our lives. If our own efforts in these areas are to be genuinely transformative, we will need an analysis that can critically disclose the roots of crisis pending in the economic, social, and political conditions of our existence. Without critical theorizing there will be no genuine cultural transformation. We must be able to envision from the conditions of the present intelligent choices about real possibilities for our future.

Philosophers from Confucius and Aristotle to John Dewey and Paulo Freire have investigated, as the axial human problem, how education is to help us in accomplishing our own humanization. What *is* the relationship of learning to beauty, truth to art, and political education to human flourishing? Herbert Marcuse would ask if it is even possible to have an informed public discussion about such matters today. We *have* had the recent highly publicized commentaries by Allan Bloom, William Bennett, E. D. Hirsch Jr., Dinesh D'Souza, and others, in the culture wars against "political correctness" in the humanities and against multicultural education reform. The field is rather fully occupied by conservative spokespersons; serious theorists and philosophers of education are read by professionals in the field, but get very little exposure to a mass audience.[1] Jonathan Kozol, bell hooks, Cornel West, and Noam Chomsky are struggling successfully to revive the Deweyian role of the progressive public intellectual. They have serious insights to communicate about education and miseducation, social inequality, and democratization. But in recent years few have done as much as Herbert Marcuse to challenge the conventional wisdom about educational and cultural matters in the United States. This book is dedicated to exploring just how Marcuse philosophized about education under conditions of oppression and alienation. Though it is not yet generally acknowledged, this concern and activity were central to his entire intellectual project: I wish to introduce a *new* Marcuse.

Even as late as 1999, an adequate understanding of the intellectual and political sources of Marcuse's philosophy and that of the Frankfurt School still requires new analytical effort. Douglas Kellner (1984, 1989), Rolf Wiggershaus (1988), and Martin Jay (1973, 1984) have made the most significant contributions to date in this regard. The critical theory of the Frankfurt School—especially as this is exemplified in the ideas of Herbert Marcuse as its foremost proponent—needs to be revisited on matters of our alienation and liberation. The core of this philosophy warrants invigorated critique for its fullest appreciation. We will find in Marcuse's work sources of immense insight into philosophical traditions largely eclipsed in the usual forms of U.S. higher education. Familiarity with these intellectual traditions is indispensable for the breadth and depth of theoretical development that is needed in philosophy and in the social sciences.

Today *we* must still inquire, as he did, into conditions for a humanistic cultural transformation. With the globalization of production activities over the past decade, we have seen the social distribution of income and wealth become increasingly polarized. Simultaneously, a destabilization has occurred in established forms of governance worldwide. In Eastern Europe and in the former Soviet Union "New Democracy" movements recently seemed to represent some of the most significant efforts against alienation that our epoch has yet seen. Mass protests that were to a large degree peaceful and motivated by the idea of a fairer social system free of repression brought "hard-line dictatorships" to relinquish state power. The massive changes that ensued soon intensified social and economic inequalities. Revitalized retail and residential districts sustain a definite sense of euphoria, while new conditions of employment have also given rise to widespread disillusionment with social change. For an examination of these consequences Peter Marcuse (1994) has recently highlighted the continuing relevance of his father's analysis in *Soviet Marxism, A Critical Analysis* (SM) and in "Protosocialism and Late Capitalism: Toward a Theoretical Synthesis Based on Bahro's Analysis" (PB). It was in PB (1978) that Herbert Marcuse extended the aesthetically motivated analysis of Rudolf Bahro (of social life in the German Democratic Republic) to a critique of the consumption model of society represented by the Federal Republic of Germany and by Western late capitalism in general. For Herbert Marcuse, the real criterion of emancipation (that which the freedom to vote for the Christian Democratic Union or Social Democratic Party and the monetary union a decade later could never actualize) was the progressive reduction of socially necessary labor time (PB, 27–28) and an end to the cultural logic of corporate power.

While the global economy has (until quite recently) generated tremendous paper wealth, it has also been systematically producing vast insecurity and want for the majority of the world's population. Major economic crises in the future may well lead vested interests to war over the world's resources and markets and to police state stabilization strategies, even as the Multilateral Agreement on Investment is on its way to becoming a global constitution that establishes the sovereignty of the world's largest corporations in economic affairs worldwide.[2] Today economically pressured elements in European societies, responding to racist bias and reactionary leaders, are displaying an exceedingly regrettable anti-immigrant backlash to economic hardship. Yet there is fortunately a very vital antifascist and multicultural youth movement astir across Europe today.

In the United States, militias and freemen are the extreme representatives of more mainstream forces working for a reactionary reconstruction of this country's lived political culture. At the fringes this program represents a violent resurgence of racism and sexism that scapegoats not just the directly targeted groups but also law-governed liberal politics in general (as in the Weimar era). This is where right-wing extremism meets mainstream neoconservatism privileging a protofascist idealized freedom of the individual and corporate power from effective forms of liberal-democratic governmental oversight. Significantly, the militias, the reactionary Republicans, and the conservative Democrats are not the only new forces that have emerged. Rejuvenated progressive political formations have also been appearing in the past few years. Some of the key signs of this rather radical democratic stirring in the nation's grass roots are the growth of independent, third-party political organizations like the Alliance for Democracy, the New Party, the Labor party, the Independent Progressive Politics Network, and the Greens, which have rather decisively broken with two-party politics-as-usual, rejecting Democrats and Republicans as two wings of a single party controlled by the interests of the most massive corporations in the United States. The new progressives bring a vital element to current debates in the public sphere because they question the legitimacy of the concentrated wealth and global exercise of power (both military and political) of corporate capitalism. They also bring a key new strategy for the left: coalition-building that can forge an activist-minded populist force to go on the offensive to end the control of large-scale corporations over U.S. culture, politics, and the economy. The widespread support for, and the dramatic success of, the August 1997 UPS strike, as well as the militant resistance to union busting by the A. E. Staley workers in Decatur, Illinois, and the newspaper workers in Detroit have forced even the leadership of the AFL-CIO to become more militant. A major regional mobilization was staged in Decatur June 25, 1994 by mid-western unions, clergy, and community groups in support of 800 protesting employees of corn syrup producer A. E. Stanley. These employees had been locked out since June 1993 for confronting management over health and safety issues and harsh labor practices. Decatur police in SWAT gear and gas masks maced the demonstrators engaging in civil disobedience (a sit-down in the driveway) at the plant gate. While this struggle ended in a stalemate, its militance energized the AFL-CIO, which has subsequently undertaken a nationwide organizing campaign. Striking journalists from the *Detroit News* and the *Detroit Free Press* have put out their own labor newspaper from 1996 to the present, the *Detroit Journal*. Numerous new progressive newspapers, presses, and web sites are also appearing, reviving a spirit of resistance that is antiracist and antisexist as well as anticorporate. The culture wars waged during the last decade by the reactionary right against progressive policies in education, the arts, and social-needs-oriented programs, testify to the latent power of contemporary progressive movements and their critical ideas. The dialectic of social and educational change today is not without emancipatory potential.

My work in the following pages is intended to support these radically democratic civic efforts, especially those involving education, as forms of cultural action for freedom. It will do so with particular attention to the principles of liberation in the social and educational philosophy of Herbert Marcuse. Marxist critical theory must also reexamine its traditional treatment of the theories of Karl Marx if it is to advance the development of educational philosophy and cultural transformation theory. What follows is based on the premise that with the real threat of social-political tumult to come, we will need to have not only optimism and energy, but also a very strong sense of direction. The future of critical social theorizing hinges on knowing its own history and on understanding the development of its analytical foundations and the political context in which it emerged.

Marcuse's work communicates the vibrancy of his German intellectual sources and an appreciation for much of the real conflict in our lives, which, as he finds, are unduly stressed and torn. The essential connection of education to the resolution of these tensions and the attainment of the social potential of the human race is an integral part of his general theoretical discourse. Marcuse's final book, *The Aesthetic Dimension, Toward a Critique of Marxist Aesthetics* (AD, 1978), deals with the aesthetic sources of our wisdom and learning and with the theory of literary art. His relatively recently (1978) published doctoral dissertation, "*The German Artist Novel*" (originally completed in 1922) is concerned with the education (*Bildung*) of *the artist* as this is *depicted in modern German fiction*. Current scholarship on Marcuse displays a new emphasis on his aesthetic philosophy (Reitz, 1996; Lukes, 1985, 1994; Nicholson, 1994; Becker, 1994; Koppe, 1992; Menke, 1992; Geyer-Ryan, 1992; Raulet, 1992). As right-wing commentators carry out their culture wars with regard to the literary canon, the place of values in schooling, and the role and function and future of the arts and humanities in higher education, Marcuse's philosophical insights into art *and education* become more relevant than ever.

Allan Bloom recently sought to "rescue" the humanities from the perils of political protest and value relativism in *The Closing of the American Mind*.[3] Similarly, Alan Charles Kors and Harvey A. Silverglate (1998) seem to think that Marcuse was the single most important philosopher of the 1960s counterculture, whose social theories have led to "the betrayal of liberty on America's campuses."[4] While higher education in the humanities is traditionally thought of as pursuing universally human aims and goals, these conservative writers are unwilling to admit that a cultural politics of class, a cultural politics of race, and a cultural politics of gender *have* set very definite historical constraints upon the actualization of the humane concerns of a liberal arts education. Bloom attributes a decline of the humanities and U.S. culture in general to the supposedly inane popularization of German philosophy in the United States since the 1960s, especially the ideas of Nietzsche, Heidegger, and Marcuse, which are regarded as nihilistic and demoralizing. Bloom argues that we have imported ". . . a clothing of German fabrication for our souls, which . . . cast doubt upon the Americanization of the world on which we had embarked. . . ."[5] In a typically facile remark, Bloom says of Marcuse: "He ended up here writing trashy culture criticism with a heavy sex interest. . . ."[6] No hint from him that one of Marcuse's prime contributions (in *One-Dimensional Man: Studies in the Ideology of Advanced Industrial Society*) to the critical analysis of American popular culture is his notion of "repressive desublimation"—how the unrestrained use of sex and violence by the corporate mass media and by other large-scale commercial interests accomplishes social manipulation and control in the interest of capital accumulation. Or that Marcuse (in some ways very much like Bloom) valued high art and the humanities precisely because they teach the *sublimation* of the powerful urge for pleasure that in other contexts threatens destruction. For Kors and Silverglate, as well as for Bloom, Marcuse's pursuit of an authentic social equality (consistent with a critical analysis of societal mechanisms already privileging wealth, race, patriarchy, and power) becomes the pursuit of injustice. Marcuse's pursuit of liberation (consistent with arguments exposing the ironies of undemocratic freedoms/ democratic unfreedom in the United States today) becomes the practice of repression. Any *opening* of the American mind that involves a trenchant critique of the conventional political wisdom is to them a *closing* of the American mind. The unremitting conservative backlash to the progressive and radically democratic educational reform efforts of the 1960s and 1970s is now in full swing. We shall see, however, that Marcuse knows the *conservative* tradition more critically than it knows itself. Conservative intellectual and cultural traditions, including a conviction about rationally defensible standards of value, are in fact pivotal to the development of his own theories of art and the humanities against alienation.

Marcuse's thought is usually viewed as an extension of the perspectives of Marx, Hegel, and Freud. I find that Marcuse is an immensely complex and sometimes contradictory thinker whose interpretation of these authors is undergirded by an even deeper appreciation of the cultural philosophy of German idealism. According to Marcuse, Hegel, Marx, and Freud each utilize a language more fundamental than that of Hegel's philosophy of history, Marx's political economy, or Freud's clinical psychology. They operate in the *literary-aesthetic idiom* associated with nineteenth-century

German philosophy and with its view of the high culture of Periclean Greece. Marcuse's writing thus has a *classical* dimension above and beyond the radical tone for which it is renowned. Wilhelm Dilthey, Goethe, Friedrich Schiller, Schopenhauer, Nietzsche, and Martin Heidegger were crucial in building Marcuse's formulation of critical theory. There is much to be learned from Marcuse's deep acquaintance with the Western intellectual tradition and classical German philosophy. This is to be appreciated and upheld. There is also much to raise to a higher level and much to overcome.

Marcuse's continuing merit and appeal stems precisely from his work on the problems of knowledge and on the political impact of education. I find his critique of the prevailing mode of enculturation in the United States as education *to alienation* and to single-dimensionality to be immensely relevant today. So too, his emphasis on the emancipatory and *disalienating potential of art and the humanities*. These topics are closely connected to the concerns articulated by Max Horkheimer and Theodor W. Adorno, who together with Marcuse, began in the 1930s and 1940s to delineate the social, historical, and political difficulties and contradictions of the era around World War II. They viewed that period as a time of incredible scientific-technological achievement, but also as an epoch indelibly marked by militarist oppression and genocide. In their subsequent critical writing they saw the entire century (from World War I to Hiroshima, and later to Vietnam) as exhibiting the simultaneous culmination and twilight of civilization. Human dignity and barbarism were inextricably interlocked. This was a repellent circumstance that they nonetheless came to accept as an inevitable condition of human life that tragic art could help us understand. Their increasingly pessimistic vision of our culture and history held science and technology to be largely responsible for the troubles of our time. "The educated made it easy for the barbarians everywhere," Horkheimer and Adorno wrote in 1944, "by being so stupid."[7] Already utilizing what were to become central tenets of postmodern theory (especially what are taken to be the illusions of progress, reason, and scientific objectivity), they rejected the political-economic categories of the Enlightenment, positivist social science, and traditional Marxist thought as they sought to understand fascism, world war, repression, and alienation more genuinely. Marcuse's writing on these themes remains fascinating and influential.

In spite of this, I find myself troubled, in particular, by the way in which *Marcuse's* theories of art, alienation, and the humanities displace *Marx's* structural analysis of social life to such an extent that the former's work also takes on ironically conservative political overtones. I want to underscore not only the gains to be made from a familiarity with Marcuse's philosophy of culture, but also the theoretical limitations of his approach. I hold that the philosophical difficulties of Marcuse's theories of art and education hinge upon his reformulation of the analysis of alienation veering attention toward a concept of reification (as *Verdinglichung*) that is ultimately detached from the materialist context of the Marxist economic analysis. As this book develops I will show why I feel that Marcuse's non-Marxist and even anti-Marxist philosophical abstractions debilitate our efforts to understand ourselves and to extricate ourselves from the oppressive conditions of our social existence.

When I say that we need to *recall* Marcuse's ideas today, I use this word primarily as German philosophy uses the concept *aufheben*. This may variously mean to lift up, raise up, hold up, take up, pick up, elevate, preserve, protect, exalt, criticize, suspend, abolish, repeal, annul, cancel, invalidate, counteract, supersede, refine, purify, and transcend. The concept signals the multidimensional movement of the mind involved in the theoretical analysis of Hegel and Marx in their description of the dialectical learning process. In addition to the positive connotations of remembrance and memorialization, I also want to play quite consciously on two further meanings of this word: the recall of a representative from parliament, and the recall of an item that has come into circulation with hidden defects and dangers. The central objective of this book is to reflect upon the cultural critique developed by Marcuse: its philosophical foundations, political prospects, and implications for the future. My effort here will be to examine, compare, criticize, counteract, extend, invalidate, refine, advance, and supersede Marcuse's work. It is a tribute to Marcuse that in the process of reading his texts one can learn much about genuinely worthwhile elements in European traditions in higher education, about ourselves and our world, and about the limitations and promise of our own political lives and our political future. Recalling Marcuse certainly does *not* mean merely reminiscing about the 1960s or about the conventional wisdom with regard to Marcuse's philosophy. It means becoming critically conscious of the fullness of his theory, including major segments that remain unfamiliar today even to those who have systematically studied other aspects of his work. The future of critical theorizing requires us to *build beyond* the philosophy of Herbert Marcuse and to liberate *the critical* in the legacy of critical theory. My work, therefore, seeks to be a critical engagement with his thought.

For the purposes of this study I use the term *critical theory* in a technical sense to refer to the theories of Marcuse, the Frankfurt School, Western Marxism, and their deconstructionist and postmodernist philosophical progeny.[8] When speaking more generically, I use the terms *critical thinking* or *critical theorizing*. Much of what is called critical theory today is rooted specifically in Marcuse's thought. Marcuse has formulated a particular approach to *aesthetic education* and a unique version of a *philosophical humanism* that he then presents *as critical theory* against the debilitating paradoxes that he sees at the core of our single-dimensional culture: alienation in the midst of affluence, repression through gratification, and the overstimulation and paralysis of mind. Marcuse's efforts at building an emancipatory theory of education are at times immensely insightful and at others they risk being elitist and unhelpful. Most importantly, he has posed a critical theory of education to us *as a problem*. The task confronting us is that of assuming sufficient philosophical perspective to enable creative synthesis to enhance our powers of learning and transformation.

I am attempting to break new ground in the study of Marcuse and critical theory by attempting to do what few academic philosophers to date have thought worthwhile: to take very seriously what Marcuse has to say about the theory and conduct of education. I contend in this investigation that Marcuse's contributions to a critical theory of art and critical theory of alienation only become fully intelligible on the basis of what he has to say about a critical theory of education. My point is that *educational* insights are the major purpose of his extensive analyses of art and alienation. By comprehensively reviewing materials from the primary sources, and by permitting him to speak for himself a good deal of the time, I hope to delineate the inner logic of his philosophical work. The body of this study will disclose the structure and movement of his thought. It will raise up (*heb auf*) some of the untranslated and relatively inaccessible materials that have rarely been critically appreciated. It will demonstrate why these are indispensable aspects of Marcuse's overall approach, and even more importantly, it will attempt to build beyond both his theoretical accomplishments and failures.

I see the philosophy of education, as my specific analytical focus, offering particular advantages that can aid in the identification of the metatheoretical basis of Marcuse's cultural and social theory. These advantages stem from the fact that Marcuse's aesthetic and social-philosophical links to educational issues are indissoluble. Marcuse stresses the *educational* value of the arts because of the qualitative difference he finds between the multidimensional kind of knowledge thought to be produced by the aesthetic imagination and the unidimensional kind of knowledge attributed to what he describes as the controlled and repressive rationalities of achievement, performance, and domination. During his most optimistic phases, Marcuse views aesthetic education as essential for the actualization of a utopian form of society, where art is also to become a material force for the revitalization of all aspects of social life. His intention is to liberate the original meaning of art from its narrow and repressive association with high culture. A theory of art must become a theory of sensuousness, pleasure, and gratification, capable of reshaping society *for life*, rather than persist as the traditional study of the beauty and form of accomplished works. Most uniquely, Marcuse formulates a dialectic of love and death that he believes is grounded in the conflicted essence of human nature. This dialectic, he contends, is preserved as paradox and tragedy in high art and in the humanities. Ultimately, Marcuse will advocate an educational and cultural philosophy that maintains a critical distance from direct forms of social intervention, stressing instead education as affective and intellectual preparation for a redefinition of need and for a restructuring of consciousness, in some ways quite consistent with the classically conservative liberal arts approach.

The thematic interconnections among Marcuse's theories of art, alienation, and the humanities constitute the decisive structural and philosophical unity of his work. Alienation, in his estimation, is thought to be the result of *training people to forget* their authentic human nature—its essential internal turmoil and social potential—*by educationally eradicating* the realm where this knowledge is considered to be best preserved, that is, *the humanities*. Marcuse was appalled at what he saw as the displacement of the humanities in the 1970s by a form of higher education that had become mainly scientific and technical and that primarily stood in service to the needs of commerce, industry, and the military. Marcuse's theory contends that our society is obsessed with efficiency, standardization, mechanization, and specialization, and that this fetish involves aspects of repression, fragmentation, and domination that impede real education and that preclude the development of a real awareness of ourselves and of our world. Alienation is seen as the result of a mis-education or half-education that leads people to accept sensual anesthetization and social amnesia as normal. Conditioned to a repressive pursuit of affluence, making a living becomes more important than making a life. This aspect of Marcuse's approach to alienation is explicitly drawn from Schiller's arguments in favor of art and against crass utilitarianism in *On the Aesthetic Education of Man in a Series of Letters* (1793).

During his militant "middle period," Marcuse, like Schiller, urges education and art as *countermovements to alienation*: an *aesthetic rationality* is thought to transcend the prevailing logic of performance and achievement in the one-dimensional society and to teach radical action toward justice and human fulfillment. He even sees a possible reconciliation of the humanistic and technological perspectives via the hypothesis that *art may become a social and productive force* for material improvement, reconstructing the economy in accordance with aesthetic goals and thus reducing alienation in the future. But there is also a "turn" in Marcuse's theorizing, almost a reversal. He finds that even the best education (to art through the humanities) can be itself alienating, if also in some continuing sense emancipatory. The artistic and cultured individual remains rather permanently separated from the broader social community and is stigmatized as an outsider in a way that precludes close identification with any group. Art, then, is held to be ultimately *un*able to respond to alienation except with a more extreme, yet higher, form of alienation. Marcuse finds himself enmeshed in oscillating, *oppositional* relationships and tensions that are projected by his analysis of the social phenomena of alienation, art, and the humanities.

My work here is based upon a rethinking of Marcuse's writing as a whole. I begin the documentation with the materials from his earliest project, the 1922 dissertation, *The German Artist Novel*, and from his important first published book, *Hegel's Ontology and the Theory of Historicity* (1932). Readers will be more familiar with Marcuse's middle period however, which extends roughly from 1932 to 1970 and encompasses those texts that articulate Marcuse's *"Art-against-Alienation"* program: *Reason and Revolution, Hegel and the Rise of Social Theory* (1941); *Eros and Civilization, A Philosophical Inquiry into Freud* (1955); *One-Dimensional Man, Studies in the Ideology of Advanced Industrial Society* (1964); and *An Essay on Liberation* (1969). The turn in Marcuse's theorizing to his *"Art-as-Alienation"* position is most evident after publication of *Counterrevolution and Revolt* (1972) and *The Aesthetic Dimension, Toward a Critique of Marxist Aesthetics* (1978). This turn is a return to philosophical tendencies latent during the middle period but explicitly present in his early period. By investigating the dual themes of art-against-alienation and art-as-alienation, the scope of the following undertaking is intended to embrace the doubled structural framework that I see undergirding Marcuse's lifetime of writings on sociocultural philosophy and education.

I intend to demonstrate that Marcuse's changing disposition as a philosopher of education not only correlates with, but also defines, his changing disposition as a social and political philosopher. Following Dilthey and

Heidegger, he finds that the very world of philosophy is external to the world of science and is constructed only in the humanities, as such. He sees aesthetic education as the basis of all genuinely philosophical (and political) education. Yet the persistence of a *duality* and tension between the ideas of art and the exigencies of everyday life in Marcuse's overall conception accounts for the enduring pessimism that stands in sharp contrast to the more utopian and radical tenor of his middle-period aspirations. In the end Marcuse retreats from the realm of struggle and advocates a kind of inner immigration.[9] I emphasize that, at both the beginning and end of his career, Marcuse relegates educational philosophy to a quietist rather than an activist function in our life and world. The educational activism of his middle period is reduced during his later phase to the movement he imputes to the aesthetic form, in and of itself, toward maturity, peace, and understanding. Marcuse ultimately articulates a concept of literary-aesthetic education in this regard standing in disjunction from the philosophical categories generally associated with a historical and materialist dialectic, but related instead to Dilthey's concepts of the emotional and political potential of the *Geisteswissenschaften* (humanistic disciplines); a *Geistesgeschichte* (intellectual history); and a *Lebensphilosophie* (life-philosophy, a philosophical precursor to depth psychology). This crucial and hitherto insufficiently elaborated aspect of Marcuse's approach, drawn from Dilthey, as well as from the cultural radicalism of Nietzsche, asserts a logical and political-philosophical priority over his treatment of the thought of Hegel, Marx, and Freud, and comes to define Marcuse's characteristic understanding of *aesthetic education as the foundation of a critical theory.*

The future of critical theorizing demands that we avoid the traditional political dangers of aestheticism and cultural conservatism that follow from the reduction of *social* theory to *aesthetic* theory. In order to liberate *the critical* in critical theory, I believe we need to examine carefully the epistemological underpinnings of Marcuse's intellectual position. To do so we must come to understand more fully what I take to be the philosophical cornerstone of the critical theory of the Frankfurt School and of Western Marxism, namely its central analysis of *alienation as reification*. This involves an analysis of Marcuse's particular theorization of the concept of reification, as involving a false consciousness of reality that is caused by a philosophical deficiency that may be *remediated* only through the deconstructive and reconstructive power of a critique grounded in the *aesthetic imagination*. This version of reification theory has also been a major influence on certain literary tendencies within much postmodern and deconstructionist cultural commentary as opposed to the more sociological and historical postmodernist perspectives.

A critique of methodological reification (as the illegitimate erasure of the researching subject from the study of the object in question) can be traced back to the epistemology of neo-Kantianism. This surfaced in European philosophical discussions during the era around World War I in various ways within the related outlooks of existentialism, phenomenology, hermeneutics, and Western Marxism (especially the early Georg Lukács). Aspects of each of these theoretical perspectives find eclectic expression in Marcuse's work, generally displacing a class-struggle analysis. Marcuse's *Reason and Revolution* perhaps most clearly furnishes us with his central elucidation of the idea of reification in terms consistent with his basic neo-Kantian concern. The concept becomes an insight of chiefly methodological significance that Marcuse claims can uniquely redeem Marxist social philosophy from the objectivistic, mechanistic, and deterministic modes he imputes to it. In Marcuse's estimation, the proper explication of the phenomenon of reification—as *Verdinglichung*—can achieve the indispensable intellectual precondition for liberation in which *economic theory* is transformed into *critical theory*.

The work of Mitchell Franklin, Eugen Fink, and Heinz Paetzold drew my attention to the problems in reification theory quite a few years ago, and I have independently investigated this philosophical terrain, especially where Marcuse's negation of reification leads to an aesthetic ontological "denial of things."[10] This is a theme that runs throughout his middle- and late-period works and will be examined carefully in chapter 3 on Marcuse's emergent critical theory of alienation.

Marcuse has addressed some of the most pressing social and cultural problems of our era, but he certainly has not done so in a fashion that is beyond question. He has much that is valuable to say about the theoretical and practical controversies that continue to confront social philosophy, critical pedagogy, and aesthetic theory. His work never deserved to be uncritically promoted or uncritically condemned. The study of Marcuse continues to be rewarding not only in those areas of his greatest strength. I want to work on the aspects of his thought that are most problematic theoretically, for it is upon this analysis that the very future of critical theorizing hinges. By stressing Marcuse's intellectual interconnections to Nietzsche, Heidegger, Lukács, and Dilthey as well as to Hegel, Marx, and Freud I hope to convey my appreciation of the complexity, ambiguity, and seeming inconsistency of

Marcuse's theoretical project in addition to what I shall disclose as its dynamic symmetry and essence.

Marcuse wrote in *Counterrevolution and Revolt*, "The inner dynamic of capitalism . . . necessitates the revival of the radical rather than the minimal goals of socialism" (CR, 5). But the social philosophy of *The Aesthetic Dimension* turns away from this position. His more radical impulse was epitomized by *Eros and Civilization*, which centered on Schiller and aesthetic education, emphasizing beauty as the key to political emancipation. This occurred within the context of a blistering critique of the highly administered oppression characteristic of the contemporary social and economic order in the United States. By the time of his final book, though, Marcuse seems to be speaking as an aesthetician in the most classical and abstract sense. *The Aesthetic Dimension* underscores the primacy of the aesthetic *form* and aesthetic *autonomy*, and favorably reevaluates such notions as "art as art" and the liberating potential of mental labor *separated from* manual labor. In so doing, Marcuse retreats from aesthetic and educational activism to a pat restatement of certain of the most well-established elements of the idealist aesthetic tradition. He develops a love/hate relationship with a materialist and historical approach to aesthetics. "In all its ideality art bears witness for the truth of historical materialism—the permanent non-identity of subject and object, individual and individual" (AD, 29). The long-standing utopian element in Marcuse's thought becomes an explicit philosophical idealism. Ideality is now the method by which to access and understand reality: "The truth of art lies in this: the world really is as it appears in the work of art" (AD, xii).

Marcuse's understanding of alienation and oppression is thus linked to art and to the aesthetic dimension in two basic ways: he has indicated that art may both act *against* alienation and oppression and to *preserve* them. In the former context, in *Eros and Civilization*, Marcuse makes reference to the aesthetic dimension's power to counteract the alienation that comes from the bureaucratization and mechanization of one-dimensional society. It is thought that the standardization of competencies and performances in the economic milieu of advanced industrial society leads quite directly to regimentation and to unthinking and unfeeling forms of social interaction. Meaning and fulfillment are eradicated from a society that is so highly engineered that it stands beyond freedom and dignity. He utilizes the aesthetic categories of pleasure and beauty as criteria by which to condemn the existing order as well as to create an alternative one. Orpheus and Narcissus are offered as aesthetic symbols of a nonrepressive Eros and lived culture that can pursue gratification and peace through artistry and beauty. These ideals are thought capable of effecting the reconciliation of humanity and nature in a sensuous totality. In *An Essay on Liberation* he advocates the development of an *aesthetic rationality* and an *aesthetic ethos* that can secure and consummate an *aesthetic world*. Alienation is understood as *anesthetization*—a deadening of the senses that makes repression and manipulation possible. Thus, art can act against alienation as a revitalizing, rehumanizing force.

Known during the 1960s as the philosopher of the student revolts, Marcuse's writings of that period were thought to embody a philosophy of protest within higher education itself. He considered higher education to be qualitatively *higher* only where the humanities fulfilled their potential to work *against alienation*: as a critique of positivism, conformity, and repression, and also as a means to political engagement. The educational goal Marcuse proposed was the restoration of *the aesthetic dimension* as a source of cultural critique, political activism, and the guiding principles for the social organization of the future. In his estimation, our technological mindlessness and social fragmentation have to be remediated philosophically through a broadened education to the human condition. He emphasized particularly the aesthetic roots of reason and the value of literary art and education in accomplishing our own mature sense of self and our liberation. While Marcuse interacted with members of the radical and international student movement of the 1960s (Angela Davis and German militant, Rudi Dutschke), these efforts were ultimately accompanied by a political distancing, an intensifying interest in art, and the emancipatory potential of a liberal education classically conceived. His attention turned to the essentially pedagogical dimensions of intellectual activity preparatory to revolution.

Marcuse ultimately comes to emphasize that art can also *contribute* to an alienated existence. Alienation is understood in this second sense as a freely chosen act of withdrawal. It represents a self-conscious bracketing of certain of the practical elements of everyday life for the sake of achieving a higher and more valuable philosophical distance and theoretical perspective. Marcuse contends that artists and intellectuals (especially) can utilize their own personal estrangement to serve a future emancipation. Art and philosophy (i.e., the humanities) can, by virtue of their admittedly elitist critical distance, oppose an oppressive status quo and furnish an intangible, yet concrete, *telos* (sense of purpose) by which to guide emancipatory social practice. Marcuse is attracted to the humanities because their subject matter and methodology are thought to focus upon questions of the meaning of human experience, rather than on the sheer description of data (this latter procedure being rejected as the nonphilosophical approach of behaviorism and the physical sciences). He regards classical learning by means of discourse and reflection on philosophy, literature, drama, music, painting, sculpture, and so forth, as liberating insofar as it is thought to impel humanity beyond the "first dimension," the realm of mere fact, to the world of significance and meaning. As Marcuse sees it, the very form of beauty is dialectical. It unites the opposites of gratification and pain, death and love, and repression and need, and therefore can authentically represent what he takes to be the con-flicted, tragic, and paradoxical substance of human life. In Marcuse's view, the insights provided by these liberal studies are "transhistorical" and are con-sidered the precondition to any political transformation of alienated human existence into authentic human existence. The liberal arts and humanities are not seen simply as transmitting or preserving (or as he says, "affirming" or apologizing for) the dominant culture. They make possible the very develop-ment of critical thinking and human intelligence itself. Here the arts relate to higher education and to advanced forms of knowledge not merely in terms of "arts instruction," but as the very basis of a *general educational theory*.

When Herbert Marcuse speaks of art, he usually does so in terms of literature, rather than painting, music, sculpture, or any other aesthetic form. This stems from his own early experiences in higher education. He was trained at the graduate level, not primarily in philosophy, psychology, or economics, but in the modern literary theory and literary history of German culture. Promoted to "Dr. Phil." by the Albert-Ludwigs University (Freiburg i. B.) in October 1922, his dissertation, *Der deutsche Künstlerroman* (KRg),—*The German Artist Novel*—focused on the special problems repeat-edly addressed in modern German fiction dealing with the artist's stress and frustration at the incompatibility of an aesthetic life and the painful exigencies of everyday existence. Marcuse perceived a harsh dissonance between the world of art and that of daily life and work. On the one hand, the ordinary realm of daily routine was thought to represent a flat and spiritless domain, subsequently described as "one-dimensional." On the other hand, this reality of social and economic habit was opposed and confronted by the infinite inner richness of the realm of human imagination and creativity (*Geist*). The tradition of German romanticism was no stranger to this aesthetic and social conflict. Marcuse's dissertation is profoundly critical, however, of the Romantic perception of the artist (as observed in the literature of the *Sturm und Drang* and involving a uniquely sensitive subjectivity caught up in an "inevitable" conflict with the social environment). Marcuse is quite cognizant of the political dangers of aestheticism. Nonetheless, the essential social philosophical position with respect to the artist that he expresses in the dissertation is this: *"Dem Künstler ist die kollektivistische Gesellschaftsordnung des Sozialismus an sich eben so fremd, so gleichgültig, wie die der kapitalistischen Bourgeoisie"* (KRg, 195—*To the artist* the collectivist social order of socialism is in itself every bit as alienating and just as much a matter of indifference as is the world of the capitalist bourgeoisie; emphasis added). Some thirty years later, while associated with the Russian Institute, Columbia University, and the Russian Research Center at Harvard, Marcuse would refine and develop a similar philosophical position (eventually elaborated in *Soviet Marxism*) indicting the social theory and practice of both the U.S. and Soviet systems as sharing similarly oppressive productive mechanisms, both of which were thought to be essentially incapable of resolving the fundamental question of human alienation.

Once a supporter of the reigning party of Weimar Germany (the conservatively Marxist SPD, the Social Democrats, led by Friedrich Ebert, see *Five Lectures—Psychoanalsyis, Politics, Utopia* [FL, 102]), Marcuse severed his political ties to the SPD in 1919 when it was implicated in the murders of the revolutionaries Rosa Luxemburg and Karl Liebknecht. Ebert struck a Faustian bargain with General Wilhelm Groener, second-in-command of the German army. Groener would allow the SPD to rule if Ebert allowed the army to crush the massive, armed street demonstrations led by the revolutionary Sparticists, Luxemberg and Liebknecht. The army, thus secure, betrayed the SPD to the Nazis (Shirer, 83–89).

Disillusioned early on with his own political activism, and disheartened at what he saw as the very limited possibilities for a truly socialist revolution, the dissertation he was then preparing would not look to economic analyses or party-oriented political action, but rather to works of art from the history of German literature for advice in the struggle against the alienating conditions of social life. It would cite Hegel, Nietzsche, Dilthey, and the early (i.e., explicitly idealist) Lukács as its philosophical sources, and conclude that the artist may never ultimately identify with popular aspirations for social revolution (KRg, 195). Although Marcuse by 1928 and 1932 would explicitly address the viability of phenomenology and historical materialism as contemporary philosophical perspectives, he did not see it as the task of his dissertation to develop a phenomenological or historical materialist interpretation of art, alienation, or the humanities. He presumed, rather, with Dilthey, that political, historical, and educational issues were better understood *out of art itself.*

Significantly, Marcuse's final book, *The Aesthetic Dimension*, again brought questions of art and alienation to the forefront of his philosophy. This again occurred within the context of a *literary* discussion that is also now a confrontation with the classical Marxist theory of literature. It brought Marcuse to reemphasize his early notion of the relative autonomy of art:

> . . . in contrast to the orthodox Marxist aesthetics I see the political potential of art in art itself, in the aesthetic form as such. Furthermore, I argue that by virtue of its aesthetic form, art is largely autonomous vis à vis the given social relations. In its autonomy art both protests these relations and at the same time transcends them. Thereby art subverts the dominant consciousness, the ordinary experience. (AD, ix)

Marcuse in *The Aesthetic Dimension* found art (as art) liberating, while socialism was thought to fail, because "art breaks open a dimension inaccessible to other experience" (AD, 72), and also because "socialism does not and cannot liberate Eros from Thanatos" (ibid.). *The Aesthetic Dimension* is convinced that the "Form" of aesthetic beauty and truth may be linked directly to humanity's innermost needs and affective essence. In this manner, Marcuse implicitly joins the aesthetic theory of his final book to his middle-period volume on Freud, *Eros and Civilization* (EC), but without the radical implications of EC. Marcuse first formulated his unique vision of the "dialectic" of Eros and Thanatos in EC, where it appears to replace the classical Marxist dialectic of capital and labor. In EC Marcuse advocated the general development of humanity's play impulse, polymorphous sexuality, phantasy and art, rather than the cultivation of an explicitly socialist consciousness or conduct. Marcuse thus sought even during his militant middle period to supplant the political-economic idea of communist revolution with that of an aesthetico-erotic negation of the phenomena of repression and alienation.

During the 1960s, Marcuse found the following to be major characteristics of what he called the totally administered, welfare/warfare, social order: (1) a high level of individual productivity, achieved through the advancing technologies of automation and mechanization, capable of supplying mass needs; and (2) an absence of mass political opposition within the repressive political apparatus. This second quality was thought to occur because: (2a) mass economic needs had been met; (2b) blue-collar jobs were giving way to white-collar occupations; and (2c) private life was being integrated into the system of commodity production.

Advanced capitalism was perceived as having deactivated the conflict of class interests and as having achieved a qualitatively different level of social homogenization. Advanced industrial society was therefore held to be structurally different from the early industrial mode of capitalism analyzed by Marx and Engels. Marcuse did not construe this to mean that these new developments refined away oppression. He saw the late twentieth-century developments as comprising an even more vile, obscene, and ugly social order—but one that required above all else an updated theoretical interpretation. His vision and revision of classical Marxist theory warrant careful attention and will be examined thoroughly as this analysis proceeds. The economic categories of orthodox dialectical materialism were deemed no longer adequate to comprehend the transformed state of affairs. Marcuse's main revision in this regard is the strategic use of Art *against* Alienation.

During this middle period, Marcuse increasingly comes to call upon the idea of the aesthetic dimension as the genuinely dialectical, life-enhancing, counterconcept to the life-restricting rationality of the established order (i.e., its profit and performance principles). His broadened Schillerian notion of the aesthetic involves what he terms "the inner connection between pleasure, sensuousness, beauty, truth, art and freedom" (EC, 172) and the aesthetic emerges as the central category of his critical theory. Anticipating charges of the dematerialization of Marx, his particular version of critical theory claims to furnish philosophy with the sensuous, practical, *and material* (i.e., *aesthetic*) foundation critical analysis needed after he and others in the Frankfurt School concluded that the Marxist materialism was obsolete. Marcuse emphasized in *Eros and Civilization*, "Schiller states that, in order to solve the political problem, 'one must pass through the aesthetic, since it is beauty that leads to freedom'" (EC, 187).

As Marcuse utilizes the concept of art during this middle period, it is no longer limited to the literary realm. The aesthetic now functions as:

1. *a dimension of his social theory*: a specific mode of thought and action that represents an alternative to the crass rationalism and positivism of "one-dimensional" thinking;

2. *a principle of cultural critique*: a rejection of the techno-bureaucratic mindedness that is seen as the starting point of anesthetized culture;

3. *a countermovement to alienation*: refinement of the aesthetic sensibility that makes possible human self-actualization, (i.e., art as rehumanization reestablishes human wholeness instead of replicating fragmentation); and

4. *the actual negation to social exploitation* in a movement principally wrought by those who understand art (students, artists, and intellectuals), rather than those who understand the history of production—and where art, as social criticism, serves as a moral and political force more compelling than an economics-oriented cultural analysis.

In these four ways, Marcuse claimed that the aesthetic could actually aid in the restoration of a multidimensional universe. The practical effectiveness of the aesthetic dimension however presupposed the formation of a widely dispersed *aesthetic social consciousness* via an *aesthetic education* that could ultimately lead to human actualization. Marcuse thus came to view *his* critical theory as *the* contemporary protest philosophy that could overcome social anesthetization through an emphasis on the pleasure principle and the erotic life instincts. He grounded a Great Refusal against the established order in this new aesthetic sensibility that he contended had historically emerged out of humanity's actual (but noneconomic) material needs: those for beauty, pleasure, and sexual gratification—rooted *not* in productive relations, but in nature, biology, and subjective human sensuousness. In contradistinction to Freud, however, who saw art and higher culture as requiring sexual repression and sublimation, Marcuse held that art might quite legitimately be regarded as a manifestation of a broadened and liberated (i.e., polymorphously expressed) sexuality. Ultimately, Marcuse wanted (during this middle period) to encompass the organization of labor and civilization within the dimensions of Eros and the aesthetic. His *Essay on Liberation* concludes with the admonition that technique must become art, and art must become reality: society must be shaped "for Life." Dilthey's *Lebensphilosophie* will be shown in this regard as the precursor to the aesthetic and social philosophy Marcuse articulates.

Marcuse's middle-period works, especially his 1937 essay "The Affirmative Character of Culture" and *Eros and Civilization*, considered the traditional definition of aesthetics as problematic. This traditional definition confined aesthetics to "the study of that which pertains to art and beauty," thus *repressing* what was thought to be its original meaning as "the study of the sensuous" (EC, 172–74). Marcuse's middle-period effort must be seen as an attempt to reformulate a contemporary aesthetic philosophy that could also incorporate a practical and critical social function by virtue of being grounded in the sensuous substance of "Life." During this period Marcuse would also oppose education to higher culture, conformity, positivism, and guilt, redirecting learning and research toward the emancipation of humanity's *sensuous practical activity.*

If art is conceived in terms of a renewal of the senses or the rehabilitation of the pleasure principle, it may be thought to achieve a therapeutic, and even redemptive, goal: gratification. Art as pleasure or beauty or consummation may fulfill, restore, and harmonize; that is, serve as a retotalizing countervailing force to alienation as loss or separation. Where alienation signifies the puzzling fragment, art implies the conscious reconstruction of the whole. Because art in this sense is thought to represent an intelligible, and even philosophical, translation of everyday affairs, it opens up our horizons and energizes our intellect. Art is seen as liberating and as overcoming deficiencies in both knowledge and satisfaction. Marcuse refers, in his later work, to art as a "second alienation" (CR, 97), however. In this philosophical turn of events, this aesthetic alienation is still considered to be emancipatory, rather than oppressive. It is a condition in which the artist "dissociates himself methodically from alienated society and creates the unreal 'illusory' universe in which art has, and communicates, its truth" (ibid.). Nietzsche pointed out just how much our aesthetic ideals entail an alienation from, or a renunciation of, the timeworn sameness of lived experience. To him, artistic mimesis and conformity represented slavish and nihilistic habituations to the historical status quo. To Nietzsche it was our task—if one was strong enough—to sublimate our loneliness into our only-ness. Alienated existence was to become our most authentic mode of being. Nietzsche writes of the ugliness of truth and of the life-preserving power of art. Likewise, Marcuse maintains in *The Aesthetic Dimension*: "If art were to promise that at the end good would triumph over evil, such a promise would be refuted by the historical truth. In reality it is evil which triumphs and there are only islands of good where one can find refuge for a brief time" (AD, 47).

The pessimism and resignation expressed in this, Marcuse's last book, completes an important line of thought in his aesthetic theory. Marcuse has come full circle, back to the disillusionment of his dissertation years. This final book is an explicit reassertion of certain of the most traditional European values and assumptions, present in muffled form during his middle period, but rooted in his early literary training.

> The more immediately political the work of art, the more it reduces the power of estrangement and the radical, transcendent goals of change. In this sense there may be more subversive potential in the poetry of Baudelaire and Rimbaud than in the didactic plays of Brecht. (AD, xiii)

Clearly, *The Aesthetic Dimension* did not simply appear as a bolt from the blue. The earliest formulations of its position occur in his dissertation. Intimations of these views occur even within his middle period. For example, in *An Essay on Liberation*, he writes: "Art remains alien to the revolutionary praxis by virtue of the artist's commitment to Form: Form as art's own reality, as *die Sache selbst*" [the thing in itself] (EL, 39). Also in "Art in the One-Dimensional Society," he maintains "art can fulfill its inner revolutionary function only if it does not itself become part of any Establishment, including the revolutionary establishment" (AO, 55). During his later period, Marcuse negotiates his "turn" and "return," highlighting his view of art *as alienation*, and the emancipatory function of high art and the humanities, tying together his "beginning" and "end" (KRg and AD).[11] Problems can arise if this periodization is adhered to too strictly or too schematically, because the analytical separation of his early and late, from his middle, works corresponds as much to logical, as to chronological, distinctions. These divisions are not so much irreconcilable breaks in continuity, as oscillations within a larger frame.

In both his earliest and latest writings Marcuse directs special attention to the emancipatory power of the intelligence gained through a study of the humanities. Marcuse's understanding of the cognitive value of art, particularly the great literatures of classical Greece and modern Europe, thus also needs to be specifically examined. It is within this context that we may perceive the overall unity of his philosophy—*in its several, interconnected attempts to extract reason from art and from the aesthetic dimension.*

Classical literature (in the Great Books tradition) has long been considered a prime art form assisting the genuine advancement of learning. The general liberal arts philosophy of education presupposes both a cognitive and an affective value in aesthetic effort and achievement. This is held to be the case because the classics are thought to represent a definite mastery of the complex art of knowing ourselves and our world. They are philosophically esteemed insofar as they render relevant human meanings sensuously apparent. Because of their particular ability to illumine human experience, they may be also considered unique in their potential to transform *alienated* human existence into *authentic* human existence. Authenticity in this sense might be thought to accrue to those who are cultivated, in cultural-educational terms. In the memorable words of Mark Van Doren, "Liberal education makes the person competent; not merely to know or do, but also, and indeed chiefly, to be."[12]

Since the venerable liberal arts tradition has been historically (and inseparably) tied to a realistic and normative concept of *eidos* and essence (as per Plato, Aristotle, Augustine, Thomas, Hegel, and Husserl), we should not be surprised to find some modification of classical realism (and *not the value relativism* that the conservative culture warriors claim) in Marcuse's aesthetics and ontology. Indeed, chapter 8 of *One-Dimensional Man* argues the historical reality of universals, and his third chapter highlights the importance of the aesthetic Form as the dimension where both reality and truth are disclosed. Marcuse also generally shares with Plato and Schiller the philosophical conviction that the most meaningful and beautiful works of art are also the soundest foundation for an education to political justice.

Much of this is an immensely valuable philosophical excursion into a discussion of the nature of emancipatory education that is usually absent in the United States, even in academic circles, and swamped by nationalism and conservative moralism at the hands of William Bennett and his colleagues. One problem here, though, is that despite Marcuse's valuable attention else-where to issues of class, race, and gender, he ultimately articulates a concept of literary-aesthetic education standing in disjunction from much sociological and historical methodology as well as from the philosophical categories generally associated with a materialist dialectic. Political, historical, and educational issues, in Marcuse's estimation, are considered better understood *out of art itself* and *out of art alone.*

An article by Barry M. Kátz on the Freiburg dissertation of Marcuse claims that it "is not a conservative work."[13] I must disagree, and will demonstrate that, in terms of its philosophical foundations, his dissertation does not transcend or reject the traditional approach to liberal arts educational theory; rather it operates well within its usual parameters. An explicit aesthetic philosophical conservatism is acknowledged by Marcuse (at AD, x), justifying his adherence to what are considered to be the permanent values and long-established criteria defining great literature and authentic art, rather than revising these criteria by bringing new philosophical or historical insight to bear on them. Furthermore, while we can also see, in retrospect, that his writings along the classical literary lines of *Der deutsche Künstlerroman* and *The Aesthetic Dimension* occur in conjunction with the militant Schillerian humanism of his middle period, this does not so much contradict Marcuse's fundamental philosophical conservatism as deepen our understanding. Both phases seek norms of moral and political reason through the mediation of the aesthetic reality.

In one of the earliest works of his middle period, "The Affirmative Character of Culture," Marcuse had understood high culture to be ideologically affirmative of the status quo, even while he regarded it also as a valuable preserve of truth. In the end, as in his beginning, the traditional and highly formalized arts are prized by Marcuse for their critical intellectual function, while their affirmative nature is tolerated as inescapable. Marcuse's inability to escape the history of affirmation that has attended the perennialist liberal arts philosophy of education and art as well as our need to transcend the failure of critical theory in this regard must also be addressed.

Marcuse's philosophy of protest within higher education criticized the multiversity vision of Clark Kerr, former head of the University of California. Kerr's educational philosophical point of view represented a decisive departure from the traditional collegiate self-conception as an "autonomous" ivory tower or grove of academe, one step removed from the practical realm, and stressed instead a logic of corporate and government involvement in higher education. Institutionalized during the 1960s at Columbia, Harvard, Berkeley, and at the state universities of Wisconsin and New York, among other places, this philosophy of the extended, service university has now been implemented almost everywhere in higher education. In the post-Sputnik, early Vietnam era, critics of the multiversity pointed out that the phenomenal growth of these conglomerate higher education systems was heavily subsidized by grants from the federal government and corporations for research into areas such as aerospace, intelligence, and weapons. A massive expansion of Reserve Officer Training Corps programs also occurred. These extra-academic interests characteristically influenced higher educational policy giving priority to many of the needs of the business and military establishments. Many also objected to the dehumanization displayed in the multiversity's new and increasing commitment to behavioral objectives in teaching and learning and performance-based criteria for intellectual competence, as well as the growing predominance of managerial language and thinking in the organization of higher education. Kerr was a major liberal spokesperson who thereafter became chairperson of the Carnegie Commission on Higher Education. His ideological and institutional innovations represented one of the most articulate and authoritative administrative points of view in the intense educational philosophical debates that occurred on this nation's campuses during the late 1960s and early 1970s. Marcuse on the other hand of course acquired a reputation in the United States and in Europe as a spokesperson for radical university reform and for the militant new left analysis of (and resistance to) the foreign and domestic policies of the U.S. government and of its allies in Europe and Southeast Asia.

Marcuse's relationship to the radical student movement was not without its problems, however. While his theories were embraced and propounded by many, his politics and philosophy also came under close critical examination.[14] Marcuse's nine year association with the U.S. government as an intelligence officer with the Office of Strategic Services (OSS) and the Department of State became a topic of debate in some circles when it was raised by the Progressive Labor Party (PLP).[15]

Paul Breines (1970) vehemently ridiculed the PLP's contentions. I have sought to examine them myself, and have found no evidence at this juncture to support any assertion that Marcuse's government work extended to his leadership role in the student movement. My review of unpublished materials that have only recently become available, produced by Marcuse during the war for use by the OSS and the Department of State, tends to substantiate that his work was that of an honest leftist theoretician working with great integrity against fascism.[16] I must add that not all of his project reports were accessible to me in 1997 (due to cataloging limitations, now overcome) at the Herbert Marcuse Archive of the *Stadt- und Universitätsbibliothek* at Frankfurt. In those that were, many of his economic and political statements are quite bluntly formulated in strong Marxist language, utilizing less Aesopian terms than he would later employ after his departure from government service. Douglas Kellner (1998) has recently collected and published several of Marcuse's key essays from this period in *Technology, War, and Fascism: the Unknown Marcuse*. This book now makes possible wide access to these documents, and several other volumes are planned which will facilitate continuing scholarly assessment.

Many intellectuals worked with the U.S. government against the Nazis in World War II, but few of them remained with the intelligence service for so long a period after the war. In late 1942 Marcuse was employed as a senior analyst in the Bureau of Intelligence in the Office of War Information. In 1943 he served with the research and analysis branch of the OSS. In 1945 he transferred to the State Department, and in 1947 he became head of the Central European Division of the State Department's Research and Intelligence unit. In 1952 he went to the Russian Institute of Columbia University, then in 1954–55 to Harvard's Russian Institute, where *Soviet Marxism* was completed. I concur with Kellner's assessment that it is ultimately *incongruous* that Marcuse stayed so long in intelligence work.

There is no question, however, that Marcuse's original impact was connected most closely to the intellectual and political, campus-based turmoil of the 1960s, and derived from his theoretical leadership in the very definition of the cultural and educational issues involved. He addressed, for example, the questions of science and research in service to the "performance principle" of advanced industrial society. He also spoke to the almost infinite facets of alienation in everyday life, that is, at school, on the job, and in recreational activities, where these were thought to be regulated by a consciousness industry and a total administration. He stressed the emancipatory potential of a renascent sensuality under the guidance of the most rational and legitimate goals of art. But one repays Marcuse badly if one takes his insights as dogmas solely to be celebrated. His philosophy must be extended, deepened, negated, and raised to a higher level. By investigating the singular interrelationships forged by Marcuse among the topics of alienation, art, and the humanities, a penetrating critical perspective on his work can be established. I am arguing that the failure to address significant issues in educational theory is responsible for the inadequate status of current scholarship on Marcuse's general philosophical orientation. The vindication of Marcuse's theory and the future of critical theorizing hinge upon this effort.

CHAPTER TWO

—◊◊◊—

Literary Art and *Bildung*:
Marcuse's Early Works

Marcuse's early affinity with aspects of the literary aesthetic philosophy of Wilhelm Dilthey and classical German idealism is a powerful underlying influence in his lifelong intellectual effort. Even in his later work this early influence is sufficiently strong as to insure that where he makes concessions to more contemporary orientations like psychoanalysis and the theory of socialism, he does so only on the basis of his early idealist orientation. In the end Marcuse returns to the "critical" domain of classical German philosophy: art, while grounded in social reality, has its *own* truth that is always the *other* of this world. Truth, for the neo-Kantians, is not *the given* in nature or society, but a knowledge of the *meaning* of being that the human *mind* develops. Dilthey's theory of the *Geisteswissenschaften* (literally mind-studies, but usually translated as the humanities or human studies) is explicitly considered by the early Marcuse to take critical regard of this subjective epistemological circumstance. Consistent with Dilthey's *Construction of the Historical World in the Humanities*, Marcuse believed that the humanities may make us more profoundly human by making us aware of the deepest contradictions of life, for instance, between love and death or barbarism and justice, in a formal, aesthetic manner that is said to be uniquely emancipatory. This is because the humanities are thought to be the preserve of art as transcendence or sublimation. They engender the *radical* kind of knowledge that is thought to be nonempirical, speculative, and dialectical in the classical Greek sense. This Greek notion of knowledge as reminiscence was also thought to be preserved in the psychoanalytic sense of recall of the

27

repressed. Literary art makes an intuitive recovery of a sense of our being that has long faded from our own consciousness. The living, ontological core of humanity is retrieved through the educative reminiscence that is the domain of art and literature. The aesthetic imagination is the means to the liberating intellectual condition that Marcuse will continue to seek throughout his later works. His dissertation, written in 1922 but unpublished until 1978, is indispensable to an appreciation of his philosophical relevance to current debates in the humanities and in higher education.

Der deutsche Künstlerroman: The German Artist Novel

Marcuse's dissertation explores the ways in which German novels have portrayed the character formation of artists. To the best of my knowledge it is as yet untranslated and unpublished in English. He finds that these novels proceed through an oftentimes tortuous process of personality development to an eventual education to maturity. James Joyce published his *Portrait of the Artist as a Young Man* in 1916 just before Marcuse was to begin his graduate literary studies. While Marcuse's dissertation confined itself to an analysis of exclusively German sources, it nonetheless shared Joyce's conviction that insight into the problems and educational stages in the life of the artist had something to teach us all. The "artist novel" or *Künstlerroman* is that singular type of narrative in which an artist is the leading figure. Among the wealth of literary materials discussed by Marcuse are Goethe's *Wilhelm Meister's Apprenticeship*, Gottfried Keller's *Der Grüne Heinrich*, and Thomas Mann's *Death in Venice*.

Marcuse's dissertation operates well within the framework of the *Geisteswissenschaften* firmly established since Dilthey.[1] It reflects the traditional assumption of the educative qualities of the process, experience, and object of art, and the value (as well as distress) inherent in an *education through art to autonomy.*

Dilthey is generally credited with academically popularizing the term *Bildungsroman* (novel of education) in modern literary studies, through his emphasis on the educational processes depicted in Goethe's novel, *Wilhelm Meisters Lehrjahre.*[2] Dilthey accomplished this through his 1906 volume, *Das Erlebnis und die Dichtung (Experience and Literary Art)*. While it is clear that the term *Bildungsroman* does not have an unequivocal or precise meaning, it *is* nonetheless taken to characterize an identifiable genre within modern German fiction. "Classics" in this regard include not only Goethe's *Lehrjahre*

(*Wilhelm Meister's Apprenticeship*), but also Keller's *Grüner Heinrich* and Mann's *Buddenbrooks* and *The Magic Mountain*, as well as his *Bildungsroman*-parody, *Doktor Faustus*.

Dilthey ardently believed that education (*Bildung*) stood centermost in the affairs of human life. His analysis contributed to the continued relevance of educational issues and political and cultural matters in the then contemporary literary circles. Ten years after the publication of his *Das Erlebnis and die Dichtung*, Georg Lukács outlined a typology of novel forms in *The Theory of the Novel* (1916). This would also include a chapter on Goethe's *Wilhelm Meister*. As a doctoral student in German literature during this period, Marcuse could not have been unfamiliar with these contemporary influences in the philosophy of literary art, nor of the centrality of the issue of education in them. Indeed the period between the two world wars witnessed a multifaceted *pedagogical reform movement* throughout the German-speaking countries.

According to Fritz K. Ringer's excellent educational history of this period (which can also shed some light on the postmodern critique of modernism today), a fundamental cultural conflict made its appearance just after World War I, resulting in a "crisis of learning" precipitated by the confrontation of educational "modernists" and "mandarins." This period was also the time of Dilthey's greatest educational philosophical influence, and as Ringer notes: "The most important and distinguished contributions to the revival in German learning after 1880 dealt with the methods and objectives of the humanistic disciplines, the *Geisteswissenschaften*."[3] Dilthey is described as a leading force in a revival of the "mandarin" movement issuing from the Southwest German School of neo-Kantianism against the philosophical encroachments of logical positivism and empiricism (the modernists). István Meszáros's book on Lukács notes that the latter's *Theory of the Novel* was hailed as the outstanding work of the *Geisteswissenschaft*-movement in this period of educational and literary revitalization. Lukács's own 1962 preface to the reissue of his *Die Theorie des Romans* mentions the "fascinating effect" of Dilthey's *Das Erlebnis und die Dichtung* on him during his early years, although he also emphasizes his book's potential to move beyond Dilthey's neo-Kantian limitations.

Andrew Arato and Paul Breines note that Lukács's participation in the Budapest wing of the *Geisteswissenschaft*-movement reflected his "ethical or mythical utopian socialism"[4] that entailed a sweeping rejection of capitalism, though without any practical elements. They mention the fact that this movement was "in the right wing of the Hungarian intellectual opposition of the war years,"[5] but that Lukács moved away from it in 1919 to join the ranks of the communists. In contrast to Lukács's leftward shift, Marcuse resigned from the Social Democratic Party in 1919 and would move further away from political practice and *closer* to Dilthey's perspective over the next ten years.

Marcuse's dissertation explicitly cites Dilthey and Lukács as providing its analytical foundations, as well as the nineteenth-century aesthetic works of Hegel and Schelling. Like Dilthey and Lukács, Marcuse's work also centers on an analysis of the novel form, and includes major subsections on the *Bildungsromane* of Goethe, Keller, and Mann. Marcuse explicitly prefers and defends the life-centered, worldly-educational approach of Dilthey against the contending Romantic interpretations of Goethe's *Wilhelm Meister* expressed in the work of Novalis and Friedrich Schlegel (KRg, 92–94). In so doing he exhibits the orientation defended by Lukács, stressing the primacy of social existence and education, over the romantic concern for metaphysics. Marcuse also utilizes Dilthey's concept of "life" and Lukács's notion of "totality" as key analytical tools.

Dilthey presupposed that the *Geisteswissenschaften* served as the organon for a critical reflection on historical human reality, and that human existence in society could best be understood out of historical works of art. The last sentence of Marcuse's dissertation highlights this same conviction. His conclusions from the study of the artist in the German novel are summed up with the following words: "Deeper perhaps than any other novel form, the *Künstlerroman* emerges from the specifically Germanic sense of the world which acknowledges the tragic duality of being, behind all unity, and the innate suffering of the individual. . . ." He continues: "The entirely dualistic sense of the world, from which the *Künstlerroman* comes, lends it a heavy and sorrowful atmosphere from the beginning—there is no drunkenness with life here, no pure joy in the senses, no festive color, that is not also born of yearning. . . . Above and beyond the literary-historical problems, a piece of human history becomes visible: the struggle of the German people for a new community" (KRg, 333). This new form of communal social organization and sense of national solidarity were goals that Marcuse thought the divided German spirit either had to create or to forego (ibid.). These traditionally conservative references to German national feeling are disconcerting, even if Marcuse would later make explicit his criticism from the left of the Weimar era SPD. Such references must be bracketed at this point in order to elucidate the purpose and method of Marcuse's dissertation.

The Artist's Education from Alienation to Maturity

Marcuse's investigation into the world of artistic self-reflection and self-examination aimed at disclosing the artist's personal concerns with the problems of being an artist. In accordance with the approach of Dilthey, *he sought insight into the infrastructure of the historical world through literature*. In Marcuse's view, the German *Künstlerroman* articulates the harsh duality of the ideal against the real, perceived by modern artists in the alienating quality of their life and activity vis-à-vis the general forms of social existence emergent from advancing civilization. As he sees it, the novel itself, as a unique literary form, is no longer the broad expression of the general social mood and feeling (as was considered to be the case with epic poetry). It is rather an expression and record of a narrower cultural sphere reflecting the increasing differentiation internal to modern civilization. Novels revolve around the aims, conflicts, and conduct of particular social strata and substrata, and the artist novel is thought to capture the special form of life represented by the artist and the artist's circle. The artist novel is said to be possible only by virtue of the fact that the artist *does* possess a *unique life-style*, and this particular life-style is taken as evidence that the other forms of social existence generally available are not adequate to the innermost being (*Wesen*, KRg, 10) of the artist. During the Homeric and classical periods in Greece, as well as during the age of Viking and Germanic culture, artists were fully integrated into their cultures. In more modern epochs, however, artists become separated, though characteristically attached to a symbiotic social sector such as the Church, the feudal aristocracy, or eventually, the bourgeoisie (KRg, 13–14). Marcuse points out that in the artist's bond with the Church, aesthetic subjectivity merges with religion. The dependence upon feudal courts resulted in the deflection of art into chivalric formalities. In the early bourgeois era, art is said to have become an acquired skill, a trade with apprenticeship and mastery supervised by guilds. The artist had not yet come into his own. Marcuse stresses: "Only those who stood outside of these ties to societal sectors, or whose exuberance at the new worldliness allowed them to tear themselves away, experienced the breakthrough to their own self-conscious subjectivity" (KRg, 13). He mentions as examples the wandering troops of mimes and players, as well as the young clerics and students, as representatives of an emancipated, vagabond life (ibid.). To Marcuse, this independence reflected simply a lyrical protest that was also unrealistic and ultimately self-destructive. The *Künstlerroman* would attempt to transcend merely lyrical aesthetic feeling and to preserve it at a higher level. It sought to balance what Marcuse considered to be the artist's pathetic-ecstatic extreme relationship to life with a tempered or *educated* reconciliation of the artist to the realities of social existence. Considering the novel form explicitly after the manner of Lukács (KRg, 10), Marcuse believed that it expressed a longing for an as yet unattained "totality of life" (ibid.). The novel reflected historical human striving for a new community, beyond the realm of individual alienation, dissociation, or subjective and illusory autonomy. Marcuse contends that for certain important literary figures (Goethe, Keller, and Mann) the artist novel inherently tends toward *Bildungsroman* (KRg, 12, 84). It searches for a mature and viable form of artistic life. Education, here, clearly implies the passage from youthful naïveté and subjective excess, to an active and practical adulthood, a process of seasoning and aesthetic self-perfection. The *Bildungsroman*, as such, is never concerned with curricular design or instructional methods or schooling in the narrower sense. Rather it addresses the problems of character formation and such issues as the harmonization of sensuousness and intellect and the conflicts between individual self-awareness and one's social potential. According to Albert Berger[6] the theory of the *Bildungsroman* presumes that it is possible for the aesthetic form of the novel to uniquely contribute to an understanding and resolution of these educational questions (precisely in virtue of its orientation toward "totality," etc.). Likewise, the German literary critic Ernst Leopold Stahl has discussed the replacement of the religious educational ideals of the Middle Ages by the humanist educational ideals of classical German philosophy, and linked these educational issues essentially to the emergence of the *Bildungsroman* in eighteenth-century Germany.[7] In this regard, Goethe is said to have written of a *natural* (rather than supernatural or religious) *human impulse* to education (*Bildungstrieb*). This aimed at the fullest possible cultivation of each human being's naturally given capabilities via the agency of practical worldly concern and the desire to attain aesthetic, rather than religious, dignity and grace. Both Goethe and Schiller also link this educational ideal to the ethereal, aesthetic existence of the Beautiful Soul. A Beautiful Soul is an individual educated to self-discovery and anamnesis through art and the aesthetic experience. Marcuse points out, with regard to Goethe's *Wilhelm Meister*, that a Beautiful Soul reaches a necessary, but not sufficient, stage in the full perfection of human development. "The Beautiful Soul" he writes "gives form to its existence from the inside out, lives accordingly and genuinely, but the goal of all education: 'perfected equilibrium—harmony with freedom,' unity of 'contradictory impulses . . .

without destruction,' has not been reached. . . . [T]hat ideal is fully actualized only in the circle around Lothario" (KRg, 80).

To Marcuse, the significance of Goethe's character, Lothario, is that he matures beyond the stage of the Beautiful Soul. He is the intimate friend and protector of certain of the central delicate aesthetes in Wilhelm Meister's life (Mignon and the harpist), and is also the model of a productive and active member of society and a representative of a Masonic-like lodge that eventually inducts Wilhelm into its order. Only at this point is Wilhelm's education considered to have attained its fullest development. Marcuse emphasizes: "In that moment when Wilhelm is accepted into this circle and recognizes its appropriate form of life, his apprenticeship years are done." Wilhelm's maturation is regarded in an Enlightenment sense: ". . . from now on he has only to absorb, to understand, and as a consequence, to act. All error dissolves itself before the calm clarity of these knowledgeable ones" (ibid.).

Marcuse seeks to understand the development of educational thought in Goethe's literary work. Through his analysis of Goethe's early efforts at the artist novel, that is, *The Sorrows of Young Werther* and *Wilhelm Meister's Theatrical Mission*, he follows Goethe's first literary attempts to resolve the problem of artistic alienation and the inability of a Beautiful Soul to effectively deal with the devastating duality perceived between the ideal and reality, and art and life. *Werther* is regarded as one of the earliest artist novels (or, more precisely, as it is noted, novel-of-letters) portraying the tragic and self-destructive consequences of extreme subjectivism in the personality formation of the artist. In the *Theatrical Mission*, Wilhelm seeks to express his artistic inwardness and subjectivity in a more realistic and objective vein than did Werther. Marcuse finds that a reconciliation of self and world, and aesthetic existence and civilization, is possible upon the basis of a "painful, but voluntary renunciation (*Entsagung*), that from here on characterizes Goethe's portrayals of artists and men" (KRg, 51–52).

Wilhelm chooses the theatrical life as a form of aesthetically oriented social existence that incorporates a social and educational program in the actualization of its artistic aims.

> The artist is assigned this "mission"—to work creatively and constructively upon the environment through the medium of the theater. (KRg, 55)

> . . . Wilhelm . . . is not like Werther, like the artist of the Werther-era, a subjectivist artist from the very beginning and fated

> to be such; instead this subjectivism is for him but a part of youth,
> he—and Goethe—strive forward toward its supersession, toward
> "maturity." (KRg, 61)

Maturity must supplant aesthetic subjectivism and resolve the problem of
the Beautiful Soul. For Goethe's Wilhelm, this maturity also emerges from
an encounter with art—the dramatic art of Shakespeare: ". . . Wilhelm
perceives in Hamlet a final justification of his own otherness, his opposition
to the environment. . . ." (KRg, 67). Wilhelm, like Hamlet, has had to
contend with inner turmoil and with the intellectual or spiritual pain that
should lead to action, but that instead makes him recoil from it. Marcuse
quotes Goethe on Wilhelm's reaction to Shakespeare: "This is not just
literary art; you feel like you are standing before the wide-open, terrifying
books of fate, through which howls the windstorm of the most agitated
life. . . ." (Goethe, at KRg, 66).

    According to Marcuse, Shakespeare has shown Wilhelm that the true
artist is aware of the intimate "interconnection of art and life, artistic existence and environment" (KRg, 66). Wilhelm is now said to realize exactly
how important it is to have experienced "the entire fullness of being" (ibid.)
rather than to flee from the tumultuous truths of sociohistorical reality to a
blessed otherworld of aestheticism, as the Beautiful Soul characteristically
does. Shakespeare's own historical artistic activity is considered eloquent
testimony to the fact that the theater may have the profoundly disalienating
and educational effect. It helps us in understanding life out of art. Wilhelm,
thus, resolves to produce Shakespeare's plays with an itinerant theatrical
company. Ultimately he is also cast in the role of Hamlet. Shortly after this,
the *Theatrical Mission* breaks off, but the narrative is picked up again in the
first half of *Wilhelm Meister's Apprenticeship*. Marcuse explains that *Wilhelm
Meister's Apprenticeship* reflects the next stage in Goethe's aesthetic and educational thinking—a stage in which artistic creativity and fulfillment are
achieved not through the theater, but through "real life, itself" (KRg, 75).
This is seen as the most appropriate realm of human gratification and
expression. "Nothing points beyond life, contrasts the reality to the idea,
because life, reality, has itself become idea" (KRg, 81).

> It is clear that this form of life is, in its depths, aesthetically founded:
> the perfected equilibrium of inner and outer, spirit and sensuality,
> essence and activity, transforms the existence of each individual in
> this quite limited circle into beauty, into artwork. (ibid.)

The aim of Goethe's *Bildungsroman* is, thus, seen as the resolution of the problem of artistic alienation and the Beautiful Soul through those forms of discipline, renunciation, and self-control (*Entsagung*) that will permit the harmonious development of each individual's innermost creative impulses and powers to live an active life in the real world. Here maturity is contrasted with youth, and this concept of full adulthood is understood as "entirely different than a resignation to a shallow realism of everydayness" (KRg, 82). Wilhelm learned to practice a voluntary and painful, yet emancipatory, renunciation of his purely subjective tendencies, because in Goethe's estimation, "humanity cannot be happy until it itself sets limits to its boundless yearning" (ibid.). By imbuing the immature and incapacitating yearnings of the Beautiful Soul with the measure and proportion of art and reality itself, an even more sublime Beautiful Soul could be *reclaimed* for this world and *for life*. Marcuse's Goethe commentary concludes: ". . . the harmonious regularity of the universe, the world-artwork, will no longer brook an artistry that stands to the side or keeps to itself" (KRg, 84).

While Marcuse does not mention it, it was, of course, Kant's essay, "*Was ist Aufklärung?*" (*What is Enlightenment?* 1784), which most vividly proposed a worldly autonomy against that theological and otherworldly "immaturity" that we inflict upon ourselves. Kant calls humanity's immaturity our *selbstverschuldene Unmündigkeit*, our dysfunctional ability to independently reproduce our own moral, political, or religious dependency. Likewise, it was this spirit of a mature, worldly, cultural enlightenment (taken up by Wm. v. Humboldt) that animated the major university reform efforts begun with the establishment of the University of Berlin in 1810, virtually replacing the dominance of the faculties of Theology and Law with the faculties of Arts and Sciences and reflecting the educational humanism that was integral to the emerging classical German idealism. Maturity signified the human being in possession of itself—its *inalienable* rights and the moral law of reason. Still enlightenment ideals were expressed differently in different countries and under different social conditions. In the United States and in France, these merged very visibly with revolutionary movements; in Germany, this explicitly political tendency remained very much in the background. In lieu of revolution, in Germany, Goethe's *Bildungs*-philosophy and Friedrich Schiller's *On the Aesthetic Education of Man in a Series of Letters* codified the prevailing educational-humanist view that art and beauty were the primary forces that could lead to political freedom.

Marcuse's dissertation points out that radical political activity *was* also one of the forms of social existence (in addition to the theatrical life, bohemia, and the life-style of the master craftsperson) experimented with in the artist novel's search for a resolution to the problem of aesthetic alienation and attainment of community and solidarity. This is exemplified in the literary efforts preceding and accompanying the February 1848 revolution, that is, the cultural movement known as Young Germany (*Jung Deutschland*). "Finally, the struggle against the established society was actively taken up in Germany," he writes of this movement's purpose and perspective. ". . . [T]he people were awakened; the masses had arisen—it appeared as if the revitalization should radiate from them. Now the artist believed to have found comrades in arms, to have attained solidarity: he stepped in on the side of the revolutionary people, accompanied their struggle and suffering, participated in their attacks against the old forms of life" (KRg, 195).

As he explains, this new generation of youthful German artists had made its aim the striving for maximal fulfillment in this life, rather than a resignation to, or a lyrical escape from, the world's failure to grant us each immediate and lasting gratification. "These artists are . . . simultaneously fighters for a social and political revolution" (KRg, 189). Marcuse emphasizes the fact that the purely subjectivistic-romantic type of artist novel was actually a literary form quite incompatible with the Young Germans, but that their socially engaged literary effort did share many of the essential cultural concerns, though not the typical solutions, which also animated the artist novel.

Marcuse's analysis of the testimony of the art of this movement, however, brings him to extremely pessimistic conclusions about the revolutionary involvement of artists in the practical struggle for social emancipation:

> When the artist sides with the revolutionary masses and joins in the struggle against the established society, he will nonetheless not find fulfillment: certainly a brief agreement on a path, but not upon a goal, for these masses battle for everything else but that for which he yearns. (KRg, 190–91)

In Marcuse's estimation, the Young Germans depicted the radical cultural goals of the artists as being destroyed in the context of revolutionary practice. As Marcuse explains Laube's novel, *Das Junge Europa* (*Young Europe*): "The attempt to achieve the ideal demands of the activist conception of the artist is shattered in the course of the revolutionary campaign" (KRg, 191). Laube is said to leave no alternative except for artists to fit themselves into the established form of society. Marcuse interprets this development, not as capitulation, but as an extension of Goethe's concept of an educated ripeness, maturity, and self-controlled renunciation (*Entsagung*, ibid.). This measured or tempered solution ". . . holds to the *middle* between both extremes" (KRg, 192, emphasis added), that is, it is thought to make possible a self-confidence and "aplomb" (Laube at ibid.) that stands apart from both an uncritical surrender to empty convention as well as from a total immersion into revolutionary mass organizations and movements. It is at this point in his early reading of what he considered to be art's analysis of history that we encounter an aspect of the *political* instruction that Marcuse believes to have wrested from art.

In what the ugly course of historical events in Europe (from 1922 to 1933 and beyond) would render an unfortunate and ironic choice of words, Marcuse highlights Gutzkow's call to a "Third Reich" (KRg, 282; Gutzkow at KRg, 200) in which the dualities between intellect and sensuousness, and art and life, could be reconciled. Certainly neither Marcuse nor the artist novel can be held responsible for the unfortunate connotations of this phrase after 1933. Nonetheless it graphically illustrates what Robert Steigerwald[8] first stressed as Marcuse's desire for a "third way," a political course apart from the capitalist and socialist paths of social development.

Marcuse's treatment of the artist novel is an extremely lengthy one: the dissertation typescript was originally bound in two volumes. I have referred to it here only where it specifically relates to Marcuse's concepts of art, alienation, and the humanities. He devotes, for example, three of his ten chapters to a critical analysis of the limitations he perceives in the lyrical romantic form of the artist novel, contrasting this subjectivistic form with the epical-realistic or objectivist modes (that also tend toward the *Bildungs-roman* or socially engaged art). In addition to his chapters on Goethe, *Jung Deutschland*, and so forth, he also treats the work of Gottfried Keller and Thomas Mann. The chapter on Mann deserves special attention.

Throughout Marcuse's dissertation, the artist is treated as a special philosophical or psychological type, whose social existence stands in abrasive opposition to the general social existence of humanity. This condition of artistic alienation is nowhere more vividly explicated than in Marcuse's chapter on Mann. Mann's work is taken as an example of the self-reflection of the artist, revolving around the estranging inner tensions that make themselves felt between art and knowledge. Knowledge, here, is not regarded in the romantic, ideal fashion of the subjectivistic artist novel, which is said to question the very right of reality to exist, but in the tragical pessimistic manner of Nietzsche and Hamlet, who represent the more seasoned and profound, epical-realistic, view. According to Marcuse's account, "The newer artist novel contains a painful and deep concept of the artist: the artist with knowledge as a disinherited and disfranchised, stigmatized and joyless individual of loneliness and yearning." In the work of Mann, he writes, "this image has found not only its sharpest focus and formation and final resolution," but also "the total problem of the artist—his painful-knowing relationship to life, his inner dividedness" (KRg, 303) is presented in a new and significant way.

Mann's early work, *Buddenbrooks* (1901), is considered central to all of his subsequent writing, because it introduces the themes of estrangement, distancing, loneliness, and homelessness, regarded by Marcuse as socially pivotal (KRg, 305). These multifaceted phenomena of alienation, revolving around the decline of a bourgeois family and life-style, are derived in Marcuse's estimation from "the killing of the capacity for life by knowledge" (ibid.). For Mann "These knowledgeable ones can no longer act. The business is sinking—however, the same compulsion that makes them unable to perform leads them to an aesthetic existence. . . ." (ibid.).

Mann's starting point appears to take up where history has forced a crisis in Goethe's approach to education and knowledge. Unlike the self-confident and active circle around Lothario and his organization, the Buddenbrooks have lost the harmonious interrelation of art and life, and life and knowledge. Marcuse stresses, however, the fact that Mann himself remained self-assured and was not demoralized. He possessed a naturalistic world view and a categorical commitment to life and humanity, over against the excesses of aestheticism. These were of such redeeming power as to permit Mann mental and emotional renewal. This naturalism and commitment are cited (KRg, 306–7) as the key stimuli to Mann's search for a viable form of social life to which the artist could again connect, and thus continue to survive. Unlike the work of Heinrich Mann, which in part looked expressly to new socialist forms of political organization, Marcuse finds superior potential in Thomas Mann's vision of the reconstituted *familial* social existence of the high-serious German burgher, who overcomes decadence and aestheticism through a transfigured (and admittedly ironic [KRg, 318]) appreciation of the "joys of the usual" (Mann at KRg, 307). In this way, Marcuse contends, Thomas Mann realistically *recaptures life for the artist*, by linking him to a social form (the middle class) that still has organic historical roots, rather than to the working class, whose rootedness Mann (in 1901) believed had not yet even developed. The necessary mediating ingredient to Mann's philosophy of reconciliation is "a strict resoluteness, a steely education" (KRg, 307), by means of which subjective yearning is directed back toward life.

Marcuse finds in Mann yet another example of a third solution between conventional capitalist and socialist forms.

After these comments on *Buddenbrooks*, Marcuse turns to Mann's several novellas. All are said to be intimately concerned with the primordial experience (*Urerlebnis*, KRg, 305) of the deadening effects of knowledge on the artist, the attendant dangers of decadence and aestheticism, and the ultimate human need to reclaim life from the most devastating blows of truth and the debilitating effects of aesthetic subjectivity. Marcuse's treatment of Mann's 1913 novella, *Death in Venice*, is designed to trace out and clarify these interconnections.

Gustav von Aschenbach, Mann's central character, is a professor of art at the University of Munich. Through renunciation and self-control he has tempered his subjectivistic aesthetic striving and yearning, and transformed it realistically into a socially acceptable, indeed prestigious, bourgeois profession. The price he paid was the gradual encroachment of an "official-pedagogical" (KRg, 326) quality into his work, but, in exchange, he was no longer stigmatized as a stranger or outsider. In this manner, Mann's character apparently represented the resolution of the artist novel's basic problem, the fundamental conflict separating the artist from society. The life-style of the master artist was, however, not at all an unconstrained or free and natural one. Rather, as Marcuse explains, it was only maintained through the strictest discipline bordering on heroism. Deep inside, Aschenbach was all too aware of the fact that his position as artistic *Meister* and teacher was a lie, that the prestige of his social existence was a pose (KRg, 327). It was ridiculous that he should function as an educator (ibid.), for he knew that he had an inborn incorrigible tendency to fall back into the abyss of a self-destructive aesthetic longing and subjectivity. Aschenbach comes to a self-awareness that Marcuse describes as follows:

> The celebrated and elevated master, the acknowledged intellectual leader of a new young generation, who had found the criterion of his rise to "honor," acceptance, civic responsibility, precisely in his consuming struggle for purity, innocence, classicism and objectivity of Form, acknowledged with a shudder, that even in this struggle for Form was hidden the Dionysian compulsion of the artist—a dark, destructive, unbourgeois power. . . . (KRg, 327–28)

Aschenbach is driven back into this subjective aesthetic nether world by a self-destructive obsession with the image and actuality of a beautiful Polish boy. Everything in his life is tossed overboard. Delusion, degradation, and death follow. His highly sublimated life-style ultimately founders in its consuming encounter with Eros-Thanatos. In Marcuse's estimation, Mann's novella is not to be considered *merely* the tragedy of an artist (KRg, 328). The desire and the suffering of Aschenbach are also considered typical of humanity at large. Marcuse claims that Mann has achieved a sweeping Homeric impact and beauty in this regard (KRg, 329), in that every reader can identify with the work's total, epical quality. It is easy to see how this book might well be considered a *Bildungsroman*-in-reverse, the undoing of the seasoned professional by unbounded sensuality. Still, Marcuse stresses (at ibid.) the fact that the problem of the artist *is* in a sense also genuinely resolved in *Death in Venice*. The artist's suffering is no longer seen as merely his or her own, but merges with what Marcuse sees as the pervasive erotic agony of humanity in general in contemporary bourgeois society. "It is the tragedy of the times that here makes itself heard, not the tragedy of an individual artist" (KRg, 331).

Marcuse also finds an important educational aspect in Mann. He highlights Mann's own reference to the "educational component in Nietzsche" (Mann at KRg, 317) according to which intelligence, knowledge, and insight are regarded as "inferior" when compared to the real exigencies of life (ibid.). These exigencies of life are, clearly, not served by the blind urge to pleasure at any cost (Thanatos), but rather through the "erotic irony" (KRg, 319, 325) that Mann considered to be the outcome of the educational thinking of Nietzsche. Here, the force of Eros ironically subordinates pleasure to the retrieval of a capacity for life in spite of the modern tendency of the intellectual to plummet toward madness, decadence, and paralysis. Eros confronts the artist's essential knowledge and yearning with an equally essential *Entsagung* or "renunciation" (KRg, 319), subduing the driving pleasure principle of Thanatos.

It is in this regard the Marcuse refers to "Nietzsche's Hamlet-epigram concerning knowledge that kills action" (KRg, 296), and connects Mann's conception of the artist also with the debilitating "insight of Hamlet" (KRg, 310). Nietzsche asks (at *Ecce Homo*, pt. 2, no. 4): "Is Hamlet understood? Not doubt but certainly drives one mad." Nietzsche is considered by Marcuse to represent a profound new understanding of the complexity and depth of human knowledge. The truth *is* ugly. Marcuse writes that in Mann's view that rare person ". . . who has 'just once been able to peer into the essence of things,' who has seen through being in its entire concreteness, and into nausea, and whom this knowledge has rendered unfit for life, who can no longer coexist with the others who do not know—, . . . 'that person' . . . becomes singular, homeless. . . ." (KRg, 308). But Nietzsche proclaims that we make art in order not to perish from the truth. Marcuse concludes that, upon this Nietzschean basis, Mann's literary work is able to develop a concept of the fragility *and strength* of the artist (ibid.). Still, the powers that destroy Aschenbach affect not only him. They are deep and generic (KRg, 328). The collapse of any one of us is entirely possible, for our solutions are "stretched over abysmal depths" (KRg, 325). Nonetheless, strength of character remains identified with the arduous retrieval of a quality of aesthetic and social sublimation that can in fact *sustain* life. In this view, human nature and the world itself demand that art and knowledge be invoked in the name of Life, not Death. This is the fundamental principle of *Lebensphilosophie* developed by Nietzsche and Dilthey to whom the value of art *for life* is the central educational lesson. It is also the essential educational meaning of Mann's aesthetic effort. This *Lebensphilosophie* will surface again in Marcuse's 1931 essay on Dilthey, and subsequently in his 1969 *Essay on Liberation.*

Marcuse's dissertation clearly turned to literary art as a source of educational insight and understanding into the problem of the artist's loneliness, homelessness, distance, and unattainable yearning. In this sense, the problem of alienation is present in his work from the beginning. Addressing the artist's personal experience of the divided self, where ideals inevitably clash with the inadequacies of the real world, his goal is social fulfillment and community. Before the ideals of community are given up, or taken up as a cultural assignment, however, he needed to consult the history of modern literature for insight into models of social practice and social understanding. He undertook an aesthetic critique of historical thinking, following Dilthey's lead toward an aesthetic of history. In pursuit of community rather than society ("*Gemeinschaft* rather than *Gesellschaft*" [KRg, 330]), he sharply criticized both the romantic-pathetic conception of the artist, and the artist's problematic accommodation and sacrifice of subjectivity to either the unreconstituted bourgeois order or to revolutionary socialist organizations and movements. In his estimation, the aspirations of the people are not those of art. The disturbing conflict between art and life has been explicated through the history of the German *Künstlerroman* as that essentially tragic ontological rift standing at the core of our being that nonetheless uniquely precipitates a breakthrough to a depth dimension of truth. His subsequent early work, as I shall show in the next section, links this alienating insight to the cultivation of a mature subjectivity not only through the artist novel, but in the *Geisteswissenschaften*, or "humanities," as such.

Marcuse and Dilthey

We have seen that Marcuse's early work derives especially from the thought of Wilhelm Dilthey. The key texts in this regard are a 1931 essay by Marcuse on Dilthey, "The Problem of Historical Reality: Wilhelm Dilthey" (GWg), and his 1932 book, *Hegels Ontologie und die Theorie der Geschichtlichkeit* [*Hegel's Ontology and the Theory of Historicity*] (HOg).

Dilthey was a philosopher at the University of Berlin during the period prior to World War I. He had written a famous biography of one of the founders of the "heroic tradition" in German higher education, Friedrich Schleiermacher, who brought a romantic conservatism and an emphasis on literary aesthetic (hermeneutic) method to the idea of the university being implemented at Berlin at the beginning of the twentieth century. In addition, Dilthey also wrote on ethical and psychological theory as well as on the theory of history. The problems of a philosophy of literary art and a philosophy of the humanistic disciplines (those of the *Geisteswissenschaften*) gradually came to be the most prominent of his interests. According to Rainer Winkel,[9] Dilthey developed his liberal arts approach to intellectual history and cultural scholarship during the late nineteenth century, and his pedagogical theory eventually became a dominant force in German educational philosophy around the period of World War I. Winkel characterizes Dilthey's educational approach as standing in contrast to empirically oriented educational schemes, emphasizing instead literary-etymological methods, especially those of phenomenology and hermeneutics. He points out that this approach to education has been criticized as methodologically one-sided in its de-emphasis on empirical research procedures and as lacking in educational scope. Winkel contends that its predominant focus on literary curricular content has been seen as a modern reformulation of the *pedagogia perennis* in the politically turbulent period following World War I that philosophically aided the conservative German universities in "beclouding and repressing" rather than illuminating the actual social, historical, and political tensions of the era.

Also according to Manfred Riedel,[10] Dilthey's substantial impact and educational influence in Germany between the two world wars had nothing ("*Nichts . . . an sich*") to do with the inherent logic or validity of his liberal arts approach as such, but that rather his ideas attained significance because of the "catastrophic" political history of the period. The German turmoil of the 1920s was held to be a consequence of the "social and scientific revolutions" of the nineteenth century that were thought to have brought about a highly specialized division of labor and to have engendered cultural fragmentation and social division. Dilthey's theory of the *Geisteswissenschaften* was viewed as a restorative countermovement to these trends. His approach, like certain of today's trends in postmodern theory, was seen as nonrevolutionary or even as "antirevolutionary" in that it opposed the "objectivism" of modern science and the "mechanistic" tendencies of modern materialism. Rejecting the historical philosophies of Hegel and Marx, Dilthey reached back to Kant, reasserting the relative autonomy of individual human reason and its basis in lived human experience. In certain ways the antimodernism of contemporary postmodernist theory reconstitutes this backlash mandarinism.

Ilse N. Bulhof[11] has also examined the social background and ideological aspects of Dilthey's work, noting that the latter's political leanings were toward patriotism and the Prussian monarchy rather than toward socialism. She contends that his attacks on socialism revealed a basic antidemocratic bias and that his attacks on positivism and science were connected with his conservative political stand. Marcuse nonetheless explicitly preferred the Diltheyian, hermeneutic approach toward the philosophy of history over the unrevised historical philosophies of Marx and Hegel.

Marcuse's 1931 essay on Dilthey proposed that Marxism had much to learn from the approach of a liberal education to culture and the arts. Not as yet translated into English, it introduced Dilthey's concept of the *Geisteswissenschaften* into the then current discussion, begun by Karl Korsch, on the relationship of philosophy to Marxism (GWg, 350). Marcuse holds Dilthey's theory of the *Geisteswissenschaften* to be a philosophical aid to Marxism (GWg, 355) in deciphering the meaning of historical reality. Marcuse emphasizes the fact that Dilthey's effort begins with an epistemological investigation into the *Geisteswissenschaften* as a theory of scholarship that is thought able to disclose the meaning of historical reality and meaning of human life (GWg, 355–56) while the methods of the natural sciences are not able to do this. The humanities are defined here not just in terms of art and high culture, but as "all of those studies that have socio-historical reality as their subject matter" (Dilthey at GWg, 356). Empathic, interpretive, and so-called phenomenological (symbolic interactionist or ethnomethodological) methods in the social sciences, but not sociostructural approaches to inequalities of wealth, power, race, or gender, would come to be associated with this definition of the human sciences. Marcuse notes that these collected human studies are considered by Dilthey to be more than the mere sum total of particular humanistic disciplines, rather they are considered to be an integrated unity arising out of the totality of sociohistorical reality and better suited to the interpretation of this reality than either the methods of the natural sciences or the sociological sciences in their present forms (GWg, 357). Dilthey proposes that access to historical reality is furnished *not* through the approaches of positivism or empiricism (which are regarded as unhistorical, static, and metaphysical), but rather, through an *aesthetic of history*.

The term *aesthetic of history* comes from Rudolf Makkreel who emphasizes the fact that Dilthey "treats the poetic imagination and the historical imagination, not merely as parallel, but as basically akin."[12] He writes that Dilthey's concept of history thus has little in common with scholarship that establishes general explanatory principles, but shares Schiller's view that history is an interpretative discipline that educes meaning from life. Marcuse finds that the enterprise designated by Dilthey's major work, *The Construction of the Historical World in the Humanities*, also represents *a new fundamental understanding of philosophy* (GWg, 358). In Marcuse's view, it is the very *world of philosophy* that is "constructed" in the humanities, and from which Marxism is thought to have much to learn.

Marcuse also claims that Dilthey's search for the dynamic substance of historical human life has immense significance for Marxism. Dilthey's emphasis on the humanities is considered absolutely necessary to capture the living *depth, complexity,* and *ambivalence* of historical human existence, which is otherwise often misapprehended in terms of sociologically or biologically fixed (and hence, ostensibly lifeless) categories and objects. Dilthey's work on the theory of the humanities, in which the human studies become the foundation of philosophical and historical understanding, is taken by Marcuse to delimit an important approach to that internal human domain where ideals and realities are thought to meet. This dimension is considered inaccessible to the methods of a mechanistic materialism or a transcendental idealism, which are both criticized as tearing apart (GWg, 366) the fundamental unity of subject and object established by Hegel. Dilthey's *Lebensphilosophie*, understood as the most logical outcome of Hegelian thought, is presented as the new foundation of social and historical theory (more important even than Heidegger's work in this regard). Marcuse writes: "In the last third of the 19th century a new actuality of philosophy emerges, a new form of its realization: the so-called *Lebensphilosophie*" (GWg, 354). He continues: "Here, we understand as *Lebensphilosophical* only those theoretical investigations that acknowledge the Being of human life as belonging to the fundamental structure of philosophy, and . . . the single genuine representative of this philosophy [is] Wilhelm Dilthey" (ibid.). Dilthey's concept of "Life" is thought to restore the human core to philosophy, and to unify humanity and nature, and body and spirit, in a vital, if also essentially conflicted and enigmatic totality. Life-philosophy is said to revitalize thought because it is considered able to pry open closed and fixed conceptual absolutes, revealing their ambiguous, internal, living core: historical human subjectivity.

Life-philosophy is thought to question critically every given piece of information by seeking to understand its theoretical and practical relevance to the concrete historical experience of the living individual. It represents Dilthey's great refusal to accept the empirical world as given in appearance, and indicates his willingness to protest the coercion of static ideals and conventions. In this regard, Marcuse cites Dilthey's reformulation of the Copernican Revolution statement made by Kant in the *Critique of Pure Reason*:

> Humanity has long sought to grasp life taking the world as starting point. But there is only an approach which begins with an interpretation of life and then moves toward the world. . . . We carry no meaning from the world into life. We are open to the possibility that meaning and relevance emerge only in humanity and its history. (Dilthey at Marcuse, GWg, 364–65)

Marcuse points out that self-reflection and introspection are the distinctive qualities that distinguish method in the humanities from that in empirical sociology and in the natural sciences. He emphasizes the fact that this turning inward is to be understood in historical rather than transcendental terms, although we shall see in a moment that *Hegel's Ontology* will identify historicity in this regard with inwardness and reminiscence. In "The Problem of Historical Reality: Wilhelm Dilthey" (GWg) the humanities are thought to be especially pertinent to the revolutionary project of Marxism, because they ostensibly furnish the philosophical knowledge that may elevate humanity toward autonomy and freedom (GWg, 367). They open up the horizon of human subjectivity to the necessities of history, unify sensuousness and intellect, and call forth the ontological meaning of mind and "reason" for a "revolution," thus *rehumanizing* philosophy.

The philosophical work that Marcuse began in this 1931 essay is continued and deepened in his treatment of Dilthey's concept of historicity in the former's first book on Hegel published a year later. Marcuse did postdoctoral work with Husserl and Heidegger from 1929 to 1933 at the University of Freiburg. He had decided to pursue an academic career, and the German university system required in this regard not only that he be "promoted" (i.e., possess the earned doctorate), but also that he be "habilitated" (i.e., complete a second, higher-level dissertation under the direction of an academic chairholder). Ten years after receiving the Dr. Phil., Marcuse published *Hegel's Ontology and the Theory of Historicity* (HOg), and sought to have Heidegger certify it as his *Habilitationsschrift*.

In this book Marcuse wanted to link the Diltheyian concept of "life" to the philosophical writings of Hegel: "Hegel's ontology is the basis and foundation of the theory of historicity (*Geschichtlichkeit*) as worked out by Dilthey" (HOg, 2). It is, indeed, this concept of historicity that provides a definite focus for Marcuse's effort. He clearly indicates Dilthey's relevance as follows:

> Dilthey's investigations represent the foremost state of this research: even today they furnish the foundation and limit of this problematic. Therefore the question of *Geschichtlichkeit* is to be taken up with him. (HOg, 1)

Marcuse's exposition of the concept of life in Hegel's texts immediately involves him in the problem of the separation of subject and object, and of other philosophical dualities, including a notion of education as one-sided and partial because of the traditional separation (*Entzweiung*, HOg, 9) of "reason from sensuousness," and "intelligence from nature." (Max Horkheimer and Theodor W. Adorno, in *Dialectic of Enlightenment*, would subsequently term this deficient sort of education *half-education*.[13]) The deficiency of this education is described as its preoccupation with an isolated and fixed understanding of partial appearances of a greater realm of Being, which still requires philosophy if it is to "restore the totality" of the "divided world" (HOg, 13), and to achieve real knowledge.

In Marcuse's Diltheyian estimation it is precisely the concept of "life" that makes possible a *philosophical* reconciliation of these opposites in a unity or totality (hence, the virtue of "life"-philosophy). *Hegel's Ontology* explicates this unity or totality in terms of Hegel's emphasis in the larger *Logic* on motion and change and the concept of self-identity in otherness as the philosophical basis for the reunification of opposites. Ultimately all of this is synthesized in "Life as *ontological* concept. . . ." [*Leben als Seinsbegriff* (HOg, 229, emphasis added)].

Much of the substance of *Hegel's Ontology* was incorporated into Marcuse's second Hegel book, *Reason and Revolution, Hegel and the Rise of Social Theory* (RR), which perhaps accounts for the fact that the former went untranslated into English until 1987. *Reason and Revolution* repeats the fundamental conclusions of HOg:

> The first concept Hegel introduces as the unification of contradictions is the concept of life . . . Hegel conceives of life as mind, that is to say, as being able to comprehend and master the all-embracing antagonisms of existence. In other words Hegel's concept of life points to the life of a rational being and to man's unique quality among all other beings. Ever since Hegel, the idea of life has been the starting point for many efforts to reconstruct philosophy in terms of man's concrete historical circumstance and to overcome thereby the abstract and remote character of rationalist philosophy. . . . (RR, 37).

Marcuse highlights the convergence of the early concept of life with the more mature Hegelian concept of mind (*Geist*):

> "Life" is not the most advanced philosophic concept that Hegel attained in his first period. The *Systemfragment* in which he gives a more precise elaboration of the philosophic import of the antagonism between subject and object and between man and nature, uses the term mind (*Geist*) to designate the unification of these disparate domains. Mind is essentially the same unifying agency as life. . . . (RR, 39)

During Marcuse's middle period, in *Eros and Civilization, A Philosophical Inquiry into Freud* (EC) especially, a dialectic of life and death replaces the classical Marxist dialectic of the social relations of production. Even his final work, *The Aesthetic Dimension, Toward a Critique of Marxist Aesthetics* (AD) also does this: "The revolution is for the sake of life, not death. Here is perhaps the most profound kinship between art and revolution" (AD, 56). In this conceptual scheme, a philosophy of life and mind is thought necessary to overcome the epistemological deficiencies of the fixed and static logic of the present-at-hand and the immediacy of factual data. Thus, all fragmentary learning is to be superseded through the deeper knowledge of the dynamism and historicity of universals disclosed through the being and the philosophy of human mind and life. As the book following *Reason and Revolution*, that is, *Eros and Civilization*, would make clear, the conflicts between reason and love, repression and life, gratification and death, find (1) their *unifying substance* in the affective depths of the living human being, and (2) their *universal form* in the imaginative and meaningful constructions of "the aesthetic dimension." *Eros and Civilization* also takes up Hegel's notion of "remembrance" (EC, 232). Twenty-three years earlier, this topic was initially investigated in *Hegel's Ontology*, and was considered there to be a foundation of Hegel's concept of "historicity":

> "Remembrance" clearly has nothing to do with the psychical phe-nomenon that we indicate by this name today: it is a universal ontological category: it is "a movement of Being itself," which "through its nature remembers itself." It is the "going-into-itself" of that which is, a going-back-to-itself, but—and this is decisive—this movement does not proceed in the dimension of immediacy itself . . . rather it goes back and into a new dimension of the "timeless" past, of essence. (HOg, 77)

> —Even the concept of "Remembrance" finds its first decisive and categorical significance in the *Phenomenology* as a fundamental category of historicity. (HOg, 79)

Remembrance in this regard is said to be intrinsically related to the past of being, also understood by Aristotle as essence (HOg, 78) and intimately con-nected to Hegel's reinterpretation of essence as historical being. Remem-brance becomes the foundation of human "historicity," as the necessary prerequisite to the comprehension of essential human motion, unity, and totality, over time. Because time is also regarded as the "form" of lived and remembered reality (HOg, 360), in contrast to "thinghood" as form of the external world, remembrance is also contrasted with reification and aliena-tion. Truth itself, is described near the end of HOg as the identity-in-difference of alienation and remembrance, as two poles of human existence. Remembrance, as a turning inward of the mind: *Er-innerung* (HOg, 359), is counterposed to alienation, as a loss of mind in outward expression or exteri-orization: *Ent-äusserung, Ent-fremdung* (HOg, 339, 354).

Inwardness and introspection are thought to provide the realistic aesthetic warrant for the "revolution" (AD, 73) in consciousness and con-duct that Marcuse desired throughout his career. Even Dilthey, however, objects to subjectivist excesses in *Lebensphilosophie* and in the theory of the *Geisteswissenschaften*:

> It is not through introspection that we may conceptualize human nature. This was Nietzsche's terrible illusion. Therefore he could never grasp the meaning of history. . . . The individual is only the point of intersection for the cultural systems and organizations into which its existence is interwoven; how could they be understood out of the individual?[14]

Despite this admonition from Dilthey, Marcuse repeatedly stresses precisely the individual's sense of *Er-innerung* as internalization in *Hegel's Ontology*.

> . . . externalized (or alienated) existence, present-at-hand, inasmuch as it is as it is, is essentially limitation, which cannot be transcended by (external) knowledge existing in alienation. Only the disappeared and remembered form of existence can ground the internalized, remembered form of the mind: this is existence enriched through true knowledge of its (essential) past being, and thus "reborn of knowledge." As long as mind lives in the realm of the world that is present-at-hand, it is in alienation. Its knowledge of itself has imprisoned it in this alienation, it cannot achieve its essence and its truth. Only in the disappearance of this external existence does this knowledge become liberated, and objectification is once and for all broken-through; only the remembered mind is emancipated in itself and for itself, and gives birth to its new existence out of the true knowledge of itself. Thus, remembrance is a genuine internalization. . . . (*So ist die Erinnerung eine wirkliche Er-innerung*, HOg, 360)

Hegel's Ontology concludes with a section explicitly on Dilthey's theory of the humanities. It repeats what it takes as Dilthey's basic position: that "life" is the fundamental fact and presupposition of both the humanities and philosophy itself (HOg, 2, 363). In the end, "mind" and the "mind"-studies, the *Geistes-wissenschaften*, function as *life*-studies and *human* studies, and are thought to be necessary and indispensable, not as sheer opposites to nature or to the natural sciences, but as bearers of the essentially human elements required to grasp the meaning of being also encompassing the natural and historical world. While Dilthey does not formulate the following point explicitly, Marcuse claims (at HOg, 367) that Dilthey increasingly tends to eliminate the distinction between the natural sciences and the human studies that had hitherto characterized his approach. It is thought that the human mind is able to penetrate human life and being intellectually, ultimately overcoming all duality. Alienation is displaced by self-knowledge. Dilthey's neo-Kantian philosophy permeates Marcuse's effort, from his first to his last works. The multidimensional knowledge that is capable of imaginatively synthesizing the external and internal realities of life is explicitly identified with the dimension of high art in the humanities. Other early essays by Marcuse, to which we turn in the next chapter, extend this philosophical perspective into his emergent critical theory of art and alienation.

CHAPTER THREE

—〰—

The Emergent Critical Theory of Alienation: The Laws of Beauty versus the Law of the Thing

Marcuse's dissertation was primarily concerned with the alienation of the artist as this was reflected in German novels of the eighteenth, nineteenth, and early twentieth centuries. The project indicated Marcuse's notion of the value of *literary* reflection on the nature of human existence in society, the search for self, and the need for a new sense of political community and solidarity. Most importantly, it demonstrated how he sought, through the testimony of art, to understand the historical human condition. He probed the ways in which reason and wisdom are disclosed through the aesthetic dimension. He was searching for the *sources of a disalienating knowledge*, and he found these in *literature* and in the *human studies*. He thus emphasized the epistemological role of art in constructing our internal sense of identity through, especially, literature's capacity to activate an historically based reminiscence and imagination. He believed that Wilhelm Dilthey's *aesthetic of history* could serve the very significant and disalienating goal of *rehumanizing philosophy*.

Marcuse's other early writings would likewise make an important contribution to the emerging development of alienation theory as well as to aesthetic philosophy. They can also be taken as evidence that his efforts to rethink the problems of alienation and the disalienating potential of art were leading him to *a shift away from Marxism, toward an ontological perspective*, grounded in the social and aesthetic theory of Martin Heidegger, Georg Lukács, and Dilthey.

51

This increasing philosophical distance from Marxism is reflected in a series of four articles on historical materialism, labor, phenomenology, and dialectics written between 1928 and 1933. Marcuse's 1932 essay, for example, "The Foundation of Historical Materialism" (HM) investigates the problems of alienation as reification, the fulfillment of our species-being and attainment of humanism, and production according to the laws of beauty (HM, 13–21). Marcuse shifts the study of alienation here from the Marxist focus on economic facts to an analysis of human factors—sensuousness, historicity, and art—utilizing theoretical approaches from Heidegger and Dilthey. In 1933 Marcuse extends his new perspective in "On the Philosophical Foundations of the Concept of Labor in Economics" (CL), where he characterizes estranged thought and action as occurring ". . . under an alien, imposed law: the law of the 'thing'. . . ." (CL, 17). By the same token, Marcuse's 1928 "Contributions to a Phenomenology of Historical Materialism" (PH) had already begun to trace the roots of the existential-phenomenological approach of Heidegger back to the cultural historical methodology of Dilthey. Dilthey's work is also more highly valued than that of Marx or Engels in Marcuse's 1930 article, "On the Problem of the Dialectic" (PD). This rejects Engels's theory of a dialectic of nature, and advocates a restriction of dialectical method to human living space and to the phenomenologically-oriented human studies. In 1941 Marcuse would publish his first book in English, *Reason and Revolution, Hegel and the Rise of Social Theory* (RR). In it he would present the collected insights of these early essays on alienation, labor, phenomenology, and historical materialism, and link them to the work he had already accomplished in *Hegel's Ontologie*.

Alienation as *Verdinglichung*: Cornerstone of Critical Theory

Even before Marcuse became formally associated with the Frankfurt Institute, he was utilizing its intellectual output for his own early research purposes. During the 1920s, the institute (pre-Horkheimer, under the more explicitly leftist philosophical direction of Carl Grünberg) worked in conjunction with the Marx-Engels Institute of Moscow to publish the collected works of Marx and Engels in German via the now famous 1932 *Marx/Engels Gesamtausgabe* (complete edition). This project presented Marx's *Economic and Philosophical Manuscripts of 1844* for the first time to the German-speaking world. Also called the *Paris Manuscripts*, these contain the key section "On

Alienated Labor." Marcuse was perhaps the first scholar anywhere to review this new primary source material in Marx's philosophy. Marcuse's work here is of particular interest because it shows the degree to which he began in these essays to negotiate a philosophical course median to Marxism and phenomenology, through Lukács and Dilthey.[1,2]

I am arguing in this chapter that the *key element* in Marcuse's new approach is the philosophical centrality of alienation as reification (*Verdinglichung*). The implications of *this* theorization of alienation are absolutely crucial for understanding Marcuse's emergent critical theory, both in these early essays, as well as in the later works like *Reason and Revolution*, *Eros and Civilization*, *Soviet Marxism*, and *One Dimensional Man*.

Marcuse's pivotal reinterpretation of Marx on the problem of alienation occurs in his 1932 essay, "The Foundation of Historical Materialism" (HM or HMg). Published in *Die Gesellschaft* and quite radical in tone, Marcuse makes it clear that Marx is writing a critique of established economics and philosophy that must be understood as a "theory of revolution" (HM, 3). Marcuse endorses Marx's effort to philosophize in a *practical* manner oriented to "the overthrow of the capitalist system through the economic and political struggle of the proletariat" (HM, 4). Marcuse restates these militant, action-oriented views at several junctures in his lengthy essay. At the same time his major goal is to present new insights from Marx's early work that will cause us to reexamine the *philosophical foundation* of the theory of revolution.

Marcuse's close inspection of Marx's newly published manuscripts leads him to assert that a "remarkable discovery" (HM, 7) is to be made here. He contends that a detailed examination of the theory of alienation, estrangement, or reification (HM, 6) being presented by the young Marx reveals that

> . . . what is here described is *not merely an economic matter*. It is the alienation of man, the devaluation of life, the perversion and loss of human reality. . . . It is thus *a matter of man as man* (and not just as worker, economic subject and the like) and of a process not only in economic history but in the history of man and his reality. (HM, 7–8, emphasis added)

Marcuse's analysis in this essay culminates in his conclusion that a *philosophical humanism*, that is, *a disalienating theory of the human person*, should be seen as *the basis* of a properly understood historical materialism.

Marcuse's interpretation stands in sharp contrast to later commentators on Marx's *1844 Manuscripts*, such as Erich Fromm, who upon an examination of the same materials, elaborate Marx's *historical materialist foundations* for humanism.[3]

It is my view that Marcuse sees Marx's newly published materials on alienation as lending a *Marxist* theoretical legitimacy to certain ideas that he already found extremely congenial stemming from the philosophical commentary on alienation and art by both Lukács and Heidegger. In what follows I will discuss Marcuse's line of reasoning, and indicate the central significance of the particular theorization of reification he shares with Lukács and Heidegger.

Marcuse's essay, like his dissertation, makes important points with reference to an ostensibly emancipatory theory of knowledge and learning. He especially highlights what he sees at the liberating power of a *knowledge of objectification*. This is described as an awareness of how both humanity and the objective world, as social relations, have become what they are (HM, 34–35). Knowledge of the social process of human becoming is *an activating and liberating knowledge*. It is thought to provide insight into the *social*, that is, *human*, construction of reality. As such, this insight is considered to be *the specific kind of knowledge* (HM, 34) that *can serve as a powerful lever* by which to break free of the constraints of alienation. According to Marcuse: "The insight into objectification, which breaks through reification, is the insight into society as the subject of objectification" (ibid.). Objectification, as the general productive or reproductive act of the social human subject is also said to condition essentially the history of nature and things. The knowledge of objectification is that kind of awareness that can achieve "the practical force and concrete form through which it can become the lever of revolution" (HM, 35). In this manner the early Marcuse is already examining the interconnections of *reason* and *revolution* that his 1941 book of that name would subsequently consolidate.

In spite of Marcuse's clear emphasis here on revolution, his philosophical approach at this point is centered *not* upon *Marx's* analysis of alienation and reification from either *Das Kapital* or the "Die entfremdete Arbeit" section of the *Economic and Philosophical Manuscripts*. Instead, he is focusing on alienation as *Verdinglichung*, thingification, as this emerges from the writings of Lukács and Heidegger. Consciously employing the polar concepts of *authenticity* versus *facticity* from Heidegger's theory of alienation, Marcuse maintains that ". . . the authentic task, when facticity has progressed so far as totally to pervert the human essence, is the radical abolition of this facticity" (HM, 29). Clarifying the anthropocentric, or humanist, basis of his *Verdinglichung* theory (in the tradition of Heidegger's *Sein und Zeit*), Marcuse appends the following sentence to the one just cited; "It is precisely the unerring contemplation of the essence of man that becomes the inexorable impulse for the initiation of radical revolution" (ibid.). It is Marcuse's belief, typical of the Frankfurt School after Max Horkheimer took its lead, that any "merely economic or political" (ibid.) facts or philosophies of class struggle or the dictatorship of the proletariat "miss the point" (HM, 30) if they do not come to grips with their "real foundation" (ibid.).

This *real foundation*, Marcuse writes, emerges from authentic knowledge of the human essence, emphasizing especially: (a) the *historical*, and (b) the *sensuous* character of this essence. Both of these aspects of Marcuse's thinking need to be examined in greater detail. First, however, I would like to point out that Marcuse defends his case for the *human* foundations of his view of historical materialism, initially by conceding certain of Marx's own criticisms of philosophical anthropology:

> We know the cruel derision with which, in his *German Ideology*, which appeared only a year after these *Manuscripts*, Marx destroyed the idle talk of Hegelians, such people as Stirner and the "true socialists," about *the* essence, *the* man, etc. (HM, 27)

Nonetheless, Marcuse claims that *his* analysis of the human essence furnished in "The Foundation of Historical Materialism" stands squarely within the philosophical framework of Marx's genuine intent: "If the real humanism outlined here by Marx as the basis of his theory does not correspond to what is commonly understood as Marx's 'materialism,' such a contradiction is entirely in accordance with Marx's intentions. . . ." (HM, 40).

Marcuse certainly allows that alienation is a proper matter for both economic and political analysis (insofar as these studies may validly elaborate alienation's "factical" dimensions). He does discuss the problems of commodification consistent with Marx's analysis of the commodity fetish. He does trace alienation's origins to private property relationships (at HM, 27), and he does acknowledge that the destruction of reification can occur, in this historical period, only as a result of the practical activities of those who labor (HM, 39). However, these points are ultimately subordinated to Marcuse's major (philosophical anthropological) objective in "The Foundation of Historical Materialism," and will later be abandoned altogether. His immediate goal is to interpret Marx's *Manuscripts* in terms of the "definition of man" (HM, 26) contained in them, a definition that Marcuse claims is Marx's very "*basis* of the critique of political economy" (ibid., emphasis added).

Marcuse claims correctly that Marx in the *Manuscripts* repeatedly identified a genuine conception of communism with a humanist worldview. Marcuse also claims correctly that Marx's alienation theory looks to the supersession of alienation through the actualization of the human essence. Marx's notion of *objectification* (*Vergegenständlichung*, HMg, 143) is seen as the decisive process in this regard. But at this point Marcuse diverges from Marx's discussion to take up the theory of reification (as *Verdinglichung*, HMg, 143). "Reification is a specific ('estranged,' 'untrue') mode of objectification" (HM, 11). Reification does not ultimately result from any "merely chance historical facts" (HM, 37) external to the laborer (e.g., the given relationships of wage-labor or private property), but emerges out of an inauthentic or ontic mode of human existence that is nonetheless rooted in the very essence of humanity.

In Marcuse's view, the human activity of objectification is the key that unlocks an understanding both of the history of humanity—and of nature. He claims to educe from Marx's early writings that this act of objectification "always carries within it a tendency towards *Verdinglichung*" (HMg, 165). As with Heidegger (and his analysis of Hegel in *Hegel's Ontology* [HO]), the immediate perception of objects as external to humanity, as nonhuman-related entities, is considered to be the result of a deficiency in the ontological and cognitive human processes, an alienating reification or thingification of existence, consciousness, and perception. In contradistinction to the classical Marxist idea of objectification as the historical process of the appropriative social interaction of labor with nature (often mediated by class conflict) that has produced the material and cultural record identifying the emergent and generic essence of humanity, Marcuse maintains that Marx "attempts to implant objectification . . . deeply into the definition of man" (HM, 18). In other words, instead of stressing the historical essence and identity of humanity as the social *outcome* of its objective forms of labor, Marcuse conversely views *real* (HM, 37) and *natural* (HM, 24) *objects* as the product of a more fundamental human activity: ". . . they only become real objects through and for him. Objects first confront him directly in an external and alien form and only become human objects, objectifications of man, through conscious historical and social appropriation" (HM, 37). Objects, thus, are held by Marcuse to possess an unreal or illusory appearance of independence from any existing human being, which may also seem to function as a "precondition of his being which does not belong to his being" (HM, 18), giving an alien and overpowering quality to them vis-à-vis human existence. For Marcuse, objectification indicates a process within human consciousness and action that also signifies the essential self-expressive unity of humanity and nature: "The objective world . . . is part of man himself" (ibid.). Furthermore, Marcuse contends that *all* real objectivity and fact are derived from the act (HM, 12) of human objectification (HM, 24) or of generic self-actualization.

> If the objective world is thus understood in its totality as a "social" world, as the objective reality of human society and thus as human objectification, then through this it is already defined as a historical reality. The objective world which is in any given situation pre-established for man is the reality of a past human life, which, although it belongs to the past, is still present in the form it has given to the objective world. . . . Not only man emerges in history, but also nature, insofar as it is not something external to and separated from human essence but belongs to the transcended and appropriated objectivity of man. . . . (ibid.)

In Marcuse's words, it is through this human activity of objectification that the history of both nature and humanity is to be understood. Statements like the one just cited document the Diltheyian philosophical anthropology standing at the foundation of Marcuse's theory of the human person.

In Marcuse's estimation, the sensuous character of the human essence is as fundamental as its historical character. Here Marcuse understands the substance of human existence in terms of human sensuousness rather than "any materialism" (HM, 19). Marcuse contends that Marx—following Kant (ibid.)—agreed that objects are given to humanity only through sensuousness and perception. In addition, Marcuse elaborates the *passive* character of this sensuousness, which he contends Marx understood following [*sic*] Feuerbach, who wanted to put "the receptivity of the senses back at the starting point of philosophy" (ibid.). Hence, Marcuse underscores that the human disposition must endure *care* and *apprehension* as fundamental characteristics of everyday human affairs. These are considered no mere consequence of any set of socioeconomic arrangements, nor as purely psychological ramifications of them:

> The distress and neediness which appear in man's sensuousness are no more purely matters of cognition than his distress and neediness,

as expressed in estranged labor, are purely economic. Distress and neediness here do not describe individual modes of man's behavior at all; they are features of his whole existence. They are ontological categories. . . . (HM, 21)

In such statements as this Marcuse is again very much the disciple of Heidegger, for whom care and anxiety (*Sorge* and *Angst*) provided the major categories of his existential analysis of humanity, *Dasein*, in *Being and Time*. It was this book that also stressed the existential identity of subject and object in the human world, describing this phenomenon of identity most vividly as *Jemeinigkeit* (ever-mineness).

According to William Barrett, this *Jemeinigkeit* signifies a condition where "mine-ness permeates the whole field of my Being."[4] Thus, Marcuse insists that his emphasis on the core human factor in the definition of objective reality distances his Marx interpretation from any association with a Lockean type of "sensualism" or Enlightenment sort of "materialism" (HM, 19). The method and approach of classical Marxism (i.e., that of a dialectical and historical materialism, which focuses on the objective and external workings of historical economic and cultural patterns) is quite categorically rejected in favor of a fundamental-ontological philosophy that can allegedly derive these patterns from an essentially internal human source.

Bourgeois political philosophy . . . disregards the essence of man and his history and is thus in the profoundest sense not a "science of people" but of non-people and of an inhuman world of objects and commodities. "Crude and thoughtless communism" . . . is just as sharply criticized for the same reason: it too does not center on the reality of the human essence but operates in the world of things and objects and thus itself remains in a state of "estrangement." (HM, 9)

According to Marcuse, Marx's theory is *revolutionary* not because it advocates a socialization of the means of production, but because it is thought to achieve a *disalienating subjectification* (*rehumanization*) *of philosophical theory itself.*

Marcuse's theory of the subjectively historical character of the human essence must be philosophically distinguished from that of the materialist conception of history embodied in classical Marxism. The latter stresses natural history and biologic evolution, as well as the emergence of historical human identity out of the social struggles for production, knowledge, domination, and the emancipation of labor. On the other hand, Marcuse, explicitly interprets the historical character of the human essence in terms of the philosophy of history developed by Dilthey (and elaborated by Heidegger) stressing the technical notion of "historicity" (*Geschichtlichkeit*).

Marcuse emphasizes *historicity* and *ontology* rather than history or dialectics in his descriptions of both Hegel and Marx. As we have seen, Marcuse's first Hegel book was written for Heidegger. Heidegger acknowledges that his particular use of the term *Geschichtlichkeit* is derived from the work of Dilthey, especially his studies in the *Geisteswissenschaften*. *Geschichtlichkeit* is characterized as "a temporal mode of being belonging to humanity itself."[5]

As with *Verdinglichung*, Marcuse presents the concept of historicity as authentic elucidation of Marx's own position: "*Für Marx . . . die Geschichtlichkeit des Menschen ist in seine Wesensbestimmung aufgenommen*" (For Marx . . . the historicity of the person is taken up into the definition/constitution of his or her essence and being [HMg, 157]). Marcuse maintains that Marx has here assumed a "new standpoint" (HM, 28) that no longer views human essence and "facticity" as "separate regions of levels independent of each other" (ibid.). Rather, these two spheres are held always to be essentially interrelated, concretely tied to the human subject at every juncture through the human quality of historicity. Where this interdependence is "forgotten," alienation is thought to ensue. In his estimation, the human quality of historicity is the condition of the possibility of overcoming alienation as facticity or *Verdinglichung*. Marcuse ultimately concludes in this essay (as he will repeat in *Reason and Revolution*) that since alienation is not "merely an economic" condition, it will require more than an economic solution, and that communism will not be able to obviate *Verdinglichung* unless it can philosophically disclose the subjective human core of economic relationships that are only ostensibly objective, in a manner similar to that of Heidegger and Dilthey. Marcuse considers that he has accomplished a distinctive interpretation of Marx capable of putting "the entire theory of 'scientific socialism' on a new footing" (HM, 3).

This theoretical shift is propounded not only in "The Foundation of Historical Materialism," but also in "Contributions to a Phenomenology of Historical Materialism" (PH). Here Marcuse asks what he considered to be the pivotal question: "does the theoretical basis whence Marxism arises . . . come from a full grasp of the phenomenon of historicity?" (PH, 3). He then proceeds to outline the neo-Kantian background to this concept following the work of Heidegger and Dilthey:

> Since the middle of the last century, the problem of historicity has again become a central problem in philosophy . . . from Dilthey on it became a central problem. Since then, it has been dealt with with a growing awareness that it may be the fundamental problem of science. (To mention some names: Simmel, Rickert, Troeltsch, Max Weber). Through rigorous phenomenology, Heidegger finally raised and answered the question in its full and radical significance. (PH, 12)

Marcuse acknowledges, however, that Heidegger neglects the social and material aspects of historicity (PH, 17, 18), and thus, Marcuse takes up Dilthey's original treatment at this point. For Dilthey human life and human activity are the concrete social and substantive bases of historicity. For Dilthey external objects and the natural world "are already in historicity" (PH, 12): they are encountered within the sphere of human life and activity. Their real meaning is considered to have been interpreted most concretely, not through the natural sciences, but as they impinge on the human world, the "life-world," the history of which has been studied most authentically in the *Geisteswissenschaften*. Dilthey identifies the historical world with human living space, and upon this basis Marcuse concludes that "all reified objectivities" (PH, 33; PHg, 67) may become historical *when living human beings become concerned with them* (ibid.). Marcuse evidently turns to the theory of historicity to center his philosophy of human nature on an analysis of subjectively lived human existence, rather than on any independently conceived, objective dialectical developments in society or nature.

The essays reviewed here, from Marcuse's early middle period, clearly understand Marx *not* as the founder of a dialectical materialist conception of history, but as a radical opponent of reification, narrowing Marx's social and political criticisms more and more to a sheer negation of *Verdinglichung*. The philosophical foundations of Marcuse's theory were not originally or primarily elaborated in this manner by Marx, but rather by Heidegger, Dilthey, and Lukács.

Marcuse employs Marx's statements in the *Manuscripts* that communism is fundamentally a "humanism" (HM, 40) to make a characteristically Heideggerian point: alienation results not simply from the objective and external workings of historical economic patterns and relationships, but rather from an internal human source. True to the fundamental-ontological philosophical presuppositions of Heidegger, Marcuse thus propounds an analysis of the human core of human existence, a new philosophical humanism, as the starting point for an understanding of alienation. This humanism is not understood after the fashion of historical materialism. Historical materialism emphasizes the sociohistorical role of the working class as revolutionary creator of the socialist political-economic order that is thought necessary to precondition the emancipation of humanity in general and to permit the cultivation and refinement of its all-sided development. Rather, the humanism of Marx's early writing is interpreted by Marcuse more in the sense of a philosophical anthropology or anthropocentrism of the sort developed by Feuerbach, Max Scheler, Arnold Gehlen, and Heidegger (which regard human factors, as such, as the primary elements in their interpretation of history, society, economics, and politics), and that eventually permit Marcuse to speak less of the political-economic than of the "biological foundation" for socialism (*An Essay on Liberation* [EL], 7). This existential, anthropological, or biologic notion of humanism is also supported by, and given additional connotations through, the literary humanism of Wilhelm Dilthey. Dilthey's theory of the human sciences (*Geisteswissenschaften*) also reverberates with the more militant aesthetic humanism of Friedrich Schiller, and conditions certain of Marcuse's interpretations of psychoanalysis as a secularized (humanistically demystified) theory of the human spirit. Marcuse's 1966 essay on "Socialist Humanism?"—note the question mark— would distinguish him sharply from the socialist humanism propounded by Soviet authors and even from the neo-Freudian social humanism of Erich Fromm.

Marcuse focused attention in "The Foundation of Historical Materialism" (HM) on revising the theory of revolution. As early as 1928 in the journal, *Philosophische Hefte*, he began calling for a redefinition of *militant action: die radikale Tat* (PH, 4; PHg, 47). Marcuse's new perspective on activism and militance stressed the *educational* point that *ontological knowledge*, that is, "the knowledge of authentic historicity" (PH, 32) is the condition of the possibility of a theory of revolution and transformative praxis. Activity, Marcuse believes, can be described as "radical," only insofar as it emerges out of an understanding of the existential core of the human condition and is directed toward altering human existence. Radical action requires *as its foundation an emancipatory knowledge and learning*: it requires *a fundamental ontologcal analysis* of the nature of our being as humans, as this knowledge is suggested by Heidegger and rooted in the thought of Dilthey.

Writing about Dilthey in "Contributions to a Phenomenology of Historical Materialism," Marcuse highlights the exceptional value to be found in the *Geisteswissenschaften's* conception of historical knowledge:

> The object of knowledge of the knower does not in this case stand "over against" him as a different entity "foreign" to him (as in the case with knowledge of physical objects), but "lives with him. . . ." (PH, 4)

Historical knowledge and historical human existence are understood as related in "a living unity" (PH, 5).

> The daily concern with the living space necessarily forces existence . . . into a rigid world of things. . . . This is the process of "reification," "objectification," or "estrangement" discovered by Marx, which achieves its sharpest expression in capitalist society. (PH, 32)

> Knowledge of authentic historicity and consciously historical existence is possible only when existence shatters reification. It is not possible to recognize that the ontic world related to concerned existence unless the world as given to existence creates the conditions which make possible the world as living space. Thus it can realize that all reified objectivities have become historical by the very fact that its living existence has become concerned with them. By recognizing the historicity of the world, it recognizes its own historicity which can create a new world. . . . (PH, 32–33)

Throughout this citation, "reification" is the translation of *Verdinglichung*, and an authentic "concern" for the human "living space" is thought to require a mode of being human capable of "shattering" this reification.

Marcuse had also written earlier that the Diltheyian theory of "living space" requires a different approach for its authentic study than that characteristic of the natural sciences. This occurs in his essay, "On the Problem of the Dialectic" (PD, 24), where Marcuse argues Dilthey's main point: *the being of man is dialectical, but the being of nature is not.* In particular Marcuse supports Lukács's polemic against Engels's theory in this regard in *Dialectics of Nature*, and grounds Marx's concept of dialectic instead in Hegel's *onto-*

logical concept of life. "Hegel's concept of 'consciousness' is from the outset to be understood so broadly that it can embrace the entire basic behavior of life" (PD, 27). "The 'dialectic' of the process of life has essentially such a 'real' character. It is not a dialectic of pure cognition, but a dialectic of praxis" (PD, 36). Marcuse elaborates here on the "dialectic of praxis," as a theory of conscious human conduct directed against phenomena of reification. Marcuse quotes Hegel: "Thus, the 'thingness which the form gets in labor, is no other substance but consciousness'. . . ." (ibid.) and as Marcuse concludes: "It is already evident from this example that Hegel here means the process of reification (*Verdinglichung*) and its transcendence (*Durchbrechung*) as a basic occurrence in human life, which Marx then represented as the basic law of historical development" (ibid.). In other words according to Marcuse, *Marx's dialectic* is also *grounded in historical human life* and his dialectical method is based on the dialectical being of the human person, *not* on a dialectics of the physical or social world, nor on the allegedly reified methods of the physical, economic, or social sciences.

Marcuse clearly states that Marx's dialectic has the singular purpose of a revolution against the commodity form of production (ibid.), but his philosophical genealogy of the dialectic leading up to Marx from Plato, Kant, and Hegel stresses the notion that the dialectic is an *ability of human reason* (PD, 16), a *cognitive power* (PD, 18) which "frees all being from its apparent rigidity and isolation . . . [and] comprehends being as a necessary moment in its totality, as a result of its becoming; it comprehends being in its true essence. . . ." (ibid.). Marcuse concludes that it is *this insight* into the dialectics of human life that triggers *genuinely* radical or revolutionary action.

Marcuse's 1933 essay "On the Philosophical Foundation of the Concept of Labor in Economics" (CL) likewise finds that an understanding of labor solely in terms of economic activity (i.e., as wage-labor) is too theoretically narrow and limiting. Marcuse wants to discover the essence and meaning of the very concept of labor, and in so doing he wants to look at economic activity within the total complexity of other human activities and human existence in general. Marcuse wants to clarify his contention that "labor is an ontological concept of human existence as such" (CL, 11). He reviews the philosophical concepts of labor presented by Hegel, Lorenz von Stein, and Marx highlighting their common emphasis on labor as self-creation and as self-objectification. Labor is seen as the key activity by which humanity exteriorizes itself and also humanizes the world. While capturing the sense in which Hegel and Marx agreed on the philosophical essence of the labor process in this essay, Marcuse *no longer discusses* the doctrine of the alienated character of the labor process. Marcuse moves away from an acknowledgment that *under certain social conditions* the human act of appropriation confronts the work force instead as expropriation. He leaves behind the recognition that the labor process, *in specific historical circumstances*, occurs *not* as human self-actualization but as self-denial.

Instead, Marcuse centers his discussion on a broadened concept of the process of objectification. He indicates now that there is a nonalienated objectifying activity that he considers to be the philosophical obverse of the (apparently now *always alienating*) labor process: the objectifying activity of *play* (CL, 14). The decisive difference between objectifying play activity and objectifying labor activity is considered to be the dimension of freedom inherent in the former, but now *entirely precluded* in his estimation from the world of work. "In a single toss of a ball, the player achieves an infinitely greater triumph of human freedom over objectification than in the most powerful accomplishment of technical labor" (CL, 14-15). Marcuse claims that from the standpoint of free play, labor as such exhibits "its essential character of being a burden" (CL, 16). Thus Marcuse now steps *outside* the labor process to develop a philosophy of play and freedom (derived evidently from Friedrich Schiller's emphasis on the play impulse and freedom vis-à-vis utilitarian labor in *On the Aesthetic Education of Man in a Series of Letters*). Schiller's twenty-third letter formulates the phrase, "according to the laws of Beauty" that is reprised with reference to production in Marx's 1844 *Manuscripts*.

For Marcuse labor is seen necessarily as burdensome and alienating because it is a process that must deal with physical facts and realities that must be ordered according to their own laws, rather than according to the free will of humanity. The burdensome character of labor is regarded as a categorical feature of human existence, an ontological attribute of human work effort. It ". . . is a result of the fact that human doing stands under an alien, imposed law: the law of the 'thing' . . . that is to be dealt with (and which remains a 'thing,' an Other to life itself even when one provides one's own labor). . . . In labor one is always distanced from one's self-being and directed toward something else: one is with others and for others" (CL, 17).

Marx originally understood reification, not as a faulty method in science or philosophy, but as capitalist society's obsession with production for profit rather than for human need, its fetish with production for exchange rather than for use. Consciousness becomes fetishized or reified when it misapprehends the social as if it were the natural in order to legitimate and perpetuate the given structure of economic power. But by redefining reification as *Verdinglichung*, Marcuse positions the concept precariously close to the metaphysics of classical philosophical idealism. Reification is held to be responsible for the "semblance" (RR, 281) of objectivity adhering to the social arrangements of human civilization.

In *Reason and Revolution* (RR) Marcuse alleges that:

> Marx's early writings are the first explicit statement of the process of reification (*Verdinglichung*) through which capitalist society makes all personal relations between men take the form of objective relations between things. (RR, 279)

> Economic relations only seem to be objective because of the character of commodity production. As soon as one delves beneath this mode of production, and analyzes its origin, one can see that its natural *objectivity* is mere semblance while in reality it is a specific historical form of existence that man has given himself. Moreover, once this content comes to the fore, economic theory would turn into *critical* theory. (RR, 281, emphasis in original)

Although the text of *Reason and Revolution* was initially published in English, Marcuse inserts the German word, *Verdinglichung*, into the statement just cited. In several other places Marcuse also ascribes *Verdinglichung* to Marx. Marcuse nowhere cites a specific passage from Marx with regard to the use of this concept, and other published scholarship on this issue is inadequate, even contradictory.[6] My comparative readings of the German-language texts of both Marx's early essay "On Alienated Labor" in the *Economic and Philosophical Manuscripts of 1844* and his subsection of *Capital* on "The Secret of the Fetish Character of Commodities" disclose *no* instance of Marx's use of the term. I find it highly improbable that Marx ever employed this word or this concept.[7]

If *Verdinglichung* represented merely a terminological change with reference to a concept of alienation whose content remained the same, this shift would not be a matter of much analytical concern. But this alteration is by no means an inconsequential semantic variation of the *original* notion of *reification as fetishization* as this appears in Marx's writings. This is a philosophically, socially, and politically substantive shift. Marcuse (on the basis of the writings of Lukács and Heidegger) ultimately allows the economic phenomenon of commodity fetishism in the dynamics of capital accumulation to recede into the deep background of his social analysis and social theory. Instead, he conceives of alienation and reification almost exclusively as a sclerosis of thought and action, as a subordination of philosophical method *not* to the exigencies of capitalism, but to mechanistic and objectivistic principles as such. By the time of his final book, Marcuse claims (echoing Max Horkheimer and Theodor W. Adorno's statement in *Dialectic of Enlightenment*): "'All reification is a forgetting,' Art fights reification by making the petrified world speak, sing, perhaps dance" (AD, 73). Art is thought to preserve a liberating memory that the social and cultural worlds are dynamic and multidimensional, not fixed or static. Reification is held to occur when this subjectively creative role (the social construction of reality) is forgotten, and when the ensuing alienation thus takes on connotations of social amnesia and cultural dehumanization. On the centrality of reification in critical theory Christoph Demmerling has recently written: "The critique of *Verdinglichung*, the core of the social theory that derived from Marx, is still a fundamental element of the critical theory of society despite the discussion in sociology of the end of industrial labor and despite the 'linguistic turn' in social theory."[8]

Martin Jay clearly considers *reification* a term introduced into the discussion of alienation and proletarian consciousness *not* by Marx but by Lukács: "Extrapolating from Marx's discussion of the 'fetishism of commodities' in *Capital*, and applying insights from Bergson, Georg Simmel and Weber, he [Lukács] introduced the notion of reification. . . . This term, not in fact found in Marx himself, meant the petrification of living processes into dead things."[9] Likewise, Rolf Wiggershaus emphasizes the roots of Marcuse's reification theory in Heidegger and Lukács: "The two important philosophers who most inspired Marcuse were Georg Lukács and Martin Heidegger who attained fame in the 1920s as the philosophers of alienation, *Verdinglichung*, and inauthenticity."[10] But the *Verdinglichung* concept causes the greatest consternation to Jürgen Habermas when he examines the uses made of it in the critical social theory of Horkeimer, Adorno, and Marcuse. "Horkheimer and Adorno understood their critique of instrumental reason as a 'negation of reification'. . . ."[11] "Horkheimer and Adorno detach the concept not only from the special historical context of the rise of the capitalist economic system but from the dimension of interhuman relations altogether. . . ."[12] "It is the 'Aesthetic Theory' that first seals the surrender of all cognitive competence to art. . . . Negative Dialectics and aesthetic theory can now only 'helplessly refer to one another.'"[13] "Horkheimer and

Adorno get ensnared in their own difficulties. There is something to be learned from these problems; indeed they furnish us with reasons for a *change of paradigm* within social theory."[14]

Habermas has made insightful contributions to the task of rethinking critical theory's aesthetic philosophy and its future. Like Marcuse, however, he states that Marx's use of *Verdinglichung* should be dropped.[15] Thus he reinforces Lukács and Marcuse's misreading of Marx, and does not question this reading as I do here. Habermas might better have written that we need to drop the *Verdinglichung*-claim originally made by Lukács (as well as the claims derived from Lukács made by Horkheimer, Adorno, and Marcuse) insofar as their version of reification theory tends to accept the permanence of alienated communication and the continuing paralysis of reason itself within the given form of society.[16]

I have tried to demonstrate in the foregoing discussion that Marcuse's particular analysis of alienation ultimately defines what he believes makes critical theory *critical*. *Verdinglichung* is central to his redirection of critical theory and to his new philosophical course. His theory of the *cognitive power and activating potential of dialectical philosophy* furnishes the foundation for his emerging confidence in the genuinely educative *rationality of art* as a major political, economic, and philosophical weapon *against alienation*. The laws of Beauty shall liberate humanity from the law of objects and facts. Already thinking in new ways about the "and" in "reason and revolution," Marcuse developed in the early essays discussed in this chapter an *ontological* ("an ontology which I believed I could locate in Marx himself" [TP, 126])[17] and a *phenomenological* ("maybe there is after all an internal, conceptual relationship between what is really good in Husserl and perhaps even in Heidegger" [TP, 131]) *rationale* for a reinterpretation of Marx's materialism and the transformation he would eventually seek of "economic theory . . . into *critical* theory" (RR, 281).

The analysis of alienation continues unabated even today, and still evokes broad patterns of controversy. It remains an issue of central importance for anyone wishing to theorize about our society critically. Perhaps the single area of agreement tying together the variety of descriptions of the nature of alienation is a rather universal reference to problems of *loss*: loss of identity, loss of interpersonal contact, loss of freedom, loss of power, loss of property, loss of meaning, loss of god, and loss of love—loss of something formerly and essentially one's own. Beyond this, however, a collision of opposing accounts is encountered. Alienation sometimes manifests itself as loneliness, forsakeness, isolation, poverty, sexual-emotional frustration, psychosis, emptiness, nausea, impotence, or absurdity. Alienated individuals may be seen as having been deserted, abandoned, repressed, disfranchised, expropriated, exploited, or dehumanized. They may appear to be bored, apathetic, depressed, anomic, indifferent, helpless, or retreatist—and conversely also as rebellious, iconoclastic, or creative.

Richard Schacht in 1994 took pains to write of the *future* of alienation, emphasizing that alienation theory shall continue to be inseparable from our ongoing philosophical inquiry into social life, values, and the human good.[18] His earlier book had already attempted to bring some order to the wealth of meaning associated with problems of alienation. Schacht shows that the initial meaning of the word *alienation* is found to carry with it a notion of *divestment*.[19] He traces the etymology of the term back to the Latin verb, *alienare*, to make something another's, to take away, remove. It was used principally in the Latin in connection with property relationships and denoted the *transfer of ownership* from one person to another. A second Latin meaning is also cited as referring to a state of disturbed consciousness, with a paralysis of one's mental faculties or a loss of one's senses. Yet a third meaning, that of interpersonal estrangement, is traced to Latin as well. In Middle English, this third meaning was used primarily in a theological sense, as estrangement from god, but gradually this usage was broadened to include alienation from other individuals. Schacht notes, in addition, that the fundamental German term for "alienation," *Entfremdung*, also finds its linguistic roots in social forms of divestment. In its verb form it means *fremd machen, berauben, nehmen, entledigen*; that is: to estrange (make alien), to rob, to take, to strip of. This word has been used in German, as have its equivalents in Latin and English, also to denote mental disorders such as amnesia, stupor, coma, or *Betäubung* (unconsciousness or anesthetization). A second German word, *Veräußerung*, has customarily been used to denote *alienation's* connection to selling and to the institutionalized transfer of property.

Proceeding from *alienation's* basic reference to loss and divestment, the term is seen to have legal, psychological, and interpersonal meanings, depending upon the specific analysis of what is alienated from what or whom, and how the particular removal, divorce, or separation takes place. These are, of course, the areas of greatest controversy in alienation theory. In addition, there is considerable debate and discussion over the extent to which reunifying remedies are possible. Schacht's careful and critical survey of the literature on this subject (from Hegel and from the early German idealists to Marx, Heidegger, Fromm, Sartre, et al.) reduces confusion on these matters considerably. His concluding chapter (Schacht 1971) is a solid effort toward systematization of the analytical approaches and basic issues involved.

Mitchell Franklin[20] has warned of "opposed conceptions of alienation" and of a "rivalry of theory" in the conflicting explications of this phenomenon encountered in its philosophical treatment since Hegel. In his estimation, both existential philosophy and historical materialism have propounded a critique of Hegel's alienation theory, and have done so in such fashion as to reflect a contest between materialist and idealist worldviews. I offer here a brief summary of the analysis presented by Franklin to present the essence of these debates in a concise fashion that will be crucial for the subsequent analysis of Marcuse. Much of this philosophical terrain on Hegel's dialectic of labor and recognition is also covered in Seyla Benhabib's chapter on "defetishizing critique" in *Critique, Norm, and Utopia*,[21] but Franklin's account is not marred by her rejection of the Hegelian and Marxist notion of objectification.

Franklin focuses on the specific connotations of the German terms for alienation typically utilized by Hegel and Marx, and by the existential philosophers. He observes that Hegel and Marx ". . . employ a series of words, *Entäußerung, Entfremdung, Veräußerung, and Aneignung. . . .*" (expropriation, estrangement, divestment, and appropriation) in their analyses of phenomena of alienation, noting that as students of law, both were primarily aware of the significance of these concepts with respect to ownership and property relationships. Citing section 66 of Hegel's *Rechtsphilosophie (Philosophy of Law)*, Franklin holds that a sociohistorical priority is assigned to the meaning of alienation: primarily as seizure of property, and appropriation of wealth, but secondarily also as the legal transactions of sale, lease, or bequest according to testament.

Franklin claims that Hegel and Marx both oppose theories of permanent alienation, citing Hegel's fundamental belief that alienation would be found to alienate itself. He points out that Hegel, as a representative of the Enlightenment, was concerned with the alienation characteristic of feudal customs and legal relationships in conflict with newer, sociohistorical developments in religion, philosophy, morality, and practical activity. The *Phenomenology* had argued the social evolution of reason, from lower to higher, which would absorb and complete the limited and "alienated" products of an earlier form of culture and education—attaining at the same time an advanced level of intelligence, art, and civilization. Hegel's theory also acknowledged that this achievement would be the *work* of the *alienated elements, themselves,* but, Franklin claims, the philosophy of alienation had to await Marx before the moment of appropriation in this process would be fully appreciated. Citing Marx's *Economic and Philosophical Manuscripts of 1844* as the seminal text in this regard, Franklin stresses the fact that these represent both a critique and a completion of the Hegelian theory of alienation. Hegel had grounded alienation in *labor* (in both the *Phänomenologie des Geistes* and the *Rechtsphilosophie*) and related this also to a discussion of social needs and the system of social production—essentially the subject matter of economics—in the *Rechtsphilosophie*, secs. 189–208. According to Franklin, Marx's contribution to this theory of alienation was to recognize the fact that whereas under slavery and feudalism, appropriation is direct and immediate, under capitalism this occurs in a concealed or disguised fashion: Marx considered alienation via the appropriation hidden in the exchange of commodities and in the leasing of the service of labor by workers. For Marx, alienation is understood as the seizure of surplus value in a social process of production that alienates laborers from the product of their labor, from control over the labor process, as well as from other laboring comrades, and from the political (as well as sensual and aesthetic) potential of the human species itself. This differs, in essence, from Hegel's social understanding of alienation as a voluntary submission of property to sale or transfer, even expropriation (*Rechtsphilosophie*, secs. 65–66).

Franklin highlights the Marxist theory of alienation as fetishization, that is, the loss of an object that has been created, and which, in turn, confronts its creator as alien or even "holy." Franklin explains that this fetishization process was considered by Marx as one involving "the social divinization of the thing, the sovereignty of the object, the subjugation of the subject, [and] as in reality the hidden consequence of the alienation of wage-labor through appropriation. . . ." (Franklin, 24–25). Instead of entailing social relations based upon human need, it is thought that capitalism, as a productive system based on profit, engenders market relationships among people as well as among wares. Social life becomes commercialized and commodified, as exchange relationships predominate in society as a whole, restricting the potential development of interpersonal relations to market modes. The very essence of being as sensuous living labor is, in the case of the working class, considered to be *in*voluntarily transformed, restricted, and distorted into an item for sale, barter, or exchange. While "free" in formalistic legal terms, labor is not considered to be free in fact.

Franklin points out, however, that ". . . a collision in regard to the theory of reification. . . ." (Franklin, 25) has emerged between the opposed outlooks of existentialism and historical materialism. The existentialist theory of reification centers on the notion of a loss of identity that results when an individual is treated as an object, in a depersonalized fashion, regardless of the economic questions of appropriation, profit, or need. Franklin links this nonappropriative meaning of reification to the work of Karl Mannheim and Max Weber and to their conceptions of the inevitably and "permanently" alienating effects of bureaucracy and scientific rationalization.

This latter formulation of the theory of reification is especially pertinent to Lukács's 1923 redefinition of fetishization—in nonappropriative terms—as *Verdinglichung*. This term is taken by Lukács to signify, in Weberian fashion, a definite paralysis of consciousness within the working-class movement, involving the restriction of its thought to calculative and deductive modes. We have seen that Marcuse adopts this analysis.

According to Franklin, Hegel did not recognize the problem of fetishism, although he conceived of *language* and *culture* to be products of the *history of human labor* that also confront human beings as objects with which they must struggle to become familiar. In this manner, Franklin indicates the *relevance of theoretical education* to the foregoing discussion of alienation in Hegel, and emphasizes the importance of the relationship of the world of language, culture, and education to the world of labor and appropriation. Franklin concludes that any fetishization of language, thought, or education must be understood in conjunction with the particular historical practices of the productive and appropriative processes of its period. It is here where Franklin has important insights that even Habermas might well consider. He concludes that no permanence of this alienation or fetishization can be philosophically justified "unless an idealism is advanced to maintain this" (Franklin, 30).

The early Lukács's major contribution to the emerging lexicon of Western Marxism was the conceptual dyad of "reification" and "totality." These were understood with special reference to the problem of epistemological reductionism that he considered to have marred what he then dismissed as "orthodox" Marxism. To Lukács the real historical world was much too complex to be understood in terms of a mechanical materialism or economic determinism that he said (inaccurately, in my estimation) characterized philosophical Marxism. His vision of the theoretical task at hand involved *a reassertion of the dialectic* in Marxist philosophy. In Lukács's view, dialectics must insist on the concrete unity of the whole. Without this, "fetishized" relationships between parts are thought to prevent consciousness from ever finding meaning. "Totality" is seen as the revolutionary philosophical category that governs historical reality, while reification as *Verdinglichung* represents a rigid and reductionist fragmentation of consciousness that afflicts both the bourgeois and the proletarian. The problems of the "reified mind" and of the reification of consciousness, and the concepts of totality and reification are thought to be more germane to this Western Marxist analysis than the primacy of economic factors in historical explanation.

Lukács developed a particular emphasis on the concept of reification in the chapter from *History and Class Consciousness* entitled: "*Die Verdinglichung und das Bewußtsein des Proletariats*"—Reification and the Consciousness of the Proletariat. Lukács's work in this regard was developed on the basis of *Das Kapital*, not Marx's early works (since the 1844 manuscripts had not yet been published in 1923).

Marx's analysis in *Das Kapital* shows how private accumulation is immensely enhanced when exchange relationships multiply and predominate in society as a whole. Because of this, social relationships oriented toward the noncommercial fulfillment of human needs are thought to be increasingly eliminated. Where these needs and relationships are not simply abandoned, they are coerced into inverted and exploitable social phenomena, subject to capitalism's conventions of commodity exchange. Alienation occurs here because genuinely social attitudes and interests in people and toward people get driven out by business relationships. Exchange in the capitalist market is thought to evoke: "... *sachliche Verhältnisse der Personen und gesellschaftliche Verhältnisse der Sachen*" (... matter-of-fact and impersonal attitudes toward persons, but social concern for matters of business) per Karl Marx.[22]

Verdinglichung-theory is redirected by Lukács, however, into a reinterpretation of alienation, away from Marx's notion of fetishization and toward Weber's work on rationalization. *Verdinglichung* comes to signify a profound fragmentation and paralysis of consciousness within the working-class movement, involving a restriction of mental activity to calculative and deductive modes that makes individuals comfortable only when handling facts and things. Lukács's German-language work cites no primary source in the writings of Marx for his use of the term *Verdinglichung*. Lukács does cite a form of the word *Verdinglichung* only with reference to Simmel's *Philosophie des Geldes* [*Philosophy of Money*].[23]

Apparently building upon Lukács, Heidegger in 1927 recapitulated *his* underlying interest in the methodological problems of *Verdinglichung*. On the last page of *Being and Time* he writes: "It has long been known that ancient ontology works with 'thing-concepts' and that there is a danger of 'reifying consciousness.' But what does this "reifying" signify? Where does it arise? Why does Being get 'conceived' 'proximally' in terms of the present at hand. . . . Why does this reifying always keep coming back to exercise its domination?"[24]

According to Heidegger, human beings are "worldly" in a non-objective way: our "being-in" is not of the "reified," spatial sort (as when a book might be said to be "in" a briefcase), but of an "unreified," unthinged, existential sort. Existence that is authentically human is held to infuse its world with meaning, at the same time as it opens itself up to an understanding of Being. In Heidegger's estimation, *alienated* human beings are "with" one another merely "ontically," as closed things, while *authentic* human beings are "with" one another "ontologically," as open potentialities or as communicative projects within the field of Being as such. In a vivid turn of phrase, Heidegger contends that *things* can never "touch" other things, "even if the space between them should be equal to zero."[25] Objective entities are considered to be "worldless" finalities, without the open and projective "ontological" dimension that is said to distinguish humanity (*Dasein*). In addition, Heidegger flatly rejects science, which he undialectically equated with positivism and with a reification of consciousness.

Because the concept of a disalienating rehumanization (subjectification) of theory has a long and venerable history in the tradition of German idealism, I would like to highlight certain developments in this major intellectual current in a few bold strokes. In so doing, I am trying to disclose an outline of the philosophical foundations of *Verdinglichung* theory in the work of Schopenhauer and Nietzsche to whom Marcuse will eventually explicitly turn (especially in *Eros and Civilization*).

German idealism has long stood in opposition to the empiricism (or sensualism) of such thinkers as Bacon and Locke. In the tradition of German idealism (especially its neo-Kantian form) ultimate "Being" in itself was rarely construed as a collection or aggregation of discrete *rei*, "entities" or "things." It was, rather, generally identified with an *un*thinged, or unconditioned potency: a dynamic spiritual or physical hydraulic, a flux, flow, force, an energy or will, a becoming or process. This is especially true of the *Lebensphilosophie* of Nietzsche and Dilthey. Schopenhauer was a vehemently anti-Hegelian successor to Kant who would proceed to assert that the world, in itself, was a darkly moving reality, throbbing with a mysterious life of its own, essentially inaccessible to rational thought. Likewise, the essence of humanity was thought to lie below the planes of consciousness or reason, at a deeper, more sensuous, and primordial level. This enigmatic and active core of all Being was termed the *Will*, or the *Will to Life*. This Will was thought to be the internal impulse or drive that motivated all change and development in both humanity and the world at large. It was thought to underlie all organic and inorganic processes, and the Will to Life in humanity was thought to stir the heart to beat and the lungs to breathe. Foreshadowing the analyses of Eros and Id in the depth-psychology of Nietzsche and Freud, Schopenhauer's chapter on "The Metaphysics of Sexual Love" from *World as Will and Imagination* (1818) contends that the strongest expression of the Will to Life is the erotic drive in humanity toward sexual reproduction. According also to his posthumously published note-books: "If you were to ask me whence comes the most intimate knowledge of the innermost essence of the world, which I have already christened 'the Will to Life,' . . . I would have to point to the ecstasy in the act of copulation. That is it! That is the true essence and center of all things, goal and aim of all existence."[26]

This sensual and emotional experience is considered profoundly "unthinglike." It overcomes the finite boundaries of human individuality both in terms of the sexual union and of the very multiplication of the species. Thought and rational analysis are thus considered entirely incapable of capturing this innermost essence of Being. Both direct observation and the logic based upon it were regarded as but simplistic and restricting impositions—reifications—of the Will. Schopenhauer believed, rather, that only music could adequately embody the immanent truth and the internal pulse of the authentic Will and Being, and that *this* art was actually the organon of philosophy. "Music is just exactly that which all the arts attempt to be, namely an echo of the world in a unique medium (*Stoff*); and that which music discloses is exactly that which the world would wish to make known."[27] In music, Schopenhauer's "art of arts," the Will was thought to have become audible. In his estimation, music represented the redemption of humanity from the confining and reified realms of utility and science. In *Counterrevolution and Revolt* (CR) Marcuse comments explicitly on Schopenhauer's aesthetic philosophy in close connection with the problem of alienation as *Verdinglichung*. He quotes Schopenhauer on music noting that ". . . the supreme points of art, seem to be the prerogative of music (which 'gives the innermost kernel preceding all form, or the heart of things'). . . ." (CR, 100). Subsequent to this he presents an example relating music to the sensuality of the living body in motion, and *Verdinglichung* to the stasis of "a fixed entity" alienated from life:

It is as if the cultural revolution had fulfilled Artaud's demand that, in a literal sense, music move the body, thereby drawing nature into the rebellion. Life music has an indeed authentic basis: *black music* as the cry and the song of the slaves and the ghettos. In this music, the very life and death of black men and women are lived again: the music *is* body; the aesthetic form is the "gesture" of pain, sorrow, indictment. With the takeover by whites, a significant change occurs: white "rock" is what its black paradigm is *not*, namely *performance*. . . . What had been part of the permanence of life, now becomes a concert, a festival, a disc in the making. "The group" becomes a fixed entity (*verdinglicht*). . . ." (CR, 114–15, emphasis in original)

In Schopenhauer's estimation, the arts and philosophy are only properly understood when they are seen to uncover the nonreified sensuous substrate that remains when appearances (*Vorstellungen*) of every sort dissolve. Modifying Kant's revolutionary "rehumanization" of theory in this sensual and aesthetic direction, Schopenhauer also maintains: "You must understand nature out of yourself, not yourself out of nature. This is my revolutionary principle."[28]

Schopenhauer's antirealist metaphysics of music and sex did much to condition the *Artisten-Metaphysik* of Nietzsche (see especially, chap. 1, "Die 'Artisten-Metaphysik,'" in Eugen Fink, *Nietzsches Philosophie*).[29] Fink like Marcuse was a student of Husserl and Heidegger at Freiburg. Nietzsche held that insight into the heart of the natural universe, as well as an understanding of the social and psychological world, could only be obtained through the thoroughly human *optics of art*. He opposed the philosophical methods of rationalism and empirical science, and sought another (aesthetic) dimension of truth. Heidegger was among the first (in his 1939 lectures on Nietzsche and art) to point out that Nietzsche conceived of art as a type of metaphysical activity, creative in an ultimate philosophical sense, insofar as art had the power to "objectify" or bring forth that which not yet is, and set it into Being. Heidegger writes: "*Künstlersein ist ein Hervorbringen-können. Hervorbringen aber heißt etwas, das noch nicht ist, ins Sein setzen.*"[30] ("The artist's essence is an ability to bring forth. Bringing forth means placing into Being something which not yet is.") According to Heidegger, Nietzsche characterized this type of aesthetic activity as *procreative*, and in this procreative view of the genesis of art, art was considered to be reproductive in an erotic rather than a "realistic" sense.

Both Nietzsche and Heidegger, thus, compared the artist (in sexist fashion) to one who "begets." This act of passionate begetting (objectification and exteriorization) was considered the key countermovement to social passivity and decadence and to the nihilistic denial of self. Aesthetic creativity was considered to represent elemental human optimism and the sensual enjoyment of life, the pivotal expression of human strength and fulfillment of the fundamental human need to sustain and enhance human life on earth.

According to Nietzsche's section on "The Will to Power as Art," entry number 800, from *The Will to Power*: "Artists, if they are any good, are (physically as well) strong, full of surplus energy, powerful animals, sensual; without a certain overheating of the sexual system a Raphael is unthinkable—Making music is another way of making children:. . . .—Artists should see nothing as it is, but fuller, simpler, stronger: to that end, their lives must contain a kind of youth and spring, a kind of habitual intoxication." In this manner, Nietzsche's aesthetic philosophy, like that of Schopenhauer, is an important precursor to the normative and teleological aesthetic theories embodied in the *Lebensphilosophie* eventually elaborated by Dilthey, Heidegger, and Marcuse.

Fink comments specifically on the epistemological implications of the views represented in Nietzsche's " Will to Power as Art," emphasizing that they involve what he terms a "Negative Ontology of the Thing."[31] In his estimation, Nietzsche asserts not only the profound falseness of thing-ideas, but also the ultimate irreality of things, as such. "Nietzsche radicalizes a Kantian tendency: the thingness of things is something 'subjective'; in Kant, objects of experience are made possible by objectivity categorically understood,—in Nietzsche, however, a thing, and a belief in things, is but an illusion, which makes life possible."[32] Fink interprets Nietzsche as saying that an alienated and unphilosophical humanity believes in "things," but "things" are not that which is actually there; alienated humanity believes in the existence of external entities, but these external entities are the creation of humanity. Fink claims that for Nietzsche, as for Heraclitus, the world is properly understood, not in terms of "beings," but in terms of becoming (*Werden*). Objectification, thus, means the subjective begetting of concepts, ideals, and the patterns of Being itself. *Verdinglichung* implies the begetting of false concepts, that is, thing-concepts, in mental acts where stasis is imposed upon movement or science freezes truth. "With concepts the thinker . . . halts the flow of becoming, and fastens into permanent images that which in truth never stands still."[33] According to this "negative ontology," it seems as if the world has become the vibrant substratum upon which traditional forms of human mental activity inscribe, define, and shape a pure potency into limited and finite things. Art, however, is thought to transport humanity beyond the illusory concreteness of "now" and "here" characteristic of positivism and empiricism, dissolving them back into their more significant, but also more ethereal and utopian "nowhere." Naive realism is considered absolutely insufficient as an epistemological approach. The sheer observation of brute facts is held to forget that there is literally human art in knowing. Nietzsche's "negative ontology of the thing" seems to be a clear philosophical precursor to the power that Marcuse finds in "negative thinking" as this approach is explained in his 1960 preface to *Reason and Revolution* called a "A Note on Dialectic" (ND).

> The power of negative thinking is the driving power of dialectical thought, used as a tool for analyzing the world of facts in terms of its internal inadequacy. I choose this vague and unscientific formulation in order to sharpen the contrast between dialectical and undialectical thinking. . . . All facts embody the knower as well as the doer; they continuously translate the past into the present. The objects thus "contain" subjectivity in their very structure. . . . Now what (or who) is this subjectivity that in a literal sense, constitutes the objective world? (ND, viii)

Marcuse answers his own question unequivocally with reference to human subjectivity. He believes that because common sense and science have purged themselves of philosophical negativity (ND, vii), cognitive power must now be sought in art. For Marcuse, it is poetry that especially represents the power "to deny the things" (ND, xi). Likewise, he would adopt this aesthetic philosophical approach in such statements as: "On its deepest level, art is a protest against that which is" (SM, 117) and "Art is a means of experiencing the Becoming of the object; that which is already there is of no importance to art" (AO, 59). The following chapter will trace the emergence of Marcuse's ingenious, yet problematic, conception of the critical function of the aesthetic dimension in breaking free from reification and attaining ontological knowledge.

CHAPTER FOUR

—⁓—

The Emergent Critical Theory of Art: Marcuse's Middle Period

Our religion, morality, and philosophy are decadence forms of man.
The *countermovement*: art.

Friedrich Nietzsche,
The Will To Power, number 794

After 1933, Herbert Marcuse enters a new phase in his intellectual development. The transition to his middle period occurs after the 1932 publication of *Hegels Ontologie* (HOg). The middle period dates from the onset of the Nazi regime in Germany and Martin Heidegger's hesitation at that time to continue academic support for Marcuse. Marcuse published *Hegel's Ontology and Theory of Historicity* as his *Habilitationsschrift* ten years after receiving his doctoral degree. He sought to have Heidegger officially sanction this work. Marcuse had cited Heidegger at the outset of this treatise on the ontological significance of the concept of historicity in Wilhelm Dilthey and Hegel—acknowledging Heidegger (at HOg, 2) as the key philosopher responsible for the scholarly accomplishments of Marcuse's own book. Nonetheless, Heidegger had reservations (Sidney Lipshires asserts these were anti-Semitic[1]) that prevented him from sponsoring Marcuse's *Habilitation*, and Marcuse left Freiburg. Max Horkheimer offered to undertake Marcuse's *Habilitation* at Frankfurt, but political circumstances led him to assist Marcuse with emigration instead. Marcuse became associated

79

with the newly established branch of the Institute for Social Research in Geneva, Switzerland, and when the Frankfurt center moved to Columbia University in 1934, Marcuse was the first to join its staff there. Thus, Marcuse's middle period, also begins with his association with Horkheimer and the Institute for Social Research, and is represented initially by Marcuse's publications in its *Zeitschrift für Sozialforschung*.

From the standpoint of this investigation two of these *Zeitschrift* articles warrant our particular attention: "Philosophy and Critical Theory" (1937) and "The Affirmative Character of Culture" (1937). These and others are translated and reprinted in *Negations, Essays in Critical Theory* (1968). Originally written and published in German, they were all composed while Marcuse was based in New York at Columbia. It is here that he begins to develop the basic pattern of his emerging critical theory of art: *Art Against Alienation*.

"Philosophy and Critical Theory" (CT) was published in the same issue of the *Zeitschrift* in which the Postscript to Horkheimer's landmark essay on "Traditional and Critical Theory" also appeared.[2] Of course, the *Zeitschrift* had become the theoretical record of those who propounded the institute's critical Marxist point of view. Marcuse's article was his first specifically on critical theory, and it stressed his concern for an adequate philosophical response to the changing state of contemporary social affairs during the period in which Nazism was being consolidated in prewar Germany. Revolutionary Marxism was thought to have provided the European working class and progressive humanity as a whole some basis for hope in the face of fascism. Marcuse raised questions however:

> What, however, if the development outlined by the theory does not occur? What if the forces that were to bring about the transformation are suppressed and appear to be defeated? Little as the theory's truth is thereby contradicted, it nevertheless appears then in a new light which illumines new aspects and elements of its object. The new situation gives a new import to many demands and indices of the theory, whose changed function accords it in a more intensive sense the character of "critical theory." (CT, 142)

Marcuse, of course, did not consider the defeat of the German left to be any longer a merely hypothetical affair: he had after all found it necessary to flee his native country after the Nazis were installed as its leaders. Because of this, he contended that the changed situation required a changed function on the part of any theory that would persist in "negating" the status quo. It required an *obstinate utopianism*.

> When truth cannot be realized within the established social order, it always appears to the latter as mere *utopia*. This transcendence speaks not against, but for, its truth. The utopian element was long the only progressive element in philosophy, as in the constructions of the best state and the highest pleasure, of perfect happiness and perpetual peace. The *obstinacy* that comes from adhering to truth against all appearances has given way in contemporary philosophy to whimsy and uninhibited opportunism. *Critical theory preserves obstinacy as a genuine quality of philosophical thought.* (CT, 143, emphasis added)

Thus, Marcuse ostensibly urged Marxists to remain steadfast in their commitment to revolutionize society. At the same time, he implied that the *dialectical materialist philosophy of history could no longer supply a scientific warrant for communist revolutionary practice*: "Theory can invoke no facts in confirmation of the theoretical elements that point to a future freedom" (CT, 145). Agreeing with one of Horkheimer's main conclusions in "Traditional and Critical Theory," Marcuse was convinced that humanity had in this regard been sadly misled by the traditional conception of Marxist social theory *as a science*: "Scientific objectivity as such is never a sufficient guarantee of truth, especially in a situation where the truth speaks as strongly against the facts and is as well hidden behind them as today" (CT, 156). Philosophical opposition to scientific method in social theory had to be developed now because he believed the desperate contemporary situation demanded it. This reversed Engels's important section of *Anti-Dühring* on "Socialism: Utopian and Scientific," which advocated the replacement of utopia by science. Marcuse stressed, instead, that only a *utopian* concept of an ultimate social goal (CT, 145) could furnish contemporary progressive forces with a social energy, a social potential, which could press forward to the desired social transformation. Guardedly maintaining that critical theory must preserve a materialist (CT, 135) and anti-theological (CT, 145) philosophical posture, Marcuse nonetheless considered critical theory's real strength to stem *not* from its *economic* analyses, but "from the force with which it spoke against the facts and confronted bad facticity with its better potentialities" (CT, 142). With an irony that has been noted by Mitchell Franklin,[3] this theoretical shift indicated Marcuse's willingness to return to certain *traditional* philosophical sources, long since critically bracketed within the classically conceived materialist dialectic. As with Horkheimer, Marcuse would return to, and employ, a version of neo-Kantian philosophy against what was perceived to be the ruinously confining character of historical materialism's scientific method.

A "critical" perspective with regard to *what ought to be* was, thus, in Marcuse's estimation, philosophically superior to what he called the scientific reductionism (positivism or scientism) of historical materialism and of other empirically oriented social theories. Consistent with the neo-Kantian nonidentity hypothesis, Marcuse also stressed the nonidentity and separation of philosophy from empirical social reality, a distinction that historical materialism was thought to have obscured: "What is true is so only to the extent that it is not the truth about social reality. And just because it is not the latter, because it transcends this reality, it can become a matter for critical theory" (CT, 152). The new emphasis that critical theory placed upon the separation of these two realms led critical theory to veer the activist role of the philosopher away from the day-to-day realities of the sociopolitical world. Classical Marxism understood its activism in terms of the eleventh Feuerbach thesis that insisted that philosophy must henceforth aid in the transformation rather than in the mere interpretation of oppressive social circumstances. Critical theory directed its attention, instead, towards the more artistic worlds of *human phantasy* and *human imagination*, and toward the theoretical sources in the history of philosophy that were thought able to preserve a critically obstinate social utopianism:

> The *transformation* of a given status is *not*, of course, the business of philosophy. The philosopher can only participate in social struggles insofar as he is not a professional philosopher. . . . *Adhering to the abstractness of philosophy is more appropriate to circumstances and closer to truth than is the pseudo philosophical concreteness that condescends to social struggles.* (CT, 147, emphasis added)

According to Marcuse's "Philosophy and Critical Theory" the *philosopher's* social task was most properly a *cultural, ideological,* or *educational* one. Horkheimer and Marcuse sought from the critical distance of U.S. exile to promote a discussion of the decisive philosophical concepts thought to be necessary for an emancipatory sociopolitical theory, through the debates occurring in the *Zeitschrift.* "With this intention, several fundamental concepts of philosophy have been discussed in the journal: truth and verification, rationalism and irrationalism, the role of logic, metaphysics and positivism, and the concept of essence" (CT, 147).

Explicitly reproducing the traditional separation of theory from politics, the academic émigrés of the Frankfurt School were trying to reach those infrequent individuals who might stand open to the complex critique of social consciousness and conduct toward which their philosophical activity aimed. Struggle in *this educational arena*, it was held, could preserve at least a minimal degree of the *utopian obstinacy of philosophical thought* that was elsewhere considered to have all but disappeared. Marcuse's acceptance of this separation of theory from politics in "Philosophy and Critical Theory" stands in sharp contrast to his simultaneous critique of precisely this dualistic conception of culture undertaken in his article on "The Affirmative Character of Culture." An understanding for Marcuse's oscillation and ambivalence in such matters will be developed in this book's concluding chapters.

While Marcuse did not directly speak of art in "Philosophy and Critical Theory," this essay nonetheless borders on a discussion of the (postmodern) role that the aesthetic dimension might play in the consolidation of a philosophical utopianism against science that was required for emancipation from social alienation. In his estimation a narrowly rationalistic or scientific (positivistic) discussion was thought to be inadequate to the fully perceived theoretical task of negating social reality:

> The abyss between rational and present reality cannot be bridged by conceptual thought. In order to retain what is not yet present as a goal in the present, phantasy is required. The essential connection of phantasy with philosophy is evident from the function attributed to it by philosophers, especially Aristotle and Kant, under the title "imagination." Owing to its unique capacity to "intuit" an object though the latter be not present and to create something new out of given material of cognition, imagination denotes a considerable degree of independence from the given, of freedom amid a world of unfreedom. (CT, 154)

This essay highlighted elements of the aesthetic philosophies of Aristotle and Kant—the key human faculties of "imagination" and "phantasy"—as having more emancipatory social potential than the traditional methods of science. Marcuse found, however, that these aesthetic faculties had remained degraded (ibid.) even where their potential had previously been propounded most diligently (in the philosophy of Kant) because they remained restricted to the realm of the a priori. Marcuse's critical theory, on the other hand, sought especially to connect these faculties to human experience and to the human need "for the construction of a more beautiful and happier world" (ibid.). His view of critical theory at this point clearly implied that the social philosopher might well enlist elements from the aesthetic domain (phantasy, imagination, beauty, and happiness) against an alienating social reality, and furthermore, that *this* kind of critical and utopian perspective was necessary in order to bring about any *qualitative* "transformation of the material conditions of existence" (CT, 135). An imaginative and critical social and cultural stance was thought to be of more practical value in the cause of human emancipation than scientific method ever had been or could possibly be.

The specific form this practical and "materialist," but nonscientific utopianism might take had already been indicated in one of Marcuse's other 1937 essays published in the *Zeitschrift*. "The Affirmative Character of Culture" (AC) presented Marcuse's first statement of the new *aesthetic direction of the political program* of his middle period, that is, of *the practical value of the arts against alienation.*

Art and the Actualization of Utopia

In a careful reading of "The Affirmative Character of Culture" one is confronted by both the immense breadth and intricate sophistication of Marcuse's theorizing. The piece is long, and stylistically difficult. It begins with a six-page consideration of the classical metaphysical separation of practice from theory in the philosophies of Plato and Aristotle and the concomitant "break between the necessary and useful on the one hand and the 'beautiful' on the other" (AC, 88). Likewise, he calls to mind the ancient and hierarchical division of the human psyche into lower and higher spheres: "The history of the human soul transpires between the poles of sensuality and reason" (AC, 90). Neither Plato nor Aristotle was thought to have questioned these separations or the accompanying devaluation of the material and "appetitive" realms. Both consigned happiness to the activities of "pure theory" and "higher culture." In Marcuse's analysis, this was, in itself, not a fundamental problem, because the philosophies of Plato and Aristotle did not ignore the social ills or the historical realities of commercial Athens in classical Greece, even though they separated theory and practice quite dualistically. In Marcuse's opinion these philosophies took up a critical stance to their social situation *precisely in their idealism.* "Plato's idealism is interlaced with motifs of social criticism. . . . And the authentic, basic demand of idealism is that this material world be transformed and improved in accordance with the truths yielded by a knowledge of the Ideas. Plato's answer to this demand is his program for a reorganization of society" (AC, 91–92).

Because Aristotelian theories were less idealistic, or more "realistic" (AC, 92), than their Platonic counterparts, however, "the reorganization of society no longer occupies a central role" (ibid.) in Aristotle's politics. Marcuse described a process at work here in which what he considered to be *the genuine intent of idealism,* that is, the *actualization of its goals, decayed and subsided:* "The history of idealism is also the history of its coming to terms with the established order" (ibid.). In his estimation, *idealism ultimately came to exonerate* (ibid.) *the inadequacies and injustices* experienced in the practical realm, by promoting an acquiescence to them at the same time as *it became abstractly preoccupied with the concepts of the good, the true, and the beautiful that were thought to belong to a "higher" or "finer" world.* In this sense, Marcuse maintained that *idealism became "tranquilized"* (AC, 93), sedated, quietist. In a term he apparently coined for this essay, idealism became *affirmative. Art is considered affirmative insofar as it confines its ideals to a transcendent realm, and leaves the social world unaltered.*

Marcuse's next eight pages define and describe the general character of culture in the *bourgeois* epoch. Likewise he is concerned here with the "affirmative character" this culture is thought to display.

> By affirmative culture is meant that culture of the bourgeois epoch which led in the course of its own development to the segregation from civilization of the mental and spiritual world as an independent realm of value that is also considered superior to civilization. Its decisive characteristic is the assertion of a universally obligatory, eternally better and more valuable world that must be unconditionally affirmed: a world essentially different from the factual world of the daily struggle for existence, yet realizable by every individual for himself "from within," without any transformation of the state of fact. It is only in this culture that cultural activities and objects gain that value which elevates them above the everyday sphere. Their reception becomes an art of celebration and exaltation. (AC, 95)

Marcuse was well aware of the paradoxical circumstance in which the aesthetic treatment of social realities could actually lead to an *anesthetic* "tranquilization" of perception and thought. Because the philosophy of Marcuse's middle period was intently concerned with emancipating aesthetic theory from this tradition of affirmation, it was necessary for him to formulate *alternative notions of art and culture* that might enable humanity *to intervene and transform the social reality in the direction of an ideal* (or utopian) conception of justice. Marcuse's effort in this regard (toward an ostensibly materialist, socioaesthetic activism) begun in this essay, was generally sustained throughout his middle period. His opposition to aestheticism was authentic, militant, and earnest, although based less on the aesthetics of classical Marxism (as developed e.g., by Mikhail Lifschitz and George Plekhanov[4]) than on the cultural philosophies of Nietzsche and Nietzsche's elder colleague at Basel, Jakob Burckhardt.

Marcuse sought to formulate an aesthetic theory in which art might surpass the "affirmation" or exoneration of social problems, and demonstrate, instead, a practical *usefulness* for the refinement and enjoyment of social life and the achievement of *happiness on earth*. Having explicitly come to grips with what had been perceived as the *harsh duality between, and separation of, art from life* in the course of his 1922 dissertation, Marcuse now wanted to develop an alternative aesthetic philosophy that could *integrate the arts and sociopolitical action*. He seemed convinced that one could construct such a synoptic theory building upon the intention of the Platonic "program for a reorganization of society" (AC, 92), and a critical appreciation of Friedrich Schiller's utopian and humanist elaboration of the emancipatory political potential of the Kantian aesthetic. Even these potentially liberating theories, however, would have to be revised, according to Marcuse, in the direction of (1) a social materialism, and (2) human sensuality. To achieve a new understanding for these particular revisions, an extensive middle section of "The Affirmative Character of Culture" is taken up with a criticism of the repressive and ideological function of affirmative culture's continual "poetization" of the soul and sublime beauty. While acknowledging, on the one hand, that great bourgeois art had a progressive character in its earlier phases, when it represented unattained and utopian goals, Marcuse claims it nonetheless "entered increasingly into the service of the suppression of the discontented masses" (AC, 98). Thus a revised, emancipatory philosophy of art and culture had now to be directed specifically against the aesthetics of the affirmative tradition.

> . . . the real gratification of individuals . . . can only be realized *against* idealist culture, and only *against* this culture is it propagated

as a general demand: the demand for the real transformation of the material conditions of existence, for a new life, for a new form of labor and enjoyment. Thus it has remained active in the revolutionary groups that have fought the expanding new system of injustice since the waning of the Middle Ages. And while idealism surrenders the earth to bourgeois society and makes its ideas unreal by finding satisfaction in heaven and the soul, materialist philosophy takes seriously the concern for happiness and fights for its realization in history. (AC, 100, emphasis in original)

Emancipatory aesthetic theory had to be directed against the prevailing conceptions of art—wherever art "surrendered the earth" to unfreedom. Marcuse's new aesthetic philosophy was to be an *earthly* one, inseparable from utopian social protest in the interest of human justice.

Marcuse recognized that the affirmative tradition in culture also included an affirmative *educational* component. Thus, the essay presents a brief philosophical critique of the particular type of cultural education propounded by such figures as the eighteenth-century German romantic, Johann Gottfried Herder. Marcuse felt that Herder's positions continued the poeticizing approach to reality, revolving around "man's noble education to reason and freedom" (AC, 101). Though Herder's educational scheme stressed an understanding of the human spirit through art (folk song and legend), in Marcuse's estimation, this romantic educational approach actually betrayed its ideals of human progress and the development of critical intelligence, and became instead regressive or apologetic. While freedom and reason were "supposed to be effected through the cultural education of individuals" (AC, 103), the real meaning of these notions was thought to have become fatally sublimated and spiritualized, and to represent "a world to be brought about not through the overthrow of the material order of life, but through events in the individual's soul" (ibid.). In their affirmative modes, education and culture belonged "not to him who comprehends the truths of humanity as a battle cry, but to him in whom they have become a posture which leads to the proper mode of behavior. . . . " (ibid.). Herder's aesthetic educational philosophy was seen as part and parcel of the history of affirmation that had attended the idea of beauty as a "noble ideal" in conventional cultural and educational theory and practice, and that has traditionally led to political quietism and social tranquilization: "By exhibiting the beautiful as present, art pacifies rebellious desire. Together with the other cultural areas it has contributed to the *great educational achievement* of so disciplining the liberated individual, for whom the new freedom has brought a new form of bondage, that he tolerates the unfreedom of social existence" (AC, 121, emphasis added).

Marcuse claimed that he wanted to restore a militant concern for material social improvement and a striving for sensual (rather than purely intellectual) happiness to the philosophies of art, education, and culture. "When all links to the affirmative ideal have been dissolved, when in the context of an existence marked by knowledge it becomes possible to have real enjoyment without any rationalization and without the least puritanical guilt feeling, when sensuality, in other words, is entirely released by the soul, then the first glimmer of a new culture emerges" (AC, 116–17).

Marcuse sought a new theory of art and culture that could act as a countermovement to culture and education that affirm the status quo. This new theory of art sought to reject the repressive effects of aesthetic spiritualization and sublimation, that is, the "affirmative character" of culture, in favor of a reassertion of the sensual and sociocritical aspects of aesthetic endeavor. Still, Marcuse did not advise the flat rejection of the great artworks of even the affirmative tradition: "There is an element of earthly delight in the works of great bourgeois art, even where they portray heaven. The individual enjoys beauty, goodness, splendor, peace, and victorious joy. He even enjoys pain and suffering, cruelty and crime. He experiences liberation. And he understands, and encounters understanding for and in response to, his instincts and demands" (AC, 120–21). It was clearly Marcuse's intention to revive the dissipated and subdued tendencies toward utopianism present in even "affirmative" aesthetic activity. This meant restoring both the sensualist component and political dimension to the philosophy of art. Marcuse praises in this regard the nineteenth-century cultural historian, Jakob Burckhardt, for his notion of the Renaissance man, as a model for "a life as extensive and full of deeds as possible" (AC, 123), noting that affirmative culture has drained the life from this model of "expansive activism" (ibid.). Affirmative culture, instead, promoted an ideal of "the person who renounces his instincts and places himself under the categorical imperative of duty" (AC, 119). Affirmative culture was thus thought to represent a conservative Protestant and neo-Kantian ethical asceticism, which Marcuse sought to redeem by stressing the sensualist aspect of Kant's own doctrines of phantasy and imagination (see CT, 154 and also *An Essay on Liberation* [EL, 30, 31]). As a result of the affirmative tendencies toward instinctual renunciation and contempt for the "lower" pleasures of the human body, Marcuse claimed that the potentially liberating countertendencies present in the aesthetic dimension were forced underground: "The artistry of the beautiful body, its effortless agility and relaxation, which can be displayed today only in the circus, vaudeville, and burlesque, herald the joy to which men will attain in being liberated from the ideal, once mankind, having become a true subject, succeeds in the mastery of matter" (AC, 116). Marcuse held that these socially and ethically marginal (or lower) forms of art and entertainment preserved an "anticipatory memory" (AC, 116) that could "foreshadow a new happiness" (ibid.), and in which a liberated sensuality actually triumphed over repressive spiritualization.

In terms of the relationship of affirmative art to repressive politics, Marcuse claimed that "the authoritarian state is due in no small measure to affirmative culture" (AC, 135). Affirmative culture was seen to have paved the way for the subservience of the individual in the fascist state to a "total mobilization" (AC, 127), acquiescence to fate, and obedience to authority. "The intensive education to inner freedom that has been in progress since Luther is now, when inner freedom abolishes itself by turning into outer unfreedom, bearing its choicest fruit" (ibid.).

Marcuse wanted to develop an aesthetic and educational philosophy that could *abolish*, rather than affirm, these repressive and alienating conditions. His search aimed at a theory that could demonstrate the practical value of art and culture for the full elimination of alienation from the material life process. He desired a theory of art and beauty that would be fundamentally incompatible with a bad present. "The Affirmative Character of Culture" represented only the very beginning of his revised aesthetic thinking. It did not clearly or adequately demonstrate how a philosophy of art or a philosophy of education could actually negate or transform or perfect the processes of material life in the direction of their fullness and concreteness (i.e., actualized ideal). His shift in aesthetic emphasis from spirituality to sensuousness was clear, as was the shift from the *contemplation* of utopia to its *realization*. Yet he had not been able to depict in detail the sources of the power of the aesthetic dimension that might enable it to accomplish the new cultural goals he thought the contemporary period required.

Marcuse had a rough idea, however, that his new aesthetic theory might involve *less of a preoccupation with works of art in the traditional sense, and more of an emphasis on shaping society and human experience in accordance with human sensuality and the aesthetic form.* "Beauty will find a new embodiment when it no longer is represented as real illusions but, instead, expresses reality and joy in reality. A foretaste of such potentialities can be had in experiencing the unassuming display of Greek statues or the music of Mozart or late Beethoven. Perhaps, however, beauty and its enjoyment will not even devolve upon art. *Perhaps art as such will have no objects*" (AC, 131, emphasis added).

Similarly, Marcuse claimed that "The assertion that today culture has become unnecessary contains a dynamic, progressive element" (AC, 130–31). This "anti-art" position, which was to cause Marcuse no little philosophical annoyance in later years, became characteristic of the aesthetic outlook of his middle period. Even while he maintained that he did not seek to demolish culture, as such, but rather merely its affirmative character (AC, 129), the aesthetic approach of his middle period would become profoundly associated with such a demolition. Marcuse apparently foresaw this association, taking it into account in the following comment: "Insofar as in Western thought culture has meant affirmative culture, the abolition of its affirmative character will appear as the abolition of culture as such" (AC, 130).

Marcuse's middle-period writings were convinced that a more synoptic aesthetic theory had to be formulated than could confine itself to "higher" cultural activities as they were traditionally defined and affirmatively practiced. Were these activities to be properly held to revolve primarily around the beautiful work of art, as such, or were they to involve something more? "The Affirmative Character of Culture" represented Marcuse's first concentrated attempt to find a new definition, emphasizing the heretofore neglected elements of *human sensuality* and *material social criticism*, combined in an aesthetic program to achieve an *earthly happiness*, rather than in an abstracted and affirmative theory of the beauty of aesthetic objects alone. It would take him nearly twenty years, that is, until his chapter on "The Aesthetic Dimension" in *Eros and Civilization*, to work out this redefinition of aesthetics in a more detailed fashion and to ground it in his unique philosophical synthesis of Kant, Schiller, Nietzsche, Freud, and others.

For the moment, the tentative character of his endeavor seemed undeniable, even to himself. "The integration of culture into the material life process is considered a sin against the mind and soul" (AC, 130). "Every attempt to sketch out the counter image of affirmative culture comes up against the ineradicable cliché about the fools' paradise" (AC, 131–32). Of course, for Marcuse, a philosophical utopianism preserved the sociocritical point of view that he held had been eliminated from all given forms of political thought and activity. Insofar as utopianism contained a basically materialistic element—in its demand for the actualization of its content—it was considered to be valuable and liberating. The false element in any utopianism was thought to be the perpetuation of its content as *mere image*, that is, the idea of a nonrepressive civilization as mere idea.

Marcuse openly sought to replace the affirmative character of art, culture, and philosophy with the critique embodied in a "genuine" utopianism. This is a goal that persists and is continually reinforced from 1937 through the late 1970s, that is, through *An Essay on Liberation, Five Lectures*, and his final book, *The Aesthetic Dimension*. His essay on "Philosophy and Critical Theory" stressed an alliance between critical philosophy and the utopian elements in phantasy, rather than an association of critical theory with a *science* of social structure, social forces, and social theories of social change. "Strong emphasis on the role of phantasy seems to contradict the rigorously scientific character that critical theory has always made a criterion of its concepts" (CT, 155). "[T]he fateful fetishism of science is avoided here in principle" (CT, 156).

Marcuse would subsequently (at EC, 72) compare and contrast the critical content of a genuinely utopian longing for an earthly paradise to what he considered to be the affirmative character of social theory as science. He was looking for a philosophy of art and culture that would go beyond an aesthetic realism grounded in the universals of history and matter (i.e., the historical materialist philosophy of art being developed by Lifschitz, Brecht, et al.), as well as beyond the social affirmation grounded in the eternalization of ideals (the romantic, literary idealist tradition in culture). Marcuse was looking for a "third way"—between (1) Marxism and (2) aestheticism—for a theory that would make sensuous (and libidinal) gratification the basis of its aesthetic and "materialist" program. Hence, the critical theory of art, worked out during Marcuse's middle period, was to be represented by a utopianism oriented toward practice, and this practice was envisioned primarily as the fulfillment of a "joy in reality" (AC, 131). It was oriented toward the gratification of the instinctual needs repressed by both affirmative art and the economic order, and characterized by the "genuinely" utopian longing for a *Schlaraffenland* (i.e., fools' paradise [ACg, 100]) *made real*. Marcuse's explicit critique of scientific socialism was thus also accompanied by a recognition and rejection of other theoretical perspectives thought to be ideological props of an affirmative quietism, as his treatment of Goethe and the problem of the Beautiful Soul had shown in *The German Artist Novel*. The Beautiful Soul represented an attitude toward intellectual inwardness, prone to hypersensitivity, which nonetheless avoided all real struggle against irritating circumstance.

There can be a beautiful soul in an ugly body, a healthy one in a
sick body, a noble one in a common body—and vice versa. There
is a kernel of truth in the proposition that what happens to the
body cannot affect the soul. But in the established order this truth
has taken on a terrible form. The freedom of the soul was used to
excuse the poverty, the martyrdom and bondage of the body. It
served the ideological surrender of existence to the economy of
capitalism. (AC, 109)

This criticism of the Beautiful Soul did not imply a sheer rejection of the
notion of spiritual freedom, however. Nor did it lead Marcuse to a conception of intellectual activity based upon the philosophical foundations of
historical materialism. Marcuse sought an emancipatory theory of human
intelligence and action that would represent an outgrowth neither of the
"gloomy science" of bourgeois (Malthusian) economic thought nor socialist
economic philosophy, but rather out of the third force of the joyful science
(*gaya scienza*) developed by such an outspoken critic of traditional culture
and scholarship as Friedrich Nietzsche. Nietzsche, in contrast to the contemplative orientation of the Beautiful Soul, called upon the activist "free
spirit" to create heaven on earth, not above it. Likewise, Marcuse's militant
utopian humanism explicitly aimed toward the achievement of the earthly
pleasure and human gratification that could not be attained in the world as
it now stood, but that *might* be obtained in the world as it could (potentially)
be. To the extent that the economic order under socialism might also "pre-
empt the entire life of individuals" (ibid.) Marcuse's activism and practice
(like Nietzsche's) would *not* be oriented toward socialism. In his estimation,
the overriding social objectives of a critical theory had to revolve around
the achievement of pleasure and beauty in actual human practice. According
to Marcuse, it was *Nietzsche* who had indicated that art and culture could
reawaken humanity's "aphrodisiac bliss" (AC, 115), and that art need not
necessarily merely "tranquilize" repressed individuals with its sublime per-
fections and perpetual ideals.

When culture gets to the point of having to sustain fulfillment itself
and no longer merely desire, it will no longer be able to do so in
contents that, as such, bear an affirmative character. "Gratitude,"
will then perhaps really be its essence, as Nietzsche asserted of all
beautiful and great art. (AC, 131)

In Marcuse's estimation, culture could, thus, *redeem its promise*, and evoke this sort of gratitude, but only when artistic activities had been transformed into sources of real gratification (rather than sublimation) and into bases for the achievement of material happiness (rather than the perpetuation of wretchedness and want). Calling for the abolition of affirmative culture and the oppressive socioeconomic relations it preserved, Marcuse sought to develop an aesthetic theory that could assist in the realization of the promise thought to be originally presented by great art. Foreshadowing both the form and content of the concluding sentence to Max Horkheimer and Theodore W. Adorno's 1944 *Dialectic of Enlightenment* ("Enlightenment which is in possession of itself and coming to power can break the bounds of enlightenment"), Marcuse's concluding sentence to this 1937 essay in cultural critique would again cite Nietzsche to the effect that: if we are ever to be happy at all, "we can do nothing other than promote culture" (AC, 133).

Marcuse was convinced that culture *could be* purged of its affirmative character, that is, of its compatibility with, and subservience to, the established society. But while *religious* and *philosophical* cultural activities had increasingly come to capitulate to positivism and empiricism, *art* remained *that particular cultural component that retained a concern for material human happiness and social justice*:

> Only in the medium of ideal beauty, in art, was happiness permitted to be reproduced as a cultural value in the totality of social life. Not so in the two areas of culture which in other respects share with art in the representation of ideal truth: philosophy and religion. In its idealist trend, philosophy became increasingly distrustful of happiness, and religion accorded it a place only in the hereafter. (AC, 117)

Thus, in Marcuse's estimation, the aesthetic dimension of culture uniquely retained the promise of happiness and freedom that modern philosophy and religion tended to "forget" (even though this promise was generally restricted to forms that also engendered resignation to the social status quo). Therefore, even affirmative art contained emancipatory potential:

> . . . art became the presage of possible truth. *Classical German aesthetics* comprehended the relation between beauty and truth in the idea of an *aesthetic education of the human species*. Schiller says

that the "political problem" of a better organization of society "must take the path through the aesthetic realm, because it is through beauty that one arrives at freedom." And in his poem "Die Künstler" ("The Artists") he expresses the relation between the established and the coming culture in the lines: "What we have here perceived as beauty / We shall some day encounter as truth"... (AC, 117–18, emphasis added)

To be sure, Marcuse felt that Friedrich Schiller's humanist emphasis on the aesthetic education of the species was affirmative, insofar as it remained, in part, satisfied with a poetization of the soul and human spirit, rather than being totally and passionately concerned with the questions of concrete human practice. But Schiller's aesthetic educational philosophy was also liberating, according to Marcuse, precisely because it was primarily motivated by an overarching utopian concern for a better organization of society. Marcuse held that Schiller's practical-aesthetic educational philosophy preserved the sensuous and sociocritical ideals that Herder's romantic-literary orientation tended to eliminate from the activities of culture and education.

Insofar as Schiller's vision of aesthetic education was thought to aid in both perceiving and fulfilling the social longings and instinctual needs (that were otherwise merely perpetuated as ideals by the established culture), it was held to assist in bringing humanity back to its senses and to enlist art against alienation. Marcuse's subsequent elaboration of Schiller's aesthetic endeavor would also aim at abolishing the affirmative character of art as such, and at permitting a renascent aesthetic philosophy to begin to reshape society for life. (Marcuse's initial treatment of the Schillerian aesthetic in AC is further developed at EC, 180–92 and at FL, 41–42.)

I would like to reflect briefly on the general meaning of Marcuse's essay on affirmative culture with regard to the interrelated topics of art and alienation. It is true that Marcuse does not speak of alienation, as such, in "The Affirmative Character of Culture." He is, however, concerned with the problems connected with humanity's lack of fulfillment in the sensual dimension of its existence, as well as the loss of its political-intellectual ability to oppose the oppressive social status quo. These phenomena are connected to the separation of art and culture from life. In Marcuse's estimation, the then contemporary form of society (in Europe and the United States during the 1930s) had so repressed and sublimated the basic human needs for material happiness, emotional gratification, and social freedom that human consciousness (in its established religion, philosophy, and traditional culture) became "tranquilized" and "affirmative." To that extent, the human intellect lost its critical autonomy and freedom; the human "spirit" was numbed into oblivion. As such, cultural philosophy was thought to have succumbed either to the contemplative passivity of the mechanical materialist or to the withdrawal of the Beautiful Soul. All aesthetic philosophy that was content to accept art as an "illusion" or as a "reflection of the real" was thought to have become an affirmative prop of just those existent social conditions that insured humanity's loss of (or alienation from) the goals Marcuse stresses: earthly happiness, instinctual fulfillment, and social freedom. Art as illusion leaves the social world unaltered. Likewise, art as a reflection of the real is considered affirmative insofar as it glorifies a "bad facticity" and does not overcome it. Thus, the human lack of sensual fulfillment and the loss of humanity's ability to oppose the status quo (i.e., problems of alienation) also disclose, to Marcuse, a crisis in aesthetic theory. Marcuse believed that an alternative approach to the philosophy of art was required, which could both supersede a romantic aestheticism and a scientific realism—in a theory that was both socially activist and philosophically utopian. Marcuse's revised aesthetic theory sought to stress the material need to redeem human experience from emotional repression and social unhappiness. It proposed a practical, political utopianism to deal with the authoritarianism and oppression of the capitalist industrial order. It defined alienation in terms of society's failure to measure up to the ideals of beauty and freedom that the affirmative culture perpetuated as mere image, and that a new form of culture had yet to make real. Because Marcuse's new aesthetic philosophical approach went beyond the appropriative economic analysis of alienation presented by Marx in the *Paris Manuscripts*, and made explicit use of utopian ideals as evaluative criteria by which to reorganize society, it secured what Marcuse perceived to be the necessary transition from a "scientific" to a "critical" theory. Critical theory rejected the "fetishization of facts," and was thought to restore human autonomy to the history of philosophy, through its stress on self-reflection, imagination, and phantasy. Alienation, in this critical philosophical framework, was a matter characterized by a state of disturbed consciousness (too highly sublimated) and distorted perception (too crudely desensitized), rather than by the seizure of surplus value or by the loss of control over one's labor in the social process of production.

Likewise, Marcuse argued in this essay *against* "affirmative" approaches to philosophy of art or philosophy of education, and pressed toward a new vision of culture as a *countermovement* to the social and ideological conditions that alienated the human spirit. He sought a cultural countermovement that would oppose both the traditional, literary-philosophical conception of critique that saw itself defined solely in terms of a higher culture, yet he also wanted to transcend the Marxist emphasis on artistic engagement and social science. "The Affirmative Character of Culture" indicated Marcuse's cultural philosophical preference for the supposed emancipatory potential of Schiller's "*On the Aesthetic Education of Man in a Series of Letters*, Plato's program (in the *Republic*) for a reorganization of society, and the radical (rather than reactionary, protofascist) side of the militant aesthetic philosophy of Friedrich Nietzsche. Marcuse's new aesthetic theory was oriented primarily toward a new conception of *art as an expression of, and a fulfillment of, species need*, which heralds a *new form of human experience and reality*. No longer narrowly concerned with works of literature, painting, sculpture, and so forth, this reconstituted (i.e., synoptic or programmatic) aesthetic theory sought instead the meaning and relevance of art for the free conduct of historical human life and experience. The critical theory and critical practice of art were thought able to preserve the autonomy and priority of human phantasy and imagination over the domination of human thought by the given data of natural or social realities. A genuinely utopian and humanist form of aesthetic education was considered necessary to cultivate and illumine these emancipatory faculties and to develop a philosophy of protest against humanity's elemental cultural alienation from its own existence as sensuous practical activity.

After a brief interval, Marcuse's philosophical treatment of the counter-cultural activity of the artist continues (in 1948) in the essay on "Sartre's Existentialism" (SE). The pertinent points here are few in number, but worthy of mention. In this essay, Marcuse objects to the particular vision of philosophy expressed in Sartre's *Being and Nothingness* (1943). This vision, he believes, has come to justify the irrationality of social existence during the Nazi era, through its apparent resignation to "living without appeal" (SE, 160) and to its theoretical adjustment to "being in an absurd world" (ibid.). In contrast to the passive version of existentialism thought to be represented by Sartre, Marcuse favors the active and rebellious philosophies of Camus and Nietzsche.

Marcuse admires Camus and Nietzsche because, in spite of the fact that the given social situation ostensibly leaves no room for hope or escape, they still do not submit to it. For them "this life is nothing but 'consciousness and revolt', and defiance is its only truth" (ibid.). According to Marcuse, both of these authors reject conformism to authoritarian ideologies, and in this respect "Camus's *Mythe de Sisyphe* recaptures the climate of Nietzsche's philosophy. . . ." (ibid.). Because Sartre on the other hand is thought to have elevated the experience of fascism into "a philosophy of the concrete human existence" (ibid.), Marcuse prefers, instead, Camus's *obstinate refusal* to rationalize the given events. "Camus rejects existential philosophy: the latter must of necessity 'explain' the inexplicable, rationalize the absurdity and thus falsify its reality. To him, the only adequate expression is living the absurd life, and the artistic creation, which . . . 'covers with images that which makes no sense. . . .'" (ibid.).

According to Marcuse, Camus is propounding a philosophy of art (based on that of Nietzsche) that obstinately persists in enunciating a utopian protest. It represents a "reconstruction of thought on the ground of absurdity" (ibid.) that need not lead to a condition of passivity or despair, nor to irrationalism, but that may actually lead to a mode of thought able to criticize and oppose the fascist mentality and social system. Unfortunately, Marcuse does not pursue this line of thought further in "Sartre's Existentialism," but rather immerses himself at this point in a detailed exposition and commentary on the basic ideas of Sartre's text, which is after all the aim of his essay, though it need not concern us further here. It can be said, however, that Marcuse recognized an emancipatory emphasis upon aesthetic imagination in the philosophy of protest of Albert Camus and sympathized with his conviction that only art can lend form and human dignity to conditions of existential chaos. Sartre's alleged willingness, on the other hand, to accommodate theory to given social facts, conflicted with Marcuse's ostensibly utopian sensibilities and with his commitment to actualize the more fulfilling social realities that "could be"—as this attitude was set forth in "The Affirmative Character of Culture."

In the ensuing chapters of this study I want to comment on the best-known Marcuse texts: *Reason and Revolution, Soviet Marxism, Eros and Civilization, One-Dimensional Man, An Essay on Liberation,* and *Five Lectures.* Marcuse's treatment of the themes of alienation, art, and the humanities will continue to guide us along the path of his thought.

CHAPTER FIVE

—∿—

Marcuse's Aesthetic Ontology

. . . we must take a leap into the metaphysics of art . . . the world is only justified as an aesthetic phenomenon.

Friedrich Nietzsche,
The Birth of Tragedy XXIV

In Marcuse's estimation the aesthetic dimension of philosophical thinking is also considered an *ontological* dimension. As such, it is held to be the best preserve of the negative, contradictory character of reality. For Marcuse, aesthetic theory is concerned more with *Being* than with *beings*, and more with ontology than with science. In 1928 Martin Heidegger classically distinguished these two dimensions with reference to *das Nicht* (that nothing or that negation) between beings and Being. "*Die ontologische Differenz ist das Nicht zwischen Seiendem und Sein.*"[1] The "ontological difference" represents what Marcuse declares to be the "inadequacy between existence and essence [that] belongs to the very core of reality" in *Reason and Revolution, Hegel and the Rise of Social Theory* (RR, 304) and he adds that a "contradictory, two dimensional style of thought is the inner form not only of dialectical logic but of all philosophy that comes to grips with reality" in *One-Dimensional Man, Studies in the Ideology of Advanced Industrial Society* (OD, 132).

I contend that by the time of Marcuse's transition to Columbia University and to the Institute for Social Research in exile there his general theory of human reality and existence is better described as an *aesthetic ontology* than

99

as any version, however complex, of historical materialism. I borrow the phrase "aesthetic ontology" from the educational philosopher, Michael L. Simmons Jr.,[2] and find it particularly appropriate with regard to Marcuse. Simmons points out that in some critical educational theories an aesthetic ontology stands in lieu of a more highly defined social philosophy, for example, of the classically conceived Marxian or Hegelian sort. It may do so, in his estimation, because this particular philosophical perspective proposes that human beings strive, in general, to reconcile the disjuncture perceived between art and life, and because it also holds that the need to resolve this tension can be a source of change toward increasingly more mature and responsible forms of human consciousness and conduct. Thus, an aesthetic ontology is linked to the essential human desire to educate, cultivate, and improve human beings as such,—in accordance with the laws of beauty—as a *precondition* to meaningful social and political action. An aesthetic ontology is thought to always involve a potentially disalienating "inward turn" toward a generic human self-awareness, as this awareness has come to be disclosed and expressed in artistic activity and aesthetic imagination. Thus, it is thought that aesthetic interests will ultimately ensure that humanity is never content to remain a stranger unto itself, and that this aesthetic kind of undercurrent is present wherever alienation explicitly surfaces as a philosophical question. Marcuse's approach to an aesthetic ontology is certainly also "ontological" in a specifically Heideggerian sense: that is, it is preeminently a theory of that being that is considered to be distinguished by its concern for Being, namely *Dasein*, or humanity. Ontology in this sense denotes a philosophical-anthropological *unity* of self and world. For Marcuse, as for Heidegger, however, this unity is simultaneously a duality, given the "nothing" or "negation" that separates the factical and ontological realms. Likewise, I must recall that Marcuse's ontology is also *aesthetic* in the Heideggerian sense (as this is derived from Wilhelm Dilthey): that is, Marcuse's theory regards art as a most profound source of truth, able to discover and convey meaning beyond the first-dimensional, functional (everyday, prephilosophical) perspective,[3] as well as a source of creative human social and intellectual power (as Heidegger derives this from Nietzsche and from the neo-Kantians) that can help externalize, and bring into being, the truest projections of the most genuine human genius and imagination.[4]

My argument, therefore, is that an "aesthetic ontology" is an especially apt designation for the theoretical approach that most adequately comprehends and describes Marcuse's essentially interrelated views on art, alienation, and the humanities. We shall see that this holds true not only during his middle period, but also in the earliest and latest stages of his thought. His reformulation of the theory of reification, in terms of *Verdinglichung* rather than in the strictly conceived doctrine of commodity fetishism, allows Marcuse to turn to the aesthetic-educational remediation of the alienation held to be hidden in everyday thought and activity. As Simmons explains, this educational emphasis is characteristic of an aesthetic ontology (and appears to stand well within the neo-Kantian interpretation of the classical tradition of Plato and Aristotle). This study contends that Marcuse's particular interpretation of Marx's alienation theory (in terms of *Verdinglichung* as well as single-dimensionality) is not adequately understood unless seen in conjunction with Marcuse's aesthetic and educational concerns.

The "Aesthetic Dimension" in *Eros and Civilization*

Aesthetic and educational concerns become most strikingly thematic for Marcuse in his 1955 volume, *Eros and Civilization, A Philosophical Inquiry into Freud* (EC). Marcuse writes that

> . . . when, on the basis of Kant's theory, the aesthetic function becomes the central theme of the philosophy of culture, it is used to demonstrate the principles of a non-repressive civilization, in which reason is sensuous and sensuousness rational. Schiller's *Letters on the Aesthetic Education of Man* (1975), written largely under the impact of the *Critique of Judgment*, aim at a remaking of civilization by virtue of the liberating force of the aesthetic function. . . . (EC, 180)

> When Schiller wrote, the need for such reshaping seemed obvious; Herder and Schiller, Hegel and Novalis, developed in almost identical terms the concept of alienation. (EC, 186)

These citations are taken from chapter 9 of *Eros and Civilization*, entitled "The Aesthetic Dimension,"—a key section of his middle-period work that is of the utmost importance to our considerations on art, alienation, and the humanities. Marcuse's chapter is divided into two roughly equal parts discussing the concept of the aesthetic as it is found first of all in Kant's introduction to the *Critique of Judgment*, and secondly, in Schiller's elaboration of Kant in *On the Aesthetic Education of Man in a Series of Letters*. Marcuse notes that his interpretation in this regard is indebted to Heidegger, who "for the first time demonstrated the central role of the aesthetic function in Kant's system" (EC, 176). Although reification is not treated as an explicit theme in this chapter of EC, Marcuse does make certain relevant statements here concerning the nature of the aesthetic *object* as well as the *objectifying* activity of the aesthetic imagination and the *objectivity* of the aesthetic judgment.

> Although sensuous and therefore receptive, the aesthetic imagination is creative: in a free synthesis of its own, it constitutes *beauty*. In the aesthetic imagination sensuousness generates universally valid principles for an objective order. (EC, 177)

> Whatever the object may be (thing, flower, animal or man), it is represented and judged not in terms of its usefulness, not according to any purpose it may possibly serve, and also not in view of its "internal" finality or completeness. In the aesthetic imagination, the object is rather represented as free from all such relations and properties, as freely being itself. The experience in which the object is thus "given" is totally different from the every-day as well as scientific experience; all links between object and the world of theoretical and practical reason are severed, or rather suspended. This experience, which releases the object into its "free" being, is the work of the free play of the imagination. (EC, 178)

Just as Marcuse's 1928–32 essays "The Foundation of Historical Materialism" (HM), "Contributions to a Phenomenology of Historical Materialism" (PH), and "On the Problem of the Dialectic" (PD) sought a phenomenological foundation for the dialectic above and beyond the philosophical foundation furnished by historical materialism, so too his aesthetic theory shows a tendency toward phenomenological development especially in its treatment of objectivity. In *Eros and Civilization*, written in 1955, Marcuse notes that his particular interpretation of the nature of the aesthetic object and the objectivity of the aesthetic judgment and imagination owes much to an article on Kant's concept of the imagination appearing in a 1930 issue of the *Jahrbuch für Philosophie und Phänomenologische Forschung*, edited by Husserl (EC, 178). This article, by Herman Mörschen, was actually a publication of the author's dissertation, and is *the* work cited by Heidegger in the latter's own 1929 interpretation of Kant's concept of imagination, *Kant and the Problem of Metaphysics*. Thus, while Marcuse excludes from consideration any direct discussion of the philosophical underpinnings of a Marxist aesthetics by choosing to *confine* (EC, 173) his attention exclusively to the early modern history of the term, the phenomenological frame of reference of his own Kant-interpretation is permitted a privileged presence. The historical materialist position is correspondingly also circumvented or displaced toward Friedrich Schiller and Kant. Marcuse, for example, while obviously inspired by Marx's comment from the *1844 Manuscripts* on production "according to the laws of beauty" (at HM, 16–17), presents Marx's allusion to the twenty-third of Schiller's letters on aesthetic education as if it were Marx's alone. Marx was extremely critical as well as appreciative of Schiller, so much so that Stefan Morawski notes that Marx turns Schiller "inside out."[5] Later (at EC, 189) Marcuse cites only Schiller, dropping reference to Marx altogether. He follows the lead of Heidegger stressing, rather, the phenomenological hypothesis of the liberating role of the *imagination* in aesthetic theory, while remaining mute on Schiller's actual status in the overall views of Marx and Engels. Marcuse's *particular* orientation to problems of alienation as *Verdinglichung* directs him to a consideration, instead, of the emancipatory potential that he believed could still be found in aesthetic imagination and aesthetic education.

With regard to the former, Marcuse claims in *Eros and Civilization* that *Kant* merges the fundamental "meaning of *aesthetic* (pertaining to the senses) with the new connotation (pertaining to beauty, especially in art)" (EC, 174). He explains, furthermore, that beauty according to Kant is dependent upon the human faculty of imagination. It is the human imagination that can depict the "pure form" (EC, 177) of an object, and it is this pure form that is considered beautiful. "An object represented in its pure form is 'beautiful.' Such representation is the work (or rather the play) of *imagination*" (ibid.). Marcuse stresses the fact that for Kant the imaginative faculty of judgment mediates between perception (which, in itself, Kant termed *blind*) and cogitation (in itself, termed *empty*). The imagination (*Ein-bildung*) is thought to *build* or *form* the sensuous and rational aspects of human experience and understanding *into a unity*: "To Kant, the aesthetic dimension is the medium in which the senses and intellect meet. The mediation is accomplished by imagination, which is the 'third' mental faculty" (EC, 179). As the *third* and *unifying* element, synthesizing the data of the senses and the categories of thought, the aesthetic imagination also stands at the foundation of Marcuse's "third way" between a Lockean sensualism and an affirmative idealism, that is, the aesthetic ontological "humanism" elaborated in "The Foundation of Historical Materialism" and *Eros and Civilization*, and designated as a philosophical anthropology by certain of Marcuse's critics (cf. Rolf Bauermann and Hans-Jochen Rötscher, E. Batalov, and Jürgen Habermas).

Heidegger's book on Kant had especially emphasized this pivotal role for the imagination. Kant wrote that "The imagination (*facultas imaginandi*) is a faculty of intuition even without the presence of an object,"[6] which may either recollect something perceived earlier, or freely invent an original form. In either case both Heidegger and Marcuse agree (EC, 181) that this makes possible the fundamental unity of sensibility and understanding in Kant's cognitive scheme. Imagination, thus, is thought to possess the inherently practical and cognitive power to produce images, a power that Heidegger terms *Bildungskraft*,[7] having the dual connotation of the capability of image-formation and the effect of education. This power is thought to stand at the core of perception and conceptualization, and is exercised in accordance with the qualities of human originality and freedom. For Marcuse the beautiful and pure forms of the aesthetic imagination may give humanity a genuinely philosophical awareness of liberation, gratification, and goodness as universally valid truths:

> The famous Paragraph 59 of the *Critique [of Judgment]* is entitled "Of Beauty as the Symbol of Morality." In Kant's system, morality is the realm of freedom, in which practical reason realizes itself under self-given laws. Beauty symbolizes this realm insofar as it demonstrates intuitively the reality of freedom. (EC, 174)
>
> The aesthetic perception is accompanied by pleasure. This pleasure derives from the perception of the pure form of an object, regardless of its "matter" and of its (internal or external) "purpose." An object represented in its pure form is "beautiful." Such representation is the work . . . of *imagination*. (EC, 176–77)
>
> Although sensuous and therefore receptive, the aesthetic imagination is creative: in a free synthesis of its own, it constitutes beauty. In the aesthetic imagination, sensuousness generates universally valid principles for an objective order. (EC, 177)

Marcuse's chapter is thus well on its way toward explaining the logic of his own conception of the "inner connection between pleasure, sensuousness, beauty, truth, art and freedom" (EC, 172), an inner connection based on the philosophical centrality of the aesthetic imagination.

Marcuse requires the neo-Kantian theory of the transcendental and synthetic quality of the human imagination in order to justify ultimately his notion of an aesthetic negation to the phenomena of reification (*Verding-lichung*), and to undergird his theory of the aesthetic origins of the critical political and philosophical potential he seeks. Because "theory can invoke no facts in confirmation of the theoretical elements that point toward future freedom" as he observed in "Philosophy and Critical Theory" (CT, 145), there thus can exist no historical or material warrant for a socially just future. Marcuse contends that "in the aesthetic imagination, sensuousness generates universally valid principles for an objective order" (EC, 177). To Marcuse the pure and beautiful forms of the transcendental or generically subjective imagination may serve as a substantive *aesthetic warrant* for a critique of human theory and human practice.

In a similar vein, Nietzsche notes in *The Birth of Tragedy* XXIV that "the world is only justified as an aesthetic phenomenon." Clearly, art has a well-established function as social criticism (e.g., Georg Grosz, Upton Sinclair, Charles Dickens, and Peter Weiss), but Marcuse's elaboration of his particular understanding of the philosophical scope and basis of this aesthetic function is what is of special interest here. Marcuse believes that the aesthetic imagination supplies the real groundwork for both perception and thought, and consciousness and conduct. Marcuse maintains, however, that this imagination has been repressed, and the aesthetic attitude distorted into the culturally affirmative modes of the museum or bohemia (EC, 176). Thus, Marcuse sought as early as 1937 in "The Affirmative Character of Culture" to refurbish the neo-Kantian doctrine, ostensibly revising it in the direction of a social materialism. Marcuse's approach (at EC, 175–96) is to revise both Kant and Schiller through Freud, and to demonstrate that certain archetypes of the human imagination, especially those that envision the fulfillment of humanity and nature through the release of libidinal forces, can prove "their truth value as symbols of a reality principle *beyond* the performance principle" (EC, 175–76). In many ways, this is a restatement of the normative *Artisten-Metaphysik* of Nietzsche, and conditions the renewed possibility that art may be educationally and politically enlisted against alienation. Wherever the imagination is restricted to calculative or deductive modes, or its sensuous human basis forgotten, *Verdinglichung* is thought to make possible the persistence of alienation. Where the imagination, instead, transcends this first dimension, moving toward the immanent but hitherto repressed realms of human pleasure and gratification, Marcuse believes that it may yet stimulate emancipatory social struggle, and thus "rescue the full content of Schiller's notion" (EC, 187).

The Rationality of Art and the Denial of Things

Marcuse's middle-period theory stresses the point that an alienating objectivity and bad facticity are persistent features of the economic aspect of human existence. As he sees it, however, even more *permanent* and more enduring than the effects of *Verdinglichung* are the social promise and also the cultural potential of *philosophy*: the philosophy of essence, the philosophy of Being, and—as becomes more and more evident—the *philosophy of art*.

We shall see that in *One-Dimensional Man* (OD), "Art in the One Dimensional Society (AO)," and *An Essay on Liberation* (EL), Marcuse comes to advocate the organization of labor and civilization within the dimension of Eros and the aesthetic, seeking to substitute an aesthetic rationality for the reified concept of reason represented by the operationalist language of objects and facts. He believed that society and human experience could be shaped in accordance with the aesthetic form and that theory could become critical if it shifted from science to utopia. The language of art provided philosophical negation insofar as it was free from the "fateful fetishism of science" and embodied, instead, a rehumanized, nonreified,—and therefore *critical*—philosophical outlook. The activities of art, rather than those of labor and economics, were considered to be both the source and the measure of the fulfillment of the species-needs of humanity.

Art was thought capable of becoming a disalienating force within existence. Art was thought able to negate the "negations" (of human essence) represented by bad facticity and reification. Art was thought capable of negating reification by virtue of its *cognitive power* to discern human meaning beyond the first dimension and because of its *practical contribution* toward a synoptic program for the aesthetic reorganization of society. In this manner, the rationality of art became Marcuse's major philosophical weapon in negating alienation as dehumanization and as *Verdinglichung*.

Certain salient features of Marcuse's notion of negation especially with regard to the philosophy of art, need to be indicated at this point. For example, Marcuse finds the "power of negative thinking" to be expressed especially in *poetry's* characteristic ability "*to deny the things*" in "A Note on Dialectic" (ND, xi). Indeed, Marcuse stresses the basic identity of dialectical and aesthetic studies, as he understands them, and these are also considered to be essentially related to a critical and negative philosophy, as such:

> Interpretation of that-which-is in terms of that-which-is-not, confrontation of the given facts with that which they exclude— this has been the concern of philosophy wherever philosophy was more than a matter of ideological justification or mental exercise. The liberating function of negation in philosophical thought depends upon the recognition that the negation is a positive act: that-which-is *repels* that-which-is-not and, in doing so, repels its own real possibilities. Consequently, *to express and define that-which-is on its own terms is to distort and falsify reality.* Reality is other and more than that codified in the logic and language of facts. Here is the inner link between dialectical thought and the effort of avant-garde literature: the effort to break the power of facts over the word, and to speak a language which is not the language of those who establish, enforce and benefit from the facts. As the power of the given facts tends to become totalitarian, to absorb all opposition, and to define the entire universe of discourse, the effort to speak the language of contradiction appears increasingly irrational, obscure, artificial. The question is not that of the direct or indirect influence of Hegel on the genuine avant-garde, though this is evident in Mallarme and Villiers de l'Isle-Adam, in surrealism, in Brecht. *Dialectic and poetic language meet, rather, on common ground.* (ND, x, emphasis added)

According to Marcuse, then, to express and define "that-which-is," on its own terms, is to distort and falsify reality: it is to succumb to oppressive quality of reification as *Verdinglichung*. In his estimation, only that *separate* language, shared alike by dialectics and art, can reflect the liberating function of negation in critical philosophy. Art is thought to preserve a reality that is "other and more" than the logic and language of facts, and poetry is thought to stand upon an external foundation (i.e., that of the negative or critical philosophy represented in the rationality of art).

In *One-Dimensional Man*, Marcuse pursues an essentially similar train of thought, asking after the emancipatory second-dimensional, conceptual elements he believes are shared as a common stock by critical philosophy and utopian art:

What is this "common stock." Does it include Plato's "ideal," Aristotle's "essence," Hegel's *Geist*, Marx's *Verdinglichung* in what ever adequate translation? Does it include the key words of poetic language? Of surrealist prose? and, if so, does it contain them in their negative connotation—that is, as invalidating the universe of common usage? If not, then a whole body of distinctions which men have found worth drawing is rejected, removed. . . . (OD, 188)

> Fiction calls the facts by their name and their reign collapses; fiction subverts everyday experience and shows it to be mutilated and false. But art has this *magic power* only as *the power of negation*. It can speak its own language only as long as the images are alive which refuse and refute the established order. (OD, 62, emphasis added)

Marcuse emphasizes the external, "outside" quality of negative reason in his controversial paper "The Concept of Negation in the Dialectic" (CN) read at the 1966 Hegel congress at Prague. In this lecture Marcuse acknowledges that his discussion of the negative in dialectical philosophy develops in explicit opposition to the concept of negation as utilized by Hegel and Marx:

> As to the concept of negation as overcoming (*Aufhebung*), for both Marx and Hegel, it is essential that the negating forces driving a system's self-evolving contradictions to a new stage develop *within* that very system. The development of the bourgeoisie within feudal society and of the proletariat as a revolutionary force within capitalism are examples of determinate negation against the whole system and yet within it. . . . Against this concept of dialectics, I ask whether the negating forces within an antagonistic system develop with historical necessity in this progressive, liberating manner. (CN, 131)

The dialectical materialist conception of contradiction classically implies more than an antinomial, paradoxical, metaphysical, or dualistic juxtaposition of contraries: it implies an *internal basis for the negation of the negation*, that is, for development to a higher level. Precisely because of Marcuse's dualistic view of the opposition between one-dimensionality and negation, however, he reads Hegel (in HOg) as *ontological* philosopher, rather than as a *dialectical* one. His negative ontology of the thing (the foundation of his *Verdinglichung*-thesis) also seems to have implicitly inspired the conclusion in "The Affirmative Character of Culture" (AC, 131): "Perhaps art, as such, will have no objects." In Marcuse's estimation, aesthetic objects may become merely affirmatively charming or decorative, but *the philosophical "dimension" of the aesthetic* is thought to preserve the full potential of human experience and reality through the synoptic integration of art and life, and through the projection of an aesthetic social program that may render liberation from alienation really possible.

> The new object of art is not yet "given," but the familiar object has become impossible, false. From illusion, imitation, harmony to reality—but the reality is not yet "given"; it is not the one which is the object of "realism." Reality has to be discovered and projected. The senses must learn not to see things anymore in the medium of that law and order which has formed them; the bad functionalism which organizes our sensibility must be smashed. (EL, 38–39)

In this manner, Marcuse's middle-period aesthetic thinking is not oriented toward the traditional work of art, as a factual artwork, but as the embodiment of the larger living human truth that the artwork is thought to symbolize or disclose (and that he would later describe in *The Aesthetic Dimension, Toward a Critique of Marxist Aesthetics* [AD] as, e.g., the tragic unity of triumph and despair and pleasure and pain). Marcuse seems to have achieved what Heinz Paetzold calls the "liberation of the aesthetic from the art object as object."[8] The aesthetic becomes a *principle* of reflection relieved of its traditional fixation on the art object as such.

Such an aesthetic is held to be primarily concerned with the negative and transcendent realm *outside* that customarily associated with science or common sense. No longer directed toward art objects, Marcuse's middle-period aesthetic is oriented instead toward an understanding of the critical, second-dimensional *rationality of art* as a general form of a negative "dialectic." Marcuse is operating with a *dualistic* and *phenomenological*, rather than with a *dialectical materialist* concept of negation. His theory is consistent with the distinctions drawn by Husserl and Heidegger separating the "science of fact" from the "science of essence" and by Dilthey's separation of "natural science" from "human science."

Husserl identified his concept of *phenomenology* with the very basis of philosophical investigation as a search for meaning and sense *beyond* the

empirically obvious aspects of reality and knowledge. He thus quite dualistically contrasted a "prephilosophical" understanding with a "truer," "deeper,"
and "purer" consciousness of universals and ideas, achieved through a process of pure conceptualization, the "phenomenological reduction." Likewise, Marcuse implies that a phenomenological reduction—or "negation" if
you will—of the functional or operational first-dimension may be achieved
through the rationality of art:

> The technological rationality of art seems to be characterized by
> an aesthetic "reduction". . . . According to Hegel, art reduces the
> immediate contingency in which an object (or totality of objects)
> exists, to a state in which the object takes on the form and quality
> of freedom . . . the artistic transformation violates the natural
> object, but the violated is itself oppressive; thus the aesthetic trans-
> formation is liberation. (OD, 239–40)

Actually, it is the *concept of dialectic* formulated by Hegel and Marx
that is transformed, even negated, by the phenomenological tenor of Marcuse's aesthetic philosophy. The real issue here is not whether Marcuse is or
is not a "genuine" Marxist. The question to be asked in this regard is to
what extent Marcuse and Husserl, Heidegger et al. have escaped the philosophical risks involved in *phenomenologically negating*, that is, proceeding
quite dualistically "beyond" (OD, 185), the spheres of fact, object, and
nature, and how this affects their analyses of alienation, art, and the humanities. Marcuse, for example, notes that art has the "magic power" (OD, 62)
of negation. Much as the occult philosopher's stone was said to be able to
mysteriously transform lead and iron into gold, Marcuse seems to propound
a negative alchemy of art: he would see humanity's "reified" social relationships (that have been turned to gold by the Midas touch of an "untrue" concept of property and a concomitant cult of efficiency and profit) resolved
back into an aesthetical phlogiston. A conscious aesthetic sensibility could
become the philosophical alkahest dissolving long-petrified reifications of
reason. By ". . . breaking the spell of the Establishment. . . ." (AO, 55) aesthetic
philosophy could also become an intellectual elixir of human freedom and life.
Marcuse refers in *Counterrevolution and Revolt* (CR) to the "alchemy of the
word" (CR, 107) in literary art. William Barrett has noted that magic and
alchemy are traditional symbols of the revolt of German romanticism against
the positivism and scientism of the present age and the materialism of bour-

geois society.[9] In this regard, Marcuse insists in *Five Lectures—Psychoanalysis, Politics, Utopia* (FL) "I am an absolutely incurable and sentimental romantic" (FL, 82).

Marcuse's emphasis on the aesthetic, romantic, or phenomenological forms of negation must be seen in connection with his theory of *Verdinglichung*, and his subsequent rejection in *Soviet Marxism, A Critical Analysis* (SM) and *One-Dimensional Man* (OD) of the classical Marxist notion of negation that also entails the postulates of progress through class struggle and the working class as the revolutionary historical subject. According to my reading of Marxism, the facts and circumstances of capitalist production, that is, the *internal contradictions* between private appropriation and social need, represent not only the negation of human existence, but also the seeds of the negation of *that* negation. An internal, economic, and political logic generates a definite form of negation that may lead to a new synthesis and to a higher stage in societal development. Marcuse, on the other hand, emphasizes the fact that the technological achievements of advanced industrial systems (of which he considered both the U.S. and Soviet societies to be variations) have led to the establishment of one-dimensional social realities and social philosophies from which all contradiction is thought to have been eliminated. In his estimation "technology has become the great vehicle of reification—reification in its most mature and effective form" (OD, 168). Marcuse's specific notion of reification attains even further significance near the end of his middle-period work. There he considers it actually to be *the* philosophical principle behind the development of the oppressive tendencies in advanced technological cultures, wherever these have forsaken the human dimension of experience and reason in favor of a strictly instrumentalist or functionalist logic of discourse and action. His notion of *Verdinglichung* actually underpins his entire theory and critique of advanced industrial society and of traditional scientific methodology with its supposed focus on nakedly calculative and operationalist modes. Ultimately, *Verdinglichung* theory permits Marcuse to misread, or misrepresent, Marx as follows:

> Marxian theory made an essential distinction between work as the realization of human potentialities and work as "alienated labor;" the *entire sphere* of material production, of mechanized and standardized performances, is considered one of alienation. (SM, 218, emphasis added)

Similarly, in *One-Dimensional Man*, alienation and oppression are described in the *Verdinglichung* sense of reification:

> This is the pure form of servitude: to exist as an instrument, as a thing. And this mode of existence is not abrogated if the thing is animated and chooses its material and intellectual food, if it does not feel its being-a-thing, if it is a pretty, clean, mobile thing. (OD, 33)

Thus, it is also *Verdinglichung* that serves as a major prop of the theoretical basis for Marcuse's *convergence* (or assimilation) thesis, first articulated in *Soviet Marxism*, and subsequently elaborated in *One-Dimensional Man*. The *Verdinglichung* theory is indispensable if Marcuse is to explain: (1) his belief in the inevitable possibility of the persistence of alienation beyond the socialization of the means of production and beyond the equalization of the distribution of value and political power, and (2) his belief in the persistence of alienation in advanced capitalism's ". . . comfortable, smooth, democratic unfreedom. . . ." (OD, 1).

In Marcuse's view, it is the reification of reason as *Verdinglichung* that has come to conceal and mystify and, therefore, perpetuate the social conditions of alienation. Hence, we find essentially similar statements in *One-Dimensional Man* and *Soviet Marxism* describing the oppressively moronizing features of the reified forms of reason that Marcuse contends have found expression in the essentially uncritical and affirmative (i.e., positivistic) rationalism characteristic of the United States and of social philosophy in the former Soviet Union. In like fashion, fascism is also seen as but a logical extension of the mechanistic, scientistic, quasi-enlightenment sort of mentality. Reification, in Marcuse's opinion, means that reason is losing touch with its human essence "behind the curtain" (OD, 185). Reason thus alienated may assume even the most inhuman tasks of the technical rationalization of methods of domination toward society and nature.

According to Marcuse, if the advanced capitalist mentality is characterized by a reification of reason, so too is the classical mentality of socialism. As he sees it, alienation is not fundamentally a result of economic processes of commodity exchange (and production for exchange rather than use), but a result of the reification of reason, which leads entire societies to be organized and administered according to instrumentalist or operationalist criteria. The problem is that reality has *two dimensions*, in his philosophical estimation, and that human beings may participate in *two forms of objectification*, one authentic, the other "untrue," one ontological in character, one merely factual and superficial. Both forms of objectifying reason may become reality principles (in a distinctly Weberian, as well as Freudian, sense) inasmuch as social institutions and social behavior are capable of being precipitated by them. All forms of objectification that lose sight of the internal dependence that Marcuse posits between fact and "human core" are, in his opinion, consigned to single-dimensionality, alienation, and *Verdinglichung*.

It is important to note that Marcuse's position is not absolutely anti-science or anti-technology (after the manner of Heidegger or Jacques Ellul). Rather, Marcuse wishes to change the form of reason that he believes defines the practice of contemporary science and technology:

> As long as the established direction of technical progress prevails, . . . change in ownership and control of the means of production would be quantitative rather than qualitative change. Prerequisite for the liberation of the humanistic content of socialism would be a fundamental change in the *direction of technical progress*, a total reconstruction of the technical apparatus. This is the historical idea of humanism today. (SH, 111)

Marcuse seeks to reconstruct the practice of science and technology around a nonreified, true, and correct form of objectification: a new *humanist* rationality—the rationality of art.

In *An Essay on Liberation* (EL), Marcuse again emphasizes his belief in the liberating cognitive and productive power of the aesthetic dimension:

> Technique, assuming the features of art, would translate subjective sensibility into objective form, into reality. (EL, 24)

> The term "aesthetic," in its dual connotation of "pertaining to the senses" and "pertaining to art," may serve to designate the quality of the productive-creative process in an environment of freedom. (ibid.)

> Emergence of a new Reality Principle: under which a new sensibility and desublimated scientific intelligence would combine in the creation of an *aesthetic ethos*. (ibid.).

Marcuse also speaks emphatically of the aesthetic as a *productive force* within society, as a "*gesellschaftliche Produktivkraft*" (EL, 26, 45).

> Released from the bondage to exploitation, the imagination, sus-
> tained by the achievements of science, could turn its productive
> power to the radical reconstruction of experience . . . the aesthetic
> . . . would find expression in the transformation of the *Lebenswelt*—
> society as a work of art. (EL, 45)

The *reification* or thingification *of reason* becomes the main problem
with which Marcuse believes an emancipatory and critical philosophy must
contend. *Verdinglichung* theory allows Marcuse to link the philosophical
revolutions of Kant and Schopenhauer to the philosophy of Marx—with
the former ultimately coming to overshadow the latter. *Reification is primarily thought to conceal humanity from itself.*

Marcuse holds positivism and rationalism, rather than metaphysics or
irrationalism, to be among the more pernicious intellectual forces con-
cealing the human dimension in the social, philosophical, and political
spheres of advanced industrial societies. Speaking of imperialism in its Nazi
phase, Marcuse maintains:

> . . . the rational rather than the irrational becomes the most effec-
> tive vehicle of mystification. The view that the growth of repression
> in contemporary society manifested itself, in the ideological sphere,
> first in the ascent of irrational pseudo-philosophies (*Lebensphilosophie*,
> the notions of Community against Society; Blood and Soil, etc.)
> was refuted by Fascism and National Socialism. These regimes
> denied these and their own irrational "philosophies" by the all out
> technical rationalization of the apparatus. (OD, 189)

> The trouble is that the statistics, measurements and field
> studies of empirical sociology and political science are *not rational
> enough.* (OD, 190, emphasis added)

In Marcuse's view romantic oppositional philosophies of protest like *Lebensphilosophie* present humanity with theories having greater rationality with
regard to human problems than the allegedly alienating results of the natural
sciences. In his 1957 analysis of the Soviet ideological system Marcuse contended that

> The progressive, critical trends in bourgeois philosophy become the
> chief target of the attack, and the chief indictment leveled against

them is that of defamation of Reason. Nietzsche and Freud, Schopenhauer and Dewey, pragmatism, existentialism and logical positivism are branded as irrationalistic, anti-intellectual. . . . (SM, 208–9)

The assault against "bourgeois irrationalism" is particularly illuminating because it reveals traits common to the Soviet and Western rationality, namely, the prevalence of technological elements over humanistic ones. Schopenhauer and Nietzsche, the various schools of "vitalism" (*Lebensphilosophie*), existentialism, and depth psychology differ and even conflict in most essential aspects; however they are akin in that they explode the technological rationality of modern civilization. They do so by pointing up the psychical and biological forces beneath this rationality and the unredeemable sacrifices which it exacts from man. The result is a transvaluation of values which shatters the ideology of progress— not by romanticist or sentimental regression, but by breaking into tabooed dimensions of bourgeois society itself. (SM, 212–3)

Marcuse continues to polarize the "technological and humanist rationalities" in this citation as he highlights a liberating, negative, that is, countercultural, value in the pessimistic, protest philosophies of Nietzsche, Schopenhauer, and *Lebensphilosophie*. These allegedly offer strategies for breaking through *Verdinglichung*.

The *unscientific, speculative character of critical theory* derives from the specific character of its concepts, which designate and define the irrational in the rational, the mystification in the reality. Their *mythological quality* reflects the mystifying quality of the given facts. . . . (OD, 189, emphasis added)

Under the repressive conditions in which men think and live, thought—any mode of thinking which is not confined to pragmatic orientation within the status quo—can recognize the facts and respond to the facts only by "going behind" them. Experience takes place before a curtain which conceals and, if the world is the appearance of something behind the curtain of immediate experience, then, in Hegel's terms, it is we ourselves who are behind the curtain. (OD, 185)

These passages are taken from the latter half of *One-Dimensional Man* that Marcuse has consciously designed as a direct attack against "The Triumph of Positive Thinking" and "One-Dimensional Philosophy" (OD, 170). They are statements of the critical potential of "Negative Thinking" (which he regards as *the customary philosophical logic of protest*). Negative thinking however, Marcuse notes, languishes today in defeat within advanced industrial societies.

Marcuse turns to Freud precisely because of his (Marcuse's) specific concern for alienation as reification. Because the philosophy of psychoanalysis is thought to achieve an understanding beyond the first-dimension (stressing, e.g., the originally unformed or amorphous character of the libido and the human need for phantasy and imagination), it is thought to enter into the realm of human universality and freedom, and to serve as a source of knowledge that may offset alienation. "Psychoanalysis elucidates the universal in the individual experience. To that extent, and only to that extent, can psychoanalysis break the reification in which human relations are petrified" (EC, 254). Reification must be broken, in Marcuse's estimation, if alienation is ever to be overcome. *Sources of emancipatory cognitive power in this regard can well emerge from the philosophy of psychoanalysis, but perhaps even more importantly, as he sees it, also from a liberating philosophy of art.*

Marx sought the objective basis of alienation in terms of his analysis of the economic function of wage-labor and the commodity fetish. Marcuse ironically conceals and shelters questions of ownership, possession, exchange, exploitation, and appropriation, as these pertain to objectively existing, factual, historical and material (private) property relations, and productive activities. His *Verdinglichung* theory of alienation deflects critical analysis instead into the supposedly debilitating thing-character of socioeconomic objects, and the distortions of reason that are thought to emerge when philosophy is out of touch with its presumably sensuous and active, that is, human, core. Critical insight into the ontologically conceived objectifying function and affective essence of humanity is considered more important than insight into the political economy of capitalism in attaining an understanding of the foundations of alienation.

CHAPTER SIX

——*◆*——

Imagination, Death, and
Educational Reminiscence

In philosophizing about alienation both Georg Lukács and his student Istvan Meszáros highlight the significance of the human imagination for the Schillerian aesthetic education of the human race. It is Martin Heidegger's 1929 neo-Kantian, *Kant and the Problem of Metaphysics*, however, that is perhaps the most striking precursor to Marcuse's theories in this regard. Heidegger had noted especially that the transcendental imagination possessed *Bildungskraft* or the power to educe and educate. As such, the imagination could serve as the "formative center of ontological knowledge."[1] A brief excursion into Heidegger's thinking in this regard is indispensable to the analysis I wish to make of death, metaphysics, and the aesthetic imagination in Marcuse's work.

Heidegger considered the essence of the imagination to be the ability to intuit without concrete presence, and he saw the clarification of the method of this knowledge as his contribution to the epistemological tasks undertaken by Kant. In his estimation, this method was not basically deductive, inductive, or representational, but rather synthetic, creative, formative, educational, and—in an essential way—apart from experience. Ontological knowledge was never considered to be empirically given, but instead grounded in imagination, and possessing an inherently transcendental character (which Marcuse tends to term its *second-dimensional* quality). By definition, this ontological knowledge was not understood at all in the objectivistic, scientific, or positivistic sense, but rather as part of "the subjectivity of the subject."[2]

117

For Heidegger, then, the human imagination stands at the very foundation of genuine philosophical knowledge and as the basis of education as well as metaphysics. It does so by intuitively projecting Being over time, thus constituting the subjective and conscious core of human historicity and objectification, as well as by also remembering human finitude and the ineradicable eventuality of death (in a manner philosophically similar to that of *memento mori*). Remembrance of the existential meaning of death, as both the most ultimately personal and completely insurmountable generic fate, is considered an imaginative process by Heidegger precisely because death is never considered to be an object, as such. It is, rather, thought to be a condition of human existence with a reciprocal effect upon human life and being when these are understood in their totality. The imaginative remembrance of death is thought to both inform thought and action and to liberate it from subservience to unreflexive empiricism and the operationalism of the realm of the present-at-hand. It is thought to signify an important break with the alienation of everyday life, as this is held to originate in the *Verdinglichung* characteristic of everyday discourse and routine. Human awareness of the ever present possibility of one's ownmost negation represents to Heidegger a break with the world of things as objects present-at-hand, and a breakthrough to an understanding of Being itself. Ultimately, it is the awareness of death that is thought to teach[3] human beings to live reverently and receptively in the field of their Being. Existential "being toward death," as a conscious intermingling of both Being and nothingness, acts as a sobering awareness (again: *memento mori*) of human limitation that sharpens an appreciation for life at the same time as it engenders the modesty, reverence, and fear that can philosophically rebuke the pragmatic and technical hubris that both Heidegger and Marcuse believe characterizes the mentality of *Verdinglichung*.

I have already indicated that in Marcuse's estimation, the imagination probes the ontological dimension of human existence. He contends that the imagination resists the worldly givens of philistinism, public opinion, science, and common sense, "breaking the spell of the Establishment" (AO, 55), and enters the inward and transcendent realm of beauty and the aesthetic form. So too, an important leitmotiv in *Eros and Civilization, A Philosophical Inquiry into Freud* (EC) is its complex and lengthy consideration of both the repressive and emancipatory philosophical significance of death. Near the end of *Eros and Civilization*, Marcuse sums up: "Death can become a token of freedom" (EC, 236). Marcuse finds that death can be a symbol for gratification, peace, consummation and pleasure—as in the notion of Nirvana: "Nirvana is the image of the pleasure principle" (EC, 119).

Here, Marcuse is speaking with explicit reference to Schopenhauer, although he also acknowledges elsewhere ("Heidegger's Politics: An Interview" [HP]) "the tremendous importance the notion of death has" (HP, 32) in Heidegger's existential-phenomenological theory. In *Eros and Civilization*, it is the philosophy of Nietzsche, however, that is considered finally to release the concept of death from the repressive form he believes it had found in the history of Western philosophy through Hegel. Nietzsche is thought to argue from a philosophical position antagonistic to the reality principle of Western civilization, in which Nietzsche's theory of being-toward-death becomes an *erotic* attitude, where fulfillment is thought to coincide with necessity (EC, 122). After quoting two substantial dithyrambic expressions from Nietzsche's *Zarathustra*, Marcuse makes the following statement:

> Eternity, long since the ultimate consolation of an alienated existence, had been made into an instrument of repression by its relegation to a transcendental world—unreal reward for real suffering. Here [in Nietzsche], eternity is reclaimed for the fair earth. . . . Death *is*. . . . The eternal return thus includes the return of suffering, but suffering as a means for more gratification, for the aggrandizement of joy. (EC, 123, emphasis in original)

For Marcuse, as for Nietzsche and Heidegger, death is not an aspect of human existence that comes "after" life, but a necessary part of life, which decisively colors life itself, when this is understood in its entirety. In like manner, human alienation is thought to persist until this separation of death from life has been superseded: "Man comes to himself only when the transcendence has been conquered—when eternity has become present in the here and now" (EC, 122).

In *Eros and Civilization* Marcuse clearly conceives of the remembrance of death as having emancipatory social, psychological, and educational potential. He is cautious enough, however, to note the repressive connotations that are generally associated with the traditional philosophical and theological understandings of the subject:

> In a repressive civilization, death itself becomes an instrument of repression. Whether death is feared as a constant threat, or glorified

as supreme sacrifice, or accepted as fate, *the education for consent to death* introduces an element of surrender into life from the beginning—surrender and submission. (EC, 236, emphasis added)

Ultimately, Marcuse even distances himself from the Heideggerian analysis of death, which he would criticize as celebrating and perpetuating these repressive associations (cf. ibid. and "Heidegger's Politics: An Interview" [HP, 33]: "I see in this philosophy, ex-post, a very powerful devaluation of life, a derogation of joy, of sensuousness, fulfillment"). As Theodor W. Adorno's book on Heidegger would derisively note: "Death is treated as a central theme in the SS-rules and regulations—and in the existential philosophies."[4]

Nonetheless, Marcuse's aesthetic theory develops what he contends to be an emancipatory dialectical relationship between the life instincts and death instincts and reminiscence through art. His final book *The Aesthetic Dimension, Toward a Critique of Marxist Aesthetics* (AD), for example, speaks of the ". . . permanence which is preserved in art—preserved not as property, not as a bit of unchangeable nature, but as remembrance of life past: remembrance of a life between illusion and reality, falsehood and truth, joy and death" (AD, 23).

In Marcuse's most mature view, *death is thought to permeate the universe of art* (AD, 68), not only as an accidental misfortune or hazard or threat, but also as *a source of philosophical negation* of the reified outlooks and attitudes that are thought to characterize the organization of a repressive and alienating reality. In his estimation, art may be emancipatory if it treats death cognitively, affectively, and socially:

> . . . death remains the negation inherent in society, in history. It is the final remembrance of things past—last remembrance of all possibilities forsaken . . . Eros and Thanatos are lovers as well as adversaries. Destructive energy may be brought into the service of life to an ever higher degree—Eros itself lives under the sign of finitude, pain. The "eternity of joy" [Nietzsche] constitutes itself through the death of individuals. (AD, 69)

The cognitive dimension that is furnished by art does not relate, in Marcuse's view, on a one-to-one basis to objects or things. Quite to the contrary, in "A Note on Dialectic" (ND) he contends that the cognitive power of art lies in its ability to imaginatively "deny the things" (ND, xi). Marcuse's early essay on *Verdinglichung* "The Foundation of Historical Materialism"

(HM) had likewise claimed that objects first confront humanity in an "external and alien form" (HM, 18), and thus are never fully understood except with explicit and imaginative reference to a definition of "the essence of man" (HM, 29) and an outline of the human factors that are thought to condition every act of objectification. Art as a mere reflection of the real was rejected by Marcuse in *Soviet Marxism, A Critical Analysis* (SM), "The Affirmative Character of Culture" (AC), *The Aesthetic Dimension* (AD), and elsewhere because it was thought to have become an affirmative prop of just those existent societal conditions that have kept humanity alienated from the more erotic goals Marcuse stresses: earthly happiness, instinctual fulfillment, and social freedom. I am endeavoring to show that he considered *Verdinglichung* the basis for the "horror of Soviet realism" (AD, 61) as well as the cultural single-dimensionality of the entertainment industry in the United States. In *One-Dimensional Man, Studies in the Ideology of Advanced Industrial Society* (OD) affirmative culture was thought *to train humanity to forget* (OD, 104) its own nature and essence by orienting its philosophy of art toward a functional or operational view of social relations and things. The sheer observation of brute fact or historical practice is held to forget the conviction that there is *more* to knowing than coarsely meets the eye: hence also Marcuse's neo-Kantian rejection of Engels's defense of the objective character of knowledge in his article, "On the Problem of the Dialectic" (PD).

Marcuse believes that *art provides cognition* not by replicating objects, but *by "recalling"* the species-essence of the human race from philosophical oblivion. He contends that the reality of death and human suffering assert themselves as pivotal phenomena in this educative process of recollection, even where the artist and work of art "draw away" from them.

> Auschwitz and My Lai, the torture, starvation and dying—is this entire world supposed to be "mere illusion" and "bitterer deception"? It remains rather the "bitterer" and all but unimaginable reality. Art draws away from this reality, because it cannot represent this suffering without subjecting it to the aesthetic form, and thereby to the mitigating catharsis, to enjoyment. Art is inexorably infested with this guilt. Yet this does not release art from the necessity of recalling again and again that which can survive even Auschwitz and perhaps one day make it impossible. (AD, 55)

It is Marcuse's belief that the educative effects of art may aid in overcoming even the most extreme forms of alienation and oppression.

Marcuse's 1955 *Eros and Civilization* represented a full-scale philosophical effort to understand the species-essence of the human race in terms of *civilization's* "dialectic" (EC, 78–79) *of death instincts and life instincts*. This book is preeminently a philosophical work because Marcuse treats these instincts quite beyond the parameters of the theory and conduct of psychoanalysis per se. They are regarded primarily for their epistemological, aesthetic, and sociopolitical importance. The book uniquely introduces a striking discussion of the interrelationships of "phantasy" and the "imagination" to a "phylogenetic" memory of humanity's "archaic heritage," death as nirvana, and the "return of the repressed." Significantly, *aesthetic education* is also considered a stimulus to the recollection of the species-essence of humanity, and simultaneously as a beacon that signals the *telos* of the social, erotic, and political potential of the human race. *Eros and Civilization* is a text that presents Marcuse *philosophizing about education*, and this specifically with *reference to conditions of alienation*. We shall here briefly reconstruct certain of Marcuse's arguments in this regard, stressing especially the concepts of reification and reminiscence.

While *Eros and Civilization* is a work profoundly concerned with an analysis of historical human oppression and manipulation, this analysis is not undertaken upon a foundation of the classical Marxist socioeconomic categories. Rather, it substitutes the concepts and content of the "hidden trend" (EC, 11) in psychoanalytical theory (much of which, as Marcuse acknowledges, has been strongly rejected by psychoanalysts, themselves [EC, 59]). Thus, instead of a discussion of reification and the cultural contradictions emergent from monopoly capitalism or imperialism, as such, Marcuse philosophically rehabilitates what he claims to be the neglected *interplay of life and death instincts found in the metatheoretical perspective of the late-period Freud*. Marcuse considers this theory of the instincts to correspond to a *"new concept of the person"* (EC, 29) emergent from Freud's final version of the psychoanalytic outline of human nature. These instincts: ". . . are defined no longer in terms of their origin and their organic function, but in terms of a determining force which gives the life processes a definite 'direction' (*Richtung*) in terms of 'life-principles.' The notions *instinct, principle, regulation* are being assimilated" (EC, 27).

Marcuse views Freud's late-period theory of the *life* and *death* instincts as a theory of human nature torn asunder by two *principles*. These serve to *regulate* and *steer* human behavior in directions that may seek to attain limitless pleasure or gratification (no matter what the cost, even self-destruction—Thanatos), or endeavor to safeguard human existence (at the price of an accrued repression of pleasure and an acquired alienation, currently represented by performance-oriented thinking and conduct—Eros). Most of Marcuse's basic ideas and terminology in this regard are well-known and require little textual explication here, except as they relate to our analysis of phantasy and imagination, death, and alienation as reification.

According to Marcuse's account, Freud felt that the death instinct was the original and primary principle governing human life—as the primordial pleasure-urge to reduce and remove internal and external tensions and stimuli in an effort to "return to the quiescence of the inorganic world" (Freud, at EC, 25). Marcuse characterizes this as the *Nirvana principle* and as the basic and "terrifying convergence of pleasure and death" (EC, 25). This is considered a regressive tendency toward equilibrium and integration, but it is superseded, Marcuse adds, by a separation of the erotic principles of life activity from the death instinct's tendency toward inertia.

> Out of the common nature of instinctual life develop two antagonistic instincts. The life instincts (Eros) gain ascendancy over the death instincts. They continuously counteract and delay the "descent towards death". . . . (EC, 25–26)

Marcuse cautions that the ultimate interrelationship of the life and death instincts remains intricate and obscure. Still, Eros is thought to gain a distinctive significance as a life-sustaining (if also alienating) force, contending against the life-destructive, sheer pleasure-urge of Thanatos.

> Freud's metapsychology is an ever-renewed attempt to uncover and to question the terrible necessity of the inner connection between civilization and barbarism, progress and suffering, freedom and unhappiness—a connection which reveals itself ultimately as that between Eros and Thanatos. (EC, 17)

Marcuse felt that this fundamental and "eternal" (EC, 79) conflict in basic principles governing the practice of historical human individuals was of the utmost importance in the analysis and elimination of cultural alienation. As he explains: the erotic impulse, while basically a principle oriented toward "pleasure," has evolved into a principle of "performance," compatible with sexual repression and surplus repression, in order to sustain a civilized form of social reality. The performance principle has, therefore, replaced the unmitigated pleasure principle (or Nirvana-impulse), and has become the life-sustaining principle in dealing with reality (i.e., the performance principle has become the reality principle). Marcuse, therefore, directs his attention toward overcoming the excessively repressing and alienating effects of the restricted and reified eroticism of this performance principle. He believes an aesthetic and philosophical consideration of Thanatos may yet release a disalienating and emancipatory mode of human sensuousness, action, and thought.

The entire content of *Eros and Civilization* is permeated with an underlying effort to understand philosophically the psychoanalytic concern for death. Thus, the second chapter maintains:

> Never before has death been so consistently taken into the essence of life; but never before has death come so close to Eros. . . . Moreover, if the "regression compulsion" in all organic life is striving for integral quiescence, if the Nirvana principle is the ground of the pleasure principle, then the necessity of death appears in an entirely new light. The death instinct is destructiveness not for its own sake but for the relief of tension. The descent toward death is an unconscious flight from pain and want. It is an expression of the external struggle against suffering and repression. (EC, 28–29)

Likewise, in chapter 4:

> . . . in terms of the eternal struggle between Eros and the death instinct: the aggressive impulse against the father (and his social successors) is derivative of the death instinct; in "separating" the child from the mother, the father also inhibits the death instinct, the Nirvana impulse. He thus does the work of Eros; love, too, operates in the formation of the superego. The severe father, who as the forbidding representative of Eros subdues the death instinct in the Oedipus conflict, enforces the first "communal" (social) relations. . . . (EC, 79)

Marcuse believes that a psychoanalytic and philosophical consideration of death holds a key potential for the negation of the repressive and alienating principles governing the established aims of the social order. Liberation, as an activity following the instinct toward death, is thought to have found long-standing and archetypal aesthetic expression in the *literary* realm:

in a world of alienation, the liberation of Eros would necessarily operate as a destructive, fatal force—as the total negation of the principle which governs the repressive reality. It is not an accident that the great literature of Western civilization celebrates only the "unhappy love," that the Tristan myth has become its representative expression. The morbid romanticism of the myth is in a strict sense "realistic." (EC, 95)

Marcuse's views on art, alienation, and death are central to the critical theory emerging in *Eros and Civilization*. In the fifth chapter of EC, Marcuse undertakes a philosophical essay relating Freudian theory to the basic tendencies of the *traditional metaphysics*, from Plato and Aristotle to Hegel. His analysis leads him to remark:

> It is the *failure* of Eros, lack of fulfillment in life, which enhances the instinctual value of death. The manifold forms of regression are unconscious protest against the insufficiency of civilization: against the prevalence of toil over pleasure, performance over gratification. An innermost tendency in the organism militates against the principle which has governed civilization and insists on return from alienation. (EC, 109)

Marcuse believes that Thanatos, thus, protests not only against the established reality principle, but in seeking fulfillment, actually aims "at another mode of being" (ibid.), and that "at this point, Freud's metapsychology meets a mainstream of Western philosophy" (ibid.). Freudian theory converges with the effort to reconcile the contradiction between alienation and gratification that Marcuse maintains characterized and animated "the inner history of Western metaphysics" (EC, 112). Aristotle, for example, in Marcuse's estimation, ascribed fulfillment to that ". . . mode of being reserved to the god; and the movement of thought, pure thinking, is its sole 'empirical' approximation. Otherwise the empirical world does not partake of such fulfillment. . . ." (ibid.). For Marcuse, the Nirvana instinct, not the repressive Eros of the reality principle, represents the urge to fulfillment and gratification rather than any accommodation to the alienating social reality. ". . . [P]rogress remains committed to a regressive trend in the instinctual structure (in the last analysis to the death instinct), that the growth of civilization is counteracted by a persistent (though repressed) impulse to come to rest in final gratification" (EC, 108). The "emancipatory" Nirvana instinct is thus taken to lie at the foundation of both social progress and metaphysics as Marcuse sees them, from Aristotle to Hegel:

> . . . the true mode of freedom is, not the incessant activity of conquest, but its coming to rest in the transparent knowledge and gratification of being. The ontological climate which prevails at the end of the *Phenomenology* is the opposite of the Promethean dynamic. (EC, 115)

> The philosophy of Western civilization culminates in the idea that the truth lies in the negation of the principle that governs this civilization—negation in the twofold sense that freedom appears as real only in the idea, and that the endlessly projecting and transcending productivity of being comes to fruition in the perpetual peace of self-conscious receptivity. (EC, 116)

Marcuse concedes that *traditional metaphysics* does not actually overcome what he considered to be the alienating negativity of the empirical world. Nonetheless, he finds that it *has preserved the spirit, or principle, of negation* that he considers to be essential to the eventual attainment of gratification and fulfillment.

Marx is nowhere mentioned in the "critical" philosophical discussion central to *Eros and Civilization*. There is also no evidence to suggest that Marcuse's "philosophical inquiry into Freud," as the book is subtitled, occurs on the basis of a Marxist philosophical analysis. Quite to the contrary, it appears that Marcuse turns primarily to Nietzsche's critique of the traditional metaphysics in this regard. Nietzsche rather than Marx is credited with the insight that metaphysics and religion have functioned to compensate the subjugated masses emotionally and to protect and maintain those who rule (EC, 121). Furthermore, "only Nietzsche's philosophy" (EC, 119) is thought actually to surmount this metaphysical tradition.

To no other philosophical author does Marcuse make such sustained theoretical reference as he does to Nietzsche. Marcuse backs away from him in only one instance, in "Political Preface 1966" (PP, xiv), and this is possibly a response to criticism of his rather categorical earlier support for Nietzsche. Marcuse points to Nietzsche as the single Western philosopher to have fully left the terrain of the repressive rationalism of the Western metaphysical tradition, although he simultaneously acknowledges that Nietzsche's thought is largely unsubstantiated or unsubstantiatable.

Nietzsche is thought to have bridged the metaphysical gap separating soul from body, and it is his concept of death and the "eternal return" which, Marcuse claims, especially distinguishes him from the Western intellectual tradition. According to Marcuse, Nietzsche's view of death represents an *erotic* will, a vision and attitude toward being in which necessity and fulfillment coincide (EC, 122). In Nietzsche's philosophy the wretchedness and finitude of self and humanity can be accepted *exactly as they are* and one's unwilled fate can be embraced, when these are courageously recognized as simultaneously the *precondition* of every real and earthly form of fulfillment and gratification.

Marcuse finds emancipatory potential in the Nietzschean philosophy of the eternal return because it essentially connects gratifying and consummatory human sensuous experience as the goal and aim of their earthly opposites, pain and want. The eternal return is a central idea of Nietzsche's *Zarathustra*, achieving its most significant formulation in his chapter on "The Convalescent." The eternal return of suffering, pain, and the wretchedness and paltriness of life—its pettiness and senselessness—is Zarathustra's "most abysmal thought." With this thought he is invaded with nausea and contempt and alienation. Zarathustra counters his revulsion by trying to establish a new earthly significance for death, and also by eliminating the repressive Nirvana-urge of the traditional metaphysical impulse.

Because of his unremitting earthly protest against everything otherworldly, Zarathustra claims he can love his life of suffering and joy throughout eternity. Writing of the eternal return, Nietzsche has Zarathustra remark: "Courage . . . slays even death itself, for it says, 'Was *that* life? Well then! Once more!'" (*Thus Spake Zarathustra*, "On the Vision and the Riddle"). Actually, the notion of the eternal return is first broached by Nietzsche at entry number 341 of *The Joyful Wisdom*:

> *The Greatest Stress.* How, if some day or night a demon were to sneak after you into your loneliest loneliness and say to you, "This life as you now live it and have lived it, you will have to live once more and innumerable times more; and there will be nothing new in it, but every pain and every joy and every thought and sigh and everything immeasurably small or great in your life must return to you—all in the same succession and sequence:. . . . Would you not throw yourself down and gnash your teeth and curse the demon who spoke thus? Or did you ever experience a tremendous

moment when you would have answered him, "You are a god, and never have I heard anything more godly."

Memento mori is thus transformed into *carpe diem*: the "earthly gratification" and "fulfillment" Marcuse emphasizes. Nietzsche's concept of the eternal return might also be said to reintroduce a categorical imperative, refashioned in terms of the aesthetic, making sensuous human existence the measure of *all things*. The passage just cited continues as follows:

> If this thought were ever to gain possession of you, it would change you as you are, or perhaps crush you. The question in each and every thing, "Do you want this once and innumerable times more?" would weigh upon your actions as the greatest stress.

Like Nietzsche, Marcuse's *Eros and Civilization* propounds a militant aesthetic humanism to advance against alienation. Marcuse contends that life is to be *regulated* according to a qualitatively different reality principle than that of contemporary civilization: a principle of fulfillment, pleasure, joy (EC, 121). This life-governing principle, aiming at ecstasy and gratification, is considered fundamentally antagonistic to the performance principle as a regulator of social life. The *performance principle (Leistungsprinzip)* is compatible with excess repression, needless alienation, and the spiritualization of happiness in the achievement of its ends of mastery and domination. The Nietzschean/Freudian/Marcusean *Lustprinzip* (pleasure principle) is not. It is thought to represent an *alternative* reality principle to the logic of domination, that is, a logic of gratification, and this alternative form of reality principle is thought to possess suppressed potential to counteract emotional repression, cultural alienation, and the spiritualization of philosophy. According to Marcuse: "The Logos of gratification contradicts the Logos of alienation. . . ." (EC, 112), and it may thus challenge the contemporary supremacy of the performance principle as reality principle. Marcuse's critique of repressive desublimation and the happy consciousness in *One-Dimensional Man* will subsequently temper his Nietzschean enthusiasm for sheer gratification. For now, we need to heed his fascination.

Nietzsche's first book, *The Birth of Tragedy Out of the Spirit of Music*, made famous the philosophical contraposition of the logic of domination and the logic of gratification via the principles of life thought to be represented by the Greek gods of Apollo and Dionysus. In the first sentence of that book Nietzsche declares that "art owes its continuous evolution to the

Apollonian-Dionysiac duality." Apollo, as a deity of light, is held to represent the cultural principles of reason, order, wisdom, and beautiful images. Dionysus, as god of the vine, represents the conflicting cultural principles of rapture, song, joy, frenzy, destruction, and fulfillment. Apollonian cultural activity revolves around a delight in the construction of timeless aesthetic monads, that is, discrete images of beauty and portrayals of discrete human individuals, and an immortalization of these. Apollonian principles are thought to predominate in the cultural world of the West, but to both Nietzsche and Marcuse Dionysus represents the more primitive and liberating principle. According to *The Birth of Tragedy*, section number 27—

> Dionysiac art, too, wishes to convince us of the eternal delight of existence, but insists we look for this delight not in the phenomena but behind them. It makes us realize that everything that is generated must be prepared to face its painful dissolution. It forces us to gaze into the horror of individual existence, yet without being turned to stone by the vision: a metaphysical solace momentarily lifts us above the whirl of shifting phenomena. For a brief moment we become, ourselves, the primal Being, and we experience its insatiable hunger for existence. Now we see the struggle, the pain, the destruction of appearances, as necessary, because of the constant proliferation of forms pushing into life, because of the extravagant fecundity of the world will. We feel the furious prodding of this travail in the very moment in which we become one with the immense lust for life and are made aware of the eternity and indestructibility of that lust.

Marcuse cites similar philosophical sentiments on the Dionysian quality of the doctrine of the eternal return in *Zarathustra* (EC, 122–23). Likewise, he finds the life-principles of the mythological personalities Orpheus and Narcissus similar to the Dionysian protest against the principles of life-regulation represented by Apollo and Prometheus.

> If Prometheus is the culture-hero of toil, productivity and progress through repression, then the symbols of another reality principle must be sought at the opposite pole. Orpheus and Narcissus (like Dionysus to whom they are akin: the antagonist of the god who sanctions the logic of domination, the realm of reason) stand for a very different reality. They have not become the culture-heroes of

the Western world: theirs is the image of joy and fulfillment; the voice which does not command but sings. . . . (EC, 161–62)

The Apollonian or Promethean principle of life-regulation might be said to approximate for Marcuse what other critical theorists have termed the *enlightenment mentality* and what he has called the "triumph of positive thinking" (OD, 170) that he believes characterizes the operationalist-oriented ideologies of advanced industrial societies. Such modes of thought, in his estimation are derived in a basic way from phenomena of alienation and reification. This is particularly so inasmuch as he understands them as a *Verdinglichung* of consciousness and conduct. Such ideologies view reality via a reduction of reality to reality's fragments, that is, in terms of "discrete entities," *rei*, which are thought to make possible human control and mastery of the world, in accordance with a violent and repressive, if also pragmatic, principle of achievement and performance. According to Marcuse's analysis, then, what is generally regarded as sociohistorical progress in science, productive capacity, and culture has only been possible by virtue of a reified principle of reality that has eschewed gratification for the systematic distortion of social existence toward the manageable fragments required for domination and power. Like Martin Heidegger, Marcuse is questioning humanity's understanding of the being of "things." He would like to see this understanding liberated from reification. A disalienating perspective is thought to be furnished via the unique constellation of his theory revolving around such concepts as Eros, Nirvana, Thanatos, *telos*, and the Orphic or Narcissistic logic of beauty and gratification:

The Orphic and Narcissistic experience of the world negates that which sustains the world of the performance principle. The opposition between man and nature, subject and object, is overcome. Being is experienced as gratification, which unites man and nature so that the fulfillment of man is at the same time the fulfillment, without violence, of nature . . . *the things of nature become free to be what they are.* But to be what they are then depends on the *erotic* attitude: they receive their *telos* only in it. The song of Orpheus pacifies the animal world, reconciles the lion with the lamb and the lion with man. The world of nature is a world of oppression, cruelty and pain, as is the human world; like the latter it awaits liberation. This liberation is the work of Eros. The song of Orpheus breaks the petrification, moves the forests and the rocks—but moves them to partake in joy. (EC, 166; first emphasis added)

Marcuse's symbols of Orpheus and Narcissus are thus thought to represent a distinctive and nonreified approach to reality, which is culturally superior to the contemporary performance principle in the genuine organization of concepts and action. Marcuse seeks to go beyond the established performance principle (EC, 127) and beyond reification.

> . . . Orpheus and Narcissus reveal a new reality, with an order of its own governed by different principles. The Orphic Eros transforms being: he masters cruelty and death through liberation. His language is *song*, his work is *play*. Narcissus' life is that of *beauty*, and his existence is *contemplation*. These images refer to the aesthetic dimension as the one in which their reality principle must be sought and validated. (EC, 171, emphasis in original)

> In associating Narcissus with Orpheus and interpreting both as symbols of a nonrepressive erotic attitude toward reality, we took the image of Narcissus from the mythological-artistic tradition rather than from Freud's libido theory. (EC, 167)

These citations clearly show how Marcuse's psychoanalytic interests and presuppositions merge with his broader analysis of the history of the theory of the human mind and learning in the West. Orphism represented one of the oldest religious tendencies in ancient Greece. It stressed the importance of underworld deities and death, and a doctrine of the immortality of the soul. The belief in reincarnation was tied to an eschatological scheme involving final judgment and penalty or reward in the life after death. As a way of life on earth, Orphism emphasized asceticism and nonviolence, with proscriptions against shedding blood or eating meat. The Platonic doctrine of reminiscence is also regarded as stemming from the teachings of Orpheus.

Because Marcuse is decidedly not dealing with the therapeutic value of psychoanalysis or its methods, but rather with the "hidden tendencies" of its metatheory insofar as these comment on the human essence and nature, my consideration of his educational philosophical observations is entirely consistent with the explicit theoretical aims of *Eros and Civilization*. Marcuse continually links the Freudian philosophy of human nature to that of the prescientific (EC, 7) perennialist and essentialist traditions. "Freud developed a theory of man, a 'psycho-logy' in the strict sense. With this theory, Freud placed himself in the great tradition of philosophy and under philosophical criteria" (ibid.). Perhaps the most significant area of overlap between Freudian theory and the philosophy of mind, reason, and learning as this has developed in Western civilization, according to Marcuse, is the concept of memory. "If memory moves into the center of psychoanalysis as a decisive mode of *cognition*, this is far more than a therapeutic device; the therapeutic role of memory derives from the *truth value* of memory. . . . The rediscovered past yields critical standards which are tabooed by the present" (EC, 18–19). In this manner Marcuse prepares to relate the psychoanalytic concept of memory to the classical philosophical (epistemological and educational) treatment of reminiscence and remembrance or *Erinnerung*. This occurs in close connection with notions of alienation as *Verdinglichung* and as "a forgetting" of our species-identity or our human essence. Ultimately, art and beauty are held to be key phenomena capable of recalling the species essence of the human race from the oblivion of a philosophical amnesia or anesthesia.

> The ability to forget—itself the result of a long and terrible education by experience—is an indispensable requirement of mental and physical hygiene without which civilized life would be unbearable; but it is also the mental faculty which sustains submissiveness and renunciation. To forget is also to forgive what should not be forgiven if justice and freedom are to prevail. Such forgiveness reproduces the conditions which reproduce injustice and enslavement: to forget past suffering is to forgive the forces that caused it— without defeating these forces. . . . The restoration of remembrance to its rights, as a vehicle of liberation, is one of the noblest tasks of thought. In this function, remembrance (Erinnerung) appears at the conclusions of Hegel's *Phenomenology of the Spirit*; in this function it appears in Freud's theories. (EC, 232)

In *One-Dimensional Man* Marcuse argues that the prevailing principle of reality—the pragmatic and operationalist performance principle—both *impedes education* and *conceals alienation*. In fact, the performance principle is considered to train humanity to forget (cf. OD, 104). In *Eros and Civilization* he makes a similar judgment:

. . . the individual's awareness of the prevailing repression is blunted by the manipulated restriction of his consciousness. This process alters the contents of happiness. . . . Happiness involves knowledge: it is the prerogative of the *animal rationale*. With the decline in consciousness, with the control of information, knowledge is administered and confined. The individual does not really know what is going on; the *overpowering machine of education and entertainment unites him with all others in a state of anesthesia.* . . . (EC, 103–4, emphasis added)

In both works, Marcuse characterizes the dominant forms of education as having submitted to the operational technological rationality of the advanced industrial societies by which they are sustained. Under such circumstances, education and research are thought to take place in a reified universe, closed by a *Verdinglichung* of discourse and action, that is, by language and conduct in the interests of the total administration. Meaning and communication, thus, become single-dimensional, lacking the contradiction between "is" and "ought." Marcuse argues, that this disjuncture in thought has been forcibly eliminated by an alienating education in accordance with a repressive reality principle, and that theory has thus become "fixed, doctored, loaded." Even "higher culture" has become integrated into the operationalist philosophical universe, dovetailing with schooling oriented toward management and production. Humanity is, in his estimation, largely lost in mental and political paralysis, though at the same time anesthetized and tranquilized. In *One-Dimensional Man*, Marcuse argues against this atrophy of mind and sensibility as it occurs in even the liberal arts approach in our era of the contemporary fragmented multiversity, and advocates the reassertion of a reunifying sovereignty of aesthetic judgment over operationalist and technical administrative concerns. This approach shares much with the traditional educational-political recommendations of Plato's *Republic*, and of Schiller's book, *On the Aesthetic Education of Man in a Series of Letters*. Marcuse's commentary on the Freudian value of memory in *Eros and Civilization* must likewise be seen in connection with the epistemological tradition established by Plato's *Meno*, *Phaedo*, and *Phaedrus*, and culminating in Hegel's *Phenomenology*. His interpretation of the role of memory in psychoanalysis hinges upon Freud's notions of the "return of the repressed" and the "phylogenetic" memory of humanity's "archaic heritage." Rebellion and revolution, in *Eros and Civilization*, are considered in terms of Freud's *Moses and Monotheism* and, thus, as having a basic relation to the "overthrow of the king-father" (EC, 68) as this occurs in the hypothetical "history of the primal horde" (EC, 63). Here, the struggle and triumph of the sons against the patriarch-tyrant, are thought to overcome the reproductive order that secured and sustained the primal system of culture for all (i.e., even the sons, albeit in a necessarily repressive manner). Rebellion is, hence, a cardinal crime and a central root of guilt because the sons are thought merely to want the same thing as the father in a slightly altered form (EC, 64). Accordingly, to Marcuse it is the repressed content of the basic drive toward pleasure that returns as rebellion against the despot-father.

> Freud assumes that the primal crime, and the sense of guilt attached to it, are reproduced, in modified forms, throughout history. The crime is reenacted in the conflict of the old and new generation in revolt and rebellion against authority—and in subsequent repentance: in the restoration and glorification of authority. In explaining this strange and perpetual recurrence, Freud suggested the hypothesis of the *return of the repressed*. . . . (EC, 69)

Marcuse highlights the "strange perpetual recurrence" (ibid.) of this return of the repressed, implicitly suggesting, much like the Nietzschean doctrine of the eternal return, that this hypothesis might also be regarded as a "most abysmal thought" unless it is assimilated to a universal human activity for real, earthy gratification. Marcuse in the end finds that the return of the repressed has potential in this regard: it helps establish a rationality of gratification that can negate the rationality of domination (currently: the performance principle) and the institutions crystallized about it (EC, 15).

The repressed content of the pleasure principle is thought to persist as a subconscious memory of past states of fulfillment and joy. The repressed material

> . . . although repelled by consciousness, continues to haunt the mind; it preserves the memory of past stages of individual development at which integral gratification obtained. And the past continues to claim the future: it generates the wish that the paradise be re-created on the basis of the achievements of civilization. (EC, 18)

Likewise, the repressed content of the pleasure-urge is considered to be universal, related more to the historical human essence than to any particular individual experience. "[T]he childhood experiences which become traumatic under the impact of reality are pre-individual, generic: with individual variations, the protracted dependence of the human infant, the Oedipus situation, and pre-genital sexuality all belong to the *genus* man" (EC, 55). Memory of the repressed content of the instincts toward pleasure is "phylogenetic" (EC, 56), because "the individual re-experiences and re-enacts the great traumatic events in the development of the genus" (EC, 20). Phylogeny refers to the evolutionary history of a species, and Marcuse devotes an entire chapter in *Eros and Civilization* to the "phylogenesis" (EC, 56) of the historical human culture and personality, stressing the fundamental value of this memory of the species past in dissolving "ossified sociological concepts into their historical content" (EC, 57). In Marcuse's estimation, the depth psychology of Freud provides this "historical" content in terms of a phylogenetic dissolution of the "reified," "ossified," and alienating aspects of performance-oriented culture.

> Psychoanalysis elucidates the universal in the individual experience. To that extent, and only to that extent, can psychoanalysis break the reification in which human relations are petrified. (EC, 254)

> Freud's . . . psychology does not focus on the concrete and complete personality as it exists in its private and public environment, because this existence conceals rather than reveals the essence and nature of the personality. It is the end result of long historical processes which are congealed in the network of human and institutional entities making up society, and these processes define the personality and its relationships. Consequently, to understand them for what they really are, psychology must *unfreeze* them by tracing their hidden origins. In doing so, psychology discovers that the determining childhood experiences are linked with the experience of the species—that the individual lives the universal fate of mankind. . . . To Freud, the universal fate is in the instinctual drives . . . subject to historical "modifications." (EC, 57–58)

The *phylogenetic* value of memory is thus held to emerge from its ability to unfreeze the realm of personal and social relations thought to be crystallized around reified principles of life-direction that have forgotten their universal human core. A phylogenetic memory is capable of breaking through the "petrified" (EC, 24) or "dead" (RR, 112) objectivity of any system of social or personal relations, disclosing that the relative independence of these relations from the core human subject is "mere semblance" (RR, 281).

Eros and Civilization's consideration of reification is an elaboration of that contained in *Reason and Revolution* and also of that in "The Foundation of Historical Materialism" (HM). Marcuse found reification to be a specific, estranged, and untrue mode of objectification (HM, 11) that had lost its internal connection with humanity's hypothesized "sensuous" and "historical" species-essence. In this early essay, reason was related to revolution in ways subsequently elaborated in *Reason and Revolution* (RR) and in *Eros and Civilization*: ". . . unerring contemplation of the essence of man . . . becomes the inexorable impulse for the initiation of radical revolution" (HM, 29). Reification was thought to denote an alienated mental attitude and principle of life-regulation (an untrue form of objectification) that concealed the human essence from humanity itself. Marcuse's phenomenological proposal in this essay to negate this reification hinged upon the restoration of a correct and true, that is, rehumanized, form of objectification (or life-regulation) that consciously understood historical human activity in terms of its primordial sensuous qualities. These were postulated as more fundamental (and as deeper) than conceived by "any materialism" hitherto (HM, 19), including the classical concerns of a Marxist political-economy in the determination of cultural patterns of thought and conduct.

As we have seen, Marcuse's *Eros and Civilization* develops the psychoanalytic elucidation of this affective essence and core in terms of life and death instincts and the regulative principles of performance and pleasure. Both the return of the repressed and the phylogenetic memory are thought to retrieve the substantive, depth dimensional emotions and insights that stand beneath the realms of alienation and reification. The subject matter of *genuinely* historical study thus is *not* considered to be political-economy as such, but rather the highly conflicted sensuous and affective essence of humanity itself. Nonreified study of the history of human society and the history of the repression of human personality (i.e., alienation) must thus essentially consider the "deposits from primitive human development present in our archaic heritage" (Freud, cited at EC, 59). This "archaic heritage" is considered to be the psychic material contained in conscious and subconscious "memory traces," (EC, 56) and likewise to constitute the "historical content" (EC, 57) of the development of human civilization and culture:

The moral principles "which the child imbibes from the persons responsible for its upbringing during the first years of its life" reflect "certain phylogenetic echoes of primitive man." Civilization is still determined by its *archaic heritage*, and this heritage, so Freud asserts includes "not only dispositions, but also ideational contents, memory traces of the experiences of former generations." Individual psychology is thus *in itself* group psychology insofar as the individual itself is still in archaic identity with the species. (EC, 56)

This disclosure undermines one of the strongest ideological fortifications of modern culture—namely, the notion of the autonomous individual. (EC, 57)

The archaic heritage is viewed as the sensuous and historical substance (cf. HM, 21, 40) or fund of essential images and affective impulses that echo past stages of human happiness and frustration. Marcuse believes that no individual human autonomy is possible apart from this archaic heritage (EC, 143). When this "past" is rediscovered and restored to consciousness, Marcuse claims its "weight" can have the impact of liberation vis-à-vis repression and reification: "The weight of these discoveries must eventually shatter the framework in which they were made and confined . . . the orientation on the past tends toward an orientation on the future. The *recherche du temps perdu* becomes the vehicle of future liberation" (EC, 19).

While Marcuse is cautious enough to explicitly state that "no part of Freud's theory has been more strongly rejected than the idea of the survival of the archaic heritage. . . ." (EC, 59), and that its value must hence only be considered "*symbolic*" (EC, 60), he nonetheless maintains that "it telescopes, in a sequence of catastrophic events, the historical dialectic of domination and thereby elucidates aspects of civilization hitherto unexplained" (ibid.).

That these "liberating" archaic symbols also belong essentially to the domain of art and literature, that is, the humanities, is indicated by Marcuse's implicit reference to the title of the vast novel of Marcel Proust, *A la Recherche du Temps Perdu* (generally translated as *Remembrance of Things Past*, and meaning literally "a quest for lost time"), as "the vehicle of future liberation" (EC, 19). Proust is generally regarded as a follower of the protopsychoanalytic vitalism and *Lebensphilosophie* of Henri Bergson, and both of these authors emphasize intuition and memory in the development of historical knowledge.

Marcuse acknowledges explicitly that he seeks the historical substance of humanity's species identity through the uniquely aesthetic agencies of phantasy and imagination. He specifically links the aesthetic value of phantasy and imagination to the traditional conceptions of the cognitive value of memory and intuition in the retrieval of humanity's species-identity from the alienating philosophical oblivion, that is, reification, accompanying the repression inherent in the dominant reality-principle:

> Phantasy plays a most decisive function in the total mental structure: it links the deepest layers of the unconscious with the highest products of consciousness (art), the dream with the reality; it preserves the archetypes of the genus, the perpetual but repressed ideas of the collective and individual memory, the tabooed images of freedom. (EC, 140–41)

> . . . imagination sustains the claim of the whole individual, in union with the genus and with the "archaic" past. Freud's metapsychology here restores imagination to its rights. (EC, 143)

Phantasy and imagination are thus considered to be fundamental mental forces capable of negating and opposing repression and alienation by virtue of their "high degree of freedom" (EC, 140) from the reigning form of reason. This negative and emancipatory capability is conceived as potential, however, because phantasy and imagination retain their independence "at the price of becoming powerless, inconsequential, unrealistic" (EC, 141).

> Obviously, the aesthetic dimension cannot validate a reality principle. Like imagination, which is its constitutive mental faculty, the realm of aesthetics is essentially "unrealistic:" it has retained its freedom from the reality principle at the price of being ineffective in the reality. . . . Before the court of theoretical and practical reason, which have shaped the world of the performance principle, the aesthetic existence stands condemned. (EC, 172)

In spite of this, Marcuse argues that phantasy and imagination retain a "strict truth value" (EC, 149). "Uncompromising adherence to the strict truth value of imagination comprehends reality more fully. That the propositions of the artistic imagination are untrue in terms of the actual organization of the facts belongs to the essence of their truth" (ibid.).

While Marcuse acknowledges a danger in abusing the discovery of the truth value of the imagination (as he claims this reprehensibly occurs in the theories of Carl Jung), recognition of the cognitive value of imagination is considered a legitimate tradition in philosophy and psychology, to which Freud has added the crucial hypothesis of the integral connection of imagination and memory to an understanding of death and the pleasure principle (EC, 141). Marcuse traces Freud's significance to his depth-psychological elaboration of the theory of the mind and learning inherited from Plato.

> the *Symposium* contains the clearest celebration of the sexual origin and substance of the spiritual relations. . . . There is an unbroken ascent in erotic fulfillment from corporeal love of one to that of the others, to the love of beautiful work and play, . . . and ultimately to the love of beautiful knowledge. (EC, 211)

As we shall see in the analysis of *One-Dimensional Man* in the next chapter, Marcuse locates a significant source of human autonomy in the ". . . experience of a divided world. . . ." (OD, 131) philosophically captured in the two-dimensional, is/ought content of the "critical" (OD, 133) Platonic dialectic. Marcuse attributes a similar, critical function to phantasy and imagination—ultimately to art and the aesthetic rationality as well. "The truths of imagination are first realized when phantasy itself takes form, when it creates a universe of perception and comprehension— a subjective and at the same time objective universe. This occurs in *art*" (EC, 143–44).

According to Marcuse, Freud's particular contribution to the philosophical history of mind and imagination is that he grounded these faculties in a generic human sensuousness, and thus furnished them with an affective, and not merely spiritual or intellectual, content. In this manner, the classical theories of Plato and Kant were thought to have been significantly revised— stressing the sensuous and historical character of human nature—and reformulating the classical educational goals of Greek culture and German idealism as (1) the remembrance of Being in terms of gratification (and through art), as well as (2) the political activation of essentially social individuals in terms of intervention toward the maximum fulfillment of sensuousness and species need. In this regard, Marcuse clearly found it necessary to move beyond the admittedly repressive aspects of the philosophical approaches of Plato and Kant (with their "affirmative" spiritualization of reason) in the direction of a Nietzschean and Freudian and Heideggerian philosophy of protest against earthly alienation. Basically Marcuse attempted to undo what he considered to have been the repressive sublimation of reason into a highly spiritualized rationality of domination. He sought to recapture the sensuous substance of that life-principle that was thought to stand before every repressive form of reality-orientation: the pleasure-urge. This explains his attempt to rehabilitate what he considered to be the primordial interpretation of being and culture in terms of Eros and Thanatos utilizing Plato, Nietzsche, and Freud (rather than in terms of the Marxist concept of the history of matter, or in terms of the dialectical materialist foundations of the history of society and thought). In this regard, Marcuse turned to Freud's metapsychology precisely because this incorporated Platonic and Nietzschean, rather than Marxist, insights. "Freud's interpretation of being in terms of Eros recaptures the early stage of Plato's philosophy, which conceived of culture not as repressive sublimation but as the free self-development of Eros" (EC, 125–26). The Nietzschean *Lustprinzip* also represented the image of a new reality principle (EC, 124) that emphasized the will to joy and gratification that preconditioned the Freudian approach.

> . . . against the conception of being in terms of Logos rises the conception of being in a-logical terms: will and joy. This counter-trend strives to formulate its own Logos: the logic of gratification.

> In its most advanced positions, Freud's theory partakes of this philosophical dynamic. (ibid.)

Marcuse also designates Nietzsche's "gay science" as a key philosophical element in shaping society for life (PP, xi, and *An Essay on Liberation* [EL, 19, 31]). Renate Brink's treatise on the educational philosophy of Nietzsche[5] elucidates the latter's conception of the philosopher as teacher, and Nietzsche's belief in a pedagogical quality adhering to all philosophical thought and activity. Brink's conclusion especially stresses the fact that *Nietzsche conceives of the social emancipation of humanity as an essentially pedagogical process*, and that in this regard Nietzsche's theory of liberation shares an educational, transcendental (or second-dimensional) approach with that of Plato. Indeed, Plato's *Phaedrus* 237d also discusses principles of human behavior in a manner that quite anticipates the principles of pleasure and performance that form the basis of Marcuse's neo-Freudian analysis: ". . . within each of us there are two sorts of ruling or guiding principles that we follow. One is our innate desire for pleasure, the other an acquired judgment that aims at what is best." Just as important as these underlying principles, however, are the theoretical imperatives to justice, gratification, and truth that Marcuse believes are embodied in certain of Plato's "extreme concepts" (OD, 132). For example, Marcuse evokes reference to Plato's *Phaedo* 64 and *Republic* 7.514 when he writes in *One-Dimensional Man* of the extreme and subversive philosophical qualities of Plato's concepts of ". . . death as the beginning of the philosopher's life, and the violent liberation from the Cave. . . ." (OD, 132). Both are viewed as symbols of liberation from the realms of single-dimensional discourse and action. To Marcuse, intuition and reminiscence (of the material conditions of gratification and need) *teach social intervention toward justice.* The aesthetic imagination, by virtue of its sensuousness and creativity, is thought able to recall the repressed substance of historical humanity. *In this manner, an education through art is held to restore the long-denied rationality of gratification to philosophical theory itself, and to reclaim the energizing potential inherent in a consciousness of the social promise of the human species for the mobilization of political action for freedom.*

Art and imagination, in Marcuse's estimation, allow humanity to sense what it wants, desires, craves, and needs, in spite of the fact that empirical reality in advanced and affluent industrial society confronts humanity with the physical absence of what are considered to be the true targets of its will and esteem: gratification, freedom, and peace. Such are the theoretical underpinnings of his *theory of education against Verdinglichung*, which I will further explore in a subsequent chapter. It suffices here to say that *Marcuse's treatment of the aesthetic imagination, death, and reminiscence represents the development of a philosophy of human nature, its alienation, and its recovery.* My analysis has endeavored to disclose the philosophical foundations of this theory as a precondition to making informed judgments about its philosophical adequacy.

CHAPTER SEVEN

—◠◠◠—

Alienation and Art in the
One-Dimensional Society

All about them the Rich create ugliness,
but they cannot bear to look at it.

—Bertolt Brecht,
Threepenny Opera

An analysis of the problems of alienation and the power of art cuts across all of Marcuse's middle-period books. Likewise, his continuing commentary on art, alienation, and the humanities accounts for the recurrent anticipations, repetitions, and elaborations that emerge across the boundaries of the various volumes that comprise this middle-period work. *Eros and Civilization* called attention to the potential of art to energize a politics of human emancipation. *One-Dimensional Man* (OD), extends the *new theory of alienation* that he had been developing since "The Foundations of Historical Materialism."

"One-dimensionality" is a concept developed by Marcuse to update his analysis of alienation for "advanced industrial society." Marcuse believed that the theory of alienation required revision especially in light of his conviction that capitalism had become a society of plenty rather than scarcity, and because the structural role of the working class had fundamentally altered. *One-Dimensional Man* is centrally concerned with new aspects of alienation resulting from the increasingly sophisticated exercise of the social control apparatus of corporate capitalism. According to the famous first sentence of *One-Dimensional Man*: "A comfortable, smooth, reasonable, democratic unfreedom prevails in advanced industrial civilization, a token of technological progress" (OD, 1).

Marcuse argues that social control mechanisms in advanced industrial society ensure the wholesale integration of the individual into mass society, obliterating specific differences among individuals, families, groups, and institutions. Alienation consists in the *total absorption of the personality* into the process of commodity production.

> . . . the concept of alienation seems to become questionable when the individuals identify themselves with the existence which is imposed upon them and have in it their own development and satisfaction. This identification is not illusion but reality. However, *the reality constitutes a more progressive stage of alienation. . . . There is only one dimension, and it is everywhere and in all forms.* (OD, 11, emphasis added)

Marcuse makes his most brilliant theoretical contribution to the analysis of alienation here in *One-Dimensional Man* with the introduction not only of his concept of single dimensionality, but also in his notion of repressive desublimation. He explains that society's social control mechanisms become even more powerful when they integrate sexually suggestive and explicitly erotic and violent content into advertising and the mass media, and infuse this also into the content of mass entertainment and popular culture. The established society's radical overthrow of the innerworldly asceticism of highly sublimated Victorian mores offers a spurious sense of liberation and has effected a sweeping desublimation of expected behavior in many of society's central institutions: in the schools, offices, shops, and workplace. Marcuse views the unrestrained use of mindless sex and violence by the corporate mass media and by other large-scale commercial interests as accomplishing more effective social manipulation and control in the interest of capital accumulation than repressive *sublimation* could possibly continue to deliver.

How much confirmation of Marcuse's insights could be offered by any observer of popular culture today in the United States! Trash TV, Bevis and Butthead, Howard Stern, Jerry Springer, Monica Lewinsky and Bill Clinton, and pornography on the Internet. To Marcuse, the prevalence of sensationalism and a counterfeit feel-good life-style and their abilities to sustain the system of commodity production that supplies them, represented the vicious circle at the core of the one-dimensional society. The most disempowering, yet characteristic, feature of this culture is that it is not perceived as unfree. Furthermore, it continually operates to mobilize bias and oppression, yet it is "without opposition" (OD, ix). Marcuse feels that the critical faculties of the contemporary human mind are basically jammed and damaged and paralyzed (ibid.) through the system of repressive satisfactions. He considers the "distinguishing feature of advanced industrial society [to be] its effective suffocation of those needs which demand liberation" (OD, 7).

Alienation, which is nearly everywhere unrecognized, is thus typified either by the "happy consciousness" that results from conditioned satisfaction with the mass-produced, common denominator, commercially available pleasures, or by a numbness or anesthesia to the everyday forms of repression suffered by the middle-class beneficiaries and the marginalized victims of the system. Marcuse reasoned that this kind of deeper alienation could occur in the booming postwar economy because the system was able to deliver consumer goods to nearly everyone. Managers of business, industry, and government now had *a real material and ideological base* from which to argue a subordination of habits of thought and behavior to the commercial needs of the productive apparatus. On their terms, a "functionalization" (OD, 86) of discourse and action made perfect sense insofar as it ensured a state of material well-being for mass society. According to Marcuse, "the fact that the prevailing mode of freedom is servitude, and that the prevailing mode of equality is superimposed inequality is barred from expression by the closed definition of these concepts in terms of the powers that shape the respective universe of discourse" (OD, 88). This continuing functionalization of discourse indicated that meaning and communication had become "fixed, doctored, loaded" (OD, 94). Communication served fundamentally to anesthetize and to alienate. Marcuse emphasizes the fact that the operationalist language of the *totally administered* order (OD, 7) excludes as nonfunctional and nonconformist all points of view that cannot be reduced to its own single-dimensional speech and action. In arguing the functional rationale of its system, such managerial language considers itself "immune against the expression of protest and refusal" (OD, 90) that might be directed against its system requirements. One-dimensional language either *excludes* oppositional elements from discussion or it *co-opts* and *absorbs* them to maintain its efficacy as a vehicle for subordination: "The unified, functional language is an irreconcilably anti-critical and anti-dialectical language" (OD, 97).

By canceling the antagonism between the human individual and the highly developed external processes of advanced economic activity, contemporary society has achieved an advanced stage of alienation. In Marcuse's estimation, alienation as one-dimensionality indicated an extreme loss of self, based upon the *false* satisfaction of material human needs.[1] It is the false projection of our needs that must be abandoned if alienation is ultimately to be overcome.

Marcuse emphasizes the fact that inauthentic needs must be replaced by genuine ones, and thus *a personal determination of authentic need* is considered *a key emancipatory task* that all individuals must accomplish *on their own*. In elucidating the distinction between false and true needs, Marcuse cites a very moving passage from the work of François Perroux:

> They believe they are dying for Class, they die for the Party boys. They believe they are dying for the Fatherland, they die for the Industrialists. They believe they are dying for the freedom of the Person, they die for the Freedom of the dividends. They believe they are dying for the Proletariat, they die for its Bureaucracy. They believe they are dying by orders of a State, they die for the money which holds the state. They believe they are dying for a nation, they die for the bandits that gag it. They believe—but why would one believe in such darkness? Believe—die?—when it is a matter of *learning to live*? (OD, 207, emphasis added)

Marcuse wants to make possible the genuine determination of need by demonstrating how to locate and to retrieve the *sources of human autonomy*. Marcuse advises us that our freedom is to be found in a special dimension of human experience, the "second dimension" (OD, 9) of human life. This is more explicitly described as being rooted in the "experience of the divided world" (OD, 131), or in the "experience of a world antagonistic in itself" (OD, 125). Second-dimensional experience is emancipatory, Marcuse theorizes, because the well-integrated, single-dimensional personality is capable of the subjective recognition of a *disjuncture* between two states of Being: the first represented by "is," and the second by "ought" (OD, 133).

In his estimation, *both human rationality and human sensuality* make possible a recognition of the inadequacy of what *is* and the discovery of what *could be*.

This discovery is the work of Logos and Eros. The two key terms designate two modes of negation; erotic as well as logical cognition break the hold of the established, contingent reality and strive for a truth incompatible with it . . . Logos and Eros are in themselves the unity of the positive and the negative, creation and destruction. In the exigencies of thought and the madness of love is the destructive refusal of the established ways of life. (OD, 127)

Marcuse is echoing a conclusion from *Eros and Civilization* here on the manipulation, restriction, and numbing of the contemporary consciousness through the prevailing modes of public communication and education (EC 103–4). Marcuse, of course, denies that the happiness or the anesthesia of affluence are at all genuinely representative of life as it ought to be, the "good life" (OD, 126). He inquires in *One-Dimensional Man* for an answer to the "time honored question: who educates the educators, and where is the proof they are in possession of 'the good?'" (OD, 40). The liquidation/manipulation of any conception of the good life or good society beyond the present form of our economy and culture is, of course, also functional insofar as it eliminates the interference of potentially disruptive elements of behavior and thought.

We submit to the peaceful production of the means of destruction, to the perfection of waste, *to being educated for a defense which deforms the defenders and that which they defend*. (OD, ix, emphasis added)

Marcuse thus emphasizes the fact that the emergence of a single-dimensional culture, the operationalist universe of theory and practice, is an *educational* as well as a "philosophical development" (OD, 104).

Functional communication is only the outer layer of the one-dimensional universe in which man is *trained to forget*—to translate the negative into the positive so that he can continue to function, reduced but fit and reasonably well. . . . (OD, 104, emphasis added)

Marcuse finds that one-dimensionality results from the circumstances by which the modern consciousness has been anesthetized and numbed. He

sees advanced industrial society's approach to education and culture as dominated by the operational needs of its technological and productive system.
These operational needs require the explicit organization of natural and
human resources as instrumentalities and entail the full-scale neglect (or in
equal measure the full-scale manipulation) of those domains of human
existence bearing only indirectly on functionality. Thus what Marcuse calls
second-dimensional knowledge gets emasculated and assimilated (when not
simply dismissed as unnecessary and irrelevant) by the established forms of
culture and education as these integrate the individual into the dominant
system of production and consumption.

> Today's novel feature is the flattening out of the antagonism
> between culture and social reality through the obliteration of the . . .
> transcendent elements in the higher culture by virtue of which it
> constituted *another dimension* of reality. This liquidation of *two-*
> dimensional culture takes place not through the denial and rejec-
> tion of the "cultural values," but through their wholesale incorpora-
> tion into the established order, through their reproduction and
> display on a massive scale. (OD, 57, emphasis in original)

Marcuse maintains that the popular culture (which advanced industrial
society finds in its interest to sustain) must conform in any of a myriad of
ways to society's commercial and operational needs. This argument may at
first glance appear to be a reiteration of the Marxist view on the class
character of culture in such matters. However, Marcuse's analysis in *One-
Dimensional Man* is distinctive in its conception of, and admiration for, the
critical, "second-dimensional" character of the realm of *higher* culture vis-à-
vis what is defined as the one-dimensional character of popular culture. To
be sure, as in his 1937 essay "The Affirmative Character of Culture," higher
culture is acknowledged as a phenomenon generally "affirmative" of the
political-economic status quo: "higher culture has always been accommodating, while the reality was rarely disturbed by its ideals and its truth" (OD,
56). Nonetheless, according to Marcuse, its authentic works also preserve a
history and *memory* of the truth with regard to those realms of human existence that stand beyond the parameters of functionality.

> The aesthetic dimension still retains a freedom of expression which
> enables the writer and artist to call men and things by their name—
> to name the otherwise unnameable.

The real force of our time shows in Samuel Beckett's novels; its *real history* is written in Rolf Hochhut's play *Der Stellvertreter*. It is no longer imagination which speaks here but Reason. . . . (OD, 247, emphasis added)

While the bourgeois order found its rich—and even affirmative—representation in art and literature (as in the Dutch painters of the seventeenth century, in Goethe's *Wilhelm Meister*, in the English novel of the nineteenth century, in Thomas Mann), it remained an order which was overshadowed, broken, refuted by another dimension which was irreconcilably antagonistic to the order of business, indicting it and denying it. And in the literature, this other dimension is represented not by the religious, spiritual, moral heroes (who often sustain the established order) but rather by such disruptive characters as the artist, the prostitute, the adulteress, the great criminal and outcast, the warrior, the rebel-poet, the devil, the fool—those who don't earn a living, at least not in an orderly and normal way. (OD, 58–59)

It is this *oppositional and contradictory dimension* that Marcuse believes popular culture has lost, and that accounts for its alienating, one-dimensional quality. This occurs, Marcuse contends, not because mass culture has eliminated characterizations of marginal or disruptive figures, but because the *disjunction between culture and the order of the day has been forcibly closed by the advancing technological society* (OD, 64).

It is to be remembered that Wilhelm Dilthey, as well as Georg Lukács and others in the *Geisteswissenschaftliche* movement after World War I, also wanted to restore a liberal arts educational philosophy as a countervailing force to what were seen by some as the destructive effects of science and technology. *One-Dimensional Man* represents the groundwork for a similar form of educational philosophy and protest oriented toward the human studies because these are seen as essential aids to humanity in gaining access to itself. A major lesson of *One-Dimensional Man* is that humanity can and must come to utilize its immense scientific and technical power in conjunction with the disalienating potential of art in order to *construct a social, sensual, and ethical world that is worthy of human ideals*, and that might then finally actualize the aesthetic dimension's ". . . 'promesse de bonheur'. . . ." (OD, 210, Stendhal's phrase for the promise of happiness and good fortune represented by the idea of beauty).

Max Horkheimer's "Art and Mass Culture" (1972b) had criticized Mortimer J. Adler's plea for general cultural and aesthetic education, because the latter took popularity to be a criterion of artistic greatness. Similarly, Marcuse objects to what he considers to be a repressive educational tendency toward the popularization of cultural insights via the mass media. In his estimation:

> The fact that the transcending truths of the fine arts, the aesthetics of life and thought, were accessible only to the few wealthy and educated was the fault of a repressive society. But this fault is not corrected by paperbacks, general education, long-playing records, and the abolition of formal dress in the theater and concert hall. The cultural privileges expressed the injustice of freedom, the contradiction between ideology and reality, the separation of intellectual from material productivity; but they also provided a protected realm in which the tabooed truths could survive in abstract integrity—remote from the society which suppressed them. Now this remoteness has been removed—and with it the transgression and the indictment. The text and the tone are still there, but the distance is conquered which made them *Luft von anderen Planeten* [ether from different planets]. (OD, 65)

In Marcuse's opinion a program for the general cultural education of a broad public, such as that proposed by Adler (or also recently by William Bennett, E. D. Hirsch Jr., and Allan Bloom) signified the integration and cooption (rather than the enhancement) of the critical potential that he ascribes to his own conception of the relationship of education to the aesthetic dimension:

> No misunderstanding: as far as they go, paperbacks, general education, and long-playing records are truly a blessing. (ibid.)

> It is good that almost everyone can now have the fine arts at his fingertips, by just turning a knob on his set, or by just stepping into his drugstore. In this diffusion, however, *they become cogs in a culture-machine which remakes their content*. Artistic alienation succumbs, together with other modes of negation, to the process of technological rationality. (ibid., emphasis added)

Marcuse argues that this general educational cultural programming surrenders, in advanced industrial society, to the manipulation of consciousness into conformity with society's operational needs and commercial interests. With the products of intellectual culture becoming increasingly familiar and incorporated into daily life, Marcuse asks: "Is their massive reproduction and consumption only a change in quantity, namely growing appreciation and understanding, democratization of culture?" (OD, 61). He explains his own understanding of the matter as follows:

> The neo-conservative critics of leftist critics of mass culture ridicule the protest against Bach as background music in the kitchen, against Plato and Hegel, Shelley and Baudelaire, Marx and Freud in the drugstore. Instead they insist on recognition of the fact that the classics have left the mausoleum and come to life again, that people are just so much more educated. True, but coming to life as classics, they come to life as other than themselves; they are deprived of their antagonistic force. . . . The intent and function of these works have thus fundamentally changed. *If they once stood in contradiction to the status quo, this contradiction is now flattened out*. (OD, 64, emphasis added)

The emancipatory potential of the aesthetic is incapacitated through the repressive overfamiliarization that occurs through the affirmative incorporation of great art into mass schemes of general education. Marcuse argues against this atrophy of the liberal arts approach. Much like Eliot, Joyce, and Dilthey, he propounds a need for *critical distance* and *aesthetic alienation* and for the reassertion of the subversive quality of aesthetic judgment against operationalist concerns.

Marcuse invokes the *Republic*'s cave allegory as explicitly involving this "subversive character of truth" (OD, 132). He also implies a subversive or revolutionary character to all second-dimensional learning and education, which permits the judgment of factual information in the light of its "essence and idea" (ibid.). Marcuse finds the *Republic*'s stress on the leadership obligation of the infrequently appearing philosopher to be Plato's indispensable political and cultural insight, and Marcuse asserts in this tradition *the interventionist mission* of philosophy, art, and education.

One-Dimensional Man criticizes the *affirmative social control function* not only of vocational training policies and operational social mentality characteristic of the management of advanced industrial societies, but also the absorption and constriction of the critical potential of great art by the one-dimensional systems of mass culture and general education that such societies permit.

Marcuse believes that it is *art* that can and must assist the individual in the experience of the "ontological" (OD, 133) disjunction between "is" and "ought" (ibid.). Guided by the broadened Platonic Eros, as a love of learning and as a love of knowledge and research, Marcuse believes that humanity may equip itself with an emancipatory mentality that can break open the closed patterns of the existent modes of discourse and behavior, and establish anew the definition of its needs. Marcuse is convinced that art allows a second-dimensional insight into the beautiful promise of both nature and human existence, and that the aesthetic may, today, be combined with the productive power of science and technology to transform humanity and the world into what they *ought to be*.

The normative ground of reason in art derives from the *substantive universals* that art, like philosophy, is able to express. "The substantive universal intends qualities which surpass all particular experience, but persist in the mind, not as a figment of the imagination nor as mere logical possibilities but as the 'stuff' of which our world consists" (OD, 213). In arguing the historical reality of these universals, Marcuse has clearly parried in advance the charges of nihilism and value relativism that culture warriors like Allan Bloom have tried to press on Marcuse. These norms and standards form the very basis of *the critical* in Marcuse's critical theory. What this means is that he is convinced that the human mind is able to approach a "second-dimensional" level of knowledge that is distinguished from that of the functionalist first dimension by virtue of its *historical*, *dialectical*, and *critical* character. Marcuse gives an example of this two-dimensional type of thinking with reference to *The Communist Manifesto* and the treatment therein provided in its analysis of the concepts "Bourgeoisie" and "Proletariat" (OD, 100). He takes pains to add that the Marxian analytical framework is merely one mode of this historical, dialectical, and critical type of knowledge that has persisted through the history of philosophy. Marcuse considers the Platonic dialectic (at OD, 131 and at AC, 91–92) to be a primordial expression of conceptually open philosophical analysis that critical theory also seeks to preserve.

Marcuse believes that the closed and one-dimensional rationality of modern positivism and science must be opened to what he considers to be the emancipatory, second-dimensional rationality and the full potential of the Platonic philosophy. Marcuse stresses the fact that Plato's *Phaedrus*, *Symposium*, and *Republic* all deal fundamentally with *the forces that may guide thought* to *recall* the second-dimensional context of first-dimensional impressions of truth. In the *Phaedrus*, Plato's *idea of love* incorporates the notion of an *impulse toward beauty* and goodness that acts as it *ought* through an inspiration to intellectual elevation over the *is*. Beauty is considered to be teleological: that is, possessing a pull factor, a "final cause," or a "cause of causes" *that can move the world* insofar as it is loved. In the *Symposium*, it is also the *love of beautiful knowledge* and the vision of the very soul of beauty that stirs and quickens imperfectly given humanity to look for its "other half," that is, toward that which it lacks as a species, but must attain, in order to achieve genuine perfection, fulfillment, and joy. Love is said to be the source of longing for ennoblement of humanity, and also of all individual contributions to that end. In the *Republic* of course it is precisely the love of wisdom that is thought to allow the philosopher to both direct the course of government and also to assist others toward an enlightened recovery of a knowledge of their hitherto obscured human nature and the Good. Platonic love thus transcends profoundly the progenitive or sexual connotations of love expanding into the love of searching and researching: the *love of learning*, as such.

Seeking to philosophize about education under contemporary conditions of alienation, Marcuse sees the revival of this particular theory of the Platonic love of humanity for learning about the Good, the True, and the Beautiful as the key *educational* stimulus to the crucial redefinition of need that he views as stimulating both individual intellectual growth and social progress.

Marcuse acknowledges here (as in "The Affirmative Character of Culture") the historical limitations of the classical Greek philosophical framework that were rooted in the social separation of mental from manual labor in the civilization of Periclean Athens. Yet (at OD, 59) he finds an underlying identity in the pretechnological rationality represented by the Platonic dialectic and by the "post-technological rationality" (OD, 238) his critical theory seeks. This attempts to reestablish the interpenetration of Logos and Eros, and reason and art. Marcuse believes that the closed and one-dimensional rationality of modern positivism and science must be opened to what is considered to be the emancipatory, second-dimensional rationality of art, and the full potential of the Platonic philosophy.

Thus, Marcuse writes of the "original link . . . between science, art and philosophy" (OD, 229), and defines the intellectual activity that unites these cognitive activities as that of the classical Greek notion of "intuition"

(OD, 125–26). This intuition is thought to represent a rational analysis of concrete, sensuous phenomena that permits a mediation by their second-dimensional development, motion, and truth. Mediation and intuition, thus, make possible the ultimate *unity of reason and art* and a new form of *technological practice*. Intuition and understanding can accomplish a normative understanding and transformation of society, nature, and humanity.

> Civilization produces the means for freeing nature from its own brutality, its own insufficiency, its own blindness, by virtue of the cognitive and transforming power of Reason. And Reason can fulfill this function only as post-technological rationality, in which technics is itself the instrumentality of pacification, organon of the "art of life." The function of Reason then converges with the function of *Art*. (OD, 238, emphasis in original)

Though Marcuse is convinced that art, alone, is powerless to actualize its intuition of the truth, he believes it has a "chance" (OD, 201) of effecting sociopolitical progress against the alienation and one-dimensionality of advanced industrial society, if it can be coupled with the transformative capacity of technology and science:

> The rationality of art, its ability to "project" existence, to define yet unrealized possibilities, could then be envisaged as validated by and functioning in the scientific-technological transformation of the world. Rather than being the handmaiden of the existing apparatus, beautifying its business and its misery, art would become a technique for destroying this business and this misery. (OD, 239)

Such is the manner in which Marcuse sought to urge art against alienation in *One-Dimensional Man*. This work was couched between *Eros and Civilization* and *An Essay on Liberation*, both of which also centrally articulate Marcuse's *art-against-alienation hypothesis*.

One-Dimensional Man stands squarely upon the shoulders of the book that most immediately preceded it, Marcuse's 1958 account of Soviet society and thought, *Soviet Marxism, A Critical Analysis* (SM). Where *One-Dimensional Man* examined certain key social issues in the context of the United States, *Soviet Marxism* did likewise in its consideration of Soviet society and thought. Both works were concerned with an analysis of highly productive economic systems that were nonetheless considered to be disturbingly alienating forms of advanced industrial civilization, with a comparable paralysis of criticism within them both. While Soviet society was clearly acknowledged to have had many characteristic and distinctive features that it did not share with contemporary capitalist societies, Marcuse felt that both the U.S. and Soviet systems revolved around parallel operational, technological, and ideological social control concerns.

> Both systems show the common features of late industrial civilization—centralization and regimentation supersede individual enterprise and autonomy; competition is organized and "rationalized;" there is joint rule of economic and political bureaucracies; the people are coordinated through the "mass media" of communication, entertainment, industry, education. (SM, 66)

His third chapter is titled "The New Rationality," reflecting Marcuse's continued willingness to utilize Weberian analytical categories, and indicating his orientation toward the discovery of those functional or operational principles around which a given social order is thought to crystallize. In this regard he observes: "It has been noted . . . how much the present 'communist spirit' resembles the 'capitalist spirit' which Max Weber attributed to the rising capitalist civilization" (SM, 169). Furthermore, Marcuse maintains: "In going through the enumerations of the highest moral values given in Soviet ethical philosophy, it is difficult to find a single moral idea or syndrome of moral ideas that is not common to Western ethics" (SM, 216). In other words, *Soviet Marxism* is a work that clearly regards Soviet society and Soviet ethical philosophy as sharing striking similarities with the system of social organization and moral thinking in the United States. The Weberian influence on Marcuse's sociocultural theory is significant. Marcuse attempts to clarify and to criticize Weber's fundamental conceptions with the aim of refining and updating his notions on productive rationality and domination through bureaucracy. Marcuse dropped what he saw as the now obsolescent emphasis on innerworldly asceticism in favor of *One-Dimensional Man's* notion of repressive desublimation and maintained a critical distance from Weber's "spiteful" (MW, 201) fight against socialism.

For Marcuse, Weber's continuing analytical validity stems from advanced industrial society's ongoing commitment to a calculable operational efficiency, despite the era's historical shift from small-scale to large-scale production (i.e., from scarcity to affluence). In Marcuse's estimation, technical progress has become incompatible with unemployment, impoverishment, and overwork; scientific management ensures increasing comforts and a rising standard of living; ultimately, this is the achievement of an advanced technological rationality that seeks to eliminate economic and social dysfunction, and to achieve a planned stabilization. In this sense, Marcuse considers the Weberian framework still eminently applicable.

> The co-existence of advanced capitalism and advancing socialism involves a competition between the two systems not only in terms of efficiency and internal growth and cohesion, but also in terms of their ability to consummate technical progress. Consummation of technical progress implies automation of material production, and elimination of the wasteful, destructive, and parasitarian jobs, goods, and services maintained by adolescent systems of domination. (SM, xiii)

Thus, Marcuse comes to speak not only of the assimilation but "perhaps even convergence of Western and Soviet society" (SM, xi). And while Marcuse does introduce a caveat[2] to this, *Soviet Marxism*'s fundamental proposition, he nevertheless made it the theoretical foundation of his original account of the persistence of alienation in Soviet society, culture, and education. He thus maintains his emphasis on ". . . the all-embracing political character of the machine process in advanced industrial society" (SM, xi). In his view, the former USSR was a highly developed example of what he would later term a *one-dimensional* civilization.

> This society, defined as socialist in terms of Marxian theory, becomes the sole standard of truth and falsehood; there can be no transcendence in thought and action, no individual autonomy because the Nomos [law] of the whole is the true Nomos. To transcend that which is, to set subjective reason against state reason, to appeal to higher norms and values, belongs to the prerogatives of class society. . . . (SM, 70)

Marcuse thus articulates his protest to this ostensibly alienating condition, stressing a need for critical transcendence. *Soviet Marxism* also presents its critique with what is Marcuse's increasingly characteristic interlocking references to problems of society and the problems of art:

"Soviet realism" is not a mere matter of philosophy and aesthetics; it is the general pattern of intellectual and practical behavior demanded by the structure of Soviet society. (ibid.)

"Soviet realism," in this sense, is a synoptic phrase that sums up Marcuse's postulate of Soviet one-dimensionality and the total administration of Soviet culture. Interpreting this aspect of the Soviet philosophy of art broadly as an ethical and political concept, rather than as a strictly aesthetic one, he stressed what he considered to be its inevitable connotations of social control through cultural conformity and intellectual integration. Just as Marcuse had emphasized the fact that the trend toward total industrialization in the West had "led to a corrosion of the humanistic liberal ethics which was centered on the notion of the autonomous individual" (SM, 179), so too he claimed that in Soviet society an essentially similar tendency toward technical progress had prevented the translation of its ideals of solidarity, cooperation, and *humanitas* (SM, 202) into reality.

To Marcuse, advancing Soviet industrialization had required and promoted the integration of its superstructural developments in culture and education. Thus, he believed that the technological interests of industrialization, on their own, had ensured that in the then Soviet Union, as in the United States, "the means for liberation and humanization operate for preserving domination and submission" (SM, xiv). Significantly, Marcuse chose a major Soviet illustration of this phenomenon from the field of educational policy and philosophy:

For example, polytechnical education, the very prerequisite for a future exchangeability of functions which would abolish man's life-long enchainment by one specialized job, is accompanied by reduction in humanistic education, and centralized planning for the satisfaction of needs includes planning for the retention of government above and against individuals. (ibid.)

In these, and similar, passages in *Soviet Marxism*, Marcuse frames an account of Soviet educational policies and philosophy in which these appeared to be baldly functional or operational adjuncts to the Soviet productive system. While Marcuse gives qualified support to the polytechnical approach to elementary and secondary educational schemes, he warned against what he perceived as an undue neglect of the humanities (ibid.) in Soviet schools.

It must be noted, however, that Marcuse's discussion of Soviet education, while approving of the notion of "exchangeability of function" to be attained through its polytechnical aspect, consistently overstates its vocational nature and thereby essentially distorts the actual role of polytechnicalization in that system. While it is clear that no part of *Soviet Marxism* was intended as a professional study in comparative education, scholars and historians in this field tend to agree that the former Soviet Union and the Eastern Bloc countries understood their approach to educational policy and philosophy in terms much broader than Marcuse's emphasis on polytechnicalization would suggest. The Western comparativists, Nigel Grant, Oskar Anweiler, and Alexander G. Korol, for example, treated polytechnicalization as an important and key aspect of the Soviet educational system, defining a *part*, but not the *whole* of its program.[3] Indeed, as the East German educationist, Gerhart Neuner, made clear, the fundamental concept describing educational policy and philosophy in the old Eastern Bloc was supposed to be that of socialism as this pertained to the system of *general education*, emphasizing the social sciences and humanities well beyond mere polytechnical training. Neuner's quantitative and qualitative breakdown of the general curriculum in the comprehensive yet polytechnically oriented secondary school clearly demonstrates the *comprehensive nature* of this educational program, and precludes the simplistic narrowing of this scheme to the vocational aspect as in Marcuse's reductionist analysis.[4] Perhaps the definitive work on the socialist theory of polytechnicalism and education is the 1958 volume compiled by the noted educational theorist of the former East Germany, Gotthold Krapp.[5] The first half of Krapp's book is dedicated to an elaboration of the many-sided nature of the historically developed human personality and character, and to both the necessity and feasibility of a system of socialist general education, which would aim at the full development of the entire spectrum of these qualities in everyone. In Krapp's detailed discussion of the polytechnical aspect of this comprehensive approach, polytechnical training is referred to as general-educational technological instruction (*allgemeinbildender technologischer Unterricht*), and the whole point of this description is that the *poly*technical aspect is not to be confused with the mono-technical, vocationalist approach that has characterized the usual relationship between work and schooling (i.e., narrowly conceived trade training) in the West. General-educational technological instruction is considered an entirely different genre of educational thinking with regard to social labor and social production. Krapp is clear in his emphasis on this new type of education as an indispensable prerequisite for informed mass participation in industrial planning decisions and overall leadership questions, in a technologically advanced socialist society. It is *not* intended to continue in the vocationalist tradition of capitalist society that has historically seemed an educational machine for the manufacture of human cogs for some overwhelming productive apparatus. Rather polytechnicalism is to break radically with that tradition, and to engender flexible, multifaceted individuals with a good general knowledge of technology, natural history, mathematics, cultural development, language arts, and socialism.

On the one hand it is interesting to note that today even in the United States reformers in vocational education are increasingly talking about agile manufacturing and the cross training of agile technologists.[6] This seems to demonstrate the material force of the logic of polytechnicalism. On the other hand we must also recall that, in contradistinction to Marcuse's thesis of cultural and educational convergence, Urie Bronfenbrenner's 1970 comparative study of the U.S. and Soviet systems of education found an ineradicable *contrast* between what to him appeared as *Two Worlds of Childhood*. Bronfenbrenner's aim was a comparison of childrearing in collective settings to childrearing practices in the contemporary United States. The polytechnical aspect of Soviet schooling does not even become thematic here, as Bronfenbrenner elaborates instead the general educational practices and methods of a collectivistic socialism as these were originally devised and implemented in educational settings by the Soviet Union's early pedagogical leaders in theory and practice: A. S. Makarenko and N. K. Krupskaia. While Bronfenbrenner found much to criticize about Soviet schooling, he also found much to appreciate. He considered remarkable the demonstrative warmth and wide diffusion of nurturant behavior expressed by Soviet adolescents and adults toward children, inside and outside the Soviet school. His comparative research found such an unusual sense of responsibility and respect for youngsters that he claimed Westerners could only view such cooperative behavior with astonishment. My point here is not to argue the virtues of public education in the old Eastern Bloc, nor is it to examine its weaknesses. Rather I wish to show that *Marcuse's* educational observations in *Soviet Marxism* appear somewhat exaggerated in their reductionist emphasis on vocational or technical training, and decidedly negligent with respect to fundamental differences in institutionalized childrearing practices. It appears that this reductionism is indispensable, however, if Marcuse is to preserve his contention that Soviet style educational innovation never adequately responded to the problems of the alienation of labor and sociocultural isolation as he defined them.

Marcuse's protest and critique in *Soviet Marxism* (as in *One-Dimensional Man* and *Reason and Revolution*) are largely predicated upon a notion of the emancipation of the individual. He believed that education could be an aid to this liberation, but quite obviously, not education as he contended it was practiced in the former Soviet Union, nor, for that matter, as he believed it to be found in its predominant modes in the advanced industrial societies of the West. For Marcuse, the key link between an emancipatory theory of education and the autonomy of the individual is the aesthetic dimension.

> The more the base encroaches upon the ideology, manipulating and coordinating it with the established order, the more the ideological sphere which is remotest from the reality (art, philosophy), precisely because of its remoteness, becomes the last refuge for the opposition to this order. (SM, 110)

Marcuse is convinced of a very tight interrelationship between social base and cultural superstructure in advanced industrial societies. In his estimation this interrelationship is that of an almost mechanical reflection of operational and functional material economic concerns in the ideological sphere leading to the formation of closed and single-dimensional totally administered systems characterized by the integration of individual interests and a paralysis of criticism. Under conditions of one-dimensionality, non-aesthetic thought tended toward functionalism and amnesia. *Art* remained as the cultural component that could retain the transcendent concern for material human happiness and social justice:

> In the Soviet system, the "general interest" is hypostatized in the state—an entity separate from individual interests. To the extent that the latter are still unfulfilled and repelled by reality, they strive for ideological expression; and their force is the more explosive to the regime the more the new economic basis is propagandized as insuring the total liberation of man under communism. The fight against ideological transcendence thus becomes a life-and-death struggle for the regime. Within the ideological sphere, the center of gravity shifts from philosophy to literature and art. (SM, 112)

To Marcuse, an education to Marxist theory in the former Soviet school system succumbed also to a repressive and functionalist realism elaborated in a supposedly inflexible and meaningless rhetoric: "the 'classics' of

Marxism . . . only recall what is preestablished. They are to be 'spelled,' learned mechanically, monotonously and literally. . . ." (SM, 72). The anti-empirical tendencies in art on the other hand, while also appearing in affirmative modes, are nonetheless thought to be capable of preserving "transcendent" images of liberation. Marcuse's thinking in this regard is clearly more closely related to the traditional metaphysical (SM, 113) tenets of perennial philosophy rather than to a dialectical and historical materialism. This is a basic theoretical shift that characterizes his critical theory.

> Metaphysics, traditionally the chief refuge for the still unrealized ideas of human freedom and fulfillment, is declared to be totally superseded by dialectical materialism and by the emergence of a rational society in socialism. (SM, 113)

> The fight against Western philosophy, "bourgeois objectivism," idealism, and so forth . . . aims at discrediting philosophical trends and categories which, by virtue of their transcendence, seemed to endanger the "closed" political and ideological system (ibid.).

> With this negation of philosophy, the main ideological struggle then is directed against the transcendence in art. Soviet art must be "realistic." (ibid.)

Marcuse does acknowledge (at SM, 113–14) that realism in art has, in certain of its forms, historically provided a sociocritical, cognitive, and political perspective on the world by contrasting the given reality to the ideals of freedom and justice humanity implicitly holds. Nonetheless, he felt that *Soviet* realism was operationalist, uncritical, and one-dimensional because it postulated the supersession of a hard-and-fast (metaphysical) disjunction between human essence and human existence under conditions of socialism.

> But it is precisely the catastrophic element inherent in the conflict between man's essence and his existence that has been the center toward which art has gravitated since its secession from ritual. The artistic images have preserved the determinate negation of the established reality—ultimate freedom. When Soviet aesthetics attack (sic) the notion of the "unsurmountable antagonism between essence and existence" as the theoretical principle of "formalism," it thereby attacks the principle of art itself. (SM, 114–15)

In this passage Marcuse clearly claims that a duality or disjunction of human essence from human existence is the very basis of art. He concludes in this regard that Soviet aesthetics, by "outlawing the transcendence of art," (SM, 116), "wants art that is not art, and it gets what it asks for" (ibid.).

Marcuse reemphasizes at this point Platonic distinctions in aesthetic theory. He emphasizes the fact that "Plato's theory of art refers to a state in which the philosopher kings guard the standards for the good, the true and the beautiful" (SM, 120), but he notes that this occurs only when the standards are rooted in transcendence, that is, in "a state antagonistic to reality" (ibid.). Marcuse thus believed that the Soviet approach retained only the repressive aspect of the Platonic aesthetic theory in which it attempts to censor and regulate aesthetic creativity in the direction of social conformity and control. He found "the most reactionary feature of Soviet aesthetics" (SM, 119) to be its ostensible "rejection of 'formalism' and of all 'abstract' and 'dissonant' structures" (ibid.).

> The Soviet state by administrative decree prohibits the transcendence of art; it thus eliminates even the ideological reflex of freedom in an unfree society. Soviet realistic art, complying with the decree, becomes an instrument of social control in the last still non-conformist dimension of the human existence. (SM, 118)

For Marcuse, the very definition of freedom is linked to an ascription of an unquestioned ethical and political value to social nonconformism (see also AD, 55–56). Because of the presumed convergence of the U.S. and Soviet systems, and their hypostatized common reliance on the suffocation of individual needs and absorption of personal interests, Marcuse was left no logical or sociological recourse but to seek liberation through a refusal to adjust to what were considered to be the alienating existential conditions of these two forms of an essentially identical productive and ideological apparatus. As in *One-Dimensional Man*, emancipation depends on an achieved autonomy, an act of self-determination that transcends all forms of "totally administered" economic satisfaction and repressive affluence. Art preserves this autonomy, according to Marcuse, because it is rooted in transcendence, that is, is grounded in a nonfunctional, second-dimensional, meta-physical domain: ". . . a protest against that which is" (SM, 117). Marcuse believes that art is fundamentally incompatible with the single-dimensional approaches of operationalism or empiricism. It can never be "pressed into the service of reality" (SM, 120) without also becoming uncritical and affirmative. Because

Marcuse was convinced that precisely this affirmation was the case with Soviet aesthetics, he stood inalterably opposed to what he considered its manipulative realism. He explicitly preferred, instead, what he believed to be the emancipatory potential of abstract and dissonant art, even in its characteristically bourgeois mode:

> The works of the great "bourgeois" antirealists and "formalists" are far deeper committed to the idea of freedom than is socialist and Soviet realism. The irreality of their art expresses the irreality of freedom: art is as transcendental as its object. (SM, 118)

Marcuse contends that art can and must retain its critical function, that is, the representation of a still transcendental truth (SM, 115), until the irreal, but emancipatory, content of art is actualized and its ideal substance lost. Politics must translate possibility into actuality. Quite obviously, in his estimation, Soviet patterns of labor and aesthetic effort failed to materialize the "promesse du bonheur expressed in art" (ibid.). Thus, art must continue (in his terms) to seek an irreal ("surreal"? [AD, 55–56]) and transcendent freedom, rather than beautify that which is.

Having thus far reviewed Marcuse's particular treatment of Soviet aesthetics, I turn at this point to a closer examination of *Soviet Marxism*'s related discussion of that alienation thought to be inherent in the labor process itself. I will show that its distinctive contributions to the theories of labor and alienation dovetail perfectly with his conception of the uniquely emancipatory potential of art.

Marcuse's analysis of advanced industrialization and bureaucratization in the United States and in the former Soviet Union entails an assertion of the necessary reduction and restriction of individual thought and behavior:

> ... progress in industrialization is tantamount to progress in domination: attendance to the machine, the scientific work process, becomes totalitarian, affecting all spheres of life. The technical perfection of the productive apparatus dominates the rulers and the ruled while sustaining the distinction between them. Autonomy and spontaneity are confined to the level of efficiency and performance within the established pattern. (SM, 69)

As Marcuse has asserted (at SM, 69–70 and at OD, 1–2), these modern developments in automation, coupled with centralized administrative technique, have rendered the individual determination of behavior and personal decision-making processes increasingly impossible, or when possible, nonetheless really dysfunctional. Unless the highly automated improvements in productive technique are at the same time also oriented toward a drastic reduction in the hours of labor and toward the satisfaction of "individual needs" in "the realm of freedom," increasing industrialization necessarily implies the intensified alienation of the individual.

> Marxist theory made an essential distinction between work as the realization of human potentialities and work as "alienated labor;" *the entire sphere of material production, of mechanized and standardized performances, is considered as one of alienation.* By virtue of this distinction, the realization of freedom is attributed to a social organization of labor fundamentally different from the prevailing one, to a society where work as the free play of human faculties has become a "necessity," a "vital need" for society, while work for procuring the necessities of life no longer constitutes the working day and the occupation of the individual. It is in the last analysis the *abolition of alienation* which, for Marx, defines and justifies socialism as the "higher stage" of civilization. And socialism in turn defines a new human existence: its content and value are to be determined by free time rather than labor time, that is to say, *man comes into his own only outside and "beyond" the entire realm of material production* for the mere necessities of life. Socialization of production is to reduce the time and energy spent in this realm to a minimum, and to maximize time and energy for the development and satisfaction of individual needs in the *realm of freedom.* (SM, 218–19, emphasis added)

By characterizing "the entire sphere of material production" in this passage, as inevitably an alienating human realm, where the individual is reduced to standardized behavior in accordance with industrial technique, Marcuse makes a clear statement of the basis of his opposition to the advanced industrial order. He understands alienation, not basically as a consequence of a specific set of social relations of appropriation and production, but in Weberian fashion, as the result of the technical rationality (*Verdinglichung*), repetitiveness, and uniformity in the activities of the labor process itself. In his view, a liberated form of human existence is predicated upon the general preponderance of "free time rather than labor time," and the reduction of number of hours and amount of energy spent in production.

Clearly Marcuse's approach stands in sharp contrast to that of Marx. For *Marx* the end of alienation is characterized *not* through the *abolition of labor*, but through the *elimination of private appropriation*, through the institution of socialist forms of production and ownership, *so that labor is free to become life's prime want, where necessity and gratification converge*. Alienation is considered the result of a specific mode of the appropriation of the products of social labor, and it is thought to be overcome through the supersession of the wage-labor system and the dynamics of capital accumulation, not simply through the supersession (or minimalization) of labor time, as such. Marcuse, quite to the contrary, takes pains to minimize the role of appropriation in alienation theory. For Marcuse, neither socialization (RR, 282) nor nationalization (SM, 222), as alternative modes of social appropriation to that of private accumulation, will necessarily "preclude alienation" (ibid.).

Given the ways in which Marcuse wanted to reshape the theory of alienation, the problem as he saw it was that up to this point in time, the "protest against the alienation of man . . . [has been] directed against the *political organization* of industry—not against industry as such" (SM, 180, emphasis in original).

Marcuse believed that he had formulated a superior theory of alienation that protested the single-dimensional operationalism of the highly developed technological rationality of advanced industrial society. Against this rationality of advancing industry as such, he counterposed a new, transcendentally oriented aesthetic rationality as the liberating principle upon which to base the construction of a genuinely free human society.

Art and the Potential for Protest

Herbert Marcuse delivered a lecture at the School of Visual Arts in New York on 8 March, 1967 entitled "Art in the One-Dimensional Society" (AO). First published in *Arts Magazine*, May 1967, he begins with a rather personal statement:

> . . . I would like to say a few words about how I came to feel the need for occupying myself with the phenomenon of art. . . . It was some sort of despair or desperation. Despair in realizing that all language, all prosaic language, and particularly the traditional language somehow seems to be dead. It seems to me incapable of communicating what is going on today, and archaic and obsolete compared with some of the achievements and force of the artistic

and poetic language, especially in the context of the opposition against this society among the protesting and rebellious youth of our time. . . . Now, this may sound romantic, and I often blame myself for perhaps being too romantic in evaluating the liberating, radical power of art . . . still, the survival of art may turn out to be the only weak link that today connects the present with the hope of the future. (AO, 53–54)

Marcuse's point of departure in this essay (and in much of his middle-period theorizing) echoes what he considered to be the debilitating and overpowering effects of the "prosaic" daily routine in advanced industrial society articulated as early as his 1922 dissertation. Now (in 1969) even war and genocide were experienced by the large majority of individuals as humdrum and unproblematic affairs; at any rate, as events against which it seemed impossible to intervene, even if one had the inclination to do so. Nonetheless, Marcuse perceived an inexplicable spark of sociocultural defiance, from time to time, which asserted itself (if only faintly, as an exception, and against the anesthesia of affluence). This seemed to portend that the routinization of mass-murder, mass-deception, and apathy need not necessarily continue. The origin of this glimmer of hope was "the liberating, radical power of art" (AO, 54). As he saw it, art could revive the "deadened" concepts, words, and images of the established order. These had become incapable of expressing the truth of the given social reality even where they explicitly sought to do so.

> . . . [S]ince the Thirties we see the intensified and methodical search for a new language, for a poetic language as a revolutionary language, for an artistic language as a revolutionary language. This implies the concept of the imagination as a cognitive faculty, capable of transcending and breaking the spell of the Establishment. (AO, 55)

In Marcuse's opinion, aesthetic endeavor (especially since the rise of German fascism) had been grappling with the problem of the *emptiness of its time-honored cultural ideals*, and struggling with the need for a new form of cultural expression and communication that might snap humanity out of its tradition-bound spiritual *stupor*. In this sense, art would become "revolutionary," and topple empires of custom and belief. But by the same token, *movements of social protest would also become functions of the revolutions in culture and art.* Marcuse held this to be the case because all genuine political change required imagination, and this creative, cognitive ability was thought to be more pertinent to the negation of existing political realities than even the naked power struggles among competing parties.

> In this sense, the Surrealist thesis as it was developed during this period (1930s) elevates the poetic language to the rank of being the only language that does not succumb to the all-embracing language spoken by the Establishment, a "metalanguage" of total negation—a total negation transcending even the revolutionary action itself. In other words, art can fulfill its inner revolutionary function only if it does not itself become part of any Establishment, including the revolutionary Establishment. (ibid.)

Marcuse believed that any genuinely emancipatory social movement had to be directed by, and responsible to, the human truths that only the aesthetic faculty of the imagination could develop. To his mind, *the aesthetic imagination had to direct the social revolution*, and not vice versa. A cultural revolution has the clear priority over a merely "political" revolution, in this framework, because the former breaks new ground (in the human dimension of experience) though the latter need not.

While Marcuse acknowledged that certain movements in art, even surrealism, had been transformed into saleable commodities, he nonetheless agreed with surrealism's demand for "the submission of the social revolution to the truth of the poetic imagination" (AO, 56). And while Marcuse also acknowledged the fact that poetic daydreamers and childlike crusaders (with or without rhythmic chants and songs of protest) had been quite mercilessly crushed throughout history whenever they actually happened to challenge power, his point was that the *rebellious spirit* of their song and their art *persisted* (AO, 57).

Apparently, it was the persistence of this mood of discontent (and its moral readiness to rebel against the social abuses that it perceived) that served Marcuse in this essay as a basis of optimism against his initial despair. While he thought science and philosophy had increasingly adjusted to the dominant social realities of one-dimensionality and affluence, the artistic aspect of culture had not: "art today responds to the crisis of our society" (ibid.). Imagination persisted in this realm in visualizing new, nonrepressive human relationships, and new approaches to nature and logic. Even where this occurred in the manner of a "destructive, disorderly, negative nonsense anti-art" (ibid.), it could nonetheless be of emancipatory political significance, precisely in taking up "a position of protest, denial and refusal" (ibid.). In fact, Marcuse observed:

> It seems that today, elements enter into art (now enter into art more than ever before) which are usually considered extraneous and alien to art, that art by itself in its own inner process and procedure tends toward the political dimension without giving up the form of art itself. And in this dynamic process, the aesthetic dimension is losing its semblance of independence, of neutrality. (ibid.)

In other words, "the historical situation of art has changed in such a manner that the purity, even the possibility of art as art becomes questionable" (ibid.). Marcuse saw art, at this point, as inextricably linked to the practical struggle for a better world. What is more, he saw "the aesthetic dimension" as a source of a humane and utopian activism. Highly imaginative art was considered a source of energy that could assist in "the construction of a qualitatively new environment, technical and natural. . . ." (ibid.) insofar as it furnished humanity with a vision hitherto unseen, or a goal never before thought possible. In general, Marcuse held that *art provided a definite negation* to the social status quo because it proposed new "forms of life" (AO, 58), that is, new systems "of needs and satisfactions in which the aggressive, repressive and exploitative instincts are subjugated to the sensuous, assuasive energy of the life instincts" (ibid.). In Marcuse's estimation in his article, "The Affirmative Character of Culture" (AC), *art could remain committed to the realization of an instinctually fulfilling and emotionally gratifying socioeconomic order.*

Marcuse also claimed that in the past art had all-too-often remained merely art, preserving and creating more "illusions," but that today art "is becoming a potential factor in the construction of a new reality" (AO, 58). Marcuse contended that "today art, for the first time in history, is confronted with the possibility of entirely new modes of realization" (ibid.). This was to say that art needed no longer to remain "mere art," in the sense of a "higher culture" above and beyond the everyday order of existence. Art no longer needed to remain the merely imaginary realization of beauty and pleasure in a sphere external to the social and physical worlds. Art in the contemporary epoch could develop and implement its highest aims, not merely in the traditionally conceived objects of art, but in the fundamental, sensuous, practical activities of human civilization. Marcuse wrote: "These propositions may indicate to what extent the aesthetic dimension is a potential dimension of reality itself and not only of art as contrasted with reality. Or we can say that art is tending towards its own realization" (AO, 60).

Marcuse clearly believed in this regard that if the promise of art were actualized in the socioeconomic, political, and emotional realms, art as "mere art" or "higher art" or "pure art" would be both canceled and transcended (AO, 58). The aesthetic process would be completed when nature and society achieved "their aesthetic Form, that is to say, the Form of a pacified and harmonious universe. . . ." (AO, 60). Marcuse asks: ". . . has now perhaps come the time to free art from its confinement to mere art, to an illusion? Has the time come for uniting the aesthetic and the political dimension, preparing the ground in thought and action for making society a work of art?" (ibid.). Marcuse, at this point in his theoretical career, is intent on reinstating the existential and sociological aspects to the aesthetic endeavor and on promoting the idea of "society as a work of art."

In 1967, the emancipatory promise of the aesthetic dimension was to be found in *art as a potential dimension of reality itself*:

> . . . we have to direct our attention to the historical character of art. Art as such, not only in its various styles and forms, is a historical phenomenon. And history is perhaps now catching up with art, or art is catching up with history. The historical locus and function of art are now changing. The real, reality, is becoming the prospective domain of art, and art is becoming technique in a literal, "practical" sense: making and remaking things rather than painting pictures; experimenting with the potential of words and sounds rather than writing poems or composing music. Do these creations perhaps foreshadow the possibility of the artistic Form becoming a "reality-principle"—the self-transcendence of art on the basis of the achievements of science and technology, and of the achievements of art itself? (AO, 65)

Marcuse believed that emancipation through art could be an historical possibility today because of the achievements of technological civilization that have allowed certain of humanity's most fanciful and utopian aspirations (flight, telecommunication, and automation) to be realized:

> If we can do everything with nature and society, if we can do everything with man and things—why can one not make them the

subject-object in a pacified world, in a non-aggressive, aesthetic environment. The know-how is there. The instruments and materials are there for the construction of such an environment, social and natural, in which the unsublimated life-instincts would redirect the development of human needs and faculties, would redirect technical progress. These pre-conditions are there for the creation of the beautiful not as ornaments, not as surface of the ugly, not as museum piece, but as expression and objective of a new type of man; as biological need in a new system of life. (ibid.)

"Art in the One-Dimensional Society" argued for the redirection of the course of technological progress and for the subordination of scientific-technical goals to the fulfillment of the mature, material, sensual, and aesthetic needs of the human race. Art was to create and express a "new system of life," and a new type of humanity. Marcuse's explicit goal was a social and cultural system in which humanity's "life instincts" need not continue to be repressed and sublimated. By focusing on the "aesthetic Form" considered to be immanent in society and nature (AO, 60), Marcuse claimed that humanity could "pacify and harmonize" the "totality" of human life. Marcuse saw his new conception of *aesthetic activity as the starting point for the rehumanization of history.*

The "revitalized" philosophy of art presented by Marcuse in this essay highlighted the practical value of art for human life and experience. Thus, this new philosophy of art was conceived as an inherently *activist and political* reformulation of the social role of aesthetic theory: "Not political art, not politics as art, but art as the architecture of a free society" (AO, 65–66). Marcuse believed that he had developed a *new political philosophical rationality* for the *construction of a free society.* This new rationality was guided not by socialist principles, but by the ideas of beauty, peace, and emotional gratification, which Marcuse demanded should be encountered today as truth in the spheres of social experience. Such a stance was (in Marcuse's parlance) a reflective, philosophical, and "utopian" one, quite at variance with the apathy of one-dimensional culture, science as Engels understood it, or "the horror of Soviet realism."

The beautiful as [a] Form of such a totality can never be natural, immediate; it must be created and mediated by reason and imagination in the most exacting sense. Thus it is the result of a technique, but of a technique which is the opposite of the technology and technique which dominate the repressive societies of today, namely, a technique freed from the destructive power that experiences men and things, spirit and matter as mere stuff of splitting, combining, transforming and consuming. Instead, art—technique—would liberate the life-protecting and life-enhancing potentialities of matter; it would be governed by a reality principle which subjugates, on the social scale, aggressive energy to the energy of the life instincts. (AO, 62)

Marcuse's vision here of a critical theory of art was opposed as a matter of principle to the *denial* of humanity's "life instincts." It was *precisely this concern for a "life-enhancing" activism in politics and culture that distinguished Marcuse's middle-period philosophizing in an essential manner*. At this point we see the vital, libidinal substance of the flicker of hope that Marcuse described as shining through in "revolutionary" languages as compared to the dim, archaic, or dead language of the politics of the left as well as right. Art in the defense of life and love spoke to a "biological need" (AO, 65) more profound than any merely economic requirements.

In this essay the foundation of the Marcusean protest and the basis of his recommended political activity is not the concrete struggle of classes, nor the historical struggle of ideas. Instead, his program is grounded in the "activism" of the aesthetic Form seeking after the earthly actualization of pleasure, beauty, happiness, and satisfaction.

Marcuse emphasizes the point that valid works of art embody something other than the sensuous: they embody Form. This Form is held to be *active*: it assembles, determines, and delimits the sensuous subject "matter" of the work in question. Form, as such, need not accomplish the beautiful; as *aesthetic* Form, however, it may do so: ". . . Form is beautiful to the degree to which it embodies this coming to rest of violence, disorder and force. Such Form is order, even suppression, but in service of sensibility and joy" (AO, 63). The Aristotelian doctrine of hylomorphism (matter is mere potency; Form is the actualizing principle of all corporeal substance) must be acknowledged as having influenced the views on form subscribed to here. So too the unnamed presence of a Freudian depth-psychology is also felt. Nonetheless, Marcuse couches this theory of the aesthetic Form largely in a quasi-Marxist (or quasi-Hegelian) terminology: ". . . in one way or another, in the setting of the lines, in the rhythm, in the smuggling in of transcending elements of beauty the artistic Form asserts itself and *negates the negation*" (AO, 64, emphasis added). The Form of beauty is thought to be the determinate negation of earthly pain, domination, and ugliness. While Marcuse undoubtedly considers this to be the critical potential of art for the pacification and harmonization of historical human existence, he certainly also recognizes that such an aesthetic vision is by no means an unproblematic one.

First of all, as he explains: art has had a history of providing "substitute gratification in a miserable reality" (AO, 63). As he had initially outlined in "The Affirmative Character of Culture," art has been content to present the illusion, rather than the reality of joy, freedom, and peace. Thus, ". . . a *catharsis*, a purification of reality occurs in art which pacifies the fury of rebellion and indictment and which turns the negative into the affirmative" (ibid.). The critical, negating, quality of the Form of beauty converts into an uncritical, "affirming," cultural characteristic wherever it is content to operate within the ethereal boundaries of "fine art" or "higher culture," fatefully separated from the activities central to the human world of sensuous and practical existence. Because the beautiful Form is considered an essential element of all art, Marcuse believes the dangers of an affirmative formalism are endemic to all types of aesthetic endeavor. Art cannot ultimately ever escape the risk of aestheticism. Once this problem has been acknowledged, however, the artist may ostensibly be on guard against it. Marcuse appears convinced that affirmative culture can only be revoked by a counterculture: "the revocation of a work of art would be another work of art" (AO, 66). The central point of "Art in the One-Dimensional Society" is that "art as art" has to be redeemed by *society as art* or by *reality as art*.

Marcuse also attempts to answer the further objection: "Why the traditional definition of art in terms of beauty, when so much of art, and of great art, is evidently not beautiful in any sense" (AO, 61)? In his response, Marcuse concludes that beauty is not something that is necessarily "evident" in an immediate sense, but rather, something that may happen to a new and estranging vision of reality, even if it initially evokes terror or revulsion. Though the particular elements of the subject matter of the work of art may indeed be mundane, grotesque, or otherwise offensive, the artist is successful as an artist only if he or she is able to teach us something of the higher level *necessity of the form* of such gruesome or ugly events (e.g., the abysmal beauty involved in tragedy). The artist discloses to the audience something more than a series of comforting or discomforting sensations. The artist is occupied with making sense out of the events or elements presented, that is, understanding that which initially appears senseless, cruel, irritating, or absurd. Marcuse rightly emphasizes that we *learn* through art: ". . . art is a cognitive faculty with a truth of its own, and . . . the language of art discovers a hidden and repressed truth." He continues: "I would like to propose to you that art in an extreme sense speaks the language of discovery. Art . . . discovers that there are things; things and not mere fragments and parts of matter to be handled and used up arbitrarily, but 'things in themselves'; things which 'want' something, which suffer, and which lend themselves to the domain of Form, that is to say, things which are inherently 'aesthetic'" (AO, 58–59).

Thus, Marcuse asserts not only the cognitive function of art, but reasserts also the time-honored (Platonic) identification of ultimate (not merely factual) truth with the Form of beauty. Art discovers "things in themselves" liberating their implicit truth as well as beauty. He writes: "The artistic process thus is the 'liberation of the object from the automatism of perception' that distorts and restricts what things are and what things can be" (AO, 59).

Art, in Marcuse's estimation, "creates a new immediacy, which emerges only with the destruction of the old" (ibid.). Thus, the ugliness or deformation of any subject matter is altered, negated, transformed (by a kind of "aesthetic reduction," [cf. OD, 239–40], akin to the "phenomenological reduction" of Edmund Husserl). Marcuse quotes a Russian aesthetician to the effect that "art is a means of experiencing the becoming of the object; that which is already there is of no importance to art" (AO, 59). Also reminiscent of Plato, Marcuse maintains that the "new immediacy" that is achieved in aesthetic cognition is the result of ". . . a process of recollection: images, concepts, ideas long since 'known' find in the work of art, their sensuous representation and—verification" (ibid.).

"Art in the One-Dimensional Society" endures as one of Marcuse's strongest statements of the interventionist mission of the artist into the day-to-day workings of advanced industrial society. Marcuse was confident that art can well fulfill a critical and emancipatory function. Nonetheless, he also recognized the fact that the critique immanent in the aesthetic Form is inadequate, taken in isolation, to the task of social reorganization that art itself proposes. As Marcuse concludes: "The rest is not up to the artist. The realization, the real change which would free men and things, remains the task of political action; the artist participates not as artist. But this extraneous activity today is perhaps germane to the situation of art— and perhaps even germane to the achievement of art" (AO, 67). While art, alone, is insufficient to the achievement of a pacified and harmonious form of social reality, it is, according to this essay, an absolutely necessary and uniquely invigorating call to action in this regard. In contradistinction to dialectical materialism, Marcuse preserves here (as in "Philosophy and

Critical Theory") a dualistic conception of the relationship of politics to art (as "extraneous activity"). While aesthetics must in*form* politics, Marcuse is adamant in emphasizing throughout his middle period the fact that "the real change which would free men and things, remains the task of *political action*" (AO, 67, emphasis added). Marcuse's major contention in this essay is, however, that no negation of the alienating conditions of social existence is even possible apart from the emancipatory potential of the aesthetic dimension.

CHAPTER EIGHT

—⁓—

Art *Against* Alienation:
Aesthetic Education as Political Praxis

... see science from the viewpoint of the artist and art from the viewpoint of life.

Friedrich Nietzsche,
The Birth of Tragedy

Throughout the foregoing I have called attention to Marcuse's many philosophical disagreements with traditional socialist theory. Elemental among them has been his reinterpretation of alienation and the economic strength and ideological stability of capitalism in its advanced industrial phase. I have highlighted Marcuse's reformulations of certain of the basic philosophical issues, especially the alienating effects he attributes to *one-dimensionality* and to *Verdinglichung*. Precisely because of his notion of the very tight, and almost mechanical, determination and distortion of social consciousness by the social order, he is led in several works of his middle period, but especially in *An Essay on Liberation* (EL), to stress the overriding need for a "radical change in consciousness" (EL, 53). This is understood in explicitly *educational* terms—as a prerequisite to emancipatory social activity:

> Under total capitalist administration ... the social determination of consciousness is all but complete and immediate: direct implantation of the latter into the former. Under these circumstances, radical

change in consciousness is the beginning, the first step in changing social existence: emergence of a new Subject. Historically, it is again the period of enlightenment prior to material change—*a period of education, but education which turns into praxis: demonstration, confrontation, rebellion.* (ibid., emphasis added)

An Essay on Liberation is Marcuse's most militant work. It furnished the activist-oriented student movement of the anti-Vietnam War era with a scorching attack on the *culture* of corporate capitalism and on the destructiveness of imperialist aggression:

> This society is obscene in producing and indecently exposing a stifling abundance of wares while depriving its victims abroad of the necessities of life; obscene in stuffing itself and its garbage cans while poisoning and burning the scarce foodstuffs in the fields of its aggression; obscene in the words and smiles of its politicians and entertainers; in its prayers, in its ignorance, and in the wisdom of its kept intellectuals. (EL, 8)

Marcuse dedicated this book to the university protesters who took to the streets in Paris during the events of May and June 1968. Its implications for a philosophy of education (at EL, 53) occur in close connection to what Lukács had originally called "a philosophy of praxis."

It is noteworthy that Andrew Arato and Paul Breines's book on Lukács and on the origins of Western Marxism discusses this sense of "praxis" in the context of their chapter on the early Lukács's theory of reification as *Verdinglichung*. In their estimation, "praxis" is the counterconcept to the deactivation and dehumanization of human beings within a productive system revolving around objective independent things. Lukács's philosophy of praxis is characterized as a Marxian reformulation of a theory of conscious human conduct as this theory is reconstructed by Lukács upon the basis of the history of German classical philosophy. They find that Lukács has here created a "powerful synthesis" of the dialectical philosophy of Hegel and Marx with Weber's understanding of "Western rationality" via the thought of Kant and Schiller. In brief, they indicate that this synthesis begins with the work of Marx (in his first Feuerbach thesis) where "praxis" is identified with the sensuous practical activity of human beings. Kant's relevance is seen in his attempt to move away from a contemplative philosophy of "pure" reason toward the questions involved in *practical reason*'s concern for moral and political problems. In this regard, Kant is said to have relied primarily upon his elucidations of the *philosophy of art* as a guide in the practical pursuit of goodness. At this juncture, Schiller is also cited as attempting to overcome the fragmentation and dehumanization of modern humanity through an aesthetic reconstruction of reality—an explicitly political extension of the Kantian philosophy. While Lukács is held to have rejected as unrealistic the aesthetic solutions offered by Schiller and Kant, and to have retained the Marxist conviction that the proletariat was the genuine bearer of cultural responsibility and potential for progressive political change, his theory of revolution depends as much upon the social philosophy of Max Weber as upon that of Marx. Where Marx was presumed to have held that the stimulus to proletarian revolution would occur almost automatically, in a deterministic fashion (an ascription to Marx, which is intensely debatable), Lukács is said to have objected on the basis of Weber, that the modern fragmentation of reason, itself, could obstruct and deactivate any revolutionary project on the part of the working class. What Weber postulated as the basic characteristics of industrial rationalization—mechanical repetitiveness, standardization, and the quantification and computation of highly simplified sets of actions in order to facilitate the goals of administration and control—were considered to debilitate the working class through a fragmentation, reification, or *Verdinglichung* of both its thought and activity. In order for the proletariat to actually assume its role as agent of a revolutionary praxis according to Lukács, it needed to develop *a new form of reason*—a retotalizing mentality that could synthesize, remediate, and transcend the isolated elements found in the given practical and theoretical spheres. As István Mészáros has noted in *Lukács' Concept of Dialectic*, Lukács was thus concerned with the inherently *problematic status of education* under capitalism, in which general educational levels are lowered to the absolute minimum required by the nakedly operationalist industrial rationality of capitalism.

I have reviewed Lukács on *Verdinglichung* and "praxis" here in order to stress the extent to which these ideas have furnished Marcuse with theoretical foundations for his own work. Many similarities are readily apparent from the presentation, thus far, of Marcuse's middle-period works. I shall recall in particular Marcuse's supportive reference to Lukács's polemic against the social implications of Engels's *Dialectics of Nature* in his 1930 essay, "On the Problem of the Dialectic" (PD, 24), and Marcuse's concomitant elaboration there of a "dialectic of praxis" (PD, 36), as a theory of conscious human conduct, directed against phenomena of reification and *Verdinglichung*. The particulars of the relationship of education to the practical supersession of

Verdinglichung that ultimately emerge for Marcuse, however, increasingly separate his thought from that of Lukács. Mészáros, for example, notes that Lukács specifically rejected the Schillerian notion of the aesthetic education of humanity as this is conceived as a separate social philosophical program designed as an antidote to the utilitarian rationality of capitalism. Marcuse, on the other hand, while criticizing Herder's romantic, educational philosophical poetization of the soul as an affirmative (that is, nonthreatening) cultural alternative to the political economic status quo in "The Affirmative Character of Culture" (AC), nonetheless exempted Schiller's call for the aesthetic education of humanity from the full impact of this criticism. Likewise, as I have indicated in the discussion of *Eros and Civilization*, Marcuse finds much political potential in the Schillerian concept of aesthetic education: "The idealistic and aesthetic sublimations which prevail in Schiller's work do not vitiate its radical implications" (EC, 192).

Mészáros emphasizes the fact that Lukács believed that aesthetic education, under capitalism, inevitably aimed at producing its desired cultural goals *in place* of the required *social* changes, rather than through them. Lukács, thus, held the emancipatory effects of aesthetic education to be predicated upon the actualization of a socialist society. Nevertheless, Lukács stressed the importance of the relationship of *education* to *reification*. According to Lukács learning emerges through the educational dynamic, originally outlined by Hegel, involving a series of necessary fragmentations and reintegrations of historically rooted information—activities which, in end-effect, also transform the learner. While Lukács's approach diverges from that of Marcuse in several places, they both emphasize the preeminent *role of theory* in the revolutionary project.

Marcuse, more than Lukács, thought that education had to be directed not against capitalism, as such, but against the *reification of reason*, that is, against *Verdinglichung*. His 1936 essay on "The Concept of Essence" (CE) emphasizes the liberating sociopolitical effects of a philosophical knowledge of the human essence, in both its distress and potential. In so doing this essay assimilates Plato's philosophy of knowledge and learning to the ostensibly materialist orientation of the newly emergent critical theory:

> Seeking the unity, universality and *permanence* of Being, and "remembering" the essence are motivated by the critical consciousness of "bad" facticity, of unrealized potentialities. (CE, 46, emphasis added)

Likewise in *One-Dimensional Man*: ". . . the concrete ground for refusal must still exist for reification is an illusion" (OD, 256). Lukács believed that precisely through the almost total reduction of the worker to an "object" within the production process, *the worker might recognize himself as this object*, that is, as an atomized and alienated being. This initial self-consciousness of alienation was thought to indicate in a minimal sense, that existence as an "object" is a problem for *human* beings. It was also believed to denote a need and interest on the part of the working class in dissolving the objective rigidity of social relationships. The reified empirical consciousness of workers could thus at times even be a spur to historical inquiry and serve as a stimulus to theoretical and practical struggle against this alienation. In this manner, phenomena of *Verdinglichung* could themselves occasion the emergence of the philosophy of praxis that Lukács sought.

Marcuse initially agreed with Lukács that existence as an "object" could be recognized as a problem by human beings, and that reification could also serve as a starting point for real change:

> In suffering the most extreme form of reification man triumphs over reification. (AC, 116)

> *Im äußersten Erleiden der Verdinglichung triumphiert der Mensch über die Verdinglichung.* (ACg, 84)

Although Marcuse originally acknowledged, in the manner of Lukács, that reification could only be broken by the practical and theoretical activities of those who labor, this particular view would subsequently be abandoned in *One-Dimensional Man*, the essay "Socialist Humanism?" and elsewhere. In *Reason and Revolution*, *Soviet Marxism*, and *Eros and Civilization* Marcuse would interpret the revolutionary political potential of philosophy as stemming from aesthetic theory and from those who best understood it. He thus came to relate a liberating concept of education not to a philosophy of labor (as in the classical Marxist conception, as well as in that of Lukács), but to a philosophy of imagination, play, and art. Art was considered educative and emancipatory insofar as it was capable of recalling the species essence of the human race from the philosophical oblivion of *Verdinglichung*.

By now it has become evident that the aesthetic dimension became perhaps the major *philosophical* resource for the middle-period Marcuse, much as it also functions as a central interest in the systems of Heidegger,

Dilthey, Nietzsche, Schiller, Schopenhauer, and Kant. In this tradition, the philosophy of art has been characteristically regarded as more fundamental and important than even *social* philosophy in matters of politics and culture. Marcuse's reformulation of the concept of the aesthetic moved away from its association primarily with works of beauty and art to what is believed to be its more primordial significance as a study of the sensuous. It was also seen as *a movement* toward earthly gratification. This is not merely an updated treatment of the philosophy of art since Schiller and Kant, but more importantly an aesthetic-educational formulation of a quasi-Marxist approach to the problem of alienation. By emphasizing the activist and political role of the aesthetic, Marcuse not only moves from economic to *critical* theory in *Reason and Revolution* (RR, 287); he also accomplishes a significant transformation and reduction of social theory to aesthetic theory. Like Schiller (and in contradistinction to Marx), Marcuse sees aesthetics as the key to philosophy and politics, and aesthetic education as the key to philosophical and political education. It is my contention that it is his treatment of alienation as *Verdinglichung* that makes this reduction possible.

Thus, for example, it has been widely noted that Marcuse opposed Freud's conception of psychoanalysis as a science and hence as part of the other emerging sciences of society. As I have already shown, Marcuse opted instead to elaborate upon a "hidden trend" in the philosophy of psychoanalysis, stressing the "mythological-artistic" (EC, 167) significance of the images of Orpheus and Narcissus, as well as the importance of a phylogenetic memory of the archaic heritage of the human species. Marcuse does not relate psychoanalysis to educational theory in the manner of the progressivist stress on the pedagogical importance of early childhood experiences, that is, developmental stages of youth, or in the interpersonal dynamics of family and social life. Unlike Wilhelm Reich, neither does he deal specifically with problems of schooling and adolescent sexuality. Marcuse's concern remains at the metapsychological level, and is opposed in principle to the practice of psychoanalysis as adjustment therapy (EC, 245–46). Instead, Marcuse, *relates psychoanalysis to educational theory by integrating it within the philosophy of mind and learning and art since Plato and Kant, stressing especially the educative value of reminiscence and imagination.* Marcuse's preface to the 1955 edition of *Eros and Civilization* also makes it clear that he explicitly intends to employ psychological categories as political categories (EC, xxvii). The former categories were to be rethought, in "critical" rather than therapeutic ways to be sure, but political and sociological effects were still to be educed from psychological and educational principles.

Marcuse's chapter on "The Aesthetic Dimension" in *Eros and Civilization* reworked traditional aesthetic notions in a similar manner: radical political implications were drawn from Schiller's aesthetic educational vision. *Eros and Civilization's* chapter on aesthetic philosophy may be said to indicate a shift in Marcuse's thinking, within the development of the book, away from "the psychoanalytical dimension" to the dimension of the aesthetic. Presaging his explicitly aesthetic-political interests in "Art and the One-Dimensional Society" (1967), *An Essay on Liberation* (1969), *Counterrevolution and Revolt* (1972), and *The Aesthetic Dimension, Toward a Critique of Marxist Aesthetics* (1977), Marcuse's preface to the 1955 edition of *Eros and Civilization* indicated the importance the aesthetic would assume in the direction of his subsequent writings:

> I have tried to reformulate certain basic questions and to follow them in a direction not yet fully explored. I am aware of the tentative character of this inquiry and hope to discuss some of the problems, *especially those of an aesthetic theory*, more adequately in the near future. (EC, xxviii, emphasis added)

Marcuse's aesthetic ontology stands not only in opposition to the affirmative tradition in culture, but also in opposition to the historical materialist philosophy of art (as this has been elucidated by George Plekhanov, Mikhail Lifschitz, Bertolt Brecht et al.). It thus also presents a qualitatively different kind of social criticism than that of classical Marxism. Beginning with *Eros and Civilization*, a dialectic of life and death supplants a dialectic of capital and labor, and aesthetic theory is said to make a more compelling argument for human liberation than economic analysis. The *aesthetic dimension* of experience is thought to define the emancipatory quality required by any future type of nonalienating social organization. Thus, Marcuse's emerging philosophy of political protest presents a different kind of critique and praxis than that represented by the class-struggle orientation of the classical Marxist parties. By seeing "art as the architecture of a free society," as he discussed in "Art in the One-Dimensional Society" (AO, 66), and hypothesizing that "artistic Form asserts itself and negates the negation" (AO, 64), Marcuse has embarked upon his "third path" to what he believes will be social and philosophical liberation. Art, for Marcuse, is not merely the organon by which he ultimately understands alienation and reification, but (by defining these phenomena in terms of *Verdinglichung*) aesthetic education actually represents the key force in their elimination. Marcuse is articulating an aesthetically oriented philosophy of "praxis," which, despite evident militance, nonetheless diverges markedly from that of Marx, Engels, Lenin, and the later Lukács. Marcuse's *Five Lectures—Psychoanalysis, Politics, Utopia* (FL) explicitly attempted a "new definition of socialism" (FL, 62) which would pivot upon the "aesthetic-erotic" (FL, 68) negation of repression and alienation:

> I believe that even Marx was still too tied to the notion of the continuum of progress, that even his idea of socialism may not yet represent, or no longer represent, the determinate negation of capitalism it was supposed to. (FL, 62)

> Today we must try to discuss and define—without any inhibitions, even when it may seem ridiculous—the *qualitative difference* between socialist society as a free society and the existing society. And it is precisely here that, if we are looking for a concept that can perhaps indicate the qualitative difference in socialist society, the *aesthetic-erotic dimension* comes to mind almost spontaneously at least to me. Here the notion "aesthetic" is taken in its original sense, namely as the form of sensitivity of the senses and as the form of the concrete world of human life. Taken in this way, the notion projects the convergence of technology and art and the convergence of work and play. It is no accident that the work of Fourier is becoming topical again among the avant-garde left-wing intelligentsia. As Marx and Engels themselves acknowledged, Fourier was the only one to have made clear this qualitative difference between free and unfree society. And he did not shrink back in fear, as Marx still did, from speaking of a possible society in which work becomes play, a society in which even socially necessary labor can be organized in harmony with the liberated, genuine needs of men. (FL, 68 emphasis added)

As early as 1928 Marcuse had called for "militant action": *die radikale Tat* (PHg, 47, 48). Activity, insofar as it is described as "radical," is thought to be emergent out of the core of human existence and directed toward altering human existence. In *Eros and Civilization*, on the other hand, Marcuse's particular concept of militance is elaborated specifically in terms of an *aesthetic* notion from Alfred North Whitehead: the Great Refusal.

In many ways the Great Refusal may be taken to summarize, combine, and symbolize Marcuse's activist approach to a protest politics of art and education. It represents an educational third way—between the two polar tendencies characterized on the one hand by strictly contemplative aestheticism, high culture, and the romantic poetization of the soul (sustained by social anxiety and repressive sublimation), and on the other hand, by the overwhelmingly practical interests of Enlightenment materialism, Lockean sensualism, or the classical Marxist conception of culture and education. The Great Refusal essentially indicates an educational philosophical response to conditions of alienation, stressing the ostensibly disalienating and emancipatory effects of *an education to art and through art*. It is a theory of education against reification (*Verdinglichung*) and of the *aesthetic ground for liberatory praxis*.

The Great Refusal and *Lebensphilosophie*

Marcuse introduces the notion of the Great Refusal in *Eros and Civilization* (at EC, 149). In his estimation, *art*, today, is *educative* precisely because it expresses the Great Refusal to accept the empirical world as given. In this regard he invokes a citation from Whitehead's 1926 volume, *Science and the Modern World:*

> The truth that some proposition respecting an actual occasion is untrue may express the vital truth as to the aesthetic achievement. It expresses the "great refusal" which is its primary characteristic. (Whitehead at EC, 149)

Marcuse considers the aesthetic imagination to be that particular human resource that can disclose those truths about the human past and human potential that are "absent" within the actual organization of society. Given the empirical realities of alienation, that is, repression, anxiety, toil, and the anesthetization of consciousness, Marcuse believes that the "realistic context" (EC, 150) of contemporary philosophy and political theory relegates them to failure. In his estimation, only art can break this alienating context of realism with impunity. The

> . . . Great Refusal is the protest against unnecessary repression, the struggle for the ultimate form of freedom—"to live without anxiety." But this idea could be formulated without punishment only in the language of art. In the more realistic context of political

theory and even philosophy, it was almost universally defamed as utopia. (EC, 149–50)

Marcuse, thus, turns to the aesthetic dimension for epistemological, emotional, and sociopolitical insight. His 1969 volume, *An Essay on Liberation*, perhaps more than any before it, revolves around an effort to derive a philosophy of praxis from a philosophy of art and a philosophy of education. The Great Refusal is predicated upon an aesthetic ontology.

Chapter 2 of *An Essay on Liberation* is titled "The New Sensibility." It elucidates Marcuse's aesthetic ontological interpretation of the philosophy of "life" and the "biologic" foundations of emancipation in human nature. The new sensibility is said to represent a liberating receptivity and a feel for "the demands of the life instincts" (EL, 19) in the manner of Nietzsche's *gaya scienza* (ibid.). Humanity needs to experience pleasure, joy, and gratification, in good conscience and without shame, where the laws of beauty become life-enhancing laws of reason (EL, 21, 27). The demands of the "life instincts" are thus held to become an organic or biologic foundation for morality and solidarity (philosophy and politics) among human beings (EL, 10). Marcuse very significantly claims that revolutionary theory and conduct

> . . . must reach into a dimension of the human existence *hardly considered in Marxian theory*—the "biological" dimension in which the vital, imperative needs and satisfactions of men assert themselves. (EL, 16-17, emphasis added)

It is at this very point that art and education may assume their emancipatory function. Because the language of reification is held to forget the human core of experience and knowledge, while the language of art preserves the memory of this fundamental substratum, Marcuse rejects political economic discussion as practiced by classical Marxist sociology in favor of his reformulated, and ostensibly more compelling, human-centered, and anthropological theory of art and education. The "new sensibility" thus updates the "real humanism" of "The Foundation of Historical Materialism" (HM) and Marcuse's other early essays of 1928–33. Marcuse explicitly acknowledges this anthropomorphist tendency in his subsequent book, *Counterrevolution and Revolt* (CR):

> Aesthetics of liberation, beauty as a "form" of freedom: it looks as if Marx has shied away from this anthropomorphist, idealistic con-

ception. Or is this apparently idealistic notion rather the *enlargement
of the materialistic base?* (CR, 66)

Such a (materialistically construed) philosophical anthropology and philosophy of "life" derives its ethical and political judgments, as well as its
judgments of truth value, from the sensuous human core that is postulated
as the center of experience. Such judgments are, thus, thought to emerge
from the ". . . 'disposition' of the organism, perhaps rooted in the erotic
drive to counter aggressiveness, to create and preserve 'ever greater unities'
of life" (EL, 10). The Great Refusal is thus thought to have its origins in a
new form of sensuousness, a new "aesthetic sensibility" (EL, 31), which can
lead the individual to shape his or her own social needs in accordance with
the liberated instincts of life, rather than as the perpetuation and extension
of the commodity form (EL, 17).

Marcuse explicitly draws on *Lebensphilosophical* themes in several of his
early works (GWg, PH, and HOg, which have already been examined). He
is intellectually attracted to *Lebensphilosophie* because it represents a philosophy
of lived human existence and a dynamic theory of human sensuousness and
instinct. It would seem that *Lebensphilosophie*, as an essentially life-centered
approach to an understanding of humanity and the world, also functions as
the foundation of Marcuse's 1969 "protest" philosophy by offering its
orientation to "life" as an alternative to the philosophy of sheer "reason"
that was thought to predominate in certain interpretations of the Hegelian
tradition in philosophy and education. It also serves as a replacement for
the utilitarianism and instrumentalism that motivated much scientific and
efficiency reform in schools and society in early twentieth-century Europe.
Lebensphilosophie, thus, related to that which was "alive" rather than to that
which was merely "rational" or "pragmatic" in order to understand human
history and culture. It rejected as lifeless and dull the classical bourgeois
materialism of the Enlightenment and the historical materialism of the
classical socialist sort. It presented itself as a vigorous philosophical hybrid,
superior to any stiff, one-sided theory of matter or mind, combining a
sensuous imaginative aesthetic sensibility and a critical consciousness.
Lebensphilosophie also emphasized critique of fixed forms and static ideas.
Otto Friedrich Bollnow's rather definitive work on *Lebensphilosophie* has the
following to say about its main theoretical characteristics:

> The foremost impulse of *Lebensphilosophie* . . . is directed against the
> coercion of static forms, because these appear to be obstructions to

the free unfolding of Life . . . and thus the typical problem for *Lebensphilosophie* develops: to inquire as to the function of these objective creations for human life. . . . The fixed forms of these creations are at every juncture traced back to Life, from which they emerged and with regard to which they have a certain function to perform. In order to define these relationships for our purposes, we speak of an *anthropological reduction.*[1]

Lebensphilosophie thus represents a protest philosophy and a cultural critique rooted in theory of the human being, as such. According to Bollnow, Nietzsche and Dilthey have been its leading representatives.

After Hitler's rise to power, Marcuse acknowledged that *Lebensphilosophie* became a part of the "heroic-folkish" (LT, 3) fascist ideology, but he did not consider that this discredited *Lebensphilosophie* as such: "This philosophy of life resembles Dilthey's *Lebensphilosophie* in name only and took from Nietzsche only odds and ends . . ." (LT, 5). In 1931 he was also quite critical, but supported Dilthey's approach nonetheless:

> Under the label of "*Lebensphilosophie*" a nonsensical amalgam of every possible philosophical and pseudophilosophical tendency, from Nietzsche and Bergson to Keyserling and Klages is emerging. We, however, understand as *Lebens*-philosophical only those theoretical investigations that acknowledge the Being of human life as belonging to the fundamental analysis of philosophy and which have researched this. As the single representative of this philosophy we refer to Wilhelm Dilthey. (GWg, 354)

Speaking of Dilthey in terms of educational philosophy, Bollnow says that Dilthey's theory of the *Geisteswissenschaften* "is not simply a consequence of *Lebensphilosophie*, but rather a contribution to the perfection and extension of it."[2]

> Just as the rational-constructive tendency in philosophy aligns itself generally with natural scientific thought, so too there is an inner relationship between *Lebensphilosophie* and the *Geisteswissenschaften*. In the earliest stages of its development, the same irrationalist currents that gave rise to *Sturm und Drang* and Romanticism are similarly influential in the development of *Lebensphilosophie* and the *Geisteswissenschaften*. In the second stage of this process, during the

last third of the 19th century, the methodological self-reflection of the humanities occurred simultaneously . . . with the emergence of *Lebensphilosophie* in its own right via Nietzsche and Dilthey. Dilthey especially welded both tendencies together in an indissoluble unity.[3]

Marxism, in its classical expressions, displayed a categorical scorn for *Lebens-philosophie*. Marcuse, nonetheless, broke with this tradition seeing it as a corrective to alienation, especially against *Verdinglichung*.[4] Writing about Dilthey in his 1928 "Contributions to a Phenomenology of Historical Materialism" (PH), Marcuse highlights the exceptional value to be found in the *Geisteswissenschaften*'s conception of historical knowledge, which is worth recalling here:

> The object of knowledge of the knower does not in this case stand "over against" him as a different entity "foreign" to him (as in the case with knowledge of physical objects), but "lives with him. . . ." (PH, 4)

Historical knowledge and historical human existence are understood as related in "a living unity" (PH, 5). The theory of *Verdinglichung* is consequently relevant to educational philosophical concerns precisely because it speaks to the problem of how the subject matter of life is to become thematic in scholarly activities. Scholarship is henceforth inseparably linked to the perspective of the artist and to the rationality of art, which are held to be rooted in the human dialectics of life and death, self-preservation and self-destruction, and suffering and joy. This rationality is considered to be the realm of concrete knowledge, and it is thought to find its home in the *Geisteswissenschaften*. Science and learning are thought to remain entirely trivial unless related essentially to a *critical aesthetic perspective*. Likewise, all education is thought to be at best partial and incomplete if it is void of reference to what is taken to be the conflicted and sensuous human core of knowledge.

Verdinglichung as the basis of Marcuse's concept of the dilemma of education in the context of alienation prepares the way to a *primarily aesthetic* conception of "revolutionary" practice. According to Marcuse, the forces that organize the social relations of production in contemporary society are *not* those classically designated by Marx as the conflicting material interests of wage-labor and capital, but the conflicting principles of pleasure and performance. Upon this basis, Marcuse argues for the substitution of a human-centered aesthetic rationality as the principle of social and cultural reorganization in place of those dehumanized forms of reason that have succumbed in his estimation to a fetishism of objects, things, and scientific laws.

Thus Marcuse ultimately counterposes the negative, critical potential of the humanities and a liberal education, in the traditional sense, against the educational "cults" of efficiency, standardization, fragmentation, and specialization that function to replicate the given social division of labor and reinforce social control. The latter processes are in fact regarded as anti-educational, as examples of a schooled stupifaction, as he stated in "Repressive Tolerance" (RT, 83) and uncritical enculturation to the reified norms of the convergent systems of conventional wisdom and conformist conduct in the United States and in the former USSR. Marcuse additionally opposes education to guilt (via sexual asceticism and repression) and passivity (via tolerance for boredom and administrative manipulation). In the tradition of Plato's *Republic*, he stresses the interventionist capacities of art and education, as well as the philosophical and political leadership obligation of those who have emerged from the cave of *Verdinglichung*. Hence, his criticism and rejection of the aestheticism, academicism, and intellectualism of higher culture in its affirmative mode. There the soul is so highly poeticized that it "appears to escape reification" (AC, 109), but "affirmative culture uses the soul as a protest against reification, only to succumb to it in the end" (AC, 108). Thus, the middle-period Marcuse advocates human familiarity not with "art as art," but with art as the radical domain of truth, the sensuous ground for judgment in ethical, epistemological, and political matters. *Praxis* emerges *from art*. Both are *of life*, and intended *for life's enhancement*. Aesthetic education (rather than an education to classical forms of communist consciousness and conduct) makes possible the "radical," human-based reconstruction of reality. Education to art and through art (rather than to the dialectics of history and matter) engenders the "*aesthetic ethos* of socialism" (EL, 48, emphasis added) and the *aesthetic theory* that Marcuse feels furnished the *telos* for society as an *aesthetic life world* (EL, 45).

Education and Social Change

For Marcuse art is always a demand for authentic freedom. It offers a vision of liberation over against the cultural logic of corporate capitalism. Thus, his aesthetic thought is permeated with a multifaceted concern for educational issues and radical action for our political future.

In one important document educational philosophy and politics are explicitly linked and become Marcuse's *primary* theme. In this hitherto unpublished manuscript theoretical learning is coupled essentially to *practical efforts at cultural transformation*. Relatively unknown even today "Education and Social Change" (ES) is a set of notes for a 1968 presentation at Brooklyn College.[5] The key ideas in this talk foreshadow Marcuse's activist approach to the practice of education in *An Essay on Liberation*. His immense respect for theoretical education and for its power to enhance human life is reflected in the manuscript's central tenet: the belief that our future and our freedom hinge on an expanded cultural emphasis on general education. While he has elsewhere pointed to the philosophies of Kant and Schiller with regard to the critical rationality of art in higher education, in this speech he highlights a new estimate that *general education* is really "a very recent concept" (ES, 1).

Marcuse's speech does not elaborate, but much effort toward general education was made in the United States during the 1940s, primarily after World War II. This was rooted in the great books movement and in the work of Robert M. Hutchins, chancellor of the University of Chicago, as well as in the Harvard University Committee Report on the Objective of General Education in a Free Society (1945). In this context, general education was a conservative cold war phenomenon hostile to social criticism and directed against progressive reform efforts in education. Marcuse had in 1964 already commented on the tendency of this version of general education to flatten out and surrender the critical potential of higher learning to single-dimensionality in culture (OD, 64–65).

In "Education and Social Change" Marcuse likewise confronts the idealized theory of general education with its conservative social reality but emancipatory potential. "*General* education, . . ." he points out, is "education previously restricted to the ruling classes. . . ." but education is "*not* general even today" (ES,1). Access to general education, he says, remains confined to the privileged few and is an upper-class phenomenon, not only because it is an expression of underlying structures of social inequality, but because it contains a potentially dangerous critical dimension. General education tends to be socially and institutionally restricted, he emphasizes, because of "the *subversive* element. . . ." in this education. Theoretical education involves ". . . knowledge, intelligence, reason as catalysts of social change—projection of the possibilities of a 'better' order; violation of socially useful taboos, illusions" (ibid.). Opposition to this general theoretical education arises "from below *and* from above" (ES, 2) due to a deeply seated anti-intellectualism in

U.S. history and culture. Still, Marcuse stresses the fact that reform efforts toward general education are gaining momentum

> on a very *material basis*: the need of industrial society to increase the supply of skilled workers and employees, especially the need for scientists, technicians, etc. for the efficient development of the productive forces and their apparatus and, more recently, the need for psychologists and sociologists for analyzing and projecting and stimulating economic and political demand. (Ibid.)

In the intervening years since Marcuse addressed the material forces impelling U.S. education toward a new emphasis on the general and the theoretical, the world has witnessed the full-fledged coming of the information age, the ascendancy of electronic technologies for information processing, the Internet, and more. Still, Marcuse stresses something in this essay that we tend to gloss over today, that is, that the social dynamics at work here have a dialectical character (and this quite apart from the aesthetic dimension). The already given tendencies of social change mandate that education must permit (for some) unrestricted access to high-quality knowledge in the humanities, natural sciences, and social sciences in order to be competitive in the global economic market and to guide the political cultures of nations in a sophisticated manner. Yet institutions of higher education must also protect this information-based global society against radical change. Marcuse's 1968 criticisms retain a contemporary relevance given the culture wars of the mid-1980s involving Allan Bloom, William Bennett, and Lynne Cheney. In the late 1990s the conservative authors Alan Charles Kors and Harvey A. Silverglate[6] centrally targeted Marcuse. All of these represent attempts to reinsinuate an elitist, Europocentric program for the liberal arts and American general education against the critical impulses *within* it toward radical perspectives on the arts, multiculturalism, social history, critical social theory, critical thinking, service learning, civic literacy, and civic action.

Marcuse emphasizes the fact that the internal political factor within general education becomes emancipatory when reason is permitted to pursue the real possibilities embedded within the established cultures that can enhance and protect human life and human freedom. The problem is that institutional power tends to constrain reason to an affirmative, apologetic role that legitimates the continued denial of these possibilities. In Marcuse's estimation, what the future needs most is higher education in the liberal arts and sciences *with critical purpose* that can politically transcend the established culture:

To create the subjective conditions for a free society [it is] no longer sufficient to educate *individuals* to perform more or less happily the functions they are supposed to perform *in this* society or extend "vocational" education to the "masses." Rather . . . [we must] educate men and women who are incapable of tolerating what is going on, who have really learned what *is* going on, has always been going on, and why, and who are educated to resist and to fight for a new way of life. (ES, 5)

Critical education, for Marcuse, is education that by its own inner dynamic *"leads beyond the classroom* . . . and may define action and behavior patterns *incompatible* with those of the Establishment" (ES, 6).

The *voice of the Establishment* is heard day and night over the media of mass communication—program as well as commercials, information as well as advertisement—and it is heard through the machine of each of the two parties.

The voice of the *radical* opposition is also heard:—sometimes, and through no machine. It has no promising jobs to give, *no money* to buy adherents and friends. Within this structure of basic inequality the radical opposition can be tolerated *up to the point* where it *tries to break through* the limits of its weakness, through the illusion of democracy, and then it meets the reality of democracy, as the police, the National Guard, the courts. Institutionalized violence . . . confronts any action by the opposition which transcends the limits set by, and enforced by established Law and Order. (ES, 9–10)

Marcuse's educational philosophy demands the abolition of domination and exploitation, and emphasizes that if democracy means the institutionalization of freedom and equality, democracy remains to be achieved. Therefore, education must become politically engaged and activist. Students and teachers must "become partisan against oppression, moronization, brutalization" (ES,14). There needs to be a key unity in education of critical thought and radical action; the need for the movements of change must be made evident in systems of schooling "preparing the ground for a better, more humane society" (ES, 11). Critical educators and students need to continue to take risks and struggle to infuse the curriculum with analysis of the "critical, radical movements and theories in history, literature, philosophy" (ES, 13).

Marcuse wanted to put critical pedagogy into practice in ways that can actually make schooling a productive, emancipatory, and transformative experience for students and for college teachers. He was attempting to discern just exactly what makes pedagogy *critical*.

Marcuse did not address the community college movement in the United States, but this sector of higher education has expanded greatly under the material imperatives he outlined in "Education and Social Change." During the 1950s and 1960s, many of the nation's locally run vocational and technical postsecondary institutions were upgraded as comprehensive community colleges. Philosophically, the curriculum was widened to offer the full range of liberal arts and sciences, as well as the traditional vocational-technical areas of training. Programs were designed to enable students to transfer to four-year liberal arts and science colleges (including into engineering curricula) in accordance with their needs, abilities, and interests. This improvement was part of a generalized philosophical approach stressing the expansion of educational opportunity to those who otherwise would have found restricted access to higher education. Open admissions policies have usually been an integral part of this philosophy, and the comprehensive community college also offers an important "second chance" to a diverse community of students with all degrees of academic ability and various cultural backgrounds. For thousands upon thousands of students the community college provides the only opportunity to encounter what Marcuse saw as the emancipatory liberal arts dimension of higher education.

The extension of opportunity through the community colleges of the United States had its objective basis in the economic and political needs of corporate capitalism. Increasingly these colleges are becoming a global model for short-cycle, inexpensive higher education reform, especially in the OECD (Organization for Economic Cooperation and Development) countries. Their perceived educational advantages stem from their work force-related technological flexibility and from their student-success approach to the core themes of general education.

From Marcuse's point of view, this could also mean that community college students worldwide may join their traditional counterparts to become an ever more potent social and political force. A critical self-appreciation of their social position—and that of their instructors—may sensitize them to the real need to break through the prevailing culture of conformity and accommodation and to pursue what they may discover as the real prospects for progressive social change that critical pedagogy can disclose.

Of course, the false promises of community colleges in the United States have been discussed over the past decades by such critical educationists as Fred Pincus, Jerome Karabel, Kevin Dougherty, L. Steven Zwerling, Burton Clark, and most recently by Penelope E. Harideen.[7] They have shown that the publicly stated functions (enhanced opportunity, mobility, personal growth, and advancement) tend to be overshadowed by the community college's unstated functions (screening, tracking, and lowering student expectations). They argue that the hidden curriculum has a social control function that primarily assists the societal process of capital accumulation. The schools maintain illusions of equal opportunity and unimpeded mobility even while they program students for differential roles in an unequal society: sorting, selecting, and channeling them in ways that preserve the current class system. In addition, they (at times sooner, at times later) actively convince or passively discourage certain types of students to opt out of post-secondary education altogether. By treating the social system(s), and sub-systems, of domination and oppression as if they were generally valid and fair, the community colleges legitimate and stabilize these systems of unjust power relations in the economy, culture, and society. Again, this is consistent with Marcuse's analysis in *One-Dimensional Man*. The overall result is the production of a labor force that tends to accept wage-labor and capitalism as normal, and whose individual members will thus tend to subjectively position themselves in ways that replicate the unequal social division of labor and wealth.

The scholarship of Pincus, Karabel, Dougherty, Zwerling, Clark, Samuel Bowles, and Herbert Gintis,[8] like that of Marcuse and Paulo Freire, presents a significant challenge to those of us working within the nation's system of mass higher education, who believe in the progressive nature of our work here, stand in solidarity with our students, and together with them endeavor toward mutual empowerment and social transformation. Today even the corporate liberal point of view acknowledges that "*Community* is a climate to be created, not a region to be served," and has recommended community-building as the key future task of the community colleges.[9] Marcuse might have asked whether this vision for the future of higher education could be extended in a radical manner toward authentically democratic cultural transformation. In fact, in a speech to students at Berkeley in 1975 Marcuse stressed just this sort of community action *outside* the university. "'Community work' based on grass roots discontent—[is] easily ridiculed by the super-radicals as 'social work' for the Establishment. But . . . in the present situation of monopoly capitalism, what was formerly harmless becomes increasingly intolerable for the power structure; the space for concessions is increasingly narrow!" as stated in "Berkeley, Oct. 18 '75" (BK, 11).

Many progressive and reform-minded college teachers are today developing initiatives with definite emancipatory power along the lines of service learning, multicultural education, critical thinking, civic literacy, and civic action. I shall return to these projects toward a critical pedagogy in higher education at the conclusion of this study. Herbert Marcuse, however, unexpectedly recoiled from his own political activism and from the counterrevolutionary culture warriors of his day, withdrawing in the end from overt political praxis. We need now to follow his thinking about education and art as phenomena entailing, in themselves, an essential alienation.

CHAPTER NINE

—᷒ᴡᴡ᷒—

Art *as* Alienation:
Marcuse's "Turn" and Return

With the 1977 German publication of *Die Permanenz der Kunst: Wider eine bestimmte Marxistische Ästhetik* (translated in 1978 as *The Aesthetic Dimension, Toward a Critique of Marxist Aesthetics* [AD]) there is a "turn" in Marcuse's theorizing, almost a reversal. Art acting as a force *against* alienation is supplanted by a notion of the need for art as alienation. Indeed, it will be argued here that "art *as alienation*" becomes the leading concept of Marcuse's late works. A Marcuse profile emerges from *The Aesthetic Dimension* (and from the book that immediately preceded it, *Counterrevolution and Revolt*) that underscores the primacy of the aesthetic *form* and aesthetic autonomy. They favorably reevaluate such notions as "art as art" and the "liberating" potential of mental labor *separated from* manual labor. In so doing, they return to certain of the oldest elements of the aesthetic tradition. These were formerly castigated as dangerously apologetic, debilitating, and "affirmative," but are now reevaluated with an emphasis on their ostensibly emancipatory cultural potential. The *interventionist* and *productive capacities* of art and aesthetic education, earlier thought to be the aspects of the aesthetic domain most in need of cultivation, now recede in importance as philosophical interest is shifted from praxis to the *formal qualities* of the once disclaimed art object, itself. Marcuse's aesthetic theory thus converts quite decisively from the militant activist positions outlined in *Eros and Civilization* and *An Essay on Liberation* to an explicit reassertion of certain of the most contemplative values and assumptions of classical European aesthetics.

The Aesthetic Dimension rehabilitates precisely this concept of *form* in art, stressing especially the autonomy and protest of highly sublimated works. It also reemphasizes what is considered to be the universally human basis of the individual and subjective dimensions of aesthetic experience (above class considerations), as well as the now decisive quality of art *as* alienation:

> the autonomy of art asserts itself in extreme form—as uncompromising estrangement. To both the integrated consciousness and also to reified Marxist aesthetics, the estranged works may well appear as elitist or as symptoms of decadence. But they are nevertheless authentic forms of contradictions, indicting the totality of society. . . . (AD, 30–31)

This reemphasis on aesthetic form and on the autonomy and estrangement of the work of art vis-à-vis the given social relations is not, however, strictly speaking, a simple turnabout in Marcuse's thinking; it is rather a return to philosophical tendencies somewhat overshadowed by the apparent militance of Marcuse's middle period work, but present there nonetheless (e.g., in *One-Dimensional Man*, [OD, 58–64]), and overt and unmistakable also in his earliest theoretical effort. As I have endeavored to point out earlier, *The German Artist Novel* treated the issue of art as alienation as a key concern: "To the artist the collectivist social order of socialism, is, in itself, every bit as alienating and indifferent as is that of the capitalist bourgeoisie" (KRg, 195). I argue that the interpenetration, reciprocity, and unity in Marcuse's "contradictory" logic on these matters reveals a symmetry and doubled structural framework, rather than sheer disjunction, in his overall intellectual effort with regard to art, alienation, and the humanities. Marcuse's beginning (*The German Artist Novel*) and his end (*The Aesthetic Dimension*) are the complementary obverse to his middle-period *art-against-alienation* thesis.

In an interview a few years before his death Marcuse's late aesthetic theory is criticized by Tilman Spengler as devolving to a "limited [*reduzierter*] concept of art, a *literary* concept of art," which appeared in *Theory and Politics: A Discussion with Herbert Marcuse, Jürgen Habermas, Heinz Lubasz and Tilman Spengler* (TPg, 49; TP, 146, emphasis added). Whereas Marcuse's famous essay "The Affirmative Character of Culture" (AC) had formerly stressed the tranquilizing and accommodating qualities that have historically defused the critical potential of high art, Marcuse now openly acknowledges a change with regard to this question: "If I were to write the essay from the 1930s today, I would modify the affirmative character of art and emphasize more its critical-communicative character" (TP, 143). Marcuse is here reiterating one of the most basic points of *The Aesthetic Dimension* and *Counterrevolution and Revolt* (CR): even "affirmative" art always has critical potential.

Counterrevolution and Revolt's third chapter reconsiders the relationship of "Art and Revolution," and anticipates *The Aesthetic Dimension* in several ways. The basic objective of that chapter is to reassess the relationship of "bourgeois culture" to the admittedly radical and progressive but decidedly less formal art of the "cultural revolution." It is here that Marcuse swings from his usual association with the revolutionary perspective on culture (established first in "The AffirmativeCharacter of Culture," then in *An Essay on Liberation* [EL]) to a favorable reappraisal of the *validity* of the culture of the bourgeois era. It is here, also, that Marcuse begins to speak forcefully of art as a "second alienation" (CR, 97), underscoring *this* alienation as emancipatory rather than oppressive. Here, the *affirmative* character of art itself is thought to become the *basis* for the ultimate negation of this affirmation. Affirmation represents a dimension of withdrawal and introspection, rather than engagement. This permits the artist to disentangle consciousness and conduct from the continuum of first-dimensional alienation, and thus to create and communicate the emancipatory truth of art:

> *The affirmative character of art* was grounded not so much in its divorce from reality as in the ease with which it could be reconciled with the given reality, used as its decor, taught and experienced as uncommitting but rewarding value, the possession of which distinguished a "higher" order of society, the educated, from the masses. But the affirmative power of art is also the power which denies this affirmation . . . *art retains that alienation from the established reality which is at the origin of art.* It is a *second alienation*, by virtue of which the artist dissociates himself methodically from the alienated society and creates the unreal, "illusory" universe in which art alone has, and communicates, its truth. (ibid., emphasis added)

In Marcuse's earlier aesthetics of liberation art and education are called upon to act *against* affirmation and alienation. Now they are esteemed precisely *because* they *contribute* to an alienated existence. This alienation is considered to be of a "second" sort, however, because it represents a methodical dissociation from first-dimensional social alienation. This second alienation becomes an alienation of dissociation and distancing, however, rather than an alienation of *Verdinglichung*.

Marcuse regrets especially the atrophy of the critical distance and perspective associated with the liberal arts approach, as well as the "disintegration" (CR, 84) of bourgeois culture in advanced industrial society. The emancipatory, second alienation, considered inherent in high-cultural phenomena, is thought to have dissipated, along with the critical potential otherwise preserved even in affirmation. Marcuse is convinced that overtly bourgeois art—because it is *art*—retains a critical dimension, and should, itself, be regarded as a source of sociopolitical opposition to domination. Marcuse maintains in fact that the art of the *bourgeois* period indelibly displays an *antibourgeois* character, and in this manner he rejects the orthodox Marxist emphasis on the class character of art:

> . . . at least since the 19th century . . . a thoroughly *antibourgeois* stance is prevalent: the higher culture indicts, rejects, withdraws from the material culture of the bourgeoisie. It is indeed separated; it dissociates *itself* from the world of commodities, from the brutality of bourgeois industry and commerce from the distortion of human relationships, from capitalist materialism, from instrumentalist reason. The aesthetic universe contradicts reality—a "methodical," intentional contradiction. (CR, 86)

Marcuse also criticizes the "living-art" and "anti-art" (CR, 85) tendencies that he associates with the politically progressive art of the leftist-oriented "cultural revolution,"[1] as representing a "desublimation of culture" (CR, 81), and an "undoing" (ibid.) of the aesthetic form. In this regard, Marcuse explicitly turns away from the immediacy of sensuousness and militance characteristic of his own middle-period aesthetic, moving instead toward a rehabilitation of the value of highly sublimated art. Marcuse asserts that art must move today, *not* toward an "immediate" (CR, 82) and politically urgent art (or "end of art") in contradistinction to the tradition of higher culture, but instead toward a reinstatement of the customary bourgeois *separation* (CR, 83) of the artistic from the material-political culture. Thus, Marcuse maintains "the revolution is in Bertolt Brecht's most perfect lyric rather than in his political plays" (CR, 117, a view echoed at AD, xiii); and as he sees it, any "uneasiness" on the part of a radical philosophy of art toward the usual domain of higher culture must be overcome:

> There is indeed a profound uneasiness toward classical and romantic art. Somehow, it seems a thing of the past: it seems to have lost its

truth, its meaning. Is it because this art is too sublime, because it substitutes for the real, living soul an "intellectual" metaphysical soul, and is therefore repressive? Or could it be *the other way around?* (CR, 102)

Even if art were to be directly motivated by political considerations, *Counterrevolution and Revolt* makes clear that it must nonetheless retain its traditional qualities of sublimation and separation. "Beauty returns, the 'soul' returns: not the one in food and 'on ice' but the old and repressed one, the one that was in the *Lied*, in the melody: *cantabile*" (CR, 117). Here, Marcuse has reversed the sense of a passage (from EL, 36) commenting favorably on soul music and soul food, and seems even to be openly sarcastic toward certain tendencies within the early Civil Rights movement (Eldridge Cleaver's *Soul On Ice*), although he is also careful not to appear as merely advocating the atavistic resurrection of archaic aesthetic modes through a "revival of classicism or romanticism or any other traditional form" (CR, 116). In calling for the elimination of the anti-art tendencies of the cultural revolution and for the reemergence of the aesthetic form, he indicates that this movement in art must assume a modern expression in contemporary society. He cites Picasso, Joyce, Beckett, and Bob Dylan in this regard, and credits Adorno (at CR, 116 and at AD, 30) for stressing the art-as-alienation hypothesis according to which

> . . . art responds to the total character of repression and administration with total alienation. The highly intellectual, constructivist, and at the same time spontaneous-formless music of John Cage, Stockhausen, Pierre Boulez may be the extreme examples. (CR, 116)

These artists are thought to have discovered certain of the most up-to-date forms of aesthetic expression capable of communicating the message of emancipation under current circumstances, where the cultural revolution is thought to have failed. In Marcuse's estimation, the classical forms of sublime and doubly alienated art transcend the everyday, alienated social reality, and represent the critical potential of art at its best. There is no question that, as he sees it, this art still represents refusal, although no longer in the immediately practical, political sense of the Great Refusal, or the demonstration-confrontation-rebellion definition of praxis (see EL, 53).

> At precisely this stage, the radical effort to sustain and intensify the "power of the negative," the subversive potential of art, must sustain

and intensify the *alienating* power of art: the aesthetic form, in which alone the radical force of art becomes communicable. (CR, 110)

Marcuse implies that his opposition to the cultural revolution does not mean that he is trying to depoliticize his aesthetic theory, but rather to clarify the form in which politics may legitimately be present in art. Marcuse is hostile to the thought of an explicitly proletarian or engaged literature because, as he sees it:

> The tension between affirmation and negation precludes any iden-
> tification of art with revolutionary *praxis*. Art cannot represent the
> revolution, it can only invoke it in another medium, in an aesthetic
> form in which the political content becomes *meta*political, governed
> by the internal necessity of art. And the goal of all revolution—a
> world of tranquility and freedom—appears in a totally unpolitical
> medium, under the laws of beauty, of harmony. (CR, 103–4)

Marcuse is here calling for an educational and cultural practice, not as a direct form of actual, social revolution, but as a call to a preparatory redefi-nition of need and to a restructuring of consciousness. He believes that what is necessary here, above all else, is an *imaginary* "creation of another reality out of the existing one" (CR, 107). This other reality may appear, in his estimation, especially in literary art due to the *"alchemy of the word"* (ibid., emphasis in original), which is derived from the literary aesthetic form, and that "transfigures, transsubstantiates the given reality" (CR, 86). We have already seen that Marcuse regards even extremely alienated *art* as a triumph over the "petrification" of *Verdinglichung* (CR, 38), and as a critical assertion of potentiality over actuality. Following Aristotle's *Poetics* in this regard, Mar-cuse looks to art to delineate "a 'second history' within the historical con-tinuum" (CR, 107); thus, he also believes that art may assist in what Wilhelm Dilthey called *Der Aufbau der geschichtlichen Welt in den Geisteswissenschaften*— or in other words the construction of a (second) historical world *in the humanities*. In this sense, Marcuse contends that both art and education must remain committed to a second level alienation and even elitism, if and where, under oppressive conditions, only a social elite has access to higher culture.

> . . . the existing society is *reproduced* not only in the mind, the
> consciousness of men, but *also in their senses*; and no persuasion, no
> theory, no reasoning can break this prison, unless the fixed, petri-

fied *sensibility* of the individuals is *"dissolved," opened to a new dimension of history*, until the oppressive familiarity with the given object world is broken—broken in a *second alienation*: that from the alienated society. (CR, 71–72)

> Art remains committed to the Idea (Schopenhauer), to the universal in the particular; and since the tension between idea and reality, between the universal and the particular, is likely to persist until the millennium which will never be, art must remain *alienation*. If art, because of this alienation, does not "speak" to the masses, this is the work of the class society which creates and perpetuates the masses. If and when a classless society achieves the transformation of the masses into "freely associated" individuals, art would have lost its elitist character, but not its estrangement from society. (CR, 103)

Even if art should ultimately outgrow its elitist character, in Marcuse's view, it would still not be thought to intervene directly toward the actualization of utopia, but rather, to furnish the transcendent goal for change.

> . . . in the work of Samuel Beckett, there is no hope which can be translated into political terms, the aesthetic form excludes all accommodation and leaves literature as literature. And as literature, the work carries one single message: to make an end of things as they are. (CR, 116–17)

In this manner, that is, as *telos*, as *the organon and logic of education*, Marcuse contends there does remain an "internal" connection between art and politics, and art and revolution, but he also concludes that the artist, as artist and educator, inevitably exists in an external and antagonistic relationship to political activism:

> In this sense, it is indeed an internal exigency of art which drives the artist to the streets—to fight for the Commune, for the Bolshevist revolution, for the German revolution of 1918, for the Chinese and Cuban revolutions, for all the revolutions which have the historical chance of liberation. But in doing so he leaves the universe of art and enters the larger universe of which art remains an antagonistic part: that of radical practice. (CR, 122)

Marcuse has made his "turn." In 1967 he was concerned primarily with a critique of the affirmative *invalidation* of *higher culture* in advanced industrial society as illustrated by the following statement from "Art in the One-Dimensional Society" (AO):

> The present situation of art is, in my view, perhaps most clearly expressed in Thomas Mann's demand that one must revoke the Ninth Symphony. One must revoke the Ninth Symphony not only because it is wrong and false (we cannot and should not sing an ode to joy, not even as promise), but also because it is there and is true in its own right. It stands in our universe as the justification of that "illusion" which is no longer justifiable. (AO, 66)

By 1972 he is, in contrast, criticizing the "cultural revolution's" attempt to eliminate the affirmative character of the traditional and dominant culture. Marcuse is seeking to avoid what he perceives as the cultural revolution's flat rejection of bourgeois culture and the neglect of aesthetic form. In his estimation, he is attempting to restore a more dialectical quality to the efforts of the cultural revolution by emphasizing the fundamental unity of affirmation and negation in all genuine art:

> . . . affirmation has its own dialectic. There is no work of art which does not break its affirmative stance by the "power of the negative," which does not, in its very structure, evoke the words, the images, the music of another reality, of another order repelled by the existing one and yet alive in memory and anticipation, alive in what happens to men and women, and in their rebellion against it. Where this tension between affirmation and negation, between pleasure and sorrow, higher and material culture no longer prevails, where the work no longer sustains the dialectical unity of what is and what can (and ought to) be, art has lost its truth, has lost itself. (CR, 92–93)

These remarks from *Counterrevolution and Revolt* were published in the same year as Marcuse authored still another important essay on art: "Art as Form of Reality" (AF). This piece should be considered the pivotal text in Marcuse's turn with regard to the validity or invalidity of higher culture. It is a sustained attack on those who categorically reject higher culture as the oppressive expression of an elitist social circle. Marcuse states his late-period position here quite unequivocally:

> There is, even in the most "impossible" verses of the traditional drama, even in the most impossible opera arias and duets, some element of rebellion which is still "valid." There is in them some faithfulness to one's passions, some "freedom of expression" in defiance of common sense, language and behavior which indicts and contradicts the established ways of life. It is by virtue of this "otherness" that the Beautiful in the traditional arts would retain its truth. (AF, 58)

As Marcuse now sees it, *the rebellion against art as art* is actually "part and parcel" (AF, 55) of the worst sort of sheer *affirmation*:

> The rebellion against the very Form of Art has a long history . . . it was an integral part of the Romanticist program. . . . The next step is to "living art" . . . . Art in motion, *as* motion. . . . Art . . . refuses to be for the museum or mausoleum . . . for the holiday of the soul . . .—it wants to be *real*. . . . All these frantic efforts to produce the absence of Form, to substitute the real for the aesthetic object . . . —are they not so many activities of frustration, already part of the culture industry and the museum culture? . . . Art cannot become reality, cannot realize itself without canceling itself as art. . . . (AF, 56)

Likewise, in this essay Marcuse emphasizes the need for an aesthetic estrangement to overcome first-dimensional alienation:

> There is a phrase of Marx: "these petrified conditions must be forced to dance by singing them their own melody." Dance will bring the dead world to life and make it a human world. But today, "their own melody" seems no longer communicable except in forms of extreme estrangement and dissociation from all imme-diacy—in the most conscious and deliberate forms of *Art*. (AF, 57)

> . . . the rebellion against "form" only succeeds in a loss of artistic quality; illusory destruction, illusory overcoming of aliena-tion. The authentic *oeuvres*, the true avant-garde of our time, far

from obscuring this distance, far from *playing down* alienation, *enlarge* it and harden their incompatibility with the given reality. . . . (ibid.)

In the work since his turn, Marcuse expresses a certain dismay that "Today the ruling class has neither a culture of its own (so that the ideas of the ruling class could become the ruling ideas) nor does it practice the bourgeois culture it has inherited" (CR, 84). In his discussion with Jürgen Habermas, Marcuse suggests (perhaps facetiously, although this is far from clear): "I think what's needed is a second bourgeois revolution because the bourgeoisie, as a result of big capital, has begun to abandon its own achievements, and because the working class has become increasingly embourgeoisified" (TP, 148). In keeping with the tenor of the last two citations, Marcuse's final book decisively replaces his former emphasis on the dangers of the affirmative character of art with a favorable reconsideration of the traditional conception of high art's *permanent value*.

Marcuse's final book was published in German a year before it was published in English. It bore the title *Die Permanenz der Kunst: Wider eine bestimmte Marxistische Ästhetik*, which translates literally as "The Permanence of Art: Against a Particular Marxist Aesthetic." It is precisely an appreciation for the permanence of art that Marcuse claims is lost to the traditional Marxist aesthetic. In his estimation, it is this classical Marxist aesthetic that has succumbed to reification (AD, 13) because "it assumes that all art is somehow conditioned by the relations of production, class position, and so on" (AD, 14). Classical Marxism, as he sees it, identifies artistic quality with transitory political content, rather than with the beautiful aesthetic form itself; it also is said to assert the artist's obligation to express revolutionary class interest as part of the work's inner logic. This is generally thought to involve a commitment to various forms of social realism in art, and to a rejection of the cultural creations of the dominant class, as hegemonic or decadent. Perhaps most importantly of all, however, the classical Marxist aesthetic is said to devalue the political function of the consciousness and subconsciousness of the individual, and to underestimate totally the general value of what Marcuse's metapsychology postulates as the entire realm of human subjectivity.

According to *The Aesthetic Dimension*, the concreteness and appeal of artwork "cannot be comprehended in terms of social theory" (AD, 12), but rather only insofar as it relates to Marcuse's updated view (i.e., via *Eros and Civilization*) of the *general nature of the human species*:

Marxist aesthetics has yet to ask: What are the qualities of art which transcend the specific social content and form and give art its universality. Marxist aesthetics must explain why Greek tragedy and the medieval epic, for example, can still be experienced today as "great," "authentic" literature. . . . (AD, 15)

This is, of course, an indirect reference to the last paragraphs of Marx's introduction to the *Grundrisse* (*Outline of the Critique of Political Economy*). In Marcuse's estimation, every great and authentic work of art, even in its affirmation of the political-economic status quo, also provides a universe of permanent human interest insofar as its sensuous imagery and logic speak to (and from) what he has conceived, following Freud, Nietzsche, and Schopenhauer, as the *depth dimensional dialectic of human nature.*

The affirmative character of art has yet another source: it is in the commitment of art to Eros, the deep affirmation of the Life Instincts in their fight against instinctual and social oppression. *The permanence of art*, its historical immortality throughout the millennia of destruction, bears witness to this commitment. (AD, 10–11 emphasis added)

The universality of art cannot be grounded in the world and the world outlook of a particular class, for art envisions a concrete universal, humanity (*Menschlichkeit*), which no particular class can incorporate, not even the proletariat, Marx's "universal class." The inexorable entanglement of joy and sorrow, celebration and despair, Eros and Thanatos cannot be dissolved into problems of class struggle. History is also grounded in nature. And Marxist theory has the least justification to ignore the metabolism between the human being and nature, and to denounce the insistence on this natural soil of society as a regressive ideological conception. (AD, 16)

Marcuse's reemphasis on the permanence of art thus appears to reconstitute a philosophical perennialism from the point of view of an elaboration of the Freudian metatheory. In *Counterrevolution and Revolt* Marcuse maintained that he was undertaking a naturalization rather than a spiritualization of beauty and freedom. He clearly believed he was enlarging the materialistic base of Marxism through his reinterpretation of many of the "apparently idealistic" conceptions of perennialist aesthetic and educational philosophy.

Marcuse also holds in *Eros and Civilization* (EC) that his dialectic of human nature's depth dimension necessarily implicates his philosophy with some of the most classical problems of educational theory, that is, the inter-relation outlined in Plato's *Symposium* between the love of the beautiful body and the love of beautiful knowledge (EC, 211), and the belief—first propounded in the *Republic*—that leadership toward freedom and justice may be genuinely exercised only by the educated (EC, 225, and in "Repres-sive Tolerance" [RT, 122]). The educational aim of an enlightened and critically self-confident human personality—emergent from a philosophical self-consciousness (or remembrance) of human nature—has indeed been a venerable component of classical pedagogical theory, from Plato to Kant.

Marcuse also seeks to recall the somatic species essence of the human race from the oblivion of repression, anesthetization, and *Verdinglichung* through a program of aesthetic education designed to retrieve what is postu-lated as the repressed, sensuous core of the human being from its historical distortion and domination by the rationality of instrumentalism and the one-dimensional logic of the present-at-hand. So too, he seeks through the agencies of "the classical aesthetic" (EL, 27) and "the long process of educa-tion" (CR, 134) to achieve a critical, self-reflection of the social potential of the species to take possession of beauty and justice, pleasure and reason, and personal happiness and communal solidarity.

According to Marcuse, the universality of art speaks to the "metabolism" (AD, 16) between human beings and nature, and illumines the "natural soil" (ibid.) of society. To this extent, *The Aesthetic Dimension* does continue Marcuse's work in *Eros and Civilization*, where a dialectic of Eros and Thanatos supplanted the classical Marxist emphasis on the dialectic of the material relations of production as the basis for societal renewal and cul-tural critique. In search of "solidarity" and "community" Marcuse looks toward a cultivation of the "natural" foundation of society that he believes may make peace and cooperation possible:

> Solidarity would be on weak grounds were it not rooted in the instinctual structure of individuals. In this dimension, men and women are confronted with psycho-physical forces which they have to make their own without being able to overcome the naturalness of these forces. This is the domain of the primary drives: of libidinal and destructive energy. Solidarity and community have their basis in the subordination of destructive and aggressive energy to the social emancipation of the life instincts.

> Marxism has too long neglected the radical political potential
> of this dimension. (AD, 17)

Insofar as *The Aesthetic Dimension* in this manner links Marcuse's vision of
humanity's innermost needs and affective essence to his theory of the
aesthetic, emphasizing an aesthetico-erotic basis for the supersession of
alienation and for the attainment of "community,"—though not the classical Marxist emphasis on the need for the theoretical and practical cultivation of an explicitly socialist consciousness and conduct—it appears to be a
rather straightforward unfolding of the positions developed in *Eros and
Civilization* and in *An Essay on Liberation* (EL) rather than a "turn" away
from them. Marcuse seems to be directly elaborating his theories of the
relationship of the human body and the human subconscious to human
sensibility and cognition and to the perception of meaning. So too, he
seems to be operating well within the parameters of a somatic, and therefore apparently materialist, approach, although his notion of the "return of
the repressed" might appear to move to the outer limits of any philosophical
materialism.

What is qualitatively different in Marcuse's late-period work, however,
is the increasing stress on the separation and alienation of art from life and
social reality, and a reemphasis on art as a work of art, rather than as a programmatic means toward the actualization of utopia. At the same time,
Marcuse begins to restore the traditional features of an idealist aesthetic,
inasmuch as he now underscores the emancipatory contribution of "nonmaterial aspects" (AD, 5) of human subjectivity, and the value of art *primarily*
as *telos*, separated from praxis, and as promise-bearing form apart from
realization:

> art is . . . the promise of liberation. This promise, too, is a quality
> of aesthetic form, or more precisely, of the beautiful as a quality of
> aesthetic form. The promise is wrested from established reality. It
> invokes the image of the end of power, the appearance (*Schein*) of
> freedom. But only the appearance; clearly, the fulfillment of this
> promise is not within the domain of art. (AD, 46)

Not only has art itself become more promise than part of an earthly program of "radical action," as formerly sought in "Contributions to a Phenomenology of Historical Materialism" (PH, 5), but even this promise is
considered precarious and uncertain:

If art were to promise that at the end good would triumph over evil, such a promise would be refuted by the historical truth. In reality it is evil which triumphs, and there are only islands of good where one can find refuge for a brief time. Authentic works of art are aware of this; they reject the promise made too easily; they refuse the unburdened happy end. (AD, 47)

The promise of art is here understood in a manner quite in contrast to the hopefulness represented in his earlier citations to art's "promesse de bon- heur" (in *One-Dimensional Man*, [OD, 210] and in *Soviet Marxism*, [SM, 115]). A pervasive pessimism has entered into Marcuse's late-period aesthetic thinking that coincides with his shift in emphasis now stressing that art is more properly understood as a transcendent end or goal of change, rather than as a force that can, directly, shape society for life. Art is no longer regarded as an emancipatory factor in the advancing technique of production, that is, as a *"gesellschaftliche Produktivkraft"* [social means of production (EL, 26)], but as a transhistorical "other," as an "ideal" (AD, 58), as something permanent and universal but nonetheless paradoxically conflicted and somber:

> . . . art militates against the notion of an iron progress, against blind confidence in humanity which will eventually assert itself. Otherwise the work of art and its claim to truth would be lies. (AD, 47)

> Art cannot redeem its promise, and reality offers no promises, only chances. (AD, 48)

> . . . Adorno has shown that the highest literary form preserves the memory of anguish in the moment of peace, . . . (AD, 60–61)

Art is no longer prized as practicable, here and now, in historical struggle, but rather for its ostensible *Permanenz*. And art's permanence is described as the beautiful representation the "inexorable entanglement" (AD, 16) of conflicting emotions in the universal human condition, arising out of a dialectic of such opposed forces as death and love, terror and gratification, and anguish and peace.

Consistent with Marcuse's theory of human nature, art is thought to preserve a permanent appeal and relevance through its reference to this dia- lectic of internal emotional and intellectual conflict. *The Aesthetic Dimension* stresses, however, that the humanist political imperative, which might correct even overt idealism in art, is now "hidden," (AD, 57) and that the actualization of art's political demands now lies "outside of" (ibid.) the domain of art itself.

> . . . We have known for a long time that our humanity does not redeem all human afflictions and crimes; rather it becomes their victim. Thus it remains ideal: the degree of its realization depends on the political struggle. The ideal enters this struggle only as end, *telos*; it transcends the given praxis. (AD, 58)

Marcuse has thus significantly revised his middle-period thinking on the internal relationship of politics and art, and art to revolution. During his middle period, Marcuse clearly wanted to develop an aesthetic and educational philosophy that could *abolish*, as he stated in "The Affirmative Character of Culture" (AC, 132), repressive and alienating conditions rather than affirm them. He wanted to revive the dissipated and subdued tendencies toward utopianism present even in affirmative aesthetic activity, but this was thought to require the restoration of the sensualist, materialist, and political dimensions to the practice and philosophy of art. Perhaps it is most important, however, in viewing Marcuse's turn, to recall the 1937 emphasis on the *false* element in an aesthetic utopianism—namely the perpetuation of its ideals as mere imagery—apart from making the materialist demand for the actualization of its content: "It is not the primitive-materialistic element in the idea of heaven-on-earth that is false, rather the eternalization of it" (ACg, 100). As we have seen, by the time of *The Aesthetic Dimension*, however, Marcuse has emphatically turned toward art as *promise*, not as *Produktivkraft*, and it is, in a certain sense, the aesthetic promise, as promise, which is thought to lend art its now most highly valued permanence. Marcuse's theory of the permanence and universality of art has philosophical roots that extend beyond the Freudian metapsychology back into the *Lebensphilosophie* of Wilhelm Dilthey and of the latter's interpretation of the early theological writings of the young Hegel. Marcuse's somatic or anthropological materialism must necessarily be viewed in this perspective. Likewise, if "socialism does not and cannot liberate Eros from Thanatos" (AD, 72), as Marcuse now especially emphasizes, it would seem that he has, actually, extended his theory of sensuousness and gratification into a theory of human nature compatible with two complementary doctrines: of the *permanence of art*, and the *permanence of alienation*.

Marcuse also derives the perennial emancipatory potential of art from what he now highlights as *art's permanent incompatibility with life.* An emancipatory duality between art and life, thus, becomes characteristic of the aesthetic theory of *The Aesthetic Dimension.* This was also the case in *The German Artist Novel.* Art as alienation—as separation and dissociation from an alienating society—is now *not* to be diminished, in his estimation, but extended:

> Not disintegration but reproduction and integration of that which is, is the catastrophe. . . . The artist's desperate effort to make art a direct expression of life cannot overcome the separation of art from life. (AD, 50)

Alienated art is thus thought to represent protest and resistance to the given social reality, but as Marcuse sees it, this alienated art no longer rebels against the established reality itself (i.e., it remains affirmative); it rebels, more precisely, against the established reality *principle*. "Art cannot change the world, but it can contribute to changing the consciousness and drives of men and women who could change the world" (AD, 32–33). Marcuse thus looks to the *consummation* of this artistic alienation. He believes that it is precisely this quality that can, and has, made literature a literature of protest and opposition:

> The degree to which the distance and estrangement from praxis constitute the emancipatory value of art becomes particularly clear in those works of literature which seem to close themselves rigidly against such praxis. Walter Benjamin has traced this in the works of Poe, Baudelaire, Proust, and Valéry. They express a "consciousness of crisis": . . . a pleasure in decay, in destruction, in the beauty of evil; a celebration of the asocial, of the anomic—the secret rebellion of the bourgeois against his own class. (AD, 19–20).

> In terms of political praxis, this literature remains elitist and decadent. It does nothing in the struggle for liberation—except to open tabooed zones of nature and society in which even death and the devil are enlisted as allies in the refusal to abide by the law and order of repression. (AD, 21)

As Marcuse sees it, liberating subjectivity may constitute itself only in an aesthetic alienation from the given network of exchange relationships and exchange values and by entering a qualitatively different realm of existence:

> Liberating subjectivity constitutes itself in the *inner history* of the individuals—their own history, which is not identical with their social existence. It is the particular history of their encounters, their passions, joys, and sorrows—experiences which are not necessarily grounded in their class situation, and which are not even comprehensible from this perspective. (AD, 5, emphasis added)

Clearly, Marcuse believes that the concreteness and appeal of art derive precisely from art's ability to comprehend the dialectic of the depth dimension—the individual's own "inner history" (ibid.) or "second history" (CR, 107), after the manner of both the Freudian metapsychology and of Aristotle's *Poetics*. Marxist categories, on the other hand, in social and aesthetic philosophy are regarded as unable to comprehend this inner dimension, and thus also unable to convey or communicate its essential truth. In short, the inner history or second history of the individual is held to be concrete and a reflection of the universals in the sensuous human condition, while the classical Marxist approach is considered to be out of touch with affective human factors, having supplanted them with political-economic categories.

As we have seen, Marcuse sought a new, *human*, foundation for dialectical philosophy, explicitly opposed to Engels's historical materialist elaborations of the historical philosophy of Hegel. Marcuse wanted to establish a new footing for the dialectic, rooted in the sensuousness and historicity of human beings themselves, rather than in a reified analysis of economic affairs.[2] We saw that Marcuse, thus, aimed at a rehumanization of philosophical theory in this regard. He held in "The Problem of the Dialectic" (PD, 23), that the humanities (*Geisteswissenschaften*) were the authentic avenue of approach to historical reality (i.e., human *Geschichtlichkeit*). Thus, Marcuse emphasized Dilthey's *literary-aesthetic philosophy of education* because this was seen as the unique gateway toward an understanding of the substance of the only genuinely historical reality, *human* existence. Consequently, a hermeneutical, rather than a historical materialist, form of analysis is considered the most appropriate method by which to arrive at the "inner history" (AD, 5) of human universals. These universals are thought to be captured in the permanence of art and represented there by the dialectic of pain and gratification, death and love, and torment and peace, subsumed under the affirmative law of the beautiful, and *alienated from* revolutionary practice as well as from life in the first dimension. Precisely art's *separation* from the immediacies of life and politics is thought to represent its potential for emancipation. Ultimately, Marcuse contends that only that form of literary art which (1) approaches the most venerable standards of perfection, and which (2) also appears as elitist because of its opposition to social integration as well as its distance from any sort of literary engagement, can function as a liberating or liberal art in the best sense. Quoting German literary critic, Michael Schneider, Marcuse writes:

> ". . . the anachronistic-elitist notion of *Dichten* [to compose poetry] as a distinguished 'higher' art assumes again an all but *subversive* character." The work of art can attain political relevance only as autonomous work. The aesthetic form is essential to its social function . . . the unity of tendency and quality is antagonistic. (AD, 53)

In asserting an antagonistic relationship between artistic quality and political tendency (a decade before conservatives began to condemn political correctness), Marcuse implies that literature with a "correct political tendency" (ibid.) just like "a totally marketed literature" (ibid.) must necessarily be bad art. Literary quality, in his estimation, must per force diminish, whenever the essential separation, now reemphasized between art and life, is closed. He writes, ". . . in the intellectual culture of our society, it is the aesthetic form which, by virtue of its otherness, can stand up against this integration" (AD, 50). The aesthetic form, as such, always remains as alienation, and this essential alienation is thought to constitute the very basis of what has long been regarded as the critical distance of perennialist philosophy.

> Thus, Büchner's *Woyzeck*, Brecht's plays, but also Kafka's and Beckett's novels and stories are revolutionary by virtue of the form given to the content. Indeed the content (the established reality) appears in these works only as *estranged* and mediated. . . . This thesis implies that literature is not revolutionary because it is written for the working class or for "the revolution." Literature can be called revolutionary in a meaningful sense only with reference to itself, as content having become form. The political potential of art lies in its own aesthetic dimension. (AD, xii, emphasis added)

The alienation of art is thus recast as protest, and its power of opposition and critique is considered a function of the "power of estrangement" (AD, xiii) inherent in the inevitable separation of art from life:

> Art breaks open a dimension inaccessible to other experience, a dimension in which other human beings, nature, and things no longer stand under the law of the established reality principle. . . . The encounter with the truth of art happens in the estranging language and images which make perceptible, visible, and audible that which is no longer, or not yet, perceived, said, and heard in everyday life. (AD, 12)

Marcuse's turn is a turn away from the *unity* he formerly found interlocking art and radical praxis, as in, for instance, the "aesthetic ethos of socialism" (EL, 48). Now, Marcuse stresses not only art as alienation, but the separation of art from radical praxis, even as he highlights the emancipatory value of art versus life. Marcuse no longer speaks of art as a "battle cry" (AC, 103) or of the aesthetic sources of "radical action," as he expressed in "Contributions to a Phenomenology of Historical Materialism" (PH, 5). Rather, he stresses the "a priori of art" (AD, 14) and the "hidden categorical imperative of art" (AD, 57), clearly separating the aesthetic dimension from direct political action.

From the very beginning of *The Aesthetic Dimension*, Marcuse acknowledges that problems of aestheticism are involved in his late-period aesthetic theory.

> *In a situation where the miserable reality can be changed only through radical political praxis, the concern with aesthetics demands justification.* It would be senseless to deny the element of despair inherent in this concern: the retreat into a world of fiction where existing conditions are changed and overcome only in the realm of the imagination. However, this purely ideological conception of art is being questioned with increasing intensity. It seems that *art as art expresses a truth, an experience, a necessity which, although not in the domain of radical praxis, are nevertheless essential components of revolution.* (AD, 1, emphasis added)

Contrary to the theories presented in *Eros and Civilization* and *An Essay on Liberation*, Marcuse finds that art is no longer related as a productive form of radical praxis or to the activities of socialist revolution. Marcuse maintains, in fact, that art must be related to revolutionary praxis as a *caveat* or *warning* in a manner that has been earlier described as analogous to *memento mori*: the sobering authenticity of a (Heideggerian) regard for death. This caveat is clearly not directed against the sensuality of the life instincts themselves (AD, 66–67), but rather as an admonition against the "one-dimensional optimism of propaganda" (AD, 14) and against "the promise made too easily" (AD, 49) of the "unburdened happy end" (ibid.).

For Marcuse, the dialectic of the depth dimension of life and death is held to temper activist fervor, perhaps even more than to stimulate it, through a remembrance of "goals that failed" (AD, 69), and thus ostensibly to deepen and balance human discourse and action.

> Art declares its caveat to the thesis according to which the time has come to change the world. While art bears witness to the necessity of liberation, it also testifies to its limits. (AD, 68)

> Compared with the often one-dimensional optimism of propaganda, art is permeated with pessimism. . . . But the pessimism of art is not counter-revolutionary. It serves to warn against the "happy consciousness" of radical praxis: as if all of that which art invokes and indicts could be settled through the class struggle. (AD, 14)

None of these statements emerge ex nihilo. Marcuse had issued warnings during his middle period separating aesthetic from revolutionary activity although these receded behind his apparent aesthetic militance and praise for the political implications of the aesthetic ethos of Schiller and of the student-worker rebellion in Paris, in 1968. *An Essay on Liberation*, maintained: "Art remains alien to the revolutionary praxis by virtue of the artist's commitment to Form: Form as art's own reality, as *die Sache selbst*" [the thing in itself] (EL, 39). *One-Dimensional Man* also emphasized the value of artistic alienation: "Now this essential gap between the arts and the order of the day, kept open in artistic alienation, is progressively closed by the advancing technological society" (OD, 64). So too, Marcuse's 1965 essay, "Remarks on a Redefinition of Culture" (RC), emphasized art and culture as modes of disjunction and alienation, and viewed this alienation in an emancipatory way. He called for "the liberation of thought, research, teaching and learning from the established universe of application" (RC, 200).

In terms of the academic disciplines, this would mean shifting the main emphasis to "pure" theory, that is, *theoretical* sociology, political science, and psychology; to speculative philosophy, etc. More important would be the consequences for the *organization* of education: the shift would lead to the establishment of "elite" universities. . . . (RC, 200)

Marcuse was thus clearly indicating the potential but suppressed value of a *pedagogia perennis* in these and in his other middle-period writings that refer to education in ways that substantially presage his reevaluation of high art in *The Aesthetic Dimension*.

Of particular interest is the line of thinking Marcuse develops as an *extension* and transformation of the obsolete doctrine of "educational dictatorship" (EC, 225; RT, 106; "Protosocialism and Late Capitalism: Toward a Theoretical Synthesis Based on Bahro's Analysis [PB, 32]) that Marcuse extracts from the educational philosophies of Plato, Rousseau, and John Stuart Mill.

> . . . the question remains: how can civilization freely generate freedom, when unfreedom has become part and parcel of the mental apparatus? . . . [W]ho is entitled to establish and enforce the objective standards?
>
> From Plato to Rousseau, the only honest answer is the idea of an educational dictatorship, exercised by those who are supposed to have acquired knowledge of the real Good. The answer has since become obsolete: knowledge of the available means for creating a humane existence for all is no longer confined to a privileged elite. (EC, 225)

The question of these intellectual standards and democracy in education is also posed in "Repressive Tolerance" where Marcuse discusses Mill's notion of "distinction in favor of education" (Mill at RT, 122) and "the democratic educational dictatorship of free men":

> The question of who is qualified to make all these distinctions, definitions, identifications for the society as a whole, has now one logical answer, namely everyone who has learned to think rationally and autonomously. The answer to Plato's educational dictatorship

is the democratic educational dictatorship of free men. . . . In Plato rationality is confined to the small number of philosopher-kings; in Mill, every rational human being participates in the discussion and decision—but only as a rational being. . . . The problem is not that of an educational dictatorship, but that of breaking the tyranny of public opinion and its makers in the closed society. (RT, 106)

The educational philosophical logic of his final period remains directed against the cultural logic of late capitalism. *The Aesthetic Dimension* was necessary, however, as a work in its own right, to clarify and disentangle much of Marcuse's seemingly contradictory thinking on these matters. In order to be true to his profound but ambivalent and underlying belief in the emancipatory value of alienated art, and "elite" higher education, Marcuse found it necessary to produce the literature of his turn away from his middle-period program and theory and to reassert an emphasis on time-honored intellectual standards. His works of the 1970s, *Counterrevolution and Revolt*, "Art as Form of Reality," and *The Aesthetic Dimension*, signaled his return to deeply held perennialist-oriented convictions though these are characteristically recast as neo-Marxist positions. This can be seen, for example, in the discussion Marcuse introduces in *The Aesthetic Dimension* associating his notion of *artistic alienation* with the aesthetic theory of Bertolt Brecht:

> Bertolt Brecht has sketched the theoretical foundations for these efforts. . . . Not empathy and feeling but distance and reflection are required. The "estrangement effect" (*Verfremdungseffekt*) is to produce this dissociation in which the world can be recognized for what it is. "The things of everyday life are lifted out of the realm of the self-evident. . . ." "That which is 'natural' must assume the features of the extraordinary. Only in this manner can the laws of cause and effect reveal themselves." (OD, 66–67)
>
> . . . Brecht's verdict recalls the essential relation between aesthetic form and the estrangement effect. (AD, 43)

Stefan Morawski also mentions Brecht's estrangement effect in the context of a discussion of the relative autonomy of art, and emphasizes the fact that Brecht's ingeniously shocking and exciting theatrical devices are employed in this regard in order to freshen perception (i.e., of content as well as

form) "so that the sense of the *Lehrstücke*, 'learning plays,' will be emphasized. . . ."[3] Marcuse argues *against* the overtly didactic or engaged qualities
of Brecht's plays (AD, xiii; CR, 117), and he reemphasizes the emancipatory
quality of the *formal* qualities of the work of art. Precisely when the form of
a work of art is unfamiliar and alien, it is nonetheless thought to be
determined by a transcendent "inner necessity" (AD, 42), by a "dialectical
logic" (AD, 55) and by the "law of the Beautiful" (AD, 62). These inevitably
invoke "the liberating images of the subordination of death and destruction
to the will to live" (AD, 62–63). In this regard Marcuse's aesthetic is led
decisively away from Brecht's classical Marxist dialectic, however, and
toward Marcuse's own vision of a dialectic of the depth dimension.

In stressing the "will to live" (AD, 63) versus the urge to "death and
destruction" (ibid.), as an aesthetic dialectic, Marcuse's theory recalls the
ontological thinking of Schopenhauer and Nietzsche, especially as this is
further developed in Dilthey's *Lebensphilosophie* and theory of the
Geisteswissenschaften. This aesthetic ontology sought to understand life out
of "life itself" and society out of the *internally conflicted universals of the
human condition*. In Marcuse's late-period theory it is the aesthetic form, as
such, that is thought to disclose life's permanencies and universals:

> . . . it is possible to transfer the action of *Hamlet* or *Iphigenia* from
> the courtly world of the upper classes into the world of material
> production; one can also change this historical framework and
> modernize the plot of *Antigone*; even the great themes of classical
> and bourgeois literature can be represented and expressed by char-
> acters from the sphere of material production speaking an every-
> day language (Gerhart Hauptmann's *Weavers*). However, if this
> "translation" is to pierce and comprehend the everyday reality, it
> must be subjected to aesthetic stylization: it must be made into a
> novel, play, or story. . . . This stylization reveals the universal in the
> particular social situation, the ever recurring, desiring Subject in
> all objectivity. The revolution finds its limits and residue in this
> permanence which is preserved in art—preserved not as a piece of
> property, but as a remembrance of life past: remembrance of a life
> between illusion and reality, falsehood and truth, joy and death.
> (AD, 22–23).

Dostoyevsky's *The Humiliated and Offended*, Victor Hugo's *Les
Miserables* suffer not only the injustice of a particular class society,

they suffer the inhumanity of all times, they stand for humanity as such. The universal that appears in their fate is beyond that of class society. (AD, 23–24)

In Marcuse's estimation, the historical milieu of the content of a particular work of art may become dated, but the universal action of the protagonistic and antagonistic forces transcends this everyday matter. The aesthetic form is ultimately said to preserve *the permanence of the internal conflicts of human life spanning the contradictions* "between illusion and reality, falsehood and truth, joy and death" (AD, 23).

> Aesthetic form, autonomy, and truth are interrelated. Each is a socio-historical phenomenon, and each transcends the socio-historical arena. While the latter limits the autonomy of art it does so without invalidating the *trans*historical truths expressed in the work. The truth of art lies in its power to break the monopoly of established reality (i.e., of those who established it) to *define* what is *real*. (AD, 9)

> [T]he social content remains secondary to the fate of individuals . . . the universal in the fate of the individuals shines through their specific social condition. (AD, 25)

In Marcuse's estimation one must look to the "inner history" of individuals to find the source and substance of the "dialectical logic" (AD, 55) and of the "inner necessity" (AD, 42) of the aesthetic form and of the "law of the beautiful" (AD, 62). This inner aesthetic dimension, when properly understood, is thought to involve a sensitivity for the tragedy embodied in the "inexorable entanglement of joy and sorrow, celebration and despair, Eros and Thanatos. . . ." (AD, 16) as contradictory forces within subjective human existence that decisively constitute reality, "for every human being" (AD, 6).

The subjective inner history of individuals, though usually described in sensual and emotional categories, is also said to have "nonmaterial aspects" (AD, 5) that are thought to shatter the class framework of the classical Marxist approaches to history, sociology, and aesthetics. These nonmaterial aspects are said to have less to do with a dialectic of the forces of production than with the dialectic of the depth dimensions of art and human existence, as these are tied together in the form of beauty. The beautiful aesthetic form is considered emancipatory because it is said to necessarily preserve a dialectical consciousness of both the essential limitations and potential of the human species.

It is *this* dialectic, of human finitude and promise, that Marcuse believes is preserved in all genuine art—even the most traditional and affirmative art. This is so in his estimation, because art, as art, sustains the "internal relation between the two poles" (AD, 59) of essentially contradictory existential states, such as human guilt and dignity, suffering and peace, terror and gratification, and love and death. Marcuse illustrates this concept of the dialectic of human existence with reference to the realm of literary art and theory, in particular the work of Goethe and Theodor W. Adorno. As he sees it, "the highest literary form" preserves this dialectic of affirmation and negation, love and repression, defiance and death. Goethe's famous poem "Wanderer's Nightsong" [Über allen Gipfeln] is taken as perhaps the supreme example of affirmative perfection of form that necessarily also contains its opposite, aesthetic critique and negation, ostensibly in its chilling identification of gratification and death.[4] Goethe describes nature not for its own sake, but as an expression of human mood or feeling, as a counterpart of the human condition. Marcuse builds upon this understanding, further elaborated by Adorno, in the sense of a critical self-reflection of humanity in nature. The affirmative and consoling aspects of the pantheistic interpenetration of humanity and nature are also seen as accompanied by a necessary human alienation that dialectically protests this world.

> In his analysis of Goethe's poem *Über allen Gipfeln* . . . Adorno has shown how *the highest literary form preserves the memory of anguish in the moment of peace*: "The greatest lyric works owe their dignity precisely to the force with which in them the Ego stepping back from alienation, invokes the appearance . . . of nature. Their pure subjectivity, that which seems unbroken and harmonious in them, testifies to the opposite: to the suffering in an existence alien to the subject, as well as to the love of this existence. Indeed their harmony is actually nothing but the accord between such suffering and such love. Even the '*Warte nur, balde / ruhest du auch*' has the gesture of consolation: its abysmal beauty cannot be separated from that which it keeps silent: the image of a world which refuses peace." (AD, 60–61, emphasis added)

Here, Marcuse has reproduced a long quote from Theodor W. Adorno testifying to his (Marcuse's) contention that the form of high art as such sustains the genuinely *human* dialectic, that is, that of the memory of anguish and peace, and of suffering and love, where even death may function as a source of philosophical negation if wedded to the form of beauty. This conception of the dialectic, however, evidently owes less to Marx or Hegel or Plato than it does to Goethe's own doctrine of polarity revised per Nietzsche, Dilthey, and Freud. According to Ronald Gray, Goethe culti- vated "the idea that 'polar' opposites (like the poles of a magnet) are com- plementary to one another, and that the highest wisdom is to realize all such opposites (good and evil, hatred and love, rejection and acceptance, male and female) in oneself."[5] As Marcuse sees it, the aesthetic form cap- tures this dialectic and, thus, characterizes the essential pathos and paradox of the universal human destiny, which is thought to unfold between the poles of happiness and unhappiness, fulfillment and denial, and hope and disappointment. *This aesthetic form* is thought to be the form immanent to human life and death itself. The sensuous power of beauty is thought able to imaginatively subordinate death and destructiveness to nonaggressive life instincts, and to herald a logic of gratification that is required precisely by its societal absence. Marcuse asks: "How can art invoke images and needs of liberation which reach into the depth dimension of human experience, how can it articulate the experience not only of a particular class, but of all the oppressed?" (AD, 40). In his view, it does so by evoking the dialectic of Eros and Thanatos and by recapturing subjective and generic human truths long since thought to have been lost or repressed—albeit through the contem- plative retreat to the dimension of the sublimation and transcendence of the aesthetic form.

> The accomplished work of art perpetuates the memory of the moment of gratification. And the work of art is beautiful to the degree to which it opposes its own order to that of reality—its non-repressive order where even the curse is still spoken in the name of Eros. (AD, 64–65)

> . . . the life instincts rebel against the global sado-masochistic phase of contemporary civilization. The return of the repressed, achieved and preserved in the work of art, may intensify this rebellion. (AD, 64)

> The ego and the id, instinctual goals and emotions, rationality and imagination are withdrawn from their socialization by a

repressive society and strive toward autonomy—albeit in a fictitious world. But the encounter with the fictitious world restruc-
tures consciousness and gives sensual representation to counter-
societal experience. The aesthetic *sublimation* thus liberates and
validates childhood and adult dreams of happiness and sorrow.
(AD, 43–44, emphasis added)

In this manner the return of the repressed (as a remembrance that seeks the
recurrence of gratification that once was) is said to be perpetuated in the
high formal achievement of the accomplished work of art. This aesthetic
sublimation, however, is thought to represent "a counter-societal experience" (AD, 44) that may intensify rebellion against the global sadomaso-
chistic phase of contemporary civilization (AD, 64).

At the outset of *The Aesthetic Dimension* Marcuse indicated that he
would reject the notion that "art as art" ultimately involves insurmountable
aestheticist dangers. However, he now considers art to be revolutionary
insofar as it is also "estranged" and transcendent: "Inasmuch as man and
nature are constituted by an unfree society, their repressed and distorted
potentialities can be represented only in an *estranging* form" (AD, 9–10). A
turning inward, into the aesthetic realms of contemplation and learning, is
held to be a permanent prerequisite to revolutionary action. Thus, Marcuse
has resuscitated the view that the liberal arts may be considered liberating,
in the most genuine sense, only by virtue of their distance, autonomy—and
alienation—from the urgencies, even the revolutionary urgencies, of day-
to-day living. Art must remain *as alienation*.

It is my contention that the educational philosophy of critical theory
must be liberated from Marcuse's final "art as estrangement" position. I
should like to develop a praxis-related form of critical theory that can also
compensate for that which is absent in Marcuse's theories of art against
alienation, the Great Refusal, general education. This approach must overcome traditional forms of academicism and connect the practice of critical
pedagogy to a politics of real cultural reconstruction. Herbert Marcuse—
like Karl Marx or John Dewey—"is both better and worse than he is."[6] I
hope to release the inner greatness of Marcuse's educational philosophy and
critical social theory by transcending the legacy of his aesthetic ontology.

CHAPTER TEN

———ʌʌ———

The *Future*—Liberating *the Critical* in Critical Theory

In order to advance social theory's power of critique and transformation I have attempted to examine Marcuse's relationship both to Marxism and to classical German philosophy. Drawing firm, defensible distinctions in this regard has been a challenge to careful scholarship for some time.[1] My own particular contribution has been to show that there is an ongoing philosophical *contest* as to just what it is that makes critical theorizing *critical*. My aim in this final chapter will be to propose that social theory and educational theory are critical if and only if they are also politically dis-alienating. They must become powerful resources in dismantling the multifold structures of domination in global late capitalism. I have tried to demonstrate that Marcuse was much less affected by Marx's concept of alienation than by the cultural critique of German idealist philosophy. Likewise, I have shown that the tradition of Western Marxism operates with a concept of alienation removed from the materialist context of Marx's dialectical and historical social theory.

I have emphasized the fact that Marcuse's aesthetic and social philosophy is riveted to educational issues. The educational philosophical tenor of this investigation has brought an essential and hitherto largely neglected perspective to bear on the study of the intellectual foundations of Marcuse's critical theory. Marcuse's voice shattered much of the silence structured into the conventional study of philosophy and educational issues in academic circles in the United States. By introducing students in the social sciences and humanities even to the Frankfurt School's view of Marxism, he furnished

223

his readers with a theoretical orientation otherwise largely untaught in this country. By the same token, the Western intellectual tradition also functions as a restorative presence within Marcuse's philosophizing. It is a living force in his social theory and educational theory, as it should be for all college teachers, but often has not been for those of us trained in the dominant patterns and habits of thought of today's system of higher education in the United States. The classical dimension in Marcuse's thought enabled him to assess critically the behaviorism, empiricism, and logical positivism still prevalent in many areas of the unreconstructed Anglo-American academy. Marcuse reclaimed elements of the classical philosophical traditions in order to confront corporate capitalism with an immanent critique of its own philistinism. In this effort, Marcuse rejected not only the prevailing utilitarian and pragmatist traditions in U.S. and British enlightenment thinking, but also much in the Hegelian and Marxist approaches to dialectic in favor of a literary-aesthetic ontology. Theories of the objective material and historical warrants for social progress were replaced with a pessimistic aesthetic idealism. He sought in this manner a reformulation of those particular elements of classical German philosophy that could intellectually support his shift from economic to critical theory, as he stated in *Reason and Revolution, Hegel and the Rise of Social Theory* (RR, 281). His approach proposed that artistic activity and the aesthetic imagination inherently possess disalienating cognitive, affective, and creative powers that can help bring into being, that is, draw out or cultivate, the finest sociocultural visions of which the human genius is capable. Nevertheless, this aesthetic ontology was also considered to involve a simultaneously alienating and subjective "inward turn" that stigmatized the artist and separated the cultured individual from society at large, precluding any lasting or unproblematic merger of such persons into the social community. This "second alienation" of the artist was thought to occur both because, and in spite of, a personal attainment of essential human self-awareness through an intimate experience of the sensuous human foundation of high art and high culture.

Marcuse dissociated his theories of art, alienation, and the humanities from the traditional Marxist doctrines of the dialectic of the social relations of production, class character of knowledge, and the identification of revolutionary art and education with the cultural forms actually experimented with by communist societies. He believed there was no objective historical warrant for the transition from capitalism to socialism as is postulated by classical Marxism, and he likewise rejected the general dialectic of historical progress developed by Hegel as "preposterous" (RR, 246). Marcuse ultimately emphasized his contention that aesthetic arguments were much more profound than historico-economic discussion as a potential source of social change. His critical theory replaced the progress-oriented philosophy of history of Hegel and Marx with his ontological aesthetic, developed upon the basis of classical German idealism following Kant, Schiller, Schopenhauer, Nietzsche, Dilthey, and Heidegger. In accordance with an underlying motif in this tradition, Marcuse held that *education through art* provides the best impetus to *philosophical and political education*. The humanities, especially, were thought to construct the philosophical-political *telos* that could orient consciousness and behavior toward emancipatory ends. The particular value that Marcuse placed on the intellectual need for aesthetic and philosophical distance in the liberal arts tended to identify the theoretical position of his beginning and end with the practice of the *Geisteswissenschaften*; a practice that was held to have socially critical as well as socially apologetic qualities, but in any case a practice sharply separated from mass revolutionary movements or from philosophical engagement for the cause of socialism.

Because Marcuse's early and late-period work was irrevocably committed to the notion of the permanence of the art/life duality, *a permanence of alienation* was also ultimately implied for the artist and for the highly educated or cultured individual. The aesthetic impulse to change was thought to remain perpetually alien and estranged from the structure of society and from the contending interests of social classes. Instead, the incompatibilities between art and existence, fact and imagination, and death and life, were considered to be the unsettling confrontations that could spark critical understanding of historical situations in ways that political-economic knowledge could not. From the time of his doctoral dissertation, Marcuse regarded an alliance between socialism and art as untenable as an alliance between capitalism and art (KRg, 195). As a consequence of this aesthetic conviction, he was to develop his own particular interpretation of historical events, ultimately arguing the aesthetic basis for the historical untenability of the classical Marxist approach to both revolution and to culture. Marcuse's Marxism is in reality non-Marxist and even anti-Marxist in its commitment to the primacy of the aesthetic methods of the *Geisteswissenschaften*. This has determined the pessimistic ontological quality of his interpretation of sociohistorical affairs, more so than any factual historical analysis of one-dimensional society or "really existing socialism" as such.

I have raised the problem of Marcuse's reduction of social and educational theory to aesthetic philosophy insofar as he sought norms of moral and political reason through the mediation of the substantive universals of the aesthetic reality. Marcuse attempted to give this dimension a quasi material foundation in the biology (and metapsychology) of art, grounding reason and knowledge somatically (or ontologically) in the suprahistorical conflicts of Eros and Thanatos, love and repression, gratification and pain, and so forth. Marcuse's ostensibly critical Marxism thus called for renewed attention to the question of the ground of reason in art. The depth dimension of the aesthetic itself was thought to capture the hidden truths of historical human existence and the very nature of the human being. The visceral and emotional permanencies of the human condition, preserved in the very form of art, also furnished reason with its ultimate foundation.

In Marcuse's estimation, the aesthetic dimension presents the emancipatory image of the social potential of the human species at the same time as it presents a depiction of factual human distress. The subject matter of genuine historical study is the highly conflicted sensuous and affective essence of humanity. The foundation of Marcuse's protest and the basis of his recommended political activity against the one-dimensional society is his theory of aesthetic negation, developed in quasi-Marxist or quasi-Hegelian terms as the negation of the negation ("quasi" because sought as an external, transcendental, ontological negation, rather than as an internal dialectical negation). We have seen that Marcuse's theory of art-against-alienation converts abruptly into a theory of art-as-alienation. His middle-period study of sensuousness (rather than the fine arts or the art object itself) converts back into an analysis of "accomplished" works. This turnabout indicates that Marcuse conceives of the interrelationship of art and alienation in an ultimately antinomial or circular fashion bereft of a dialectical ground for forward motion and the eventual supersession of estrangement (say, through a theory of cultural revolution that he derides in *Counterrevolution and Revolt*). His perspective on negation also shifts discussion away from the material contradictions between capital and labor toward those supposed to exist between subject and object. Investigation is then directed not toward social production processes, but toward the self-formative processes of self-reflective individuals as individuals. He veers our attention away from the political economy of culture toward an understanding of life out of art and life as art. Revolutionary action, as the definite negation of alienation, on his analysis may well be necessary, but it is never sufficient. The need for critical cultural commentary remains perennial.

Authentic historical scholarship is identified by Marcuse with the *aesthetic recall of the depth dimensional conflicts of the human species essence*, as these are ostensibly spanned by the ontological concept of Life. *The Aesthetic*

Dimension extended *Hegel's Ontology* in this regard, through its set of references to the "inexorable entanglement of joy and sorrow, celebration and despair, Eros and Thanatos" (AD,16). These are the core conflicts of human nature whose ambiguity and ambivalence is not thought to be adequately understood or comprehended by the classical Marxist dialectic. Marcuse's revised dialectic in this regard, however, admits only of a polar reciprocity or circularity: hence, the sweeping oscillation between the art-against-alienation thesis and the art-as-alienation position.

We have seen that Marcuse reads Hegel's dialectic ontologically, and this ontological perspective entails a specific relationship between art and knowledge. As Marcuse sees it, the form of beauty is itself conflicted, tragic, and paradoxical. It unites gratification and pain, death and love, and repression and need in the conflicted, tragic, and paradoxical substance of human life. The artist knows, in his estimation, when aesthetic memory and imagination resonate with the harmony and discord present in the very nature of the human being. Marcuse's final book cites Theodor W. Adorno's reference to Goethe's poem, "Wanderer's Nightsong," as evidence that the highest literary form preserves the "abysmal beauty" (Adorno, at AD, 61) of "the memory of anguish in the moment of peace" (ibid.). Likewise, remembrance of death is taken to be a simultaneous stimulus to life, after the tragical aesthetic insight of Nietzsche and the existential analysis of Heidegger. Art is considered educative by virtue of its ability to reveal and juxtapose paradoxically life's complexities, tensions, and polarities. The *disclosure of the tragical-beautiful paradox* becomes, in fact, *the critical* task of *education* as well as the hallmark of *truth*.[2]

The notion of a depth dimensional paradox between the social potential of the human species and its factual neediness is a very particular and idiosyncratic understanding of the subject matter of genuine historical study and aesthetic concern. As ingenious and thought-provoking as Marcuse's theory is in this regard, it is not without its problems. These revolve around his replacement of the historical materialist theories of nature, society, and thought with his catastrophic pseudodialectic of art and life, and forgottenness and recall. Marcuse has postponed an end to the cultural alienation of the artist and intellectual "until the millennium which will never be" (CR, 103). The very *Permanenz* of this contradiction makes it antidialectical and *un*critical in the Hegelian and Marxist sense. When paradox is taken to express permanent opposition, rather than real (historically surmountable) contradiction, it is not dialectical at all. It masks rather than reveals truth, and obstructs one's ability to understand the real roots of reason in art, the real basis for art as knowledge, and the real value of aesthetics against alienation.

The Irony of the Beautiful Soul of Herbert Marcuse

As early as 1970 Mitchell Franklin asked scholars of critical theory to consider the "problem of Marcuse's Diltheyian-Freudian-existential aesthetic theory,"[3] and to weigh carefully Marcuse's use of aesthetic categories in dealing with the actuality of alienation in social and educational settings. He gave his essay on Marcuse the title that I have reprised in this heading. I concur with Franklin that "Marcuse . . . is in reality anti-Marxist and anti-Hegelian, even though his widespread influence rests on the assumption that he is a theorist of Marxist and Hegelian thought."[4] Franklin's essay emphasizes especially the anti-Hegelian nature of Marcuse's posture, which he believes consciously displaces the dialectical quality of classical Hegelian and Marxist philosophy toward a metaphysical or antinomial (neo-Kantian) notion of the permanence of contradiction and paradox. While Marcuse (as I have shown in my discussion of *The German Artist Novel* and "The Affirmative Character of Culture" explicitly criticizes certain problems of the Beautiful Soul, Franklin's point is that this recognition does not, in the end, deter Marcuse's own aesthetic theory from succumbing to aestheticism and to art's history of accommodation to the culture of class domination.

Hegel's critical discussion of the term *Beautiful Soul* in the *Phenomenology* emphasizes that he uses the concept to designate an incapacity to think or to act in such a manner as to overcome contradiction. Instead, the Beautiful Soul treats contradictions as insoluble, and upon recognizing one pole of a contradiction as harmful, negative, or inferior, it flees to the opposite pole in an attempt to completely dissociate itself from the former. Hegel maintains that this attitude is undialectical insofar as it assigns an exaggerated independence of existence to both poles of the contradiction, failing to appreciate their interpenetration and unity. This results instead in a dualistic vacillation. In Hegel's estimation, both poles are to be obviated in a synthesis at a higher level. The Beautiful Soul, on the other hand, is thought to remain perennially trapped within the existing contradiction, no matter how momentarily detached or withdrawn from the "pernicious" pole its attitude appears to be.[5] Marcuse, as we have seen, was aware of Goethe and Hegel's call for the critical supersession of the Beautiful Soul. Thus *even the aesthetic tradition of German historical idealism confronts Marcuse with the pathos of his own withdrawal.*

After his turn, Marcuse's classical dimension rehabilitates the notion of learning identified with estrangement and distance. Contemplation seems to be the most emancipatory option Marcuse sees after 1972, just as exile to Columbia University was the alternative in 1934.

The prevailing contempt for "aesthetic snobbism" should no longer deter us. . . . (CR, 129)

Where radical mass action is absent, and the Left is incomparably weaker, its actions must be self-limiting. . . . Strategies must be adapted to combat the counterrevolution. The outcome depends, to a great extent, on the ability of the young generation—not to drop out and not to accommodate, but to learn how to regroup after defeat, how to develop, with the new sensibility a new rationality, to sustain the long process of education—the indispensable pre-requisite for the transition to large-scale political action. For the revolution will be the concern of generations, and "the final crisis of capitalism" may take all but a century. (CR, 133–34)

These citations, from the conclusion of *Counterrevolution and Revolt*, seemed to some radicals at the time, who were at the height of anti-Vietnam, antiracist, antisexist organizing and activity, to make a premature declaration of the strategic need to postpone revolutionary action. Instead of confrontation and militance, Marcuse now prescribed "the long process of education" as preparation for a societal transition in the very distant future. Yet to others in the movement, Marcuse's admonition seemed a challenge to perservere in a protracted, low intensity, contest for change. The first page of *Counterrevolution and Revolt* reminded readers of the killings of student protesters at Jackson State and Kent State, the police murders of Fred Hampton and George Jackson, and the assassination deaths of Malcolm X and Martin Luther King (CR, 1). At a time when society was anything but calmly onedimensional or demoralized, Marcuse confounded students impatient for transformation with the infuriating proposal that the proper response of the artist (and the educator, as I infer) to the factual oppression of the "counterrevolution"—is withdrawal. This stood in stark contrast to his demonstrationconfrontation-rebellion statement in *An Essay on Liberation* (EL, 53). Apparently patient waiting was now required until the historical opportunity comes again, and the long process of education is to sustain the *memory* of militant action as if it were the long last chord of a requiem.

In contradistinction to Hegel's concept of an historically oriented form of intellectual-cultural education, as this was both modified and assimilated in the educational theory of classical Marxism, Marcuse extended Wilhelm Dilthey's eminently anti-Hegelian "critique of historical reason" and Dilthey's rejection of the Hegelian-inspired philosophy of history. Marcuse adopted instead the "aesthetic of history" worked out by Dilthey, on the basis of Nietzsche, calling upon art as a painted and sculpted critique of knowledge (EL, 41) to get at the "truth which is persecuted in history," as he observed in "Repressive Tolerance" (RT, 90).

Classical Marxism's educational aims are clearly thought to be attained through the agency of philosophical knowledge, as this knowledge is gleaned from the interdisciplinary (or as Kellner suggests *supradisciplinary*) study of social history, natural history, art history, and intellectual history. The artist in this scheme is thought to know, not through instinct, intuition, introspection, reminiscence, or *Erinnerung* (as these are related to the concept of *Geschichtlichkeit* or historicity), but through a critical philosophical assimilation of actual historical and cultural materials and events. A study of art must simultaneously preserve a material sense of the dialectic in history, philosophy and nature. Art education is never to be considered merely an affair of the pseudohistory of inwardness or *Geschichtlichkeit*. Rather, it is an affair of the historical and material world and of the changing social condition of the individual and humanity within it. Aesthetic education involves the construction of a consciousness of the concrete socio-historical possibilities of the given material form of social existence as it tracks the emergence and trajectory of social conflict, social aspiration, and social conscience.

For the classical Marxist, theoretical advances are dependent upon the cultivation of the material, aesthetic, historical, and ethico-practical sources of human intelligence. Marx and Engels were educated according to the humanist ideals of a liberal arts university training. They strove, however, not merely to refine the institutionally given forms of culture and education, but to advance beyond them. They developed a highly selective revolutionary form of intellectual criticism that reflected the mastery of the materials both assimilated and refuted. Although Marcuse indicated that he looked toward eliminating the separation between humanistic education and higher education in the natural sciences (RT, 122) as he claimed Dilthey ultimately desired (HOg, 367), his approach nonetheless echoes a formerly prevailing educational idealism and dualism. By stressing as he does especially the "nonmaterial" (AD, 5) aspects of the individual's "inner history" (ibid.), and by retaining the atavistic epistemological notion of an Orphic recollection, which sees even science as a recall and rediscovery of the true Forms of things (CR, 69), his thought inevitably relates meaning to an enigmatic, third-path interpretation of what he considers to be the intellectual and affective core of being, separate from an understanding of social, historical, and political-economic realities. By likewise maintaining that "the authentic utopia is grounded in recollection. 'All reification is a forgetting,'" as he observed in *The Aesthetic Dimension* (AD, 73), and underscoring the key human factors (aesthetic phantasy and imagination) that are thought to stand at the center of all knowledge, he has ensured that *his* elaboration of both social philosophy and the *pedagogia perennis* occurs within a subjective and mythical-teleological framework. Marcuse's metatheoretical affinities with the dualistic and cyclic qualities of the perennialist tradition also tend to identify his historiographical position as retrogressive and incompatible with the Marxist and Hegelian aspiration to assimilate and advance the rational kernel of classical philosophy.

Marcuse has taken theoretical precautions to protect himself from exactly these sorts of objections. He considers the historical and material contradictions posited by classical Marxist theory to be an inadequate explanation of the genuine forces of history. Historical materialism has supposedly obliterated the subjectivity of the subject from its "reified" concept of dialectic. Marcuse introduces, instead, the alternative, depth dimensional theory of the interrelation of affective human essence and the "activism" of the aesthetic form, as the dialectic of the sensual and intellectual forces that he believes may (if subjectively sensed and recognized, i.e., *learned*) act as sources of emancipatory development within the historical continuum.

Hegel's *Phenomenology* argued for the historical evolution of reason, from lower to higher stages, which would absorb and complete the limited and alienated products of earlier forms of culture and education. This process of advancing education is not however associated exclusively, or even primarily, with a turning inward of the human mind toward realms of subjectivity and inwardness; this is precisely the illegitimate refuge of the Beautiful Soul that is refuted by Hegel himself.

In spite of this Marcuse develops a theory of educational knowledge that claims that there is no truth unrelated to the subjective core human factors of sensuousness and historicity (reminiscence). These are thought to be most vividly preserved and presented in the paradox and *Permanenz* of art. Genuinely educational knowledge in this scheme is "ontological" knowledge, that is, considered to be part of the subjectivity of the subject. A transcendental concept of human life and spirit is thought to stand at the center of philosophical truth, replacing the critical and dynamic naturalism of dialectical materialism. The latter is misapprehended by Marcuse and the Frankfurt School and rejected as a thingified and distorted form of reason. In their view ontological knowledge is never natural—that is, never considered to be directly or empirically perceptible, but rather grounded in the transcendental powers of human imagination and memory, and shaped by the form of the beautiful. The problem of the hermeneutic circle is ostensibly resolved by identifying the arts and the human studies with a concept of narcissism that is held to be both essential and liberating. A self-consciousness of the transhistorical human condition (especially the disjunction between human essence and human existence) is thought to be required to grasp the meaning of Being also encompassing the natural and historical realms.

Orpheus and Narcissus are offered as aesthetic symbols of an essentially nonrepressive erotic attitude and philosophical pantheism or solipsism, in which humanity longs for an unattainable unity with nature and an ego restored to a primordial oneness with the world. Marcuse elaborated this perspective in his chapter on Orpheus and Narcissus in *Eros and Civilization, A Philosophical Inquiry into Freud* (EC) where he also cites Andre Gide's yearning embodied in a Narcissus myth: "Everything strives toward its lost form. . . ." (EC, 140), and "Forms, divine and perennial forms which only wait for rest in order to reappear! O when, in what night, will you crystallize again?" (ibid.). It appears evident that Marcuse's particular readings of Hegel, Marx, and Freud may be said to represent an atavistic ontologizing of their theories, in which a residual idealism distorts even the elements of truth embedded in his ingenious elaborations of the theory of art, alienation, and the humanities.

> Deeper perhaps than any other novel form, the artist novel emerges from that specifically Germanic sense of the world which acknowledges the tragic duality of being, behind all unity, and the innate suffering of the individual. . . . The entirely dualistic sense of the world, from which the artist novel comes, lends it a heavy and sorrowful atmosphere from the beginning: there is no drunkenness with life here, no pure joy in the senses, no festive color, that is not also born of yearning. (KRg, 333)

The "dialectic" of human tragedy and paradox actually derives from Marcuse's propensities to Orphic aestheticism and isolation. According to J.-P. Guepin's *Tragic Paradox: Myth and Ritual in Greek Tragedy*, ". . . Orphic theology formed the intellectual background to original tragedy."[6] Guepin's volume investigates the profound conflict he perceives in the performance of Orphic (and Dionysian) tragedies simultaneously with spring rituals in ancient Greece. The former choral dramatizations of the horrors of murder, sacrifice, and broken sexual taboos, with the concomitant lamentation for the guilt associated with these crimes, initially seem to be ill-fitted to what might be expected of spring celebrations dedicated to the gods of plenty and gratification. These *tragedies are understood as rites of atonement for the paradoxical destruction of life that is held to be repellently inherent in the very maintenance of life itself* (especially as this refers to the consumption of the fruits of the earth in order to reproduce the fruits of humanity). Against what might be said to be the aestheticism of the Beautiful Soul, however, Guepin remarks quite tellingly that *"Plato wants to ban tragedy from his ideal city because the poets satisfy the plaintive part of the soul too much when the listeners are not sufficiently educated."*[7]

Contrary to Plato's theory of the education of the philosopher, and despite his ostensible respect for it, Marcuse reconstitutes the Orphic doctrine of reminiscence on the basis of the Heideggerian aesthetic ontology, Diltheyian *Lebensphilosophie*, and the Freudian metatheory to allow the "recall of the repressed," recapturing the "historical" human identity ("archaic heritage") from its alienation in amnesia. When human nature is aesthetically "remembered," the death instinct is thought to be disclosed as an immanent principle intimately also affecting human life. Defeat and death are held to contribute essentially to educative and emancipatory processes. The objective political-economic, that is, "reified," categories of the classical Marxist analysis, in his estimation, simply do not and can not really educate or communicate truth (CR, 38). As Marcuse sees it, his particular theory of the aesthetic education of humanity better serves the practical and philosophical goals of human liberation than does the analysis furnished by Plato or by the revolutionary communist left, in their classical expressions.

We have seen that Marcuse, like Georg Lukács, was deeply concerned with the status of liberal arts education under capitalism and socialism. Lukács ultimately rejected Schiller's notion of the "aesthetic education of man" in this regard, and in conjunction with explicit Communist party activity also criticized Dilthey and the approach of the *Geisteswissenschaften*. Marcuse's career took him progressively further away from classical Marxist theory and practice and brought him closer to Dilthey and to the Schillerian notion of aesthetic education as the foundation of genuine philosophical and political education. Where Hegel and Marx emphasize the role of science, dialectically conceived, Marcuse increasingly looks to an ontology of art located in the subjective but ostensibly universal human condition. Marcuse considers the aesthetic dimension to be the most authentic preserve of a liberating negation and critique of the empirical or phenomenal world, becoming the soundest foundation for an emancipatory social theory. It is my contention, then, that *aesthetic theory* ultimately emerges, in Marcuse's estimation, as *the most* critical theory of all, providing him with a new foundation for his social philosophy and a new theoretical standard for critique.

The Frankfurt School tends to substitute this ontological aesthetic (developed upon the basis of classical German idealism following Kant, Schopenhauer, Nietzsche, Dilthey, and Heidegger) for the progress-oriented philosophy of history of Hegel and Marx and call it critical theory. In accordance with a prominent motif in this tradition, Marcuse holds that education through art provides the best impetus to philosophical and political education, and he thereby reduces social and educational philosophy to aesthetic philosophy.

There can be no question that the truths made sensuously apparent in the humanities *do* present warrants for political critique and action. The debate is about what exactly does form the ground of reason and resistance in art? This is a truly crucial question raised by Marcuse's aesthetic philosophy even while his attempts to answer it must be superseded. What is it about art, as a medium of intellectual insight as well as affective understanding, which can help us perfect our freedom, our conduct, our humanity? Marcuse's philosophical humanism is grounded in a depth-dimensional ontology of sensuousness that the aesthetic imagination ostensibly captures as the eternal interplay and opposition of Eros and Thanatos, desire and destruction, and gratification and alienation. At this level of analysis it is a version of philosophical anthropology that utilizes the humanities as a means of understanding what are held to be the universal characteristics of human needs, conditions, and conflicts. But how can we best understand the social, cultural, and economic diversity of the human experience today and the multiple forms of oppression that we continue to challenge? Can we adequately understand this multidimensional reality primarily through the undifferentiated essentialist ontology furnished by Marcuse in both his philosophy of art and theory of alienation? Even if Marcuse and the Frankfurt School were correct in analyzing human beings at the level of an abstract philosophical anthropology, we, and they, still need to account for human sociocultural specificity and the historical aspects of political-economic exploitation. This diversity *is* manifested in the arts and a place must be found for it in critical theorizing. The issue here is really one of working with an ontological as opposed to a dialectical materialist aesthetic and educational philosophy.

Two paradigms for theories of art and alienation emerge from my discussion, each with distinctive criteria for critical insight. The aesthetic ontological or hermeneutic paradigm is subjectively self-contained and considers meaning in self-encapsulated "human" terms. For Marcuse this involves self-interpretation of the internal turmoil and distress supposedly inherent in the depth dimension of the human condition (with Eros and Thanatos as the core sensual forces). This conflict is revealed, enclosed, and preserved by the aesthetic form, and its truth is untethered to societal and historical particulars. The limits of such a position are noted by the feminist literary critic, Aeron Haynie, who has written, ". . . it is important not to posit an essential, pre-existing sexuality-as-truth. . . ."[8] Following Edward Said, Michel Foucault, and Gayatri Spivak, she contends, through an analysis of mid-Victorian literary art, that an adequate interpretation of sexuality in art requires a recontextualizing of a work's supposed inherent meaning in terms of the historical and political impacts of forces such as imperialism and social sex roles. In my view, a historical materialist paradigm gains greater explanatory and transformational power and retains a malleability and freedom from a priori categorization in this regard, because it remains externally referential. It continually implicates art and knowledge in a structural and historical analysis of social life, so it possesses a capacity to construct and engage that context in a variety of ways in accordance with several appropriate intellectual concerns. It can also raise the problems and possibilities of intervention against the material structure of oppression and alienation in ways that the self-reflexive logic of the aesthetic ontological approach cannot even consider.

Marx never desired to sever the reflective quality of the humanities and social sciences from the critique of political economy. Rather, he strove to maintain a reciprocal interconnection here through the distinctive philosophy of history (which involved neither mechanical materialism nor economic determinism) initially developed by Hegel. As such, this philosophy of history furnishes the paradigm that allows us to develop more adequately an underpinning for the social sciences and the humanities. In contrast, Dilthey's theory of the humanities and social sciences (*Geisteswissenschaften*) rests upon what Rudolf Makkreel[9] has called a *poetics of history* or an *aesthetics of history* that clashes with Marx's philosophy of art as a *social history of art*.

I highlight these two lines of thinking to contrast Marcuse's aesthetic ontology and the dialectical theory of Hegel and Marx. The debate here can be seen in the context of the controversy among the Marxists, Ernst Bloch, Bertolt Brecht, and Georg Lukács in the late 1930s.[10] This also revolved around the issues of subjectivism (expressionism) versus realism. Yet in the current context this is cast as a confrontation between two forms of realism, one ontological and the other dialectical—each of which claims to be more critical than the other. In 1938 the mature Lukács criticized the subjectivism and irrationalism of modernist and expressionist literature and defended the critical social realism of the later Hegel and Marx. He argued for a realism in art that was not the cynical objectivism of the *Neue Sachlichkeit* (1920s German Realism in painting, which "neutrally" depicted societal degeneration), but rather the classical aesthetic realism of writers such as Thomas and Heinrich Mann. In contrast, Marcuse's *Soviet Marxism, A Critical Analysis* had defended irrationalism in art as emancipatory, citing Schopenhauer and *Lebensphilosophie*, much as the expressionists did. Marcuse's *The Aesthtic Dimension* also reflects on the permanent human turmoil of alienation and the dialectic of Eros and Thanatos.

Habermas's commentary on the epistemological weakness of the aesthetic theory of the Frankfurt School (primarily that of Adorno and Horkheimer, but also Marcuse) and the art-against-*Verdinglichung* thesis is clearly insightful.[11] In "Theory and Politics: A Discussion with Herbert Marcuse, Jürgen Habermas, Heinz Lubasz, and Tilman Spengler" (TP, 132–33), Habermas explicitly suggests that Marcuse succumbs to the asociological or philosophical anthropological weaknesses that are associated with the Heideggerian existential ontology and the Freudian metapsychology. His own new paradigm (set forth in *Theory of Communicative Action*), grounded in social communication theory, aims at the active involvement of all citizens in public dialogue about the need for an authentic form of democratic society rooted in a competent analysis of the historical context of social action.

Critical discourse is absolutely essential if we are to develop critical intelligence and radical political power. Habermas, like Marcuse, has more than once modeled the requisite intellectual action and political leadership in this regard, most visibly during the German *Historikerstreit*, or historian's dispute. During the late 1980s, Habermas, the outspoken public intellectual, entered into the German version of the academic culture wars. He issued a warning about the political implications of how we interpret the past, and criticized the revisionist historical writing of Michael Stürmer, Andreas Hillgruber, and Ernst Nolte, who, in his estimation, represented the most conservative politics of the contemporary German historical profession. The controversy centered on the way in which these German historians were trying anew to come to terms with the Holocaust and with the nature of German national identity. Habermas found in their work a reactionary tendency toward both subtle and overt apologetics and damage control in the revisions they presented during the 1980s of the nature of the fascist government and German military action during the war. As a nonhistorian, but arguably as the most eminent critical intellectual in Germany, he initiated a transformative discussion of politics in scholarship and held the work of these historians up to critical examination.

Habermas also led the way philosophically when he argued that even within critical theory a paradigm shift is necessary away from its ontological aesthetic theory of culture. He quite plausibly suggests the need for a linguistic turn. Certainly from Socrates through Hegel, to Mill, and to the philosophy of Habermas himself, the Western intellectual tradition has found the meaning of *logos* and *dialectic* as constituted in the process through which reason emerges from social and cultural discourse. Communicative competence is absolutely necessary in this regard, but I find it must not be understood apart from structured social conduct, nor be considered a *sufficient* condition for emancipatory social action. In contrast to both Habermas and Marcuse, I want to stress the need to compensate for critical theory's aestheticist deficits through renewed inquiry into class structure and material social forces. This must be undertaken precisely *in order to be able* to speak critically and to empower action for democratic renewal. The goal of democratic cultural transformation requires us to more effectively rematerialize critical social theory than Habermas himself has done with his concepts of human interest, system, and lifeworld. The sociality of knowledge needs to be more fundamentally captured by critical philosophy. Communicative action for social justice and freedom must itself be based on a freshened critical materialist paradigm for philosophy.

Stefan Morawski has also linked problems of art to problems of politics in a promising fashion, and has stressed the cognitive, educative, and social aspects of the theory of art in his essays on aesthetics (including one on the "Major and Marginal Functions of Art in a Context of Alienation").[12] His work reflects the tradition of Hegel and Marx insofar as it holds cultural theory to be intimately related to objective, sociohistorical considerations. He builds upon the effort of Plekhanov, Mikhail Lifschitz, and Lukács in this area, as well as such non-Marxists as Monroe C. Beardsley, concluding among other things against Schiller and Marcuse that politics must rescue art, rather than art rescue politics. In a similar fashion, Avner Zis sees art generally as a form of social consciousness that may be either oppressive or liberating, depending upon its class character as a creative reproduction of reality.[13] Zis also addresses the problem of alienation (with reference to Ionesco and Marx), and underscores the informational, communicative, pedagogical, and political functions of the art object and experience. Lee Baxandall likewise developed an approach to aesthetic thinking along socio-political lines and focused specifically on the theme of aesthetic activity over-coming alienation in his *Radical Perspectives in the Arts*.[14]

Marxist philosophies of art and education have been fundamentally con-cerned with problems of modern industrial civilization, especially capitalism's commodity fetish. This pivotal cultural warp is illustrated by a striking citation from Marx's *Poverty of Philosophy*:

> . . . there came a time when everything that men had considered inalienable became an object of exchange, of traffic and could be alienated [*veräußert*]. This is the time when the very things which till then had been communicated but never exchanged; given, but never sold; acquired, but never bought—virtue, love, conviction, knowledge, conscience, etc.,—when everything finally passed into commerce. It is the time of general corruption, of universal venality, or, to speak in terms of political economy, the time when every-thing, moral or physical, having become a marketable value, is brought to the market to be assessed at its truest value.[15]

These remarks demonstrate Marx's profound revulsion to the intense commercialization of social and cultural affairs more than a century ago. This famous passage was perhaps first cited with reference to matters in the phil-osophy of art by the historical materialist theoretician, George Plekhanov, in his 1912 essay "Art and Society." In explication, Plekhanov wrote:

> While combating philistinism verbally, our contemporary bour-geois aesthetes worship the golden calf as much as any bourgeois philistine. "They imagine there is a movement in the sphere of art," says Mauclair, "While in reality the movement is only in the picture market, where speculation goes on also in undiscovered genius."[16]

In 1933, Lifshitz devoted the two concluding chapters of his *Philosophy of Art of Karl Marx* to a consideration of culture and the commodity fetish. He noted sardonically that

Viewed from the standpoint of the objective relations of capitalist
society, the greatest work of art is equal to a certain quantity of
manure.[17]

Phekhonov and Lifshitz, as dialectical materialist commentators on aesthetic
problems, emphasize the fact that modern art stands under the influence of
objective social relations, including those of commodity exchange and private appropriation, which can adversely affect it, even in devastating ways.
In their estimation, not only the sphere of material capitalist production,
but also the spheres of art and human culture, remained to be liberated
from these material constraints. They contended that if the commodity
fetish is not eradicated (along with the productive system that sustained it),
the affective and cognitive potential of art would remain obstructed. Likewise, they implied that the cultural education of humanity—to an awareness
of the meaning of our being in natural and social terms—would also be
decisively impeded by this form of reification.

Marxist theories of art and education emphasize the fact that an oppressive and alienating society will tend to oppress and alienate even the most
personal human experience of art and education as well. Art and education
are highly susceptible to fetishization and distortion. On the one hand, withdrawal might be seen as the only effective way of avoiding market commodification. Oftentimes taking the form of a conservative and elite protest,
liberal arts professors do oppose the corporate takeover of the academy.
However, Marcuse's middle works acknowledge that this form of protest
cannot hold the line against commodification and tends to be assimilated
into a one-dimensional culture. The early twentieth century saw, as a contrast to aestheticist withdrawal, for a short time, the combative surrealists,
futurists, critical realists, and other fighting art movements, allied with
political revolutionaries. Certainly, even an oppressed art or artist may
"strike back" seeking the social truth and the place and status and meaning
of the authentic self. But even the most critical contemporary cultural products cannot simply remain aloof and remote. Like also the most ancient
and venerable works of art and the classical literary contents of education,
all require an historical and social analysis in order to be fully appreciated.
In my estimation this analysis needs to disclose the necessity of struggling
against the institutionalized seizure of social wealth as private property.
Marxist artists and educators must aim at overcoming humanity's privatized,
commercialized pursuit of knowledge and expression. Until this is accomplished, cultural phenomena will succumb, in subtle and crude ways, to the

fetishization of commodities, and it is *this* distortion that must be eradicated before the authentic meaning and beauty of the historical development of nature, society, and art itself can be recognized. Anything less than noncommodified art and culture indicates not only the persistence of theoretical or ideological weakness, but also *artistic* weakness.

The Dialectics of Liberation and Learning

Today critical theory and its philosophy of education are in crisis. We have seen how the emancipatory potential of Marcuse's structural social analysis is too often displaced by a quietist aesthetic withdrawal. Yet key insights from Marx and Marcuse can be recalled and recrafted so that critical social theory and educational action may have a greater expectation of success in overcoming economic, cultural, and aesthetic estrangement. By what criteria can we measure the advance of educational philosophy (amid rival theories of art and alienation) toward the material goals of transformation and liberation?[18] Hegel's classic treatment in the *Phenomenology* of the consciousness of those who serve and the consciousness of those who are served discloses something of enduring importance here for the critical theory of education and for a pedagogy of the oppressed. Following the contemporary insights of the feminist philosophers Sandra Harding (1993) and Nancy C. M. Hartsock (1983), we should recall that for Hegel *only the oppressed* have the power to recognize the dialectic of interdependence that binds the "autonomous" subjectivity of the master to the subjugated condition of the servant. The social power imbalance prevents the master from recognizing this truth, but disposes the servant toward it. A serving consciousness becomes aware, through labor, that those served are dependent on it and that the master is *not* absolutely independent or free. The liberation of consciousness for both the master and servant requires this dialectification of consciousness, which I would also call, following J. N. Findlay,[19] a socialization of consciousness. The very concept of selfhood is grounded in this social interdependence and social relationality. Knowing ourselves begins when each of us sees that we are who we are through our own doing and the doing of others, and that this reciprocal doing is objectively framed and structured. Alienation begins to be understood when we come to understand that self-awareness is more than an awareness of the subjective individual self—no matter how "deeply rooted." A dialectical and materialist epistemology of oppression means that we come to see social structure in ourselves and ourselves in social structure. We come to see ourselves in others, even in those who fail to acknowledge our service, our work, or our worth, but who could not exist as they do or dominate as they do without us or a class of persons like us. Through individual and collective struggle, domination may be obviated as Marx and Hegel indicate. The structural social polarities of master and servant may be reconstructed, transformed, canceled, and overcome. This requires intelligent, emancipatory, and collective action moving along a path of empowerment with others toward an awareness of ourselves as sensuous living labor and our collective/communal realization as social beings. This is the disalienating activity that educates and humanizes.

Marx denied that social progress unfolded smoothly. He understood contradiction primarily as the real dialectical opposition between social classes in their concrete interconnection. He thought that class conflict had historically engendered opposing ideologies, each bearing the stamp of the class it served, and thus believed that *critique* had a *class character* and did not merely reflect a single perspective within a multiplicity of individualized viewpoints. Neither did it refer to the (neo-Kantian) universal subjective contribution of humanity to knowledge claims vis-à-vis an "uncritical" objectivist theory of knowledge. Furthermore, critique was never a debate involving abstract theses: critique was seen as the intellectual extension of the material contradictions between economic classes. As conflicts between these social groupings were considered irreconcilable except through the material defeat and subjugation of one class by the other, critique, for Marx, leads to civil war and to revolutionary war. For the subjugated class critique was not merely an ideological battle against false consciousness; it was part of an historical battle against oppression and exploitation. For the class in power, control is secured by its political police as well as by its oppressive cultural, educational, and judicial establishments.

Douglas Kellner, who has written extensively on critical theory and its future, has argued that it is time that a new class analysis and a new class politics revitalize critical social theory.[20] The crisis of the critical theory of education today requires the transformation of the frayed academic credo of liberation through the arts into a more philosophically advanced form of educational theory and political action for social justice. What have been called the civilizing forces of our age, the organized social struggles against racism, sexism, poverty, war, and imperialism, have *educated this nation* about alienation, oppression, power, and empowerment. The professoriate, as such, certainly did not lead in this educational effort, although many individual college teachers, like Marcuse, played important and even key roles.

Education cannot legitimately be considered merely an affair of inwardness or the supposedly unchanging nature of the human essence or condition. Education means apprehending the dialectic of the historical and material world and the changing social condition of humanity within it. It aims at an understanding of the principles of action required for human beings, as creative living labor, to grasp theoretically, possess politically, the productive processes that now divest us from ourselves, such that these processes might be restructured to alleviate and/or eliminate alienation. Human intelligence is emergent from the need to overcome material, historical, and cultural oppression. This inherently political process centers on debate and struggle around the central problems of labor, alienation, the inequalities of power and wealth, and how these affect education. Yet critical theory often equates praxis with philosophical and literary criticism and the development of an aesthetic taste for cosmic ironies. Operating fully within the conventional division of mental from physical labor and the relations of power that these divisions represent in monopoly capitalist society, critical theory is largely divested of a dimension of defiance and the power of transformation. Martin Jay, Rolf Wiggershaus, and Kellner point out how rapidly the struggle dimension of the work of the Frankfurt School atrophied.[21] The legacy of Marcuse, Horkheimer, and Adorno threatens to transform the dialectics of nature, society, and thought into a mere *Geisteswissenschaft*, an academic rather than a transformative practice. Similarly, postmodernists such as Jean-François Lyotard also leave the world exactly as it is while they condemn theory as but a reified nest of ungrounded propositions that serves only to rigidify discourse. Like much of critical theory, postmodernism profoundly castigates social science that seeks an analysis of social structure, stressing instead methodological empathy, social interactionism, and the unavoidable ambiguities of interpretation. Luce Irigaray calls for new forms of writing and thinking that counter reification by being open, fluid, and nonlinear. Meaning is seen as a free aesthetic or literary choice effected through the creative acts of reading and the interpretation of texts. The problems of philosophy and social reality require more than insightful interpretation however, they require creative strategies for change.

Marcuse does acknowledge the need for social action and social transformation: "In a situation where the miserable reality can be changed only through radical political praxis, the concern with aesthetics demands justification" (Marcuse at AD, 1). Yet, the epistemological assertions he makes about *Verdinglichung*, as well as similar claims from the early Lukács to Lyotard, just reviewed, serve only to encapsulate us within the aesthetic dimension. They displace the needed economic and political analysis and disarm our ability to overcome alienation.

While appreciating the unique contributions furnished to critical theorizing by Marcuse's discourse, the critical potential of social and political philosophy must be liberated from the constraints of his aesthetic theory. The militant and adversarial dimension of Marcuse's philosophy must overcome the Beautiful Soul. I would like to rephrase the Nietzschean epigram at the top of chapter 1: If the truth is ugly, we have *political education* and *radically democratic praxis* that we may not perish of the truth. In so doing alienated labor undertakes its own *collective education*. By fits and starts and assiduous study, individuals help each other rise to critical theoretical consciousness and *collective political action* against our own commodification and expropriation. This effort humanizes and sustains our lives and builds upon the real insights that the history of art also furnishes for this effort. Dialectic must be set free from critical theory's tendency to reduce it to an ahistorical aesthetic form. Both art and society must be understood historically, and our economic system liberated from the commodity fetish and the unequal distribution of life chances that ensues from it. Our natural and social materiality must be de-coupled from the philosophy of mere sensuousness (whether in a positivist guise or in postmodernism's preoccupation with lifeworld and the body). Truth needs emancipation from both empiricism and aesthetic de-materialization.

The advancement of educational philosophy involves the analysis and resolution of basic contradictions of the economics of exploitation and power, not simply a critique of the philistinism and provincialism of one-dimensional pedagogy or culture. Marx emphasized the dialectical nature of socially reconstructive activity as a materialist and simultaneously *educative* practice: "We say to the workers: You have 15, 20, 50 years of civil war to go through in order to alter the situation and to train yourselves for the exercise of power. . . ."[22] On the one hand, this would seem to undergird Marcuse's prescription of the long process of education in *Counterrevolution and Revolt*. But, for Marx, the advancement of learning is tied inextricably to militant struggle and to the advancement of the work force in the direction of its self-abolition as an oppressed class (through its own increasingly radical and emancipatory class action and class consciousness).[23] A labor movement thus become structurally aware of itself and its latent power can bring into being new conditions of culture more nearly adequate to the universal political and aesthetic potential of what Schiller and Marx called the human *Gattungswesen* (species being). Any movement toward genuinely critical aesthetic education must also derive from the learning involved in practical efforts toward the international elimination of the political-economy of advanced capitalist exploitation and alienation.[24] It is absolutely essential that the humanities, the liberal arts, and sciences, help us attain the full social, political, and philosophical potential of the human species. But how to redefine the humanities, consistent with what we have learned in the context of global struggles against oppression? If philosophy is the general theory of education, critical theory is not merely a study to be reserved for graduate courses in philosophy, sociology, or literary criticism. Critical theorizing must inform the total curriculum and also the analysis of the human relations and values structured into the schools and the society that sustains them.

I believe that there is a kind of education in the humanities, social, and natural sciences that can help the individual overcome powerlessness in the face of global and local processes of alienation. This begins with the rational kernel of Hegel's historical philosophy of education against alienation, which never confined dialectic to an aesthetic ontological dimension. Education in the dialectical spirit of Hegel and Marx must afford a world-historical, international, and multicultural perspective on learning that examines the pivotal social and intellectual struggles that have led to the emergence of standards of criticism in ethics, in logic, and in the worlds of art, science, and production. These standards constitute the *criteria* of judgment that critical intelligence requires. Over time the alienated products of earlier periods will be assimilated, opposed, absorbed, and transcended. Because philosophical standards collide, develop, and transform, critical education continually requires inquiry, analysis, seeing new connections, and revaluation as the ongoing methods of critical science and critical realism.[25] Dialectical educational philosophy is rooted in the social dimension of knowledge: active learning through questioning, with the emergence of reason through argument, the development of logic through debate. No side in any controversy is programmed a priori to win, and truths that are real are neither permanent nor merely perspectival. They are generative of greater truth. The public and democratic methods of critical social science discern contradictions within a nonetheless unitary and changing social reality. A living and combative philosophy fully engaged with reality derives its drama from this debate and simultaneously produces real insight into history. As a recent example of this see the 1998 debate among socialists (Bertell Ollman, James Lawler, David Schweickart, and Hillel Ticktin) on whether or not it is "necessary to have a totally market-less society for there to be some significant degree of control of society over its productive life, some important degree of reappropriation by society of its alienated powers."[26] Both sides of this discussion are fruitful for considering the transformation of the established social order in the direction of democratic and humanistic culture. As Kwame Ture (the former Stokley Carmichael) has said of the dialectical thought/action process: "Our strength is our unity of action, our weakness is unity of thought."[27]

The criteria of dialectification, historical and materialist analysis, struggle for liberation and democracy, empowerment, reconstruction in society and education (favorably resolving for labor the basic contradiction of exploitation and redefining the humanities consistent with a disalienating pedagogy of the oppressed), and so forth, disclose that today's challenges lie far beyond the current functioning (even if not necessarily the theoretical capacities) of our present institutions. Nonetheless, reform struggles make the most sense when they are not divorced from revolutionary aspirations and ends. Marcuse was inspired by Marx's view of the democratic society of the future having the shape of a humanist commonwealth, where we freely labor according to the laws of beauty. But Marcuse's pessimistic utopianism takes this idea of commonwealth-as-liberation, divorces it from the processes that can lead to it, and declares it beautiful but tragically beyond humanity's actual reach. Marcuse's vision was dependent upon Marx, but he ultimately rejected the idea that an emancipatory society could grow up from inside of capitalism. It is because of this that I find it necessary to overcome the limitations of both his Great Refusal to accept the world as it is given and his ultimate retreat to the Beautiful Soul. I offer here some very basic suggestions, for purposes of discussion, of an activist agenda of philosophical and political reform strategies organically connected both to current conditions and to longer-range radically democratic goals. I contend that an activist reconceptualization of the liberal arts and sciences *can* play a pivotal role in the process of cultural and infrastructural transformation.

Innovative teaching and learning strategies need to be developed upon a critical materialist analysis of society (and its internally grounded, i.e., historically real, prospects). New methods must be found that can render productive the current tensions between the classroom and the community, theory and practice, involving students as coinvestigators with teachers into the study and solution of the problematic aspects of structured social experience. A dialectical educational theory such as I am defending here against both the art-as-estrangement aspect of Marcuse's thought and his aesthetic ontology is not pessimistic about the possibilities of education transcending the positivistic acceptance of the status quo or its customary frame of thought. Educators, students, and community members can and must become coworkers in social transformation toward genuine democracy.[28] Even when civic action occurs today in gradualist or ameliorist fashion, the practical and intellectual requirements of these activities can become intolerable to the establishment and release the emancipatory power of social learning (as Marcuse held in *An Essay on Liberation* and in his 1975 remarks on education at Berkeley). Critical theorizing about education ultimately needs to support both an adversarial approach to the cultural logic of corporate capitalism and, when coordinated at the national level as critical pedagogy, to become a progressive social movement demonstrating the public force of democratic action. Activist education (education as life, not preparation for life) can become a lived experience of the fact that coercive corporate and government policies can be affected by a public political opposition and radically democratic deeds, altering social life in a profoundly disalienating and empowering fashion. In his 1975 address to students at Berkeley, Marcuse wrote adamantly in the upper case: "IT CAN STILL BE DONE" (Marcuse, at BK, 12). This is the Marcuse I should like to valorize and vindicate by tracing and extending the application of critical theorizing to contemporary educational problems and settings. Civic education and community service programs, combined with critical theoretical analysis, make possible the dialectical discovery of the complexities that must be sorted out before a free and just future can be secured. These forms of social practice perfect our core powers as creative producers, thinkers, and leaders. They provide the practical and intellectual foundations for liberation.

The critical pedagogy of Paulo Freire[29] suggests that a dialectical educational philosophy also needs to elicit basic student-generated themes and that these will require ongoing dialogical investigation. Freire suggests that this process should focus on three areas of inquiry:

1. into the most serious and disturbing *limit situations*, obstacles, contradictions, and negations that students (and by extension, all of us) need to know more about as challenges to our fulfillment and humanization;

2. into student actions in response to these limit situations, both actual and possible; and

3. into the structures of society and institutional realities that require transformation in order to obviate these limit situations in the future.

Students should interact as they compare their own assessments with those of others in class and in the community, and teachers should be able to probe into causality in a highly sophisticated way, stressing multiple and complex factors that lead to deeper inquiry and deeper understanding. Teachers, aware of the biases of the dominant culture, must be able to build a context for reflection on points of view that can simultaneously generate further student discourse. Students also need to be invited to evaluate whether and how the themes generated can become pivotal in developing the course's academic line of inquiry and content. If in the past much education has been a contest between students and teachers, this tension must now become productive, analagous to any democratic debate. As much as possible, however, *teacher attitude and tone* must establish an active rapport and solidarity with students. This involves real teacher commitment to developing the theoretical and practical talents of students and to facilitating student success in spite of institutionalized obstacles. This includes challenging students, though it contrasts sharply with the complaint of certain otherwise perfectly competent faculty members who long simply for "better" students. Even where faculty laments are justifiable, based on the hard facts of low skill levels, the fault lies not primarily with the individual student but with the public education system and society in general, which cheats students out of their right to a solid basic education both inside and outside of educational institutions.

Freire's idea of cultural action for freedom is ingeniously operationalized today in an importantly critical new citizenship education initiative emanating from the Hubert H. Humphrey Center for Democracy and Citizenship at the University of Minnesota. This has emerged quite separately from Marcuse's efforts or from those of Freire himself, drawing instead on the community-building techniques of Saul Alinsky. It addresses the disalienating potential of public schooling for *public* work in the public sphere. The approach owes its origins to Harry C. Boyte and Nancy N. Kari and is elucidated in their *Building America: The Democratic Promise of Public Work*.[30] Like John Dewey and Jane Addams they contend that public work is at the center of a participatory approach to citizenship and has a unique capacity to democratize power relationships. Thus they aim to develop public leadership skills in students beyond their expected roles as voters or taxpayers, stressing especially "the critical tools to participate as confident, powerful actors in the affairs of the public world."[31] Boyte and Kari ground their perspective historically in the educational efforts toward democratic renewal in American higher education by going as far back as the 1862 Morrill Act and the formation of land-grant colleges. Higher education in the United States at that time was restructured and expanded in the direction of the secular and public (rather than in the traditionally private and religious bases of the early American colleges). The shift toward the practical and professional was an extension of Horace Mann's ideal of education as the great American equalizer. Likewise, the reconceived mission of the land-grant colleges was consistent with the political ideals of Jacksonian democracy. Boyte and Kari emphasize the unfulfilled promise of these traditions, turning today to schooling and urban worksites both of which are held to be particularly relevant to public life, citizenship, and a future commonwealth of freedom. They link their own contemporary theory to that of both Hanna Arendt and Jürgen Habermas, who are credited with bringing the idea of "public" back into legitimate intellectual discussion. They further suggest the philosophy of Simone Weil, who, in *Oppression and Liberty*, is said to tie public work to everyday labor. Their new approach to citizenship advises especially journalists, educators, and social workers to transform these professions into public work. This is also recommended in other occupational areas wherever possible. Within ordinary work activity and resistance, they contend, extraordinary moments of collectivity and free community can emerge that generate a strengthened strategic capacity against alienation. Boyte and Kari advise that college students can also benefit from having their studies in education, politics, or ethics connected to a public service kind of work experience as coaches with teams of younger pupils in schools undertaking democratically determined civic action projects. This experimental effort is known as the *Public Achievement* program, which to my mind has significant potential as an experience-based, critical and active pedagogy. I believe my analysis of the critical educational potential of Marcuse and Marx reinforces, and also deepens, the social philosophical insights and the educational philosophical logic of both Freire, and Boyte and Kari, each of whom in their own right has significantly advanced the received progressive tradition.

Boyte and Kari also tie their theory to the ideals of citizenship within classical Greek political philosophy, which I would augment as follows. Plato asked to what extent we were enlightened or unenlightened about our being. The Greek word for "enlightenment" is *paideia*. Plato was asking whether we are educated or uneducated about our existential condition, its problems, and its prospects. The Greeks acknowledged that this was a *public* and not merely a private concern, and that *societal* support was the precondition for any of us to come to know ourselves. Likewise, for Plato as for Confucius and for Buddha, the enlightened person commits himself or herself to the service of others in a this-worldly rather than otherworldly way. From the axial age through Hegel, Marx, and Freire, education embodied a disalienating, humanizing social philosophy-in-action. Avoiding the paternalism that would adhere to teachers approaching students with a gift of wisdom, in this alternate pedagogy the educators themselves get educated as they talk and work with students coinvestigating the most serious problems life poses.

In the classroom, the teacher must become *"the guide on the side, not sage on the stage."*[32] Guidance consists in *providing study questions* for reading assignments and for small group work and *discussion opportunities* that will facilitate collaborative learning and personal development. This may also involve coaching students in group projects on or off campus. According to genuinely dialectical methods, we must acknowledge that this guidance requires a dialogical process that needs to be deftly directed. The teacher's guidance is absolutely indispensable to bring the theoretical analysis of problems and prospects appropriately to bear and to facilitate dialogue in a manner consistent with Freire's insights. The teacher's own analysis must be critically informed by an activist conception of the arts and by the theory of the liberal arts, the philosophy of social science, and critical materialist sociological insights from research analysts.[33] While there is much to be said for a commonsense commitment to justice, without an adequate and accurate knowledge base, inaccurate or anachronistic sets of background beliefs and worldviews on the part of teacher and student will severely limit critical thinking. Standard heuristic techniques have been tentatively worked out in order to pose critical thinking questions methodically.[34]

Collegiate level term assignments could take the form of *Study/Action Projects* that aim at getting students to assess the prospects of engaging in effective civic work aiming at a democratic vision of the public good. These projects should address a social or philosophical problem of significance to the student. A project could combine a critical interrogation of a selected academic article on the issue in question with a student search for local, regional, or national organizations that are also publicly attempting to address this problem or related themes. Students could identify an action-oriented group (or groups) within the community from whom they could *learn more* about the nature of the problem and assess possible solutions. They could be asked to devise a plan by which they could be of service to one of these groups on a relatively short-term volunteer basis. Utilizing strategies developed in class for critical thinking, students might make short presentations to small groups of their classmates about the ideas of the author they chose. They could also report on what they have learned from their civic activity, and assess its effectiveness/ineffectiveness in problem solving.

Toward the end of the semester students could *formally write up* their analysis of the essay they chose and couch this within an evaluation of their community action or service experience. The point here is to promote a critical kind of *Community Impact Education* where involvement leads to experiential civic learning that also assesses prospects for reconstructing the social order.[35] It should lead both to community-building and to the development of academic skills in communication, critical thinking, analysis of social structures, and real world problem solving.

College course content needs to be reconstructed in accordance with aesthetic, multicultural, and supradisciplinary interests, and emancipatory prospects. Each section of each course might start off in an intellectually participatory way by the teacher posing *thematic questions* with regard to theories such as: What makes higher education *higher*? What is the difference between getting a degree and getting an education? What makes critical thinking *critical*? These questions *introduce students to a transformed approach* both toward the institution of higher education and toward the academic subject matter. Teacher and student both view the process and the disciplinary content as a set of *problems* needing attention and ingenuity. For example, philosophy always involves *problems* of knowledge and logic, and *problems* of ethics. We all may make many choices about what to believe and what to do, but *what makes* a choice a *moral* choice, a *logical* choice? Discussion of these theoretical problems invites participation in a thought process that teacher-centered moralizing or single-dimensional reasoning would choke off.

Critical education theory also needs to be grounded in the social history of art and to be able to form the mature emotions and sensuality as well as powers of critical thinking and ethical reflection. As Michael L. Simmons Jr. emphasizes, art is the sensuously meaningful objectivity that creates subjectivity.[36] Artworks achieving greatness do so at least in part because of extraordinary skill and care expended in their production. Even if today many artists in many media (literature, visual arts, performing arts) are unable to support themselves by means of their art, the arduously crafted and perfected art object nonetheless symbolizes the promise of the product of unalienated labor. Artists and fine craftspeople do not labor today under nonalienating conditions; still their artistic accomplishments against tremendous odds also seem to carry an essentially moral worth. The lingering vision of perfection that is created may portend even political wisdom beyond the immediately heightened sensuous experience. Whether in exuberance or awe, we may be materially (and *not* mystically) transfigured—dialectically energized by witnessing the actualization of seemingly unattainable goals from really existing yet coarser stuff or conditions. At the same time, the power of the aesthetic to help us understand the past and build confidence in ourselves and our critical capacities—the social power of art—must be more than just acknowledged; it must be democratized. Critical education must in practice disclose the real need and real possibility of egalitarian and humanized forms of productive relations, relations to nature, and interpersonal dynamics that cultivate the aesthetic worth of these core life activities. Morality, politics, and emancipation are based on sensuous as well as conceptual grounds.

Inquiry must probe the material grounds of reason in art every bit as much as the material grounds of in/justice and oppression. Gloria Watkins (bell hooks), for example, does this expertly in *Reel to Real: Race, Sex and Class at the Movies* (1996). Similarly, students need to be able to discuss why it is that hip-hop, rock, punk, rap, spirituals, folk music, soul, bebop, and so forth can each tell us in their own way that we must come to grips with alienation and act against it. Teachers also need to be able to discuss the historical and material foundations for music education, world literatures, studio art, and foreign languages, and must be able to defend these studies in mass approaches to higher education against the forces of cost-cutting, vocationalism, and entertainment. Can we articulate the real grounds of their *general educational function* and why these studies deserve to be *at the core* of the critical educational paradigm.[37]

Above and beyond advocacy for a renewed liberal arts and sciences curriculum based on these critical pedagogical elements, college instructors are sometimes able, through special effort and often struggle, to make definite *institutionalized changes* in school policy and structure to accomplish radically democratic goals. For example, union activities can be undertaken not just to achieve job security or protection against harassment or infringements of academic freedom, but as part of a governance system of checks and balances that can struggle to liberate the mission of public education from its social control function and address, as an organized force, social issues pertinent to educational progress. Faculty have been able to infuse multicultural education across the curriculum and to include the study of *oppression* and student/faculty involvement in *community action* and *community development in their divisional (or college-wide) objectives for curriculum, educational activities, and future assessment purposes*. On many campuses professors are successfully resisting defining outcomes in terms of replication of oppressive social division of labor and wealth. (Where we do not succeed, we nonetheless better come to know the structural limitations of our positions, and may devise new strategies upon the basis of this knowledge.) Other faculty work with students and their college's office of student activities to establish recognized student groups that have as their purpose campus-wide discussions of contemporary social problems and issues bringing a critical perspective to bear on U.S. politics and culture.

In general teachers must unite with students and parents and with the interests of the work force. Here the necessity of *building coalitions* is to be stressed—locally, regionally, and nationally—with progressive organizations and individuals, as Marcuse suggested catalyst groups must do in "Proto-socialism and Late Capitalism: Toward a Theoretical Synthesis Based on Bahro's Analysis" (PB, 1978). These cooperative efforts may take a wide variety of forms. Certainly progressive college instructors usually develop friendships with progressive faculty at other local academic institutions.[38] One such coalition has made a significant attempt to formulate a common ground declaration with regard to the practical political shape that its members would like to see this country take in the future. This has become the document, *Charter 2000: A Comprehensive Political Platform.*[39] It presents a positive vision of desirable social outcomes, and is already being circulated widely to stimulate discussion of its contents. It addresses concretely the problems and prospects of justice, peace, abundance, ecology, human rights, democracy, education, health, child care, and so forth, and it attempts to be a comprehensive political program around which progressive individuals can unite. While in many ways consistent with Marcuse's values and aspir-ations, it also advances beyond his program and political limitations. For purposes of further debate, and because of its visionary power and rich detail, I include *Charter 2000* here in full as an appendix.

While the *Charter* is a valuable tool in coalition-building, it is even more useful as a pedagogical instrument. David Brodsky, an author of the primary version of this discussion document, highlights its relevance to critical education as follows:

> Although it is not written in discursive prose, and despite being published in the form of a political platform, *Charter 2000* raises a strong progressive voice for radically democratic alternatives to the usual corporate parameters of political control. In a concentrated form and with a breadth of coverage unavailable anywhere else, it provides specific suggested solutions for a wide range of contem-porary difficulties. Its points can well serve the purpose of political

debate and analysis in critical classroom discussion, and could well stimulate progressive political activity in the larger society on issues otherwise generally suppressed or marginalized in public discourse and public education. The *Charter* is a very condensed textbook of progressive thought with a minimum of 156 discussion topics/questions (planks). Any one of them, reformulated if necessary for pedagogical purposes, could provide the opportunity for broad discussion and debate, research topics and papers, civic projects, community activism, etc. Not only courses in ethics, social problems, and education, but also political science and American government students would clearly benefit from reading and responding to *Charter 2000*. If some readers were to write in response to it (negatively or positively), or even make original contributions suggesting new or revised planks, then the *Charter* would be fulfilling its main function, to circulate progressive solutions and thus values, and to start a discussion that will advance community building in a progressive direction. Such further development of the *Charter* can take place in educational settings, and the results of particularly fruitful classroom discussions can be reported in the *Progressive Clearinghouse Bulletin* [the address of which is included in the appendix].[40]

I recommend all of these educational insights and strategies knowing full well that the larger tendencies of social change worldwide seem to be generally regressive. In most venues economic and political globalization are leading *not* toward multiculturalism and mutuality, but toward the politics of polarization, privatization, and war. A reactionary racialization in politics is also occurring (the mobilization of bias against immigrants and ethnic minorities through mainstream political parties as well as through the militias and the corporate media). Reactionary politics also involves the justification for reactionary ideas within culture (from resurgent religious fundamentalism and new age millennialism and escapism, to philosophy without foundations and to the several nihilistic versions of postmodernism). Yet in this period of destabilization new forces are also emerging globally and in the United States bringing previously isolated groups of progressives together in working coalitions and alliances. Catalyst groups within higher education institutions have quite remarkably moved educational theory and practice forward in recent decades, especially through the antiracist and antisexist multicultural education reform movement. Additionally, voices like those of Ira Shor advise a sophisticated reconsideration and reemphasis on a class-based politics and educational philosophy, given the intensity of recent economic polarization and the obsolescence of the ideology of the Soviet threat. Rebellion is once again afoot, and the support for it more widespread. Witness the astonishingly successful August 1997 UPS strike; the broadly-based resistance to union-busting recently in Decatur and in Detroit; the formation of the Labor Party; the dozens of teach-ins on Democracy and Corporate Control on U.S. campuses during October and November 1996 and March 1998 against corporate hegemony within the economy, culture, and politics; massive union-organizing drives by graduate teaching assistants on a number of campuses; and the uprisings in Chiapas, Mexico, in Peru, and particularly of students in Indonesia. Critical pedagogy must synthesize critical theorizing, the liberal arts, and a movement sense of solidarity and community among these emergent forces and furnish the future with the cultivated political philosophical foundation that genuinely cultured human beings require. It must embody the basic conclusion of Frederick Douglass: *no struggle, no progress.*

It is quite interesting to note that, as we approach the year 2000, a nearly thirty-five-year-old (and almost entirely forgotten) statement on social and educational philosophy written during Marcuse's most militant middle period has come under sharp attack (in 1998) by Alan Charles Kors and Harvey A. Silverglate in *The Shadow University: The Betrayal of Liberty on America's Campuses.*[41] Kors and Silverglate assert that "The contemporary movement to restrict liberty on campus arose specifically in the provocative work of the late Marxist political and social philosopher Herbert Marcuse. . . ."[42] They focus on Marcuse's 1965 essay, "Repressive Tolerance" (RT), to demonstrate that Marcuse was not tolerant of all political views. It is certainly true that Marcuse was not a relativist nor a value pluralist. He did not tolerate all views as equally valid or invalid. Far from it: "This pure tolerance of sense and nonsense. . . ." (RT, 94), practiced under the conditions prevailing in the United States today, ". . . cannot fulfill the civilizing function attributed to it by the liberal protagonists of democracy, namely protection of dissent" (RT, 117). "To treat the great crusades *against* humanity . . . with the same impartiality as the desperate struggles *for* humanity means neutralizing their opposite historical function, reconciling the executioners with their victims, distorting the record" (RT, 113).

Kors and Silverglate allege that campus radicals are today making vocal criticisms of the First Amendment and calling for restrictions on the principles of liberty of thought and action, and that Marcuse's writings have been the philosophical inspiration to contemporary forms of political correctness on college campuses in the United States. In their view, ". . . Marcuse's prescriptions are the model for the assaults on free speech in today's academic world."[43] As they see it, campus codes against hate speech are themselves responsible for what they characterize as an atmosphere of repression and fear in higher education today and must be viewed as suppressive of speech itself. Following the current thinking of the U.S. Supreme Court they argue that the core of the First Amendment is "content neutrality"[44] and because Marcuse's critical theory is not content neutral, it undermines freedom of speech. In so doing Kors and Silverglate present a conservative view of student rights that is simultaneously an opportunistic defense of pluralism and relativism where this is thought to be useful against Marcuse's radically democratic politics as well as against his commitment to more classical (and rational) standards of expression.

It is particularly ironic that Kors and Silverglate present Marcuse as a stark antipode to John Stuart Mill, whom they see as "the classic intellectual spokesperson for freedom of thought and action. "The struggle for liberty on American campuses is, in its essence, the struggle between Herbert Marcuse and John Stuart Mill."[45] I wish to indicate briefly how Kors and Silverglate have shifted the ground away from Marcuse and Mill's progressive political emphasis on rationality and on the emancipatory nature of oppositional thinking (i.e., the higher level learning attained through the collision of opposing *arguments*, not merely opposing *opinions*). Instead, they read Mill according to their own conservative emphasis on an abstract and indiscriminate defense of what they believe is the *absolute public* right of any person to express *any* opinion *regardless of its content or meaning or repressive societal impact.*

Marcuse, like J. S. Mill, maintained that directly and in the first instance we are all free to hold whatever opinion we choose, but that even true opinion *as mere opinion* is worth little in the public sphere if it is bereft of an intellectual foundation. The second part of Mill's famous chapter "Of the Liberty of Thought and Discussion," in his book *On Liberty*, stresses our obligation to know the *grounds* of our convictions, so that even true opinion might not abide "as a dead dogma" or "as a prejudice, a belief independent of, and proof against, argument, . . ."[46] but be understood as the outcome of reasoned discourse.

In this sense, Marcuse builds explicitly upon Mill stressing the fact that intellectual legitimacy is ". . . not a matter of value preference but of rational criteria" (RT, 101), and rather than advocating the content neutrality or value relativism of Kors and Silverglate, Marcuse writes that ". . . in Mill, every rational human being participates in the discussion and decision—but only as a rational being" (RT, 106). Both Marcuse and Mill conceive of authentic democracy as possessing a political culture that honors the collision of opposing accounts as a precondition for the pursuit of truth. In their common estimation authentic democracy presupposes that society is free and that there is an educational and cultural context that facilitates autonomous thought. But it is just this genuine democracy that remains to be accomplished in the United States (even today, in the Marcusean view), and Marcuse contended that this must still be accomplished for emancipatory philosophical as well as for political reasons.

Kors and Silverglate do not discuss Marcuse's *One-Dimensional Man, Eros and Civilization, An Essay on Liberation,* or *The Aesthetic Dimension.* Thus they do not really make a substantive analysis of his historical arguments to the effect that we do not yet possess the societal conditions for a universal political freedom, nor do they mount a critique of his sociological study of knowledge and control issues in education and culture. These First Amendment absolutists simply acquiesce when confronted with evidence of the discriminatory effects of class-, race-, and gender-based forms of oppression. They do not seem to think that an absolute right to abusive speech is profoundly problematic in a culture like ours where there is no shortage of voices of hate and acts of persecution. Marcuse, to the contrary, believed that the doctrine of "pure tolerance" was systematically utilized by reactionary forces to abuse equality guarantees and to derail or destroy even the possibility of democratic egalitarianism.

According to Marcuse, what we *do* have in our advanced industrial societies is a contest of ideas and a contest for control within cultures generally and within educational institutions in particular. If we all have a de jure right to express any opinion in public, the de facto condition is that left opinions are usually marginalized and often suppressed, while right-wing ones, which benefit the ruling class, are given free play. Mill recognized an analogous problem in his own time which I shall discuss below. The problem today is really one of which ideas are distributed and amplified by the mass media, so that through repetition and placement in powerful media sources they become dominant, legitimized, and authoritative. Marcuse developed a critical theory of advanced industrial society and its ideological impacts, and participated in the waves of student protest against the forms of unfreedom accepted as natural or inevitable. What we *need* in his view is a new social framework where authentic democracy would first make universal tolerance possible. Marcuse argued in the mid-1960s that we did not yet possess the conditions of pure freedom of thought in contemporary societies such as the United States, England, or Germany. He emphasized the fact that the formation of public opinion was largely controlled by oligopolistic media owned by concentrated capital, and that dissenters had but a slim chance of influencing the debate because the price was generally out of reach of the radical opposition (RT, 118). Furthermore, the established doctrine of content neutrality served to reinforce the conventional pretense to freedom while obscuring its factual absence. Thus critical theorizing can stress the concepts of rationality and de facto instead of de jure as keys to discrediting the center-right view feigning a concern for human and civil rights. Following Brodsky,[47] the principle of *universality* should also be emphasized here so as to preclude a "right" to oppose its intended outcome of universal entitlement. This argument with regard to universality is a first step in counteracting the inadequacy of the process-in-a-content-free-vacuum approach (of both conservatives and liberals) and to suggest effective remedies. The main progressive weapon here is a set of specifically enumerated economic and social rights for all that define general and enforceable conditions of justice, such as *Charter 2000*, and that also imply legitimate limitations on the abstract idea of freedom. Another major weapon is the United Nations' *Universal Declaration of Human Rights*, to which I shall turn momentarily.

But first, can we really accept the doctrine of content neutrality, as Kors and Silverglate would have us do? They cite Justice Antonin Scalia's 1992 ruling upholding this doctrine in *R.A.V. v. City of St. Paul, Minnesota*. The Court found the antihate crime law of St. Paul to be so one-sided or lopsided in its impact (purportedly "discriminating" against racist speech but not other types of fighting words) that a fair fight (to use Justice Scalia's metaphor) on a substantive social issue is impossible under it. Justice Scalia expresses the Court's thinking in the second paragraph of section 2 of the decision formulating the following statement that I take to be twisted and racist. "In its practical operation, moreover, the ordinance goes even beyond mere content discrimination, to actual viewpoint discrimination. Displays containing some words—odious racial epithets, for example,—would be prohibited to proponents of all views. But 'fighting words' that do not themselves invoke race, color, creed, religion, or gender—aspersions upon someone's mother, for example—would seemingly be usable ad libitum in the placards of those in favor of racial, color, etc., tolerance, and equality but could not be used by that speaker's opponents. . . . St. Paul has no such authority to license one side of a debate to fight freestyle, while requiring the other to follow the Marquis of Queensbury Rules."

Kors and Silverglate (and the Supreme Court majority in the case they invoke) presumably would not condone racist violence. Should hate speech lead to violence, they would doubtless support intervention against actions motivated by hate. But in their ardent defense of an abstract freedom of speech they suppress aspects of even Mill's views on the subject. For the right-wing culture warriors it seems like this is just another case of reverse discrimination. Mill would *not* have agreed. Along with his several arguments in defense of freedom of thought and speech, and consistent with his defense of dissent, Mill writes:

> It is proper to state that I forgo any advantage which could be derived to my argument from the idea of abstract right as a thing independent of utility. I regard utility as the ultimate appeal on all ethical questions; but it must be utility in the largest sense, grounded on the permanent interests of man as a progressive being. Those interests, I contend, authorize the subjugation of individual spontaneity to external control only in respect to those actions of each which concern the interest of other people. If anyone does an act hurtful to others, there is a *prima facie* case for punishing him by law, or where legal penalties are not safely applicable, by general disapprobation.[48]

Mill also writes:

> Undoubtedly, the manner of asserting an opinion, even though it be a true one, may be very objectionable and may justly incur severe censure . . . whatever unfair advantage can be derived by any opinion from this mode of asserting it accrues almost exclusively to received opinions . . . unmeasured vituperation employed on the side of the prevailing opinion really does deter people from professing contrary opinions and from listening to those who profess them. . . . For the interest, therefore of truth and justice it is far more important to restrain this employment of vituperative language than the other; and, for example if it were necessary to choose, there would be much more need to discourage offensive attacks on infidelity than on religion.[49]

When conservative commentators deride multicultural and antiracist educational reformers as barbarians at the gate, at least they get right the general state of power relations in higher education. Kors and Silverglate, on the other hand, assert that multiculturalism has brought to higher education an oppressive intolerance of dissent that has become the "regnant political orthodoxy" constraining expressions of subtle or overt racism and sexism. Reacting against certain comparatively rare instances where campus speech codes have been utilized to sanction individuals whose questionable/negative/abusive speech was directed against minority students and women, Kors and Silverglate try to turn the tables against campus judiciaries and come to the aid instead of those cited for harrassment, and who are said (in a manner both disproportionate and fallacious) to have suffered a far greater harm: ". . . we wanted among other things to bear witness to the victims of unbearable oppression and intrusion and to name for public obliquy their unjust tormentors."[50]

Thus, Kors and Silverglate turn their attention to Marcuse. They impugn his motives in an ad hominem appeal made in that chapter of their book called "Marcuse's Revenge," a heading they make no attempt to elucidate or explain. Having been forced to flee from Germany's fascist *Gleichschaltung* and worse in the 1930s, Marcuse exposed the repressive and destructive nature of indiscriminate tolerance in the essay that Kors and Silverglate deride. Writing of the Nazi organizers of institutionalized violence Marcuse said:

> . . . if democratic tolerance had been withdrawn when the future leaders started their campaign, mankind would have had a chance of avoiding Auschwitz and a World War. . . . Such extreme suspension of the right of free speech and free assembly is indeed justified only if the whole of society is in extreme danger. . . . Withdrawal of tolerance from regressive movements *before* they can become active; intolerance even toward thought, opinion, and word, and finally intolerance in the opposite direction, that is toward the self-styled conservatives, to the political Right—these anti-democratic notions respond to the actual development of the democratic society which has destroyed the basis for universal tolerance. The conditions under which tolerance can again become a liberating force have still to be created. (RT, 110–11)

Mill's ideas as well as those of Marcuse, do have their own structural limitations.[51] They fail to emphasize adequately the role of economic conflict and the centrality of class divisions within contemporary societies and governing institutions. The problem is not just that of the reactionary use made of an abstractly defined freedom of speech, but of concrete political and economic domination and oppression. The state is an expression of material inequalities, and, having been captured by the exploitative forces, the state is not neutral even when it defines an aspect of justice in terms of content neutrality. Mill, and to some degree also Marcuse, continue in liberalism's epochal false consciousness about restrictions on freedom as deformations of culture within a democratic frame, when the frame is but form, and the deformations the substance. Within the current forms of unfreedom that are yet called democracies, the prevention-of-harm criterion used by Mill to legitimate government prohibitions has been, and will continue to be, utilized against the left, often simply by imputing some threat to democracy as in the case of McCarthyism or antihate crime regulations, while many real crimes by the right will be tolerated in practice (e.g., systematic police brutality; supplying arms and training to governments and armed groups around the world that commit torture, political killings and other human rights abuses; depriving millions of Americans from comprehensive health care; treating asylum seekers as criminals; and implementing the death penalty in a racially biased manner).[52]

Supreme Court justices are chosen on the basis of the lens through which they interpret legal matters, that is, politically, not in any sense because they are democratically representative of the interests of the governed. Nor is there any systematic way to ensure a balance of political perspectives, which tend to be center-right. Yet the deliberations of nine individuals settle the "rules of the game" in this political culture, and there is no tribunal beyond it (unless this be the United Nations). Federal judges have recently come under nationwide criticism for not disclosing the fact that they have substantial investments in the very companies involved in cases over which they preside. (See *The Kansas City Star*, January 14, 1999, p. A-8, "Memo again warns judges to avoid conflicts of interest") The unstated assumption in this criticism is that federal judges are not able to detach themselves from their material interests, a consideration I would also extend to the material interests of justices serving on the U.S. Supreme Court.

As I revise this manuscript in mid-1999, I feel compelled to mention three nationally significant incidents involving hate crimes and hate speech that have lately been viewed as repellent by much of the public.[53] First, the brutal bashing, binding, and robbery (ultimately fatal) of a gay student, Matthew Shepard, in Laramie, Wyoming. Second, the racially motivated killing last summer of James Byrd Jr., who was dragged to death by racists in a pickup truck. On 10 October 1998 the KKK rallied for white rights at the courthouse in Texas where three white men were scheduled to stand trial for Byrd's murder/lynching. Third, a New York City police officer was fired for mocking black people and for reenacting a racist killing (that of Byrd) on a float in a parade. Of late the New York Police Department operates with a policy against association with organizations that advocate hatred, oppression, or prejudice toward a racial or religious group. The New York Civil Liberties Union (ACLU) argues, however, that this officer, off duty at the time of the incident, was illegally fired for merely exercising his free speech rights. The ACLU has been captured by political libertarians and has become the handmaiden of the right-wing and corporations, betraying its historical constituency. Besides Nazis and hate speech, it defends the rights of corporations as if they were persons and unrestricted campaign contributions as the equivalent of unrestricted speech.

Essential to this libertarian Free Speech absolutism is the "pure" tolerance that Marcuse criticizes as being "extended to policies, conditions, and modes of behavior which should not be tolerated because they are impeding, if not destroying, the chances of creating an existence without fear and misery" (RT, 82). The doctrine of pure tolerance functions today to subvert the authentic defense of human rights and liberty. The United Nations' *Universal Declaration of Human Rights* (1948) recognized this danger in the aftermath of World War II and clearly articulated an egalitarian and antiracist defense of human rights (see especially its preamble and articles 1 and 2). Broader than the Supreme Court's current reading of the U.S. Constitution, the U.N. *Universal Declaration* confirmed and sealed these rights in its articles 29 and 30, the latter of which reads: "Nothing in this Declaration may be interpreted as implying for any State, group or person any right to engage in any activity or to perform any act aimed at the destruction of any of the rights and freedoms set forth herein."

In the U.S. context, I see the current skewed use of the First Amendment to protect the speech and action of those intent upon destroying the liberty rights or civil rights of others to be a clear infringement of the criterion of universality embedded in these provisions. *Charter 2000* likewise maintains in "Section V. Democracy" that "democratic process and procedures must not be used to restrict civil and human rights, or to enable or further undemocratic outcomes."

Ten years before the U.N. *Universal Declaration*, and almost thirty years before Marcuse, the mature Georg Lukács defended a similar notion:

Authentic freedom, i.e. freedom from the reactionary prejudices of the imperialist era (not merely in the sphere of art) cannot possibly be attained through mere spontaneity or by persons unable to break through the confines of their own immediate experience. For as capitalism develops, the continuous production and reproduction of these reactionary prejudices is intensified and accelerated. . . . If we are ever going to achieve a critical distance from such prejudices, this can only be accomplished by hard work, by abandoning and transcending the limits of immediacy, by scrutinizing all subjective experiences and measuring them against social reality. In short it can only be achieved by a deeper probing of the real world.[54]

This is where the educational applications of critical theorizing would be especially pertinent. In the dominator systems that characterize global cultures today, not even the oppressors or their children are capable of coming to self-knowledge strictly through the agency of those educational institutions committed fundamentally to the reproduction of an oppressive social division of labor. In such societies, educational institutions essentially replicate our fundamental class-based alienation. Only through the practical and intellectual opposition to established systems of domination can *any* theorist emancipate himself or herself from the mystifications of even the most consoling fabrications of oppressor systems. And only thus does practice or theory become critical.

Through collective emancipatory struggle we equip ourselves with a comparative and critical view of the multidimensional experience of being human and being oppressed. We learn outside as well as inside of these institutions of domination, often in spite of them. But we must come to understand the history of competing warrants for knowledge claims, moral judgments, and political goals. In dialectically theorizing the supersedure of our alienated lives and labor, we find the central criteria that are indispensable if social and educational theory are to be emancipatory.

A Concluding Backward Glance

In 1929 Marcuse was a graduate student in a lecture of Martin Heidegger's called "Introduction to Academic Study." Marcuse was *Protokollant*: he was assigned to transcribe Heidegger's presentation that centered on the theory of learning and empowerment in Plato's myth of the cave. This transcript is preserved in the Herbert Marcuse Archive in Frankfurt. According to Marcuse's notes, Heidegger stressed the fact that academic study had become to him a cause for consternation: the university had become too much like a *Warenhaus*, a "department store," where students absentmindedly pursue credentials (even in law or medicine) without ever examining philosophically weighty matters such as crime, guilt, death, sickness, and unfreedom. "Today we do not even know *what* we are to be liberated *from*. Yet it is exactly this knowledge that is the condition of every genuine emancipation."[55] This is the standard conservative reaction to the chaos of the 1920s, the weak Weimar democracy, and the collapse of imperial authoritarianism, but this is not our problem today when globalized corporate capitalism represents probably the most widespread authoritarian structure in the history of the world.[56]

Heidegger's *Being and Time* (1927) had indicated that we must be liberated from the alienation we experience in everyday, factical modes of being, by being philosophically redeemed through an authentic awareness of death as our ownmost possibility. This seems to be clerical metaphysics in a secular guise, and perhaps it has something in common with the Nazi death cult. In Kant's classic formulation, we needed to be liberated from our tendencies toward voluntary servitude (*selbstverschuldene Unmündigkeit*). Marx argued that *critical* knowledge is knowledge that enables the social negation of the social negation of human life's core activities, the most central of which are neither being-toward-death, nor subservience, but creative labor. The legal usurpation of the product of this labor by owners of capital, is *what* (according to his analysis in the *1844 Manuscripts*), we, *as sensuous living labor, are to be liberated from*. The political restoration of this product and the democratization of the production and distribution processes would be the most potent forces restoring us from our alienated to our proper selves. Marx's theory of the supersession of alienated labor provides the fundamental norm of justice for the future.

In this lecture, however, held after the publication of *Being and Time*, Heidegger argues that we need to free ourselves from the inauthentic comfort and security represented by immediate forms of consciousness (e.g., religion) which are simply accepted and conventional. Heidegger says the core question confronting a human being is *Who am I?* Like Socrates we must dare to discover our authentic selves through self-examination. Like Plato we must strive to see not merely with our eye, but with the light of intelligence that brightens thought. Plato asks about *paideia*, whether or not we have come to know ourselves, our real fiber and substance, our real identity. According to Heidegger, once imprisoned in a world of things, we discover that we are not things; we are capacities or powers. Following Aristotle (but breaking through his formal logic) we must endeavor to actualize these capacities (our virtue urging us to become theoretically and morally accomplished). In so doing human beings resolve to overcome alienation and become what we essentially are: free, flourishing social animals.

This is of course an articulate insight into the foundation of the Western intellectual tradition, but despite these worthy efforts, Heidegger and Marcuse and much of this century's radical theorists of alienation have generally deflected attention away from Marx and Engels's theory of the dynamics of capital accumulation and the economy's central cultural fetish with production for exchange rather than for use, not to mention their dialectical and materialist analysis of the dynamics of nature and the historical emergence of human identity through social interaction with the world mediated by the objectifying activities of labor and art. In pursuit of a disalienating aesthetic or ontological authenticity, apart from the Marxist economic and political agenda that stresses the necessity of labor's revolutionary emancipation, the existential/hermeneutical approach has preserved and protected the capitalist obsession with the commodification of labor and life, even while philosophically distancing itself from it. Marx's analysis of alienation—and program against it—are absolutely essential to the achievement of what Marcuse highlights as the goal of Kant's educational philosophy: "the better future condition of the human race" (CR, 27). While the abolition of the wages-system is not absolutely *sufficient* to secure the conditions for each of us to become all that we are capable of being, the alienation and exploitation of labor is the enabling material core that permits, if not to say requires, society to legitimate a variety of other forms of social oppression. We have learned from the movements against racism and sexism that class relations do not wholly demarcate structures of dominator power. Racism, patriarchy, anti-Semitism, homophobia, and other forms of discrimination, disrespect, and inequality sorely inhibit our powers of actualization. To theorize scientifically the cultural transformation of each of these negations and to be engaged politically and culturally with the labor force to end them must be the essential logic and manifesto of all future critical theory.

Such a critical materialist theory would also be consistent with Kant's insight that humanity (and that is to say each of us individually) creates something of real moral value when our hearts and minds combine to generate good will toward one another. John Rawls recently gave this ethic of classical

German idealism a concrete quality when he theorized the common good as a social formation having institutions serving equally the needs of all.

Looking toward the future, the feminist theorist Riane Eisler has stressed the fact that there is a link between world peace and a politics of partnership and equality, especially equality between men and women. Like Marcuse in *Eros and Civilization*, she returns to ancient Greek society (in *The Chalice and the Blade*) for a model of the politics of pacification. Where Marcuse looked to the images of Orpheus and Narcissus, Eisler looks to the Minoan culture of ancient Crete as a form of partnership, as distinguished from dominator, culture. She maintains that this early Minoan culture crystallized around mores of linking and sharing rather than hierarchy. Masculine and feminine roles were socially differentiated, but not politically unequal. *Gylany* is a term she coins to describe this condition of female (*gy*) and male (*an*) partnership in contrast to patriarchy and privilege. She notes that the high artistic achievements of Minoan culture never glorified war or military life, but rather the beauty of aquatic flora and fauna and the relaxed human body confident and at ease with itself. These are viewed as exhibiting gylanic values of gentleness and peace. This is not to say that art in partnership societies must be merely decorative, rather Minoan art appears to exhibit authentic human flourishing. Eisler's findings resonate deeply with Marcuse's aesthetic vision and with his desire for an economy based on caring rather than domination. In her view we must choose to move the future toward a time when "all institutions, not only those specifically designed for the socialization of children, will have as their goal the actualization of our great human potentials."[57]

The liberation of these philosophical tendencies latent in the core interests of critical social theory can facilitate cultural transformation. Reconstituted in this sense, critical theory can help generate the political ingenuity and action required to advance significantly toward the nonalienated character, conscience, and culture that our needs require us to envision. Critical theorizing must have sufficient social and political scope to generate an energizing sense of solidarity in face of the manifold material conditions of alienation. It can do so only if it is intent upon resolving the multiple problems of human and civil rights, militarism, the environment, exploitation, and education *on the basis* of what this analysis has tried to vindicate as the most necessary and critical elements in the writings of Marx and Marcuse. A rematerialized analysis of the dynamics of capital accumulation—the increasing concentration of wealth and the dramatic polarization of the global economy—is key to comprehending the intensifying interpersonal ramifications of estrangement: isolation, disrespect, disunity, and disempowerment. Critical theorizing in this form rethinks both rationality and the economic order and provides us with the necessary and developing standards of informed judgment about alienation and democratic social transformation. These criteria enable us to build from within the realities of the present the partnership organizations and institutions of the future that will permit new ways of holding resources and real opportunities for all persons to reclaim the full social power of labor, leadership, and learning.

Appendix
Charter 2000: A Comprehensive Political Platform

Kansas City Progressive Network
Ratified May 1996

Contents Summary

Charter 2000

Introduction

Charter 2000 summarizes in highly concentrated form the issues, policies, and goals the signatories believe should become part of a national debate on the future of this country. We offer it to progressive individuals, political organizations, and parties with the objective of circulating it throughout the United States, and indeed, around the world, to stimulate discussion of its contents. Since this document is still in the process of evolution, we solicit on an individual and a group basis your thoughts, revisions, and additions, as well as the platforms, programs, mission statements and the like that you or your organization have developed.

To provide an open democratic public forum for discussion, the Kansas City Progressive Network established the PROGRESSIVE CLEARINGHOUSE BULLETIN, a newsletter devoted to Charter 2000 and the issues it raises. To participate or subscribe ($10/year for four issues) write:

Progressive Clearinghouse
Box 8744
Prairie Village, KS 66208 U.S.A.

Charter 2000 is the latest version of a document initiated four years ago and circulated nationally and internationally in various forms, with contributions by some 60 people. It has also drawn on a variety of published sources (acknowledged below), the work of individuals and groups with special expertise. It was further developed and adopted in its current form in May 1996 by the Kansas City Progressive Network, whose members represent a wide spectrum of progressive opinion.

We believe it is high time to formulate a comprehensive, sustaining vision and program around which fragmented progressive constituencies can unite. Such a vision is an indispensable mass organizing tool for long-term change. A careful reading of the Charter shows that it is not a random laundry list but a broad and coherent political orientation grounded in fundamental human values. While the merits of each point should be debated separately, the Charter stresses their interconnectedness. The achievement of individual goals depends in large part on the enduring attainment of many others.

This Charter envisions a generous, inclusive, fair, and democratic society where the value of the work its members do is one of the foundations on which it rests. It is genuinely democratic because everyone is empowered, not just the privileged few. It honors the democratic process and works for democratic outcomes, maximizing the potential of all members of the community without excluding, marginalizing, discriminating against, or exploiting any individuals or groups. It guarantees each person the basis for a decent life of his or her own choice and encourages a productive one, and it lives in peaceful relations with itself, other societies, and the natural environment.

The vision on which *Charter 2000* draws is summarized in the CAPITAL-
IZED NUMBERED HEADINGS of each section of the document: PEACE,
JUSTICE, SOLIDARITY/COMMUNITY, RIGHTS, DEMOCRACY, PUBLIC
DOMAIN AND SERVICES, ABUNDANCE, AND ECOLOGY. A separate sec-
tion details the basic rights which we believe should be constitutionally guaranteed
to all members of a society: JOBS/INCOME, HOUSING, ACCOMMODATIONS,
FOOD, CLOTHING, UTILITIES, HEALTH CARE, TRANSPORTATION,
COMMUNICATION/MEDIA, EDUCATION, CULTURE AND THE ARTS,
CHILD CARE, CITIZEN/CONSUMER POWER, and MOBILITY. These
rights, intended not to replace but to supplement already existing rights, are at best
spottily supported in U.S. constitutional and statutory law and available in practice
to increasingly fewer people here and abroad.

The signatories to Charter 2000 agreed unanimously on the overwhelming
majority of its contents (most favor some form of mixed economy). The seven statements on which consensus could not be reached are marked with double asterisks
(**). There was unanimous agreement that all its ideas, both consensual and dis-
puted, should be given the widest possible circulation and discussion.

The Charter presents a set of desirable outcomes unified by a common vision
without specific recommendations on strategy. (But see item 3 under section VII.
ABUNDANCE for proposals about funding a just socio-economic system.) Some of
the Charter's goals could be attained in short order, while others are more long range.
Strategy and actions will come from experience. We prefer flexibility: any strategy
that furthers the broad progressive transformation of American society is a good one.

There are many effective ways of advancing progressive goals, ranging from
educational efforts to testimony before public bodies, community and labor organizing, electoral and media campaigns, and actions in the streets (rallies, marches,
demonstrations, picketing, and civil disobedience). We recommend immediately
deploying some of the principles and concepts found in the Charter to challenge
those running for office in this election year.

The radical right has successfully formulated its own comprehensive program.
In spite of claims to the contrary, in practice it consists of greed benefiting the few,
stinginess and meanness for the many, and intolerance and punishment of all who
don't fit their reactionary vision of life and society.

So far the alternatives have been limited to piecemeal defensive measures. We
believe that it is now imperative for us all to set our own agenda, together. We must
hammer out what we really do want, rather than make do with what we are "given."
Instead of being reactive, we must become proactive, seizing the initiative around a
set of fundamental principles and persisting in our vision no matter how long its
achievement may take.

It is now time to complete the Revolution of human rights and the age-old dream
of Justice, begun by Paine, Jefferson and our other courageous ancestors 200 years ago.

If you wish to become a signatory, to the document as a whole or to specific
parts of it, we will add your name.

SIGNATORIES (in alphabetical order)

Herbert Aptheker
Dee Berry
David Brodsky
Patricia Brodsky
Vincent Ferrini
Roena Haynie
Ben Kjelshus
Meridel LeSueur
Peter Meyers
Barbara Morrison
Tom Page
Charles Reitz
Mary Stuart
Art Thomas
Fred Whitehead

Platform

I. Peace

1. peaceful, nonviolent, and civilian economy and society; teach nonviolent conflict resolution
2. dismantle national security state system (including its military and police agencies), convert to peacetime society, eliminate political surveillance
3. foreign relations based on peaceful cooperation and international grassroots solidarity; end U.S. aggression against other nations and peoples: military training (e.g. School of the Americas) and intervention, corporate colonization, propaganda agencies (e.g. AID, National Endowment for Democracy, American Institute for Free Labor); abolish CIA and transfer its non-covert and legal information gathering functions to a new agency with full democratic oversight
4. severe reduction in military budget and in size of armed forces; nuclear and conventional disarmament; end research, testing, and production of biological, chemical, and nuclear weapons
5. end military sales to foreign countries, especially repressive regimes; eliminate U.S. military bases in foreign countries and territories
6. honor democratically established laws and treaties, national and international, including with Native Peoples
7. end embargoes that punish civilian populations

II. *Justice*

1. end classism, racism, sexism (gender and sexual orientation), ageism, domination by single culture or religion; support affirmative action
2. legitimate aim of economic activity is to optimize the common good
3. equal rights under just laws for all individuals, people before profits
4. democratic and fair distribution of wealth, property, and power
5. priority of resource allocation to the poorest and most oppressed
6. fair tax system, with genuine/steep progressivity; reduce tax burden on lower and middle incomes, wealthy and corporations pay fair share; wealth tax on net worth over $5 million; taxes on largest corporations raised to at least 50%; tax capital gains as ordinary income; replace state property and sales taxes with progressive income taxes
7. end corporate welfare, public giveaways, 14th Amendment protection of corporations (corporations as persons); rewrite corporate charter law, abolish charters in case of corporate crime; strict personal civil and criminal liability of corporate officers and agents
8. democratize, abolish, or replace U.S. Federal Reserve, IMF, World Bank, NAFTA, GATT, WTO; write off or reduce third world debt; low or zero interest rates for international lending to third world for non-military purposes

III. *Solidarity/Community*

1. encouragement of human solidarity and cooperation, locally, regionally, nationally, and internationally
2. sensible balance of community and individual values
3. build toward national and international progressive coalitions (democratic labor and citizens' movements, grass-roots-based NGOs)
4. open international borders to ordinary people, e.g. Mexican border
5. empower people in their communities, consistent with fairness, social responsibility and human rights, to meet local needs and defend communities against exploitative forces
6. discouragement of cutthroat competition (between individuals, groups, institutions, cities, states, nations); end discrimination and scapegoating
7. oppose fascism in all its forms

IV. *Rights:*

Constitutionally guaranteed unconditional universal social, political, and economic ENTITLEMENTS, many in the public domain, for all individuals, no exceptions

A. categories of basic rights/entitlements [also see "RIGHTS/ENTITLE-MENTS, detailed treatment"]

NB: these rights are generally absent in U.S. constitutional and statutory law; they do not replace but supplement already existing rights; for other rights see section b. below

1. jobs/income,
2. food, clothing, housing, accommodations, utilities,
3. health care,
4. transportation,
5. communication/media,
6. education,
7. culture/arts,
8. child care,
9. citizen/consumer empowerment,
10. mobility

B. basic freedoms, civil and human rights
   See U.S. Bill of Rights, Civil Rights Amendments and Acts, U.N. Universal Declaration of Human Rights (includes economic rights), Youth Bill of Rights April 95, plus rights to personal privacy and sexual and reproductive choice

V. Democracy:

genuine democracy for everyone; political, social, economic; democratic process and outcomes

Democratic process and procedures must not be used to restrict civil and human rights, or to enable or further undemocratic outcomes (see II. Justice, above, and V.C. below)

A. Democratic process and structure [also see RIGHTS, 11. CITIZEN/CONSUMER POWER]
   1. power belongs to the grass roots, rank and file; empowered by democratic institutions
   2. decision-making power, especially economic decision-making, resides in all individuals affected by a decision (workers, consumers, communities); e.g. workers' control over investment of their own pension funds, to be used for meeting community needs; shareholder democracy
   3. democratic control of all public and private institutions; accountable to the community they serve
   4. democratic management: a) fundamental policy decisions made by all individuals affected; b) major policy decisions made by elected board fairly representing all constituencies affected; c) day-to-day decisions made by workers on the job
   5. Simplify and clarify legal language to eliminate jargon and obscurity and make it accessible to non-specialists

B. Electoral reform
  1. public financing of elections, available to all qualified candidates; prohibit corporate campaign contributions and political activity (e.g. lobbying, PACs); strict limits on individual campaign contributions, including by candidates
  2. free and fair access to media, fair media reporting, for all qualified candidates
  3. remove obstacles to voting; easy universal voter registration; voting day holiday
  4. remove qualification and maintenance obstacles to independent candidates and parties; legalize fusion, cross-endorsement, proportional representation; binding none-of-the-above ballot option
  5. eliminate unreasonable petition requirements, closed primaries, voter purges (except when voters die or move away)
  6. expand binding initiative, referendum, recall
  7. direct election of president, eliminate electoral college
  8. guaranteed living wage for persons holding political office (permits non-affluent individuals, who must quit current jobs, to hold office)

C. Democratic outcomes
  1. political-economic
    a. no concentration of wealth, property, and power in the possession of privileged individuals or groups, elite classes, undemocratic institutions
    b. moderate (not excessive) income differential between highest and lowest income/pay scales
    c. democratic economy: democratic public financing, ownership, and management of all large enterprises (e.g. social services, education, transportation, petroleum, utilities, mass communication media, construction, large manufacturing) and financial institutions (e.g. banks, S&L's, insurance companies); low interest loans, rates capped at rate of inflation; no public lending for speculation
    d. massive public works program, for community investment and revitalization, especially of infrastructure; providing good jobs with good pay; through democratically financed, owned, and managed public employment (no public funding of private contractors, bar former military contractors from managing industries converted to non-military production); will help prevent flight of capital and factories, deindustrialization, and pork barrel for private profiteering
    e. encourage development of co-ops, credit unions, non-profit and employee owned small businesses
    f. mandate socially and ecologically responsible investing

g. interest-free federal loans to local communities and entities listed in e. above

2. social (diversity, no regimentation)

   a. equal rights under law and respect for all individuals, with regard to class, race, gender, sexual orientation, age, different abilities, language, culture, national origin, religion and its absence

   b. no discrimination against, underprivileging, or abuse of individuals and groups, based on criteria in paragraph 2a. above or on other criteria (e.g. marital status, immigrant status, political convictions, medical condition)

   c. end violence against women and children, lesbians, gays, and bisexuals, immigrants (e.g. rape, assault, battery, domestic abuse, sexual harassment in workplace and schools, female genital mutilation)

   d. separation of church and state, no official or mandatory religion

   e. no mandatory "patriotism", loyalty oaths

   f. treat drug addiction as a health matter, not a crime, establish national addiction-treatment system; classify alcohol and tobacco as dangerous drugs

   g. effective discouragement of and protection against crime, in streets or suites, whether perpetrated by individuals, groups, or institutions, private or governmental; fair and strict enforcement; penalties commensurate with the power of the criminal(s) and seriousness of the crime

   h. community controlled law enforcement for lesser offences and disputes and to maintain community order; community courts and justice centers emphasizing intervention, prevention, mediation; alternative sentencing for juvenile and nonviolent offenders; for more serious offenses guarantee non-affluent accused a qualified public defender

   i. end prison construction binge, eliminate super maximum security prisons; fair and humane treatment of prisoners, strengthen prisoners' rights to appeal, timely provision of needed medical care, no sensory deprivation, no automatic or protracted lockdowns, abolish chain gangs, eliminate death penalty

VI. Public Domain and Services

1. large and healthy public domain; restore privatized public enterprises and institutions to public sector; oppose privatization of public domain, private contracting of public services

2. public regulatory agencies encourage, protect, and enforce high standards

3. democratic public ownership and management of public enterprises and institutions
4. ban corporate use of public lands and resources on and under them, especially national parks
   Examples of public domain institutions, many of them traditional: 1) education, 2) libraries, 3) parks, 4) community centers, 5) social services, 6) post office, 7) telephone service, 8) utilities, 9) computer networks, 10) the media, 11) weather service, 12) housing, 13) culture/arts, 14) child care, 15) transportation, 16) streets, roads, highways, bridges, 17) regulatory agencies, 18) product testing institutions, 19) fire department, 20) police, 21) the military

VII. *Abundance*

1. Universal abundance, fairly distributed, based on ecological sustainability and efficiency; no (profitable) waste, planned obsolescence, accumulation of wealth and property beyond reasonable personal needs
2. necessities have priority over luxuries
3. funded by shifting from military to peacetime spending, converting military industry to productive peacetime uses; through fair taxation of corporations and the wealthy, of assets of banks, insurance companies, and financial institutions; through public acquisition at scrap prices of companies fleeing to areas with lower labor and environmental standards

VIII. *Ecology*

1. promote biodiversity and conserve natural resources; protect ecosystems and endangered species
2. promote source reduction, reuse, recycling; stop export of wastes, especially hazardous ones
3. develop environmentally friendly, energy-efficient technologies, e.g. renewable (non-nuclear) energy, including solar; close nuclear power plants and weapons facilities
4. promote sustainable organic agriculture; local or regional food production, processing, distribution, and consumption
5. prohibit environmental poisoning and damage, severe criminal penalties for non-compliance; eliminate toxic, nuclear, other harmful substances
6. convert or shut down environmentally hazardous industries; clean up toxic waste sites; use Superfund money for cleanup, not litigation
7. oppose environmental racism and classism (exposure in workplace and community to environmental hazards, toxic waste facilities, energy and mining industries)

8. include cost of pollution and environmental degradation in calculating full cost of production

Rights/Entitlements

1. *Jobs/Income*

a. secure jobs for all **who want to work** (100% full employment policy); rewarding work with a decent living; achievable in part through shorter work week (30 hours) with no cuts in pay; **double the minimum wage to $10/hour, index it to inflation**

b. guaranteed livable income for everyone; comfortable subsistence income (not punitively low) for those without jobs (e.g. students, sick, disabled, retired; unemployed, workers between jobs, on sabbatical, in school for retraining, on parental or home health care-giver leave); subsistence income permanently adjusted for inflation, financed through tax system, e.g. negative income tax

c. free choice in employment (dependent on qualifications of individual and democratically determined societal needs); **when, where, in what occupation, at what job to work**

d. motives for working: positive contribution to society and personal satisfaction with accomplishments; not restricted to coercion (e.g. survival) or greed (accumulation of wealth and property beyond reasonable personal needs)

e. remunerated work not limited to marketable labor; any labor that is useful or necessary to individuals or society is a job deserving fair pay (cf. volunteer work, housework, child rearing, caring for sick and elderly, free-lance intellectual and artistic work)

f. jobs with fair wages, fair hours, safe working conditions that don't damage health; no mandatory overtime, mandatory part time work, or mandatory unemployment; no underpaid part-time work for full-time labor

g. WORKERS' RIGHTS: guaranteed equal rights, benefits, and protections under law (e.g. no discrimination in the workplace, equal pay for comparable work) for all workers, in public and private enterprises, full or part-time, permanent or temporary, citizens or immigrants, in all occupations, including domestic, agricultural, intellectual, and artistic

   1) to organize: card check-off certification; guaranteed first union contract; legalize minority unions (bargaining units that receive less than a majority vote); severe (criminal) penalties for employers who interfere with organizing **through threats or coercion**; no company unions; repeal Taft-Hartley Act (1947)

2) to bargain collectively: effective penalties for employers that refuse to bargain or stall

3) to strike, to organize sympathy strikes and boycotts: no lockouts, firings, permanent replacement workers, government interference, court injunctions

4) to occupational health and safety; strengthen OSHA

5) to free speech, free assembly, and decision-making power in the workplace; strengthen NLRB

6) no child labor, forced labor, or slave labor (including in prisons)

7) thorough vocational education, job training, and job retraining; encouraging creativity, social solidarity, and pride in quality; jobs matched to individual's training and talents; retraining and new jobs for ALL displaced workers (not only in military, police, defense industry)

8) adequate leisure, time off, paid vacations (minimum 4-6 weeks per year); sabbaticals (for all workers, not just academics); secure and decent retirement (fully vested and transferable pensions); 1-2 years fully paid parental leave; up to a year's leave caring for sick, disabled, or elderly relatives at home

h. international trade agreements should require other nations to support workers' rights, (e.g. to organize, bargain, and strike, to decent pay, conditions, and vacations), and environmental protection

2. *Housing, Accommodations, Food, Clothing, Utilities*

a. subject to minimum standards of quality and safety; available to all (no discrimination permitted)

b. elimination of homelessness, **and of housing as an investment**; public financing of home buying, low interest rates

c. energy efficient construction of new homes, retrofitting of old ones

d. downsize public buildings (e.g. airports, shopping centers); require clear and reliable directions; eliminate mazes, prison and fortress style architecture

e. food: adequately labelled, organically grown; no pesticides, irradiation, genetic, biological, or chemical tampering

f. clothing: encourage design that is both practical and attractive, standardized sizes to fit all people, not just mannequins

g. local, state, or federally owned public utilities

3. *Health Care:*
(Canadian style single-payer system satisfies following requirements)

a. universal coverage and eligibility (no exclusions), standard package of high quality comprehensive benefits, patient's right to choose providers, provider's right to base decisions primarily on health criteria, affordable and fair financing, portability (including travel away from home and abroad), quality and cost controls

b. emphasis on prevention, education, public health, primary care, long term home care, service to underserved rural and urban areas, training of health care workers; community owned and controlled public nursing home system

c. democratic governance and oversight at all levels of system; patient-provider dialogue basis of all treatment, with no interference from third parties (e.g., private insurance companies, government)

d. treatment should minimize traumatic intervention

e. protected privacy of patient's records, to which patient has right to full access

4. *Transportation*

a. local and long distance: reliable, safe, low cost, fuel efficient; convenient access, scheduling, service, connections; accessible to disabled

b. fair distribution of service by geographical region of country

c. restore and rebuild urban mass transit, local and long distance rail service

d. design communities to eliminate long commutes and to encourage non-motorized transport (walking, bicycles, etc.)

e. restore strictly regulated and rationally planned air transport

f. public (local, state, or federal) ownership, control, and funding of airlines and other transport

g. minimize border and customs hassles and restrictions for ordinary people

5. *Communication/Media*

a. Public/community (local, state, or federal) ownership and democratic management of all mass communication media, especially broadcasting, with democratic access and accountability

b. Mail, phone, fax, computer and other communication services reliable, low cost, confidential, uncensored, with universal access

c. regulation of commercial advertising in all media

6. *Education*

a. tuition free

b. educational equity, massively increase funding levels for pupils and public schools in non-affluent communities

c. promote egalitarian structure in educational institutions, eliminate privileges across fields of specialization, including pay inequities for teachers

d. encourage life-long education, no arbitrary limits to developing abilities and skills

e. theoretical and practical education; analytical, critical, and vocational skills; social sciences, natural sciences, humanities (history, cultures, languages, and the arts); political, historical, and ethical education as the basis of an informed democracy

f. promotes individual self-esteem and community values

g. no "official" language, but required proficiency in at least one other language besides one's native tongue

h. oppose militarization in the schools and promote peace education

7. *Culture and the Arts*

a. pluralistic/multi-cultural; promotion of social and individual cultural expression; traditional and innovative; concerning potentially any aspect of individual and social life

b. preservation of and access to knowledge of the past, access to knowledge of the present

c. restricted neither to elites nor mass audiences, irreducible to model of (professional) production and (leisure) consumption, neither trivialized (e.g. as entertainment) nor cosmically over-inflated (e.g. as a cult)

d. generous and equitable public/community funding for cultural activities, whether research oriented or creative-artistic

e. cultural life free from commercial or bureaucratic domination

f. require public reports (lectures, exhibits, performances, etc.) for all public/community funded research or creative-artistic products

8. *Child Care*

a. low cost, conveniently located public centers, including at worksites and educational institutions, as well as in-home service

b. publicly regulated for safety, competence

c. low ratio of caregivers to children

d. fair and adequate pay for staff

9. *Citizen/Consumer Power*
[also see PLATFORM, V. DEMOCRACY, A. Democratic process and structure]

a. full legal standing for democratic grass-roots taxpayer, citizen, consumer, union, and community groups to monitor, regulate, and challenge public and private institutions and enterprises, in court or other official public forums, concerning issues like quality, safety, fairness, or legality of services, practices and products, including by means of class-action suits

b. encourage establishment of and access to consumer action watchdog, negotiating, and advocacy groups (e.g. through periodic inserts in utility and bank bills and statements, paid for by consumer groups)

c. legal protection of whistleblowers (individuals and groups), with severe penalties for interfering with their activities

d. public education campaign teaching citizen action, in schools, media, union, consumer, taxpayer, and other community groups

e. free, easy, and timely access to public and government information (e.g. through mail, telephone, faxes, public and home computers, prime time radio and TV programs, up-to-date and prominently displayed printed and other materials in public libraries and post offices)

f. increase citizen power over public purse, investment decisions, allocation of resources

10. Mobility

a. geographical: right to live and work where an individual chooses

b. vocational: right to change jobs or occupations and to receive education or training for new jobs or occupations

c. travel: right to travel freely, within U.S. and abroad, right to associate with whom one chooses

Published sources on which Charter 2000 draws:

"Common Ground Declaration." Final Document of the Third Parties '96 Conference, Wash., D.C., June 4, 1995.

Dugger, Ronnie. "Real Populists Please Stand Up" and "Altered State" *Nation*, August 14-21, 1995, pp. 159–164.

Freedom Charter, African National Congress, 1955.

The Greater Kansas City Greens. "Green Platform for Kansas City." Kansas City, MO: Sycamore Press, 1992.

Labor Party Discussion Bulletin. Issues of December, 1995, Jan-Feb, March, April 1996.

"Labor Party Platform Discussion." *Kansas City Area Labor Party Advocate*, March, 1995, pp. 6–8.

Nader, Ralph. "The Concord Principles: An Agenda for a New Initiatory Democracy." February 1, 1992.

National People's Progressive Network brochure, 1994.

Montague, Peter. "A High-Wage, Low-Waste Future, Part 3: A Democracy Campaign." *Rachels' Environment & Health Weekly* 460, September 21, 1995.

Sklar, Holly. "Economics for Everyone: Breaking the Cycle of Unequal Opportunity." *Z Magazine* Vol. 8, No. 7-8, July-August, 1995, pp. 44–50.

"UE Worker's Bill of Rights." Adopted at founding meeting of UE Local 893, Des Moines [nd].

"Universal Declaration of Human Rights." Adopted by United Nations General Assembly, 1948.

"Youth Bill of Rights, April 95." *Z Magazine* Vol 8. No. 9, September 1995, p. 25.

Notes

Chapter One

1. I have in mind commentators like Martha C. Nussbaum, Joseph Liberatore Devitis, Maxine Greene, Richard A. Brosio, Neil Postman, Henry A. Giroux, Peter McLaren, Ira Shor, Guy Senese, Ralph Page, Samuel Bowles, Herbert Gintis, Michael Apple, and Douglas Kellner.

2. See especially Maude Barlow and Tony Clarke, *MAI, The Multilateral Agreement on Investment and the Threat to American Freedom* (New York: Stoddart, 1998).

3. Allan Bloom, *The Closing of the American Mind* (New York: Simon & Schuster, 1987).

4. Alan Charles Kors and Harvey A. Silverglate, *The Shadow University: The Betrayal of Liberty on America's Campuses* (New York: Free Press, 1998).

5. Bloom, *Closing of the American Mind*, p. 152.

6. Ibid., p. 226.

7. Max Horkheimer and Theodor W. Adorno, *Dialectic of Enlightenment* (New York: Herder and Herder, 1972) p. 209. I stress here Marcuse's general philosophical agreement with the social analysis of Horkheimer and Adorno although several interesting theoretical and political conflicts have been well documented. On the many ways in which Horkheimer, Adorno, and Friedrich Pollock distanced themselves from Erich Fromm, Marcuse, Franz Neumann, and Jürgen Habermas, see Rolf Wiggershaus, *Die Frankfurter Schule* (München, Germany: Deutscher Taschenbuch Verlag, 1988).

285

8. Marcuse's philosophy is foundational to subsequent work in critical theory that has also developed on the basis of the general philosophical innovations of the Frankfurt School and Western Marxism (Albrecht Wellmer, Trent Schroyer, Douglas Kellner, Ben Agger, Paulo Freire, Henry A. Giroux, et al.). In addition, the legacy of this form of critical theory, especially its aestheticized, Nietzschean challenge to objectivist theory of knowledge, is felt within the more contemporary and related theoretical perspectives of deconstructionism and postmodernism (Jacques Derrida, Michel Foucault, and Jean-François Lyotard) and also the relativist epistemologies of some forms of feminist philosophy (Luce Irigaray). It is imperative that we analyze and transcend certain of the epistemological foundations of this kind of critical theory, especially with regard to the notion of alienation, if we wish to pursue our own critical theorizing to its highest levels.

9. Timothy J. Lukes points this out in *The Flight into Inwardness* (Selinsgrove, PA: Susquhanna University Press, 1985).

10. Charles Reitz, "Herbert Marcuse: Art, Alienation and the Humanities—On the Philosophical Foundations of Critical Theory of Culture and Education" (Ph.D. dissertation: State University of New York at Buffalo, 1983).

Eugen Fink, *Nietzsches Philosophie* (Stuttgart, Germany: W. Kohlhammer Verlag, 1968).

Mitchell Franklin, "On Hegel's Theory of Alienation and Its Historic Force," *Revolutionary World*, No. 9, 1974.

Franklin, "The Irony of the Beautiful Soul of Herbert Marcuse," *Telos*, No. 6, Fall 1970.

Heinz Paetzold, *Neomarxistische Ästhetik II: Adorno-Marcuse* (Düsseldorf, Germany: Schwann, 1974).

11. Barry M. Kátz, "New Sources of Marcuse's Aesthetics," *New German Critique*, No. 17, Spring 1979, p. 187.

12. Mark Van Doren, *Liberal Education* (Boston: Beacon, 1959) p. 67.

13. Kátz, "New Sources of Marcuse's Aesthetics," p. 186.

14. On the tensions between Marcuse and important leadership sources in the international student movement of the 1960s, see especially:

Franklin, "The Irony of the Beautiful Soul of Herbert Marcuse."

Paul Breines, "Marcuse and the New Left in America," in Jürgen Habermas (ed.), *Antworten auf Herbert Marcuse* (Frankfurt/M, Germany: Suhrkamp, 1968); also his article "From Guru to Spectre: Marcuse and the Implosion of the Movement," in Breines (ed.), *Critical Interruptions* (New York: Herder and Herder, 1970).

Shierry M. Weber, "Individuation as Praxis," in *Critical Interruptions*, pp. 22–59.

Jack Woddis, *New Theories of Revolution: Frantz Fanon, Regis Debray, Herbert Marcuse* (New York: International Publishers, 1972).

E. Batalov, *The Philosophy of Revolt* (Moscow: Progress, 1975).

15. Jared Israel and William Russell, "Herbert Marcuse and His Philosophy of Copout," *Progressive Labor Magazine*, Vol. 6, No. 5, October 1968; also Progressive Labor Party, "Marcuse: Copout or Cop?" *Progressive Labor Magazine*, Vol. 6, No. 6, January 1969.

16. See, for example, the 1942 typescript "The New German Mentality: Memorandum on a Study in the Psychological Foundations of National Socialism and the Chances of their Destruction," (Frankfurt Marcuse Archive manuscript number 0119.00; also *Technology, War and Facism: Collected Papers of Herbert Marcuse* [WF, 141]). Marcuse neither attributes fascist behavior to the "mass psychology of fascism" as Fromm, Horkheimer, and Reich would later do, nor to the widespread eliminationist anti-Semitism among the ordinary German people as does Daniel Goldhagen in his recently much publicized book *Hitler's Willing Executioners* (New York: Random, 1996). More like Franz Neumann's subsequent *Behemoth: Struktur und Praxis des Nationalsozialismus 1933–1944* (Frankfurt/M, Germany: Fischer, 1988) or Robert A. Brady's (1937) *Spirit and Structure of German Fascism* (London: Victor Gollancz, 1937), Marcuse's piece links an ostensibly psychological discussion of the authoritarian mentality of fascism to the material social forces that made it possible: "This character will therefore dissolve when the social forces are defeated which are responsible for the transformation of an industrial into an authoritarian society. In National Socialist Germany, these forces are clearly distinguishable: they are the great industrial combines on which the economic organization of the Reich centers, and the upper strata of the governmental and party bureaucracy. The breaking up of their dominion is the prerequisite and the chief content of re-education" (manuscript number 0119.00, p. 55; also WF, 171).

Similarly Marcuse's "Presentation of the Enemy" (manuscript number 0129.01) analyzes the problem of how to mobilize the German population for active collaboration with the United Nations after the Nazis were militarily defeated. He writes: ". . . at every possible occasion, expose the real beneficiaries and instigators of Nazi policies . . . the actual beneficiaries of these measures were, not the small merchants and traders, but big business itself. . . . A comparison of the earnings of the big German corporations and the real wage level would provide good illustrative material" (pp. 6–7, see also *Feindanalysen: Über die Deutschen* [FAg, 77–78]).

These excerpts are published with permission of the Literary Estate of Herbert Marcuse, Peter Marcuse, Executor. Supplementary material from previously unpublished work of Herbert Marcuse, much now in the Archives of the Goethe University in Frankfurt/Main, has been and will be published in a six-volume series by Routledge Publishers, England, edited by Kellner. All rights to further publication are retained by the Estate. Peter-Erwin Jansen is engaged in a similar project publishing German-language versions of Marcuse's archival materials.

Visit the website of the Frankfurt Marcuse Archive at http://www.stub.uni-frankfurt.de/archiv.htm.

See also Kellner (ed.), *Technology, War, and Fascism: The Unknown Marcuse* (New York: Routledge, 1998); and Peter-Erwin Jansen (ed.), *Feindanalysen: Über die Deutschen* (Lüneburg, West Germany: Verlag Dietrich zu Klampen, 1998). In addition, see Kátz, *Foreign Intelligence, Research and Analysis in the Office of Strategic Services 1942–1945* (Cambridge, MA: Harvard University Press, 1989).

Chapter Two

1. Douglas Kellner also argues that Marcuse's approach is traditional. See Kellner's *Herbert Marcuse and the Crisis of Marxism* (Berkeley: University of California Press, 1984) p. 18. Barry M. Kátz thinks otherwise, contending that Marcuse was attracted to Freiburg because it was a center for experimentation in the *Geisteswissenschaften*. See his "New Sources of Marcuse's Aesthetics," *New German Critique*, No. 17, Spring 1979, p. 177.

2. See in this regard Albert Berger, *Ästhetik and Bildungsroman: Goethe's Wilhelm Meister's Lehrjahre* (Vienna: Wilhelm Braunmuller, 1977) p. 4.

3. Fritz K. Ringer, *The Decline of the German Mandarins: The German Academic Community, 1890–1933* (Cambridge, MA: Harvard University Press, 1969) pp. 315–16.

4. Andrew Arato and Paul Breines, *The Young Lukács and the Origins of Western Marxism* (New York: Seabury, 1979) p. 76.

5. Ibid.

6. Berger, *Ästhetik and Bildungsroman.*

7. Jürgen Scharfschwert, *Thomas Mann und der deutsche Bildungsroman* (Stuttgart, Germany: Kohlhammer, 1967).

8. Robert Steigerwald, *Marcuses Dritter Weg* (Köln, Germany: Pahl-Rugenstein Verlag, 1969). As Marcuse's writings begin to display a growing *theoretical* distance from both Marxism and phenomenology, his "third" philosophical perspective will ultimately be called critical theory.

9. Rainer Winkel, on "Geisteswissenschaftliche Erziehung," in Eberhard Rauch and Wolfgang Anzinger (eds.), *Wörterbuch Kritische Erziehung* (Starnberg, Germany: Raith Verlag, 1973).

10. Manfred Riedel (ed.), Wilhelm Dilthey, *Der Aufbau der geschichtlichen Welt in der Geisteswissenschaften* (Frankfurt/M, Germany: Suhrkamp, 1970) p. 310.

11. Ilse N. Bulhof, *Wilhelm Dilthey; A Hermeneutic Approach to the Study of History and Culture* (The Hague: Martinus Nijhoff, 1980).

12. Rudolf Maakreel, *Philosopher of the Human Studies* (Princeton: Princeton University Press, 1975) p. 26.

13. Max Horkheimer and Theodor W. Adorno, *Dialectic of Enlightenment* (New York: Herder and Herder, 1972) p. 195.

14. Wilhelm Dilthey, *Der Aufbau der geschichtlichen Welt in der Geisteswissenschaften* (Frankfurt/M, Germany: Suhrkamp, 1970) p. 310.

Chapter Three

1. Paul Piccone and Alexander Delfini, "Herbert Marcuse's Heideggerian Marxism," *Telos*, No. 6, Fall 1970.

2. Douglas Kellner, *Herbert Marcuse and the Crisis of Marxism* (Berkeley: University of California Press, 1984); see especially chapters 2 and 3, "Phenomenological Marxism?" and "Studies in Marxian Philosophy."

3. What Marcuse did for the German-speaking world, Erich Fromm accomplished for English speakers, perhaps with greater fidelity to Marx. Cf. Fromm, *Marx's Concept of Man* (New York: Ungar, 1964). This book was a breakthrough for the study of Marx in the United States. It brought Marx's *1844 Manuscripts* and the Marxist theory alienation to the attention of English speakers *on its own terms*.

4. William Barrett, *Irrational Man* (Garden City, NY: Doubleday, 1962) p. 219.

5. Martin Heidegger, *Being and Time* (New York: Harper, 1962) p. 41. N.B.: this Macquarrie and Robinson translation of *Sein und Zeit* renders *Geschichtlichkeit* as "*historicality.*" According to Heidegger: "The definition of historicity has priority to what is called history (world-historical events). Historicity signifies the ontological constitution of the 'events' of humanity as such, and only upon this basis is anything like 'world history' possible. . . ." My translation, *Sein und Zeit* (Tübingen, Germany: Max Niemeyer, 1967) pp. 19–20.

6. For example, P. Berger and S. Pullberg, in their "Concept of Reification," *New Left Review*, No. 35, 1966, pp. 56–71, attribute "reification" and *Verdinglichung* to Marx. Piccone and Delfini concur that Marx also used the term *Verdinglichung* and also ascribe the use of this term to Husserl in their article "Herbert Marcuse's Heideggerian Marxism." Other scholars claim, with greater warrant in my estimation, that *Verdinglichung* is a term introduced not by Marx but by Georg Lukács. See Andrew Feenberg, "Reification and the Antinomies of Socialist Thought," *Telos*, No. 10, Winter 1971. Also Joachim Israel, *Alienation from Marx to Modern Sociology* (Boston: Allyn, 1971).

7. If scholarship were to disclose some instance of Marx's use of the term, its bearing, if any, on *Capital*'s rather full elaboration of reification as the fetishization of commodities would be only incidental. Actually, Marx speaks famously against any sense of negating alienation by negating *Verdinglichung* where he encountered a similar doctrine (that of *thinghood*) in Hegel: "A non-objective being is a *non-being*." See Marx, *Early Writings*, translated and edited by T. B. Bottomore, (New York: McGraw-Hill, 1963) pp. 203–7.

8. Christoph Demmerling, *Sprache und Verdinglichung* (Frankfurt/M, Germany: Suhrkamp, 1994) p. 10. See also Feenberg, *Lukács, Marx and the Sources of Critical Theory* (Totowa, NJ: Rowman and Littlefield, 1981); and Peter L. Berger

and Thomas Luckmann, *The Social Construction of Reality* (Garden City, NY: Doubleday, 1966).

9. Martin Jay, *Marxism & Totality* (Berkeley: University of California Press, 1984) p. 109, see also p. 114.

10. Rolf Wiggershaus, *Die Frankfurter Schule* (München, Germany: Deutscher Taschenbuch Verlag, 1988) p. 113.

11. Jürgen Habermas, *Theory of Communicative Action*, Vol. 1 (Boston: Beacon, 1984) p. 355. See also his "Von Lukács zu Adorno: Rationalisierung als Verding-lichung," in *Theorie des kommunikativen Handelns*, Band I (Frankfurt/M, Germany: Suhrkamp, 1981).

12. Habermas, *Theory of Communication Action*, Vol. 1, p. 379.

13. Habermas, ibid., p. 384. On Adorno's perspective on art and *Verding-lichung*, see also Dieter Kliche, "Kunst gegen Verdinglichung. Berührungspunkte im Gegensatz von Adorno und Lukács," in Burkhardt Linder and W. Martin Lüdke (eds.), *Materialien zur ästhetischen Theorie Th. W. Adornos Konstruktion der Moderne* (Frankfurt/M, Germany: Suhrkamp, 1980) pp. 219–61.

14. Habermas, ibid. p. 366.

15. Habermas, *Theory of Communicative Action*, Vol. 2, p. 374; Habermas, *Theorie des kommunikativen Handelns*, Band II, p. 548.

16. Indeed Habermas earlier explicitly derives his *Verdinglichung* theory from Georg Lukács. See Habermas, *Theory of Communicative Action*, Vol. 1, p. 355.

17. In 1978 Habermas interviewed Marcuse ("Theory and Politics," *Telos* No. 38, Winter 1978–79, pp. 125–26) on the matter of historicity:

HABERMAS: Precisely if one looks at Heidegger from a Marxist point of view, one sees not concreteness, but a quasi-transcendental, fundamental ontological conceptual system being developed for the terms of history, for historicity, but not for grasping a material process of history.

MARCUSE: Yes. For Heidegger history evaporates in the concern for historicity.

HABERMAS: You nevertheless latched onto this fundamental ontology....

MARCUSE: Yes, but that wasn't Heidegger anymore. That was an ontology which I believed I could locate in Marx himself.

18. Richard Schacht, *The Future of Alienation* (Urbana and Chicago: Illinois University Press, 1994) p. 3.

19. Schacht, *Alienation* (Garden City, NY: Doubleday, 1971) p. 9.

20. Mitchell Franklin, "On Hegel's Theory of Alienation and Its Historic Force," *Revolutionary World*, Vol. 9, 1974.

21. Seyla Benhabib, *Critique, Norm, and Utopia* (New York: Columbia University Press, 1986).

22. Marx, *Das Kapital* (Stuttgart, Germany: Alfred Kroener Verlag, 1965) p. 52.

23. Lukács, *History and Class Consciousness*, p. 217 cites Georg Simmel's *Philosophie des Geldes* (München und Leipzig, Germany: Verlag von Duncker & Humboldt, 1922) p. 531.

24. Martin Heidegger, *Being and Time* (New York: Harper, 1962) p. 487.

25. Ibid., p. 81.

26. Arthur Schopenhauer, *Urwille und Welterlösung* (n.p., n.d., Sigbert Mohn Verlag, p. 361).

27. Ibid., p. 336.

28. Ibid., p. 119.

29. Eugen Fink, *Nietzsches Philosophie* (Stuttgart, Germany: W. Kohlhammer Verlag, 1968).

30. Heidegger, *Nietzsche*, Vol. 1 (Pfüllingen, Germany: Gunther Neske Verlag, 1961) p. 82.

31. Fink, *Nietzche's Philosophie*, pp. 160–70.

32. Ibid., p. 167.

33. Ibid., p. 79.

Chapter Four

1. Sidney Lipshires, *Herbert Marcuse: From Marx to Freud and Beyond* (Cambridge, MA: Schenkman, 1974) p. 3.

2. See Max Horkheimer, "Traditional and Critical Theory," in *Critical Theory, Selected Essays* (New York: Herder and Herder, 1972).
Horkheimer's critical theory is "critical" in a sense quite different than that of Marx. In this defining essay (pp. 242–43), Horkheimer wrote:

> There are no general criteria for judging critical theory as a whole, for it is always based on the recurrence of events and thus on a self-reproducing totality. Nor is there a social class by whose acceptance of the theory one could be guided. It is possible for the consciousness of every social stratum

today to be limited and corrupted by ideology, however much, for its circumstances, it may be bent on truth. . . . *The future of humanity depends on the existence today of the critical attitude*, which of course contains within it elements from traditional theories and from our declining culture generally. Mankind has already been abandoned by science which in its imaginary self-sufficiency thinks of the shaping of practice, which it serves and to which it belongs, simply as something lying outside its borders and is content with this separation of thought and action. Yet the characteristic mark of the thinker's activity is to determine for itself what it is to accomplish and serve, and this not in fragmentary fashion but totally. Its own nature, therefore, turns it towards a changing of history and the establishment of justice among men. (emphasis added)

Horkheimer's neo-Kantianism is clearly indicated in these last sentences given their implicit references to Kant's central idea of self-determination in *What Is Enlightenment?* While Horkheimer's critical theory sought a transition to a just society, it did not consider this transition to be necessarily accomplished with a shift from capitalism to socialism. Indeed, should one ask: of what, more exactly, did Horkheimer's critical theory become critical?—the answer (propounded in his subsequent book with Theodor W. Adorno, *Dialectic of Enlightenment* [New York: Herder and Herder, 1972]) would revolve around the following five topics: (1) the critique of "orthodox" and Soviet communism, as well as the critiques of (2) fascism; (3) anti-Semitism; (4) "traditional" social philosophy and epistemological theory; and (5) the "mass" character of the cultural media, mores, and mind in advanced industrial societies.

Horkheimer's essay was to distinguish sharply between "positive" fact and the "transcendental" reflexivity of theory, at the same time he also established an interconnection between them both. This unity he claimed was grounded in the legitimate "kernel" of the Kantian epistemology: "At least Kant understood that behind the discrepancy between fact and theory which the scholar experiences in his professional work, there lies a deeper unity, namely the general subjectivity upon which individual knowledge depends" (p. 203). Horkheimer's critical theory was opposed to "naive" realistic thinking whether of a common sense or scientistic sort. It emphasized the fact that complicated and subjective social, and historical and political mediations necessarily intervened in any of the sciences traditionally conceived as "pure."

Horkheimer's neo-Kantian emphasis on the doctrine of the epistemological role of human subjectivity actually provided a distinctive philosophical foundation for critical theory's uniquely epistemological, rather than political, concepts of activism and praxis. It is this doctrine that also becomes one of critical theory's most decisive characteristics, insofar as it regards the meaning of social and individual realities to be primarily the product of the efforts of conscious human subjectivity, rather than in any sense a reflection or recognition of the effects of more fundamental external forces.

Horkheimer's critical theory emphasized the fact that there is a partisan (i.e., human, but not class-based) characteristic to social knowledge and social policy. He was convinced that "present day man" should no longer look to the "neutral" methods that had "abandoned" him in the past, but toward a critique "dominated at every turn by a concern for reasonable conditions of human life" (p. 199).

This broad concern for human justice, in contradistinction to a class interest in politics, was also utilized by Horkheimer to confront any Marxist theoretician who was ostensibly "satisfied to proclaim with reverent admiration the creative strength of the proletariat and . . . in canonizing it" (p. 214). Horkheimer reasoned that if critical theory "consisted essentially in formulations of the feelings and ideas of one class at any given moment, it would not be structurally different from the special branches of science" (ibid.).

Like Husserl and Heidegger's phenomenological approach, critical theory was only considered "critical" insofar as it opposed and contrasted (i.e., "negated") the given and factual aspects of social existence (said to be predominant in theories traditionally conceived) with their most advanced theoretical possibilities, that is, in accordance with a comparison to what it considered to be the highest intentions of human reason and the most essential requirements of human need. This was taken as the philosophical justification for a refusal to accept empirically given solutions to political and theoretical problems as ready-made or premature. Horkheimer assumed a "critical distance" from any type of solidarity with social movements and countermovements. This was not a philosophical perspective without considerable difficulties for ostensible Marxists, like Marcuse, however.

3. Mitchell Franklin, "The Irony of the Beautiful Soul of Herbert Marcuse," *Telos*, No. 6, Fall 1970.

4. Mikhail Lifschitz, *The Philosophy of Art of Karl Marx* (London: Pluto Press, 1973); George Plekhanov, *Art and Society & Other Papers* (New York: Oriole Editions, 1974).

Chapter Five

1. Martin Heidegger, *Vom Wesen des Grundes* (Frankfurt/M, Germany: Vittorio Klostermann, 1965) p. 5.

2. Michael L. Simmons Jr. "On James Herndon's Aesthetic Ontology," *Educational Theory*, Vol, 26, No. 2, Spring 1976.

3. See in this regard, C. D. Keyes, "Truth as Art: An Interpretation of Heidegger's *Sein und Zeit* (sec. 44) and *Der Ursprung des Kunstwerks*," in John Sallis (ed.), *Heidegger and the Path of Thinking* (Pittsburgh: Duquesne University Press, 1970) p. 66.

4. Cf. George H. Douglas, "Heidegger on the Education of Poets and Philosophers," *Educational Theory*, Vol. 22, No. 4, Fall 1972, p. 449.

5. Stefan Morawski, *Inquiries into the Fundamentals of Aesthetics* (Boston: MIT Press, 1974) p. 328—"Marx, with his probing of contemporary society, was to

turn Schiller's conception inside out; it was *political* man who was required for the rescue and realization of aesthetic humankind."

6. Heidegger, *Kant and the Problem of Metaphysics* (Bloomington: Indiana University Press, 1962) p. 135.

7. Ibid., p. 136.

8. Heinz Paetzold, *Neomarxistische Ästhetik II: Adorno-Marcuse* (Düsseldorf, Germany: Schwann, 1974) p. 125.

9. William Barrett, *Irrational Man* (Garden City, NY: Doubleday, 1962) pp. 128, 130.

Chapter Six

1. Martin Heidegger, *Kant and the Problem of Metaphysics* (Bloomington: Indiana University Press, 1962) pp. 136, 154.

2. Ibid., p. 213.

3. James M. Demske, *Sein, Mensch und Tod, Das Todesproblem bei Martin Heidegger* (Freiburg, Germany: Karl Alber Verlag, 1963) pp. 152–56.

4. Theodor W. Adorno, *Jargon der Eigentlichkeit* (Frankfurt/M, Germany: Suhrkamp, 1970) p. 74.

5. Renate Brink, *Die Selbstverwirklichung des Menschen als pädagogische Aufgabe in den Frühschriften Nietzsches* (Düsseldorf, Germany: Michael Triltsch Verlag, 1972). Cf. pp. vii, 101–5.

Chapter Seven

1. This is clearly an elaboration of his *Verdinglichung* analysis of reification undertaken in "The Foundation of Historical Materialism" (HM) and defined there, following Martin Heidegger, as a false mode of objectification. *One-Dimensional Man* (OD) returns to the terrain of Heidegger's existential ontology via Sartre, whose *Being and Nothingness* is an explicit commentary on Heidegger's *Being and Time* (New York: Harper, 1962). Marcuse utilizes in this regard the Heideggerian concepts of *object* and *project*. "The object world is thus the world of a specific historical project. . . ." (OD, 219). "The way in which a society organizes the life of its members . . . is one 'project' of realization among others" (OD, xvi).

2. Marcuse's 1960 preface to *Soviet Marxism, A Critical Analysis* (SM) inserts a caution against the book's tendency toward a technological determinism. Speaking of his convergence thesis, he writes:

This would imply that the common technical base (the machine process as ensemble of institutions, functions, attitudes) would assert itself even through such fundamentally different economies as nationalized and private enterprise. And if one attributes such a determining role to the technological base, one might easily be induced to see in the contemporary conflict between capitalism and communism the conflict between two forms of one and the same complex industrial society. I should like to dissociate myself from this position, while maintaining my emphasis on the all-embracing political character of the machine process in advanced industrial society. (SM, xi)

Similarly, Marcuse's 1978 essay, "Protosocialism and Late Capitalism: Toward a Theoretical Synthesis Based on Bahro's Analysis" (PB), explicitly dissociates itself from convergence theory even while it extends the "aesthetic motivation" (PB, 27) of Rudolf Bahro's social critique of the GDR also to that of Western late capitalism.

3. See especially, Nigel Grant, *Soviet Education* (Baltimore: Penguin Books, 1964); Oskar Anweiler, *Geschichte der Schule und Pädagogik in Russland* (2 vols.) (Berlin: Quelle and Meyer, 1964); and Alexander G. Korol, *Soviet Education for Science and Technology* (Boston: MIT, 1957).

4. Gerhart Neuner, *Zur Theorie der sozialistischen Allgemeinbildung* (East Berlin: Volkseigner Verlag Volk and Wissen, 1973) p. 157: Mathematics and Natural Sciences 29.8%; Introduction to Socialist Production and Productive Work Experience 10.6%; Social Sciences and Language Arts and Literary-aesthetic Studies 41.1%; Foreign Languages 10.6%; and Physical Education 7.9%.

5. Gotthold Krapp, *Marx & Engels Über die Verbindung des Unterrichts mit produktiver Arbeit und die polytechnische Bildung* (Frankfurt/M, Germany: Verlag Roter Stern, 1971).

6. Brian H. Maskell, *Software and the Agile Manufacturer* (Portland, OR: Productivity Press, 1994).

Chapter Eight

1. Otto Friedrich Bollnow, *Die Lebensphilosophie* (Berlin: Springer Verlag, 1958) pp. 76–77.

2. Ibid., p. 141.

3. Ibid., p. 134.

4. Cf. Martin Jay, *The Dialectical Imagination* (Boston: Little, Brown, 1973) p. 49 on Horkheimer's tendency in this direction, seeing *Lebensphilosophie* as a corrective to scientism and socialism.

5. Excerpts from "Education and Social Change" are published with permission of the Literary Estate of Herbert Marcuse, Peter Marcuse, Executor. Supplementary material from previously unpublished work of Herbert Marcuse, much now in the Archives of the Goethe University in Frankfurt/Main, Germany, has been, and will be, published in a six-volume series by Routledge Publishers, England, edited by Douglas Kellner. All rights to further publication are retained by the estate.

6. Alan Charles Kors and Harvey A. Silverglate, *The Shadow University: The Betrayal of Liberty on America's Campuses* (New York: Free Press, 1998).

7. Fred L. Pincus, "The False Promises of Community Colleges," *Harvard Educational Review*, Vol. 50, No. 3, August 1980.

Pincus, "Tracking and the Community Colleges," *The Insurgent Sociologist*, Vol. 4, No. 3, Spring 1974.

Jerome Karabel, "Community Colleges and Social Stratification," *Harvard Educational Review*, Vol. 42, No. 4, November 1972.

L. Steven Zwerling, *Second Best, The Crisis of the Community College* (New York: McGraw-Hill, 1976).

Burton R. Clark, *The Open Door College: A Case Study* (New York: McGraw-Hill, 1960).

Kevin J. Dougherty, *The Contradictory College* (Albany: State University of New York Press, 1994).

Penelope E. Herideen, *Policy, Pedagogy, and Social Inequality: Community College Student Realities in Post-Industrial America* (Westport, CT: Bergin & Garvey, 1998).

8. Samuel Bowles and Herbert Gintis, *Schooling in Capitalist America* (New York: Basic, 1976).

9. Ernest L. Boyer et al., *Building Communities* (Washington, DC: American Association of Community and Junior Colleges, 1988) epigraph.

Chapter Nine

1. This phrase is, of course, generally associated with the Socialist Education Movement in China during the late 1960s, although Marcuse makes no explicit reference to these events. Instead, he cites Herbert Read's aesthetic rejection of classicism (for its repressive conservatism) in *Counterrevolution and Revolt* as typical of the approach of the cultural revolution (CR, 91–92).

2. Christopher Caudwell believed, in contrast to Marcuse, that reification in art was represented not by acknowledging the social character or social function of a work of art, but by adopting the abstract "art for art's sake" position that he saw as a parallel to commodity fetishism, that is, as production for exchange, not use. This information according to David N. Margolies, *The Function of Literature* (New York: International Publishers, 1969) p. 73.

3. Stephan Morawski, *Inquiries into the Fundamentals of Aesthetics* (Boston: MIT Press, 1974) p. 101.

4. "Wanderer's Nightsong" (Wandrers Nachtlied)

> Above the mountains is repose.
> In the treetops stillness reigns.
> You cannot even apprehend
> If yet the wind doth breathe.
> Silent forest birds ponder their fate,
> And just wait:
> Soon you too
> Shall find your peace.

> (my free rendition—CR)

5. Ronald Gray, *Poems of Goethe* (London: Cambridge University Press, 1966) p. 49.

6. Simmons, Michael L. Jr. "Certainty, Harmony, and the Centering of Dewey's Aesthetics," *Philosophy of Education 1997* (Urbana, IL: Philosophy of Education Society, 1998).

Chapter Ten

1. See especially the following works:

Batalov, E. *The Philosophy of Revolt* (Moscow: Progress, 1975);

Bauermann, Rolf and Hans-Jochen Rötscher, *Dialektik der Anpassung* (Frankfurt/M, Germany: Verlag Marxistische Blätter, 1972);

Beyer, Wilhelm Raimund. *Die Sünden der Frankfurter Schule* (East Berlin: Akademie Verlag, 1971);

Franklin, Mitchell. "The Irony of the Beautiful Soul of Herbert Marcuse," *Telos*, No. 6, Fall 1970;

Holz, Hans Heinz. *Utopie und Anarchismus: Zur Kritik der Kritischen Theorie Herbert Marcuses* (Köln, Germany: Pahl Rugenstein Verlag, 1968);

Jansohn, Heinz. *Herbert Marcuse* (Bonn: Bouvier Verlag Herbert Grundmann, 1974);

Jay, Martin. "Anamnestic Totalization; Reflections on Marcuse's Theory of Remembrance," *Theory and Society*, Vol. 11, No. 1, January 1982;

———. *Marxism & Totality* (Berkeley: University of California Press, 1984);

Kellner, Douglas. "Introduction to Marcuse's 'On the Philosophical Foundation of the Concept of Labor in Economics,'" *Telos*, No. 16, Summer 1973;

———. *Herbert Marcuse and the Crisis of Marxism* (Berkeley: University of California Press, 1984);

———. *Critical Theory, Marxism, and Modernity* (Cambridge and Baltimore: Polity Press and Johns Hopkins University Press, 1989);

Korf, Gertraud. *Ausbruch aus dem "Gehäuse der Hörigkeit"?—Kritik der Kulturtheorien Max Webers und Herbert Marcuses* (Frankfurt/M, Germany: Verlag Marxistische Blätter, 1971);

Lehrke, Wilfried. *"Kritische Bemerkungen zu den frühen philosophischen Auffassungen Herbert Marcuses,"* in Dieter Bergner (ed.), *Die philosophische Lehre von Karl Marx und ihre aktuelle Bedeutung* (East Berlin: VEB Deutscher Verlag der Wissenschaften, 1968).

2. Evidence that this beautiful disclosure of paradox is the typical critical strategem emerging from Marcuse's writing is prolific. See, for example, his chapter on "The Dialectic of Civilization" in *Eros and Civilization, A Philosophical Inquiry into Freud* (EC) ". . . in the centers of industrial civilization, man is kept in a state of impoverishment, both cultural and physical . . . the goods and services that the individuals buy control their needs and petrify their faculties . . . they have innumerable choices . . . which are all of the same sort. . . . The discrepancy between potential liberation and actual repression has come to maturity. . . ." (EC, 99–101). Similarly ". . . people are . . . being made ignorant by their daily intake of information and entertainment" (EC, 102). "The theory of alienation demonstrated the fact that man does not realize himself in his labor, that his life has become an instrument of labor, that his work and its products have assumed a power independent of him as an individual. But the liberation from this state seems to require, not the arrest of alienation, but its consummation. . . . The elimination of human potentialities from the world of (alienated) labor creates the preconditions for the elimination of labor from the world of human potentialities" (EC, 105).

Marcuse also very graphically maintains, in *An Essay on Liberation* (EL), that "The opposition is thus sucked into the very world which it opposes. . . ." (EL, 64). Emphasizing the fact that "compliance" and "complicity" with the established system are rational technological attitudes, he also stresses that this is a form of ". . . 'voluntary' servitude. . . ." (EL, 6), echoing the antinomial Kantian formulation of enlightenment as emancipation from *selbstverschuldene Unmündigkeit* (from the independent reproduction of dependence).

One-Dimensional Man, Studies in the Ideology of Advanced Industrial Society (OD) of course, states that "A comfortable, smooth, reasonable, democratic unfreedom prevails in advanced industrial civilization, a token of technical progress" (OD, 1). It also claims: "This ambiguous situation involves a still more fundamental ambiguity. *One-Dimensional Man* will vacillate throughout between two contradictory hypotheses: (1) that advanced industrial society is capable of containing qualitative change for the foreseeable future; (2) that forces and tendencies exist which may break this containment and explode the society" (OD, xv).

Counterrevolution and Revolt (CR) reiterates this emphasis on "objective ambivalence" (CR, 49), and concludes with a summary statement of a "critical" approach to cultural revolution: "What has become intolerable is the overwhelming unity of opposites in this world: unity of pleasure and horror, calm and violence, gratification and destruction, beauty and ugliness, which hits us tangibly in our daily environment" (CR, 129).

3. Mitchell Franklin, "The Irony of the Beautiful Soul of Herbert Marcuse," *Telos*, No. 6, Fall 1970, p. 12.

4. Ibid., p. 5.

5. See G. W. F. Hegel, *Phänomenologie des Geistes* (Hamburg: Felix Meiner Verlag, 1952) pp. 445–72.

6. J.-P. Guepin, *The Tragic Paradox: Myth and Ritual in Greek Tragedy* (Amsterdam: Adolf M. Hakkert, 1968) p. xiii.

7. Ibid., p. 303.

8. Aeron Haynie, "Imperialism and the Construction of Femininity in Mid-Victorian Fiction" (Gainesville: University of Florida, Ph.D. dissertation, 1994) p. 13. Haynie argues that women's roles and sexuality do not merely symbolize the deferential domesticity of a colonized land or people, but also become emblematic of colonial ambitions and colonial authority. Constructions of femininity are traced to the commodification of culture and issues of overproduction ("surplus" women being advised to emigrate to the colonies) as well as to the presumed moral superiority of the female-centered colonial ruler, Queen Victoria, vis-à-vis the ostensible barbarism of colonial insurrectionism.

Two feminist critical theorists, Silvia Bovenschen and Marianne Schuller seriously challenge Marcuse's use of female imagery (to represent liberation, hope, or sensuousness) as typically male projections developed without any feminist input and against which women must actually defend themselves. See Bovenschen and Schuller, "Weiblichkeitsbilder: Ein Gespräch mit Herbert Marcuse," in *Gespräche mit Herbert Marcuse* (Frankfurt/M, Germany: Suhrkamp, 1978, 1996).

The feminist philosopher Riane Eisler's *Chalice and the Blade* (San Francisco: Harper, 1988) finds early historical evidence in Crete and elsewhere for a type of partnership society prior to patriarchy where the female principle was the emblem of a divine and peaceful actualization power. In some ways this scholarship can help to vindicate Marcuse's use of female imagery for the condition of the pacification of society.

See Nancy Fraser's "What's Critical about Critical Theory," in Johanna Meehan (ed.), *Feminists Read Habermas* (New York: Routledge, 1996).

9. Rudolf Makkreel, *Dilthey: Philosopher of the Human Studies* (Princeton: Princeton University Press, 1975).

10. Theodor Adorno, Walter Benjamin, Ernst Bloch, Bertolt Brecht, and Georg Lukács, *Aesthetics and Politics* (London: Verso, 1980).

11. Jürgen Habermas, *Theory of Communicative Action*, Vol. 1 (Boston: Beacon, 1984), p. 384.

12. Stefan Morawski, *Inquiries into the Fundamentals of Aesthetics* (Boston: MIT Press, 1974).

13. Avner Zis, *Foundations of Marxist Aesthetics* (Moscow: Progress, 1977).

14. Lee Baxandall (ed.), *Radical Perspectives in the Arts* (Baltimore: Penguin, 1973).

15. Karl Marx, *The Poverty of Philosophy*, in Marx and Friedrich Engels (eds), *Collected Works*, Vol. 6 (New York: International Publishers, 1976) p. 113.

16. George Plekhanov, *Art and Society & Other Papers* (New York: Oriole Editions, 1974) p. 63.

17. Mikhail Lifschitz, *The Philosophy of Art of Karl Marx* (London: Pluto Press, 1973) p. 93.

18. Several of the ideas presented in this section are the result of specific suggestions from my colleagues David Brodsky, Patricia Pollock Brodsky, Morteza Ardebili, and Steve Spartan, whose help has significantly strengthened the manuscript. Weaknesses that remain are my own.

19. J. N. Findlay, *Hegel: A Re-examination* (New York: Collier, 1958) p. 93.
For an insightful discussion of this educational dynamic in which class considerations are also impacted by multiform race and gender-based power relations, see bell hooks, *Teaching to Transgress* (New York: Routledge, 1994) pp. 93–110. Also Angela Y. Davis, *Women, Race & Class* (New York: Vintage, 1983).
See also Leonard Harris, *Philosophy Born of Struggle* (Dubuque, IA: Kendall-Hunt, 1983) for an account of emancipatory trends in African-American philosophizing. Also Norman R. Allan Jr., *African-American Humanism* (Buffalo: Prometheus, 1991); Cornel West, *Race Matters* (Boston: Beacon, 1993).

20. Douglas Kellner, *Critical Theory, Marxism, and Modernity* (Cambridge and Baltimore: Polity Press and Johns Hopkins University Press, 1989) pp. 228–29.

21. Martin Jay, *Dialectic Imagination* p. 286. See also Kellner, "Theory and Practice: The Politics of Critical Theory," in his *Critical Theory*. In addition consult Rolf Wiggershaus, *Die Frankfurter Schule* (München, Germany: Deutscher Taschenbuch Verlag, 1988).

22. Karl Marx and Friedrich Engels. *Collected Works*, Vol. 10 (New York: International Publishers, 1978) p. 626.

23. Bogdan Suchodolski, *Einführung in die marxistische Erziehungstheorie* (Köln, Germany: Pahl-Rugenstein Verlag, 1972).

24. István Maszáros, *Marx's Theory of Alienation* (New York: Harper Row, 1970) pp. 290–93.

25. Interesting philosophical elaborations of critical realism have recently emerged in the work of Marvin Farber, Rom Harré, Tony Lawson, and Roy Bhaskar. See Andrew Collier, *Critical Realism* (London: Verso, 1994); Farber, *The Search for an Alternative: Philosophical Perspectives of Subjectivism and Marxism* (Philadelphia:

University of Pennsylvania Press, 1984). Bhaskar's influential writings include *Plato, etc.* (London: Verso, 1994); *Dialectic: The Pulse of Freedom* (London: Verso, 1993); *Reclaiming Reality* (London: Verso, 1989); *The Possibility of Naturalism* (Brighton, Sussex, United Kingdom: Harvester Press, 1979); and *A Realist Theory of Science* (London: Verso, 1975).

26. James Lawler, "Marx as Market Socialist," in Bertell Ollman (ed.), *Market Socialism: The Debate Among Socialists* (New York: Routledge, 1998) p. 185.

27. Kwame Ture, as cited in Julie Wyss, "Kwame Ture inspires students," Kansas City Kansas Community College *Advocate*, Vol. 25, No. 11, March 5, 1993, p. 1.

28. For an extraordinarily powerful discussion of learning as democratic revolution, teaching as the practice of freedom, and engaged pedagogy informed by the classical ideas as well as a nuanced awareness of the social dimensions of unfreedom, see bell hooks, *Teaching to Transgress* (New York: Routledge, 1994).

29. Paulo Freire, *Pedagogy of the Oppressed* (New York: Continuum Publishing, 1993) pp. 75, 80, 107.

30. Harry C. Boyte and Nancy N. Kari, *Building America: The Democratic Promise of Public Work* (Philadelphia: Temple University Press, 1996) p. 2.

31. Ibid., p. 4.

32. See Idalynn Karre's *Busy, Noisy, and Powerfully Effective: Cooperative Learning in the Classroom* (n.p., 1993).

33. I have in mind the works of D. Stanley Eitzen, Maxine Baca Zinn, Joe R. Feagin, G. William Domhoff, Michael Parenti, Jonathan Kozol, Samuel Bowles, Herbert Gintis, Noam Chomsky, Holly Sklar, Barbara Ehrenreich, Neil Postman, and so forth.

34. See Paul J. Baker and Louis E. Anderson, *Social Problems: A Critical Thinking Approach* (Belmont, CA: Wadsworth, 1987). The work of Howard Kahane, *Logic and Contemporary Rhetoric* (Belmont, CA: Wadsworth, 1988) on standards of cogency is also immensely helpful here, as is that of John McPeck, *Critical Thinking and Education* (New York: St. Martin's, 1981) and Evert Vedung, *Political Reasoning* (Beverly Hills, CA: Sage Publishers, 1982).

35. College campuses can become an engine for *Community Development and Transformation* pushing beyond the usual corporate parameters. Stephen Spartan, former community research and development director at Kansas City, Kansas, Community College, has suggested that research centers for the analysis of local social issues could be established. These could be umbrella organizations that would bridge the gap between campus and community by tapping the talent of faculty as resource persons analyzing community problems, questions, and needs, as well as helping to formulate and mobilize appropriate community responses. Students could be involved as coinvestigators into significant community issues. Another

proposal of Spartan's involves the development of CONTACs (Community Organizations Network and Training Assistance Centers) to encourage and coordinate civic activism, and GAINs (Government Agencies Information Networks) to access and exchange community data. "Introduction to Local Development" courses could enroll some members of a college's own social science faculty as well as local government and business personnel. Faculty involved here could learn from, and network with, practitioners in the field, as all share experiences and debate points of view.

36. Michael L. Simmons Jr., "The Success of Bebop: Model and Cautionary Tale for the Theory and Practice of Multicultural Education," paper presented to the American Educational Studies Association annual meeting, Montreal 1996.

37. David and Pat Brodsky stress the fact that foreign language study in particular makes possible a knowledge of the historical construction of our basic tools of thought and communication, and this becomes a critical awareness of the social nature of our mental habits and symbolic cultural gestures. When this is combined with hands-on experience with a foreign culture, social science theory no longer remains a vague abstraction to students. Like language education, music from different cultures exposes monocultural students to often radically different ways of listening, moving, and even thinking, which sometimes become essential parts of our mental and social lives. Music and art can be critical, and even confrontational, articulating both alienation and the demand for emancipatory social transformation. Music education and foreign language study thus have irreplaceable critical social and intellectual power.

38. Attempting to formalize this somewhat, a loosely knit *Kansas City Progressive Network* has been established. We hold monthly pot luck dinners on Saturday nights or Sunday afternoons at activists' homes. Students are invited as well as others not working in higher education. Members of the Green Party, the Labor Party, and the Alliance for Democracy are actively involved in this network. Our common goal is *ending corporate control* of the economy and government. We have been meeting now for just about three years. We have organized local conferences, brought in speakers, run candidates locally, and overcome much of the isolation that is from time to time quite debilitating to serious critics of our culture.

39. David and Patricia Pollock Brodsky deserve special acknowledgment as primary drafters of this (subsequently revised and expanded) discussion document.

40. David Brodsky, personal communication.

41. Alan Charles Kors and Harvey A. Silverglate, *The Shadow University: The Betrayal of Liberty on America's Campuses* (New York: Free Press, 1998). For another perspective see Mari J. Matsuda, Charles R. Lawrence III, Richard Delgado, and Kimberle Williams Crenshaw, *Words That Wound: Critical Race Theory, Assaultive Speech, and the First Amendment* (Boulder, CO: Westview Press, 1993).

42. Ibid., p. 68.

43. Ibid., p. 71.

44. Ibid., p. 67.

45. Ibid., p. 110.

46. J. S. Mill, *On Liberty* (Harmondsworth, Middlesex, England: Penguin, 1985) p. 97.

47. Brodsky, personal communication.

48. Mill, *On Liberty*, pp. 69–70.

49. Ibid., pp. 116–18.

50. Kors and Silverglate, pp. ix, 3.

51. I owe the general line of thought expressed in the next two paragraphs to my colleague, Morteza Ardebili.

52. Amnesty International, *United States of America: Rights for All* (London: Amnesty International Publications, 1998).

53. *Kansas City Star*, Sunday, 11 October 1998, pp. A–8, A–9.

54. Georg Lukács "Realism in the Balance," in Theodor W. Adorno, Walter Benjamin, Ernst Bloch, Bertolt Brecht, and Lukács, *Aesthetics and Politics* (London: Verso, 1980) p. 37.

55. Martin Heidegger in Marcuse's *Protokoll* to lecture, "*Heidegger*, Einführung in das akademische Studium. Sommer 1929," Herbert Marcuse Archiv of the *Stadt- und Universitätsbibliothek*, Frankfurt, manuscript number 0013.01, p. 6. Heidegger's *Platons Lehre von der Wahrheit* (Bern: A. Franke, 1947) also elaborates these themes. Marcuse's discussion of Plato in *One-Dimensional Man* clearly owes at least some of its inspiration to this Heidegger lecture on the philosophy of higher education. Excerpts from this manuscript are published with permission of the Literary Estate of Herbert Marcuse, Peter Marcuse, Executor. Supplementary material from previously unpublished works of Marcuse, much now in the Archives of the Goethe University in Frankfurt/M, Germany, has been and will be published in a six-volume series by Routledge Publishers, England, edited by Kellner. All rights to further publication are retained by the estate.

56. Again thanks to David Brodsky for pointing this out.

57. Riane Eisler, *The Chalice and the Blade* (San Francisco: Harper, 1988) p. 202. See also Nancy C. M. Hartsock, *Money, Sex and Power: Toward a Feminist Historical Materialism* (Boston: Northeastern University Press, 1983).

Glossary of Selected Foreign Terms and Phrases

alienare	to take away, remove; to transfer ownership, divest, rob
Angst	anxiety, dread
Artisten-Metaphysik	Eugen Fink's description of Nietzsche's "metaphysics of the artist," the power of the artist to create a reality
aufheben	to lift up, to annul, to supersede, to preserve, to negate, and elevate simultaneously (through social action as well as social thought)
Aufklärung	Enlightenment
Bewußtsein	consciousness
Bildung	education, process of the formation of the self
Bildungskraft	the power to educe and educate (Kant)
Bildungstrieb	Goethe's phrase for a drive toward education and culture
Buddenbrooks	novel by Thomas Mann about the decline of the upper middle class Buddenbrooks family
cantabile	with a songlike flowing style
carpe diem	seize the day
Dasein	Heidegger's term for the Being of humanity, literally, "there-being"
Der Deutsche Künstlerroman	Marcuse's dissertation, *The German Artist Novel*
Der Grüne Heinrich	novel by Gottfried Keller, *Green Henry*

dichten	to compose poetry
Dichtung	poetry, literary art
"die entfremdete Arbeit"	Marx's notes "on alienated labor" in 1844 manuscripts
die radikale Tat	the radical deed, radical action
Dr. Phil	Ph.D.
Durchbrechung	literally, "breaking through," transcendence (Heidegger)
Ecce Homo	Nietzsche's autobiography, literally "behold the man"
eidos	idea and reality
Einbildung	imagination, literally "building into one"
Entäusserung	relinquishment, divestment, giving up property, alienation of property
Entfremdung	estrangement, alienation
Entsagung	renunciation, to get along without
Entzweiung	division into two
Erinnerung	reminiscence, remembrance, interiorization
Erlebnis	an experience of, or living through something
Eros	spirit of erotic love, desire to live
ethos	ethical spirit, principle of morality
ex nihilo	out of nothing
Faktizität	facticity; Heidegger's term for our inauthentic apprehension of our world in terms of facts, things, and beings rather than Being
gaya scienza	joyful wisdom, gay science; method of inquiry that is life-positive rather than life-denying
Geist	intellect, mind, spirit
Geistesgeschichte	intellectual history
Geisteswissenschaften	human sciences; humanities and social sciences; cultural studies, methodologically distinct from natural sciences according to Dilthey
Gemeinschaft	community, with strong sense of solidarity, partnership
Gesamtausgabe	publication of complete works in one edition
Gesellschaft	society, often having a division of labor and class inequality or other conflicts that must be mediated

gesellschaftliche Produktivkraft	social means of production
Geschichtlichkeit	historicity (in Dilthey, Heidegger)
Gespräch	conversation
gleichgültig	a matter of indifference, having no significance
Gleichschaltung	rigid control of policy, culture, and thought by Nazi leadership, crushing all dissent
Habilitation	qualification to enter a university faculty
Habilitationsschrift	second dissertation, beyond the Ph.D., prepared for a chairperson in the German academic system
Historikerstreit	historians' dispute; late 1980s over conservative reinterpretations of fascist period in Germany
Jemeinigkeit	the ever-mine-ness of our existence (Heidegger)
Jung Deutschland	nineteenth century German literary and revolutionary movement: Young Germany
Kapital, das	*Capital*, major critical work by Karl Marx
Kunst	art
Künstler	artist
Leben	life
Lebensphilosophie	philosophical vitalism of Nietzsche, Dilthey; grounded in affirmation of life instincts; also associated with tendencies in fascism
Lebenswelt	life-world
Lehrjahre	Goethe's novel *Wilhelm Meister's Apprenticeship*; literally, "years of learning"
Leistungsprinzip	performance principle; drive toward achievement
Lied	song, melody
logos	logic, rationality, word
Lust	joy, pleasure
Lustprinzip	pleasure principle; drive toward erotic gratification
Meister	master, as in master craftsperson, master artist
memento mori	remember death; a sobering yet disalienating awareness
Neue Sachlichkeit	critical realism in German painting during the 1920s (Georg Grosz, Otto Dix)

Nicht, das	Heidegger: the "nothing" between Being and beings
Nichts an sich	nothing in itself
nomos	a rule, a law, a governing principle
Ontologie	ontology: theory of beings/Being; a theory of the Being of humanity as the essence of reality itself
organon	instrument, logic, method of research and learning
paideia	Greek term for education or enlightenment
pedagogia perennis	perennialist educational philosophy, stressing universal human nature in need of cultivation and actualization
Phänomenologie	phenomenology, for Heidegger a method of accessing reality and truth
Philosophie des Geldes	*Philosophy of Money*, major work of Georg Simmel, German sociologist
Philosophische Hefte	journal of critical philosophical analysis in early twentieth century Germany
praxis	theoretically informed practice; for Marcuse this can emerge from art
Produktivkraft	productive power
promesse du bonheur	promise of well-being, good fortune, happiness represented by beauty
Protokollant	note taker
Rechtsphilosophie	Hegel's *Philosophy of Law*
recherche du temps perdu	remembrance of lost time (Proust)
rei	things, understood as entirely separate entities
reification	(1) a fetishization of the social dynamics of wage-labor and capital accumulation; (2) rendering a unthing-like process into a "thingified" form; (3) a form of alienation
Richtung	direction, principle of motion or conduct
Roman	novel
Sache selbst, die	the thing (matter), in itself, as it genuinely is
Schlaraffenland	fool's paradise
Seiendes	an entity, a thing, a being in its facticity

Sein	the Being of a being; transcendental reality of existence for Heidegger
Seinsbegriff	concept of being
Sein und Zeit	*Being and Time*, major work by Heidegger
Sorge	care; for Heidegger the core structure of our authentic mode of human Being
Stadt- und Universitätsbibliothek	library of the city and university of Frankfurt am Main, Germany
Stellvertreter, der	*The Deputy*, play by Rolf Hochhuth
Stoff	stuff, material
Sturm und Drang	storm and stress, romantic style of young Goethe
Symposium	Platonic dialogue on love
telos	"cause of causes" for Aristotle; a goal, aim, end, such as beauty which may move the world because it is loved
Thanatos	deep urge to pleasure at any cost, even self-destruction
Theorie des Romans, die	Lukács's major work, *The Theory of the Novel*
"Über allen Gipfeln"	Goethe poem: "Above the peaks" (Wandrers Nachtlied)
Urerlebnis	primordial experience, deepest experience
Veräußerung	alienation, sale of that which is properly one's own; sale of property
Verdinglichung	rendering something essentially unthinglike as if it were a thing, a fixed, finite object; literally "thingification," reification, alienation
Verfremdungseffekt	the alienation effect; utilized as a theatrical technique by Brecht
Vergegenständlichung	objectification, producing objects, culture, and identity through social labor process
Vorstellungen	images, ideas
Warenhaus	department store
Warte nur balde / ruhest du auch	last line of Goethe's "Wanderers Nightsong:" "just wait / soon you'll rest [in peace] too"

Weiblichkeitsbilder   depictions or images of femininity

Werden   becoming, come into being

Wesen   essence, being, reality

Zeitschrift für
  Sozialforschung   *Journal of Social Research* published by the Frankfurt
                             Institute of Social Research also while in New York
                             exile at Columbia University

zoon politikon   humanity as political animal, inter-connected beings
                             not disconnected beings

Bibliography

Adorno, Theodor W. *Jargon der Eigentlichkeit* (Frankfurt/M, Germany: Suhrkamp, 1970).

Alcoff, Linda and Elizabeth Potter (eds.) *Feminist Epistemologies* (New York: Routledge, 1993).

Allan, Norman R. Jr. *African-American Humanism* (Buffalo: Prometheus, 1991).

Anderson, Perry. *In the Tracks of Historical Materialism* (London: Verso, 1988).

———. *Considerations on Western Marxism* (London: Verso, 1987).

Apple, Michael. *Education and Power* (Boston: Ark, 1985).

———. *Ideology and Curriculum* (Boston: Routledge, 1985).

Apresyan, Z. *Freedom and the Artist* (Moscow: Progress, 1968).

Aptheker, Herbert. *Marxism and Alienation* (New York: Humanities Press, 1965).

Arato, Andrew and Paul Breines. *The Young Lukács and the Origins of Western Marxism* (New York: Seabury, 1979).

Augstein, Rudolf and Günter Grass. *DEUTSCHLAND, einig Vaterland?* (Göttingen, Germany: Steidl, 1990).

Axelos, Kostas. *Alienation, Praxis and Techne in the Thought of Karl Marx* (Austin: University of Texas Press, 1976).

Baker, Paul J. and Louis E. Anderson. *Social Problems: A Critical Thinking Approach* (Belmont, CA: Wadsworth, 1987).

Barrett, William. *Irrational Man* (Garden City, NY: Doubleday, 1962).

Batalov, E. *The Philosophy of Revolt* (Moscow: Progress, 1975).

Bauermann, Rolf and Hans-Jochen Rötscher. *Dialektik der Anpassung* (Frankfurt/M, Germany: Verlag Marxistische Blätter, 1972).

Baxandall, Lee (ed.) *Radical Perspectives in the Arts* (Baltimore: Penguin, 1973).

———— and Stefan Morawski. *Marx and Engels on Literature and Art* (Saint Louis: Telos Press, 1973).

Becker, Carol. "Surveying *The Aesthetic Dimension* at the Death of Postmodernism," in John Bokina and Timothy J. Lukes (eds.) *MARCUSE: From the New Left to the Next Left* (Lawrence: University of Kansas Press, 1994) pp. 170–86.

Benhabib, Seyla. *Critique, Norm, and Utopia* (New York: Columbia University Press, 1986).

Berger, Albert. *Ästhetik and Bildungsroman: Goethe's Wilhelm Meister's Lehrjahre* (Vienna: Wilhelm Braunmuller, 1977).

Berger, Peter and Thomas Luckmann. *The Social Construction of Reality* (Garden City, NY: Doubleday, 1966).

Best, Steven and Douglas Kellner. *Postmodern Theory* (New York: Guilford, 1991).

Beyer, Wilhelm Raimund. *Die Sünden der Frankfurter Schule* (East Berlin: Akademie Verlag, 1971).

Bhaskar, Roy. *Plato, etc.* (London: Verso, 1994).

————. *Dialectic: The Pulse of Freedom* (London: Verso, 1993).

————. *Reclaiming Reality* (London: Verso, 1989).

————. *The Possibility of Naturalism* (Brighton, Sussex, United Kingdom: Harvester Press, 1979).

————. *A Realist Theory of Science* (London: Verso, 1975).

Bloom, Allan. *The Closing of the American Mind* (New York: Simon & Schuster, 1987).

Bokina, John and Timothy J. Lukes (eds.) *MARCUSE: From the New Left to the Next Left* (Lawrence: University of Kansas Press, 1994).

Bollnow, Otto Friedrich. *Die Lebensphilosophie* (Berlin: Springer Verlag, 1958).

Bovenschen, Silvia and Marianne Schuller, "Weiblichkeitsbilder: Ein Gespräch mit Herbert Marcuse," in *Gespräche mit Herbert Marcuse* (Frankfurt/M, Germany: Suhrkamp, 1978, 1996).

Bowles, Samuel and Herbert Gintis. *Schooling in Capitalist America* (New York: Basic, 1976).

Boyer, Ernest L. et al. *Building Communities* (Washington, DC: American Association of Community and Junior Colleges, 1988).

Boyte, Harry C. "The Pragmatic Ends of Popular Politics," in Craig Calhoun (ed.) *Habermas and the Public Sphere* (Cambridge, MA: MIT Press, 1996).

———— and Nancy N. Kari. *Building America: The Democratic Promise of Public Work* (Philadelphia: Temple University Press, 1996).

Brady, Robert A. *The Spirit and Structure of German Fascism* (London: Victor Gollancz, 1937).

Breines, Paul. "From Guru to Spectre: Marcuse and the Implosion of the Movement," in Paul Breines (ed.) *Critical Interruptions* (New York: Herder and Herder, 1970).

————. "Marcuse and the New Left in America," in Jürgen Habermas (ed.) *Antworten auf Herbert Marcuse* (Frankfurt/M, Germany: Suhrkamp, 1968).

Brink, Renate. *Die Selbstverwirklichung des Menschen als pädagogische Aufgabe in den Frühschriften Nietzsches* (Düsseldorf, Germany: Michael Triltsch Verlag, 1972).

Bronfenbrenner, Urie. *Two Worlds of Childhood* (New York: Simon & Schuster, 1970).

Brosio, Richard A. *The Frankfurt School: An Analysis of the Contradictions and Crises of Liberal Capitalist Societies* (Muncie, IN: Ball State University, 1980).

Bulhof, Ilse N. *Wilhelm Dilthey; A Hermeneutic Approach to the Study of History and Culture* (The Hague: Martinus Nijhoff, 1980).

Chomsky, Noam et al. *The Cold War and the University* (New York: New Press, 1997).

Clark, Burton R. *The Open Door College: A Case Study* (New York: McGraw-Hill, 1960).

Collier, Andrew. *Critical Realism* (London: Verso, 1994).

Daniel, Lloyd. *Liberation Education: A Strategy for the 21st Century* (Kansas City, MO: New Democracy Press, 1995).

Davis, Angela Y. *Women, Race & Class* (New York: Vintage, 1983).

Decker, Peter and Karl Held. *Der Anschluß: Eine Abrechnung mit der neuen Nation und ihrem Nationalismus* (München, Germany: Resultate Verlag, 1990).

Demmerling, Christoph. *Sprache und Verdinglichung* (Frankfurt/M, Germany: Suhrkamp, 1994).

Demske, James M. *Sein, Mensch, und Tod, Das Todesproblem bei Martin Heidegger* (Freiburg, Germany: Karl Alber Verlag, 1963).

Devitis, Joseph Liberatore. "Marcuse on Education: Social Critique and Social Control," *Educational Theory*, Vol. 24, 1974.

————. "The Concept of Repression in the Social and Educational Thought of Erich Fromm and Herbert Marcuse" (University of Illinois at Urbana-Champaign, Ph.D dissertation, 1972).

Dickens, David R. and Andrea Fontana. *Postmodernism and Social Inquiry* (New York: Guilford, 1994).

Dilthey, Wilhelm. *Der Aufbau der geschichtlichen Welt in der Geisteswissenschaften* (Frankfurt/M, Germany: Suhrkamp, 1970).

Domhoff, G. William. *State Autonomy or Class Dominance?* (New York: Aldine de Gruyter, 1996).

————. *Who Rules America?* (Englewood Cliffs, NJ: Prentice-Hall, 1967).

Dougherty, Kevin J. *The Contradictory College* (Albany: State University of New York Press, 1994).

Douglas, George H. "Heidegger on the Education of Poets and Philosophers," *Educational Theory*, Vol. 22, No. 4, Fall 1972.

Dubiel, Helmut (ed.) *Kritik und Utopie im Werk von Herbert Marcuse* (Frankfurt/M, Germany: Institut für Sozialforschung, 1992).

Eisler, Riane. *The Chalice and the Blade* (San Francisco: Harper, 1988).

Ermarth, Michael. *Wilhelm Dilthey: The Critique of Historical Reason* (Chicago: University of Chicago Press, 1976).

Farber, Marvin. *The Search for an Alternative: Philosophical Perspectives of Subjectivism and Marxism* (Philadelphia: University of Pennsylvania Press, 1984).

————. *The Foundations of Phenomenology* (Albany: State University of New York Press, 1968).

————. *The Aims of Phenomenology* (New York: Harper, 1966).

Feenberg, Andrew. *Lukács, Marx and the Sources of Critical Theory* (Totowa, NJ: Rowman and Littlefield, 1981).

Findlay, J. N. *Hegel: A Re-examination* (New York: Collier, 1958).

Fink, Eugen. *Nietzsches Philosophie* (Stuttgart, Germany: W. Kohlhammer Verlag, 1968).

Fischer, Ernst. *The Necessity of Art* (Harmondsworth, Middlesex, England: Penguin, 1975).

Foley, Barbara. *Radical Representations* (Durham, NC: Duke University Press, 1993).

Foucault, Michel. *The History of Sexuality*, Vol. 1 (New York: Vintage, 1980).

Franklin, Mitchell. "On Hegel's Theory of Alienation and its Historic Force," *Revolutionary World*, No. 9, 1974.

————. "The Irony of the Beautiful Soul of Herbert Marcuse," *Telos*, No. 6, Fall 1970.

Fraser, Nancy. "What's Critical about Critical Theory," in Johanna Meehan (ed.) *Feminists Read Habermas* (New York: Routledge, 1996).

Freire, Paulo. *Pedagogy of the Oppressed* (New York: Continuum Publishing, 1993).

Fromm, Erich. *Marx's Concept of Man* (New York: Ungar, 1964).

Fry, John. *Marcuse—Dilemma and Liberation* (Uppsala, Sweden: Almquist and Wiksell, 1974).

Geogehagen, Vincent. *Reason and Eros: Social Theory of Herbert Marcuse* (London: Pluto Press, 1981).

Geyer-Ryan, Helga. "Das Paradox der Kunstautonomie: Ästhetik nach Marcuse" in Helmut Dubiel (ed.) *Kritik und Utopie im Werk von Herbert Marcuse* (Frankfurt/M, Germany: Institut für Sozialforschung, 1992) pp. 272–85.

Giesen, Bernhard. *Die Entdinglichung des Sozialen* (Frankfurt/M, Germany: Suhrkamp, 1991).

Giroux, Henry A. (ed.) *Postmodernism, Feminism, and Cultural Politics* (Albany: State University of New York Press, 1991).

Goldhagen, Daniel. *Hitler's Willing Executioners* (New York: Random, 1996).

Gray, Ronald. *Poems of Goethe* (London: Cambridge University Press, 1966).

Greene, Maxine. *Teacher as Stranger: Educational Philosophy for the Modern Age* (Belmont, CA: Wadsworth, 1973).

Guepin, J.-P. *The Tragic Paradox: Myth and Ritual in Greek Tragedy* (Amsterdam: Adolf M. Hakkert, 1968).

Habermas. Jürgen. "Eine Art Schadensabwicklung: Die apologetischen Tendenzen in der deutschen Zeitgeschichtsschreibung" *Die Zeit* 11. Juli 1986, reprinted in Ernst Reinhold Piper (ed.) *Historikerstreit* (München und Zürich: Piper Verlag, 1987) pp. 62–76.

————. *Theory of Communicative Action* (Boston: Beacon, 1984).

————. *Theorie des kommunikativen Handelns* (Frankfurt/M, Germany: Suhrkamp, 1981).

————. *Legitimation Crisis* (Boston: Beacon, 1973).

————. *Toward a Rational Society: Student Protest, Science and Politics* (Boston: Beacon, 1968).

————. *Knowledge and Human Interests* (Boston: Beacon, 1968).

————. (ed.) *Antworten auf Herbert Marcuse* (Frankfurt/M, Germany: Suhrkamp, 1965).

Harding, Sandra. "Rethinking Standpoint Epistemology: What Is 'Strong Objectivity'?" in Linda Alcoff and Elizabeth Potter (eds.) *Feminist Epistemologies* (New York: Routledge, 1993).

Harris, Leonard. *Philosophy Born of Struggle* (Dubuque, IA: Kendall-Hunt, 1983).

Hartsock, Nancy C. M. *Money, Sex and Power: Toward a Feminist Historical Materialism* (Boston: Northeastern University Press, 1983).

Harvard University Committee Report on the Objective of General Education in a Free Society, *General Education in a Free Society* (Cambridge, MA: Harvard University Press, 1945).

Haug, W. F. *Critique of Commodity Aesthetics: Appearance, Sexuality and Advertising in Capitalist Society* (Minneapolis: University of Minnesota Press, 1986).

Haynie, Aeron. "Imperialism and the Construction of Femininity in Mid-Victorian Fiction" (Gainesville: University of Florida, Ph.D. dissertation, 1994).

Hegel, G.W.F. *Phänomenologie des Geistes* (Hamburg, Germany: Felix Meiner Verlag, 1952).

Heidegger, Martin. *Vom Wesen des Grundes* (Frankfurt/M, Germany: Vittorio Klostermann, 1965).

————. *Being and Time* (New York: Harper, 1962).

————. *Kant and the Problem of Metaphysics* (Bloomington: Indiana University Press, 1962).

————. *Nietzsche*, Vol. 1 (Pfüllingen, Germany: Gunther Neske Verlag, 1961).

Heiseler, Heinrich von, Robert Steigerwald, and Josef Schleifstein (eds.) *Die "Frankfurter Schule" im Lichte des Marxismus* (Frankfurt/M, Germany: Verlag Marxistische Blätter, 1970).

Herideen, Penelope E. *Policy, Pedagogy, and Social Inequality: Community College Student Realities in Post-Industrial America* (Westport, CT: Bergin & Garvey, 1998).

Hildreth, Robert. *Building Worlds, Transforming Lives, Making History: A Guide to Public Achievement* (Minneapolis, MN: Center for Democracy and Citizenship, 1998).

Holz, Hans Heinz. *Utopie und Anarchismus: Zur Kritik der Kritischen Theorie Herbert Marcuses* (Köln, Germany: Pahl Rugenstein Verlag, 1968).

hooks, bell. *Reel to Real: Race, Sex and Class at the Movies* (New York: Routledge, 1996).

———. *Teaching to Transgress* (New York: Routledge, 1994).

Horkheimer, Max and Theodor W. Adorno, *Dialectic of Enlightenment* (New York: Herder and Herder, 1972a).

Horkheimer, Max. *Critical Theory, Selected Essays* (New York: Herder and Herder, 1972b).

Iggers, Georg G. *Geschichtswissenschaft im 20. Jahrhundert* (Göttingen, Germany: Vandenhoeck und Ruprecht, 1996).

———. *The German Conception of History* (Middletown, CT: Wesleyan University Press, 1983).

———. *New Directions in European Historiography* (Middletown, CT: Wesleyan University Press, 1975).

Israel, Jared and William Russell, "Herbert Marcuse and his Philosophy of Copout," *Progressive Labor Magazine*, Vol. 6, No. 5, October 1968.

Jameson, Fredric. *Postmodernism: Or, The Cultural Logic of Late Capitalism* (Durham, NC: Duke University Press, 1995).

Jansen, Peter-Erwin. *Befreiung denken—ein politischer Imperativ* (Offenbach, Germany: Verlag 2000, 1990).

Jansohn, Heinz. *Herbert Marcuse* (Bonn: Bouvier Verlag Herbert Grundmann, 1974).

Jay, Martin. *Marxism & Totality* (Berkeley: University of Califorinia Press, 1984).

———. "Anamnestic Totalization; Reflections on Marcuse's Theory of Remembrance," *Theory and Society*, Vol. 11, No. I, January 1982.

———. *The Dialectical Imagination* (Boston: Little, Brown, 1973).

Kahane, Howard. *Logic and Contemporary Rhetoric* (Belmont, CA: Wadsworth, 1988).

Karabel, Jerome. "Community Colleges and Social Stratification," *Harvard Educational Review*, Vol. 42, No. 4, November 1972.

Karre, Idalynn. *Busy, Noisy, and Powerfully Effective: Cooperative Learning in the Classroom* (n.p., 1993).

Kátz, Barry M. *Foreign Intelligence, Research and Analysis in the Office of Strategic Services 1942–1945* (Cambridge, MA: Harvard University Press, 1989).

———. *HERBERT MARCUSE: Art of Liberation* (London: Verso, 1982).

Kavanaugh, John Francis. "Whole and Part in Hegel, Marx, and Marcuse" (Washington University, St. Louis, Ph.D dissertation, 1973).

Kellner, Douglas (ed.) *Technology, War, and Fascism: The Unknown Marcuse* (New York: Routledge, 1998).

———. *Media Culture* (New York: Routledge, 1995).

———. "A Marcuse Renaissance?" in John Bokina and Timothy J. Lukes (eds.) *MARCUSE: From the New Left to the Next Left* (Lawrence: University of Kansas Press, 1994) pp. 245–67.

———. "Marcuse in the 1940s: Some New Textual Discoveries," in Helmut Dubiel (ed.) *Kritik und Utopie im Werk von Herbert Marcuse* (Frankfurt/M, Germany: Institut für Sozialforschung, 1992) pp. 301-311.

———. *Critical Theory, Marxism, and Modernity* (Cambridge and Baltimore: Polity Press and Johns Hopkins University Press, 1989).

———. *Herbert Marcuse and the Crisis of Marxism* (Berkeley: University of California Press, 1984).

———. "Introduction to Marcuse's 'On the Philosophical Foundation of the Concept of Labor in Economics,'" *Telos*, No. 16, Summer 1973.

Keyes, C. D. "Truth as Art: An Interpretation of Heidegger's *Sein und Zeit* (sec. 44) and *Der Ursprung des Kunstwerks*," in John Sallis (ed.) *Heidegger and the Path of Thinking* (Pittsburgh: Duquesne University Press, 1970).

Kisiel, Theodore. *The Genesis of Heidegger's Being and Time* (Berkeley: University of California Press, 1993).

Kliche, Dieter. "Kunst gegen Verdinglichung. Berührungspunkte im Gegensatz von Adorno und Lukács," in Burkhardt Linder und W. Martin Lüdke (eds.) *Materialien zur ästhetischen Theorie Th. W. Adornos Konstruktion der Moderne* (Frankfurt/M, Germany: Suhrkamp, 1980).

Kneller, George F. *Existentialism and Education* (New York: Wiley, 1966).

Koppe, Franz. "Durchsichtig als Situation und Traum der Menschheit: Grundzüge einer Kunstphilosophie im Ausgang von Herbert Marcuse," in Helmut Dubiel (ed.) *Kritik und Utopie im Werk von Herbert Marcuse* (Frankfurt/M, Germany: Institut für Sozialforschung, 1992) pp. 247–61.

Korf, Gertraud. *Ausbruch aus dem "Gehäuse der Hörigkeit"?—Kritik der Kulturtheorien Max Webers und Herbert Marcuses* (Frankfurt/M, Germany: Verlag Marxistische Blätter, 1971).

Kors, Alan Charles and Harvey A. Silverglate. *The Shadow University: The Betrayal of Liberty on America's Campuses* (New York: Free Press, 1998).

Korten, David C. *When Corporations Rule the World* (West Hartford, CT: Kumarian Press, 1996).

Kozol, Jonathan. *Savage Inequalities* (New York: Crown, 1991).

———. *Children of the Revolution* (New York: Dell, 1978).

———. *Free Schools* (New York: Bantam, 1972).

Kraushaar, Wolfgang (ed.) *Frankfurter Schule und Studentenbewegung* (Frankfurt/M, Germany: Rogner & Bernhard 2001, 1998).

Kulikova, I. and A. Ris (eds.) *Marxist-Leninist Aesthetics and Life* (Moscow: Progress, 1976).

Lang, Berel and Forest Williams (eds.) *Marxism and Art* (New York: McKay, 1972).

Lapoint, Francois H. and Claire C. Lapoint, "Herbert Marcuse and His Critics: A Bibliographic Essay," *International Studies in Philosophy*, Vol. 7, Fall 1975.

Lawler, James. "Marx as Market Socialist," in Bertell Ollman (ed.) *Market Socialism: The Debate Among Socialists* (New York: Routledge, 1998).

———. *The Existentialist Marxism of Jean-Paul Sartre* (Amsterdam: B. R. Gruner, 1976).

———. "Heidegger's Theory of Metaphysics and Dialectics," *Philosophy and Phenomenological Research*, Vol. 35, No. 3, March 1975.

Lawson, Tony. *Economics and Reality* (London: Routledge, 1997).

Lehrke, Wilfried. *"Kritische Bemerkungen zu den frühen philosophischen Auffassungen Herbert Marcuses,"* in Dieter Bergner (ed.) *Die philosophische Lehre von Karl Marx und ihre aktuelle Bedeutung* (East Berlin: VEB Deutscher Verlag der Wissenschaften, 1968).

Leiss, William. "Critical Theory and Its Future," *Political Theory*, Vol. 2, August 1974.

———. "Technological Rationality: Marcuse and His Critics" *Philosophy of the Social Sciences*, Vol. 2, March 1972.

Lerner, Gerda. *The Creation of Patriarchy* (New York: Oxford University Press, 1986).

Lifschitz, Mikhail. *The Philosophy of Art of Karl Marx* (London: Pluto Press, 1973).

——— (ed.) *Karl Marx und Friedrich Engels, Über Kunst und Literatur* (East Berlin: Verlag Bruno Henschel und Sohn, 1949).

Lipshires, Sidney. *Herbert Marcuse: From Marx to Freud and Beyond* (Cambridge, MA: Schenkman, 1974).

Lukács, Georg. *Die Seele and die Formen* (Neuwied, Germany: Luchterhand, 1971).

———. "Reification and the Consciousness of the Proletariat," in *History and Class Consciousness* (Cambridge, Mass: MIT Press, 1971).

———. *Theorie des Romans* (Neuwied, Germany: Luchterhand, 1965).

———. *Beiträge zur Geschichte der Ästhetik* (East Berlin: Aufbau Verlag, 1954).

———. *Existentialismus Oder Marxismus* (East Berlin: Aufbau Verlag, 1951).

Lukes, Timothy J. "Aesthetic Reduction of Technology," in John Bokina and Timothy J. Lukes (eds.) *MARCUSE: From the New Left to the Next Left* (Lawrence: University of Kansas Press, 1994) pp. 227–42.

―――. *The Flight into Inwardness* (Selinsgrove, PA: Susquehanna University Press, 1985).

Maakreel, Rudolf. *Dilthey: Philosopher of the Human Studies* (Princeton: Princeton University Press, 1975).

Macedo, Donaldo. *Literacies of Power* (Boulder: Westview, 1994).

Maier, Charles S. *The Unmasterable Past: History, Holocaust, and German National Identity* (Cambridge, MA: Harvard University Press, 1988).

Mandel, Ernst. *The Marxist Theory of Alienation* (New York: Pathfinder Press, 1973).

Mander, Jerry and Edward Goldsmith. *The Case Against the Global Economy* (San Francisco: Sierra Club, 1996).

Marcuse, Peter. "Marcuse and Real Existing Socialism: A Hindsight Look at *Soviet Marxism*," in John Bokina and Timothy J. Lukes (eds.) *MARCUSE: From the New Left to the Next Left* (Lawrence: University of Kansas Press, 1994) pp. 57–72.

―――. *Missing Marx: A Personal and Political Journal of a Year in East Germany, 1989–1990* (New York: Monthly Review Press, 1991).

Margolies, David N. *The Function of Literature* (New York: International Publishers, 1969).

Martin, F. David. "Heidegger's Being of Things and Aesthetic Education," *Journal of Aesthetic Education*, July 1974.

Martineau, Alain. *Herbert Marcuse's Utopia* (Montreal: Harvest House, 1986).

Marx, Karl. *Das Kapital* (Stuttgart, Germany: Alfred Kroener Verlag, 1965).

Mattick, Paul. *Critique of Marcuse* (London: Merlin Press, 1972).

McCarthy, Thomas. *The Critical Theory of Jürgen Habermas* (Cambridge, MA: MIT Press, 1982).

McMullen, R. *Art, Affluence and Alienation* (New York: Praeger, 1968).

McPeck, John. *Critical Thinking and Education* (New York: St. Martin's, 1981).

Meehan, Johanna (ed.) *Feminists Read Habermas* (New York: Routledge, 1995).

Menke, Christoph. "Schrecklich schön: Bemerkungen zu Marcuse und Koppe im Blick auf Bacon" in Helmut Dubiel (ed.) *Kritik und Utopie im Werk von Herbert Marcuse* (Frankfurt/M, Germany: Institut für Sozialforschung, 1992) pp. 262–71.

Mészáros, István. *Beyond Capital* (New York: Monthly Review Press, 1998).

————. *The Power of Ideology* (New York: New York University Press, 1989).

————. *Lukács' Concept of Dialectic* (London: Merlin Press, 1972).

————. *Marx's Theory of Alienation* (New York: Harper, 1970).

Morawski, Stefan. *Inquiries into the Fundamentals of Aesthetics* (Boston: MIT Press, 1974).

Morris, Van Cleve. *Existentialism in Education* (New York: Harper, 1966).

Neumann, Franz. *Behemoth: Struktur und Praxis des Nationalsozialismus 1933–1944* (Frankfurt/M, Germany: Fischer, 1988).

Neuner, Gerhardt. *On the Theory of Socialist General Education* (East Berlin: Verlag Volk und Wissen, 1973).

Nicholsen, Shierry Weber. "The Persistence of Passionate Subjectivity: Eros and Other in Marcuse, by Way of Adorno," in John Bokina and Timothy J. Lukes (eds.) *MARCUSE: From the New Left to the Next Left* (Lawrence: University of Kansas Press, 1994) pp. 149–69.

Nisbet, Arthur Lee. "A Comparative Analysis of Herbert Marcuse's and John Dewey's Conceptions of Freedom" (State University of New York at Buffalo, Ph.D. dissertation, 1974).

Norris, Christopher. *Uncritical Theory: Postmodernism, Intellectuals, and the Gulf War* (Amherst, MA: University of Massachusetts Press, 1992).

Nussbaum, Martha C. *Cultivating Humanity* (Cambridge, MA: Harvard University Press, 1997).

————. *The Therapy of Desire: Theory and Practice in Hellenistic Ethics* (Princeton: Princeton University Press, 1994).

————. "Allan Bloom's American Mind," *The New York Review of Books*, November 5, 1987.

Ollman, Bertell (ed.) *Market Socialism: The Debate Among Socialists* (New York: Routledge, 1998).

————. *Alienation* (Cambridge, London: Cambridge University Press, 1971).

Outhwaite, William. *Habermas: A Critical Introduction* (Stanford, CA: Stanford University Press, 1994).

Paetzold, Heinz. *Neomarxistische Ästhetik II: Adorno-Marcuse* (Düsseldorf, Germany: Schwann, 1974).

Parenti, Michael. *Blackshirts and Reds: Rational Fascism and the Overthrow of Communism* (San Francisco: City Lights Books, 1997).

————. *The Sword and the Dollar: Imperialism, Revolution and the Arms Race* (New York: St. Martin's, 1989).

————. *Democracy for the Few* (New York: St. Martin's, 1987).

————. *Inventing Reality* (New York: St. Martin's, 1986).

————. *Power and the Powerless* (New York: St. Martin's, 1978).

Piccone, Paul and Alexander Delfini. "Herbert Marcuse's Heideggerian Marxism," *Telos*, No. 6, Fall 1970.

Pincus, Fred L. "The False Promises of Community Colleges," *Harvard Educational Review*, Vol. 50, No. 3, August 1980.

————. "Tracking and the Community Colleges," *The Insurgent Sociologist*, Vol. 4, No. 3, Spring 1974.

Piper, Ernst Reinhard (ed.) *Historikerstreit* (München, Germany and Zürich, Switzerland: Piper Verlag, 1987).

Plekhanov, George. *Art and Society & Other Papers* (New York: Oriole Editions, 1974).

Progressive Labor Party, "Marcuse: Copout or Cop?" *Progressive Labor Magazine*, Vol. 6, No. 6, January 1969.

Rauch, Eberhard and Wolfgang Anzinger (eds.) *Wörterbuch Kritische Erziehung* (Starnberg, Germany: Raith Verlag, 1973).

Raulet, Gerard. "Die Form ist die Kunst: Kritische Überlegungen zur Ästhetik Marcuses" in Helmut Dubiel (ed.) *Kritik und Utopie im Werk von Herbert Marcuse* (Frankfurt/M, Germany: Institut für Sozialforschung, 1992) pp. 286–300.

Rawls, John. *A Theory of Justice* (Boston: Harvard University Press, 1971).

Read, Herbert. *Education Through Art* (New York: Pantheon, 1956).

Reitz, Charles. "Elements of EduAction: Critical Pedagogy and the Community College," *The Journal of Critical Pedagogy*, April 1998 (www.lib.wmc.edu/pub/jcp/issueI-2/reitz.html).

————. "Liberating *the Critical* in Critical Theory," *Researcher*, Vol. 11, No. 2, December 1996 (www.lib.wmc.edu/pub/researcher/issueXI-2/reitz.html).

————. "Racism, Capitalism and the Schools," *Urban Education*, Vol. 18, No. 4, January 1984.

————. "Imperialist Rivalry and Industrial Education," *The Insurgent Sociologist*, Vol. 6, No. 4, Spring 1976.

Rescher, Nicholas. *Dialectics: A Controversy-Oriented Approach to the Theory of Knowledge* (Albany: State University of New York Press, 1977).

Reynolds, David. *Democracy Unbound: Progressive Challenges to the Two Party System* (Boston: South End Press, 1997).

Riedel, Manfred (ed.) Wilhelm Dilthey, *Der Aufbau der geschichtlichen Welt in der Geisteswissenschaften* (Frankfurt/M, Germany: Suhrkamp, 1970).

Ringer, Fritz K. *The Decline of the German Mandarins: The German Academic Community, 1890–1933* (Cambridge, MA: Harvard University Press, 1969).

Ross, Ralph. "Art as Knowledge," *Sewanee Review*, Vol. 69, No. 4, Autumn 1961.

Rühle, Otto. *Karl Marx* (New York: New Home Library, 1943).

Said, Edward. *Culture and Imperialism* (New York: Knopf, 1993).

———. *Orientalism* (New York: Pantheon, 1978).

Schacht, Richard. *The Future of Alienation* (Urbana and Chicago: Illinois University Press, 1994).

———. *Alienation* (Garden City: Doubleday, 1971).

Scharfschwert, Jürgen. *Thomas Mann und der deutsche Bildungsroman* (Stuttgart, Germany: Kohlhammer, 1967).

Schiller, Friedrich. *On the Aesthetic Education of Man in a Series of Letters* (New York, Ungar, 1965).

Schoolman, Morton. *The Imaginary Witness: The Critical Theory of Herbert Marcuse* (New York: Free Press, 1980).

Senese, Guy with Ralph Page. *Simulation, Spectacle, and the Ironies of Education Reform* (Westport, CT: Bergin & Garvey, 1995).

Sessions, George (ed.) *Deep Ecology for the 21st Century* (Boston: Shambhala, 1995).

Shapiro, Gary. "Hegel's Dialectic of Artistic Meaning," *Journal of Aesthetics and Art Criticism*, Vol. 35, Fall 1976.

Shirer, William L. *The Rise and Fall of the Third Reich* (Greenwich, CT: Fawcett, 1960).

Simmel, Georg. *Philosophie des Geldes*, (München and Leipzig, Germany: Verlag von Duncker & Humboldt, 1922).

Simmons, Michael L. Jr. "Certainty, Harmony, and the Centering of Dewey's Aesthetics," *Philosophy of Education 1997* (Urbana, IL: Philosophy of Education Society, 1998).

———. "The Success of Bebop: Model and Cautionary Tale for the Theory and Practice of Multicultural Education," paper presented to the American Educational Studies Association annual meeting, Montreal 1996.

———. "On James Herndon's Aesthetic Ontology," *Educational Theory*, Vol, 26, No. 2, Spring 1976.

———. "Open Education and Social Criticism," in David Nyberg (ed.) *The Philosophy of Open Education* (London: Routledge and Kegan Paul, 1975).

Sklar, Holly. *Chaos or Community* (Boston: South End Press, 1995).

Solomon, Maynard (ed.) *Marxism and Art* (New York: Random, 1974).

Spate, Virginia. *Orphism: The Evolution of Non-figurative Painting in Paris 1910–1914* (Oxford: Clarendon Press, 1979).

Spivak, Gayatri. "Three Women's Texts and a Critique of Imperialism," *Critical Inquiry*, Vol. 12, 1985, pp. 243–61.

Steigerwald, Robert. "Wie Kritisch ist Herbert Marcuses 'Kritische Theorie,'" in Heinrich von Heiseler, Robert Steigerwald, and Josef Schleifstein (eds.) *Die "Frankfurter Schule" im Lichte des Marxismus* (Frankfurt/M, Germany: Verlag Marxistische Blätter, 1970).

———. "Dialektik and Klassenkampf bei Herbert Marcuse," *Deutsche Zeitschrift für Philosophie*, Vol. 17, March 1969.

———. *Marcuses Dritter Weg* (Köln, Germany: Pahl-Rugenstein Verlag, 1969).

Suchodolski, Bogdan. *Einführung in die marxistische Erziehungstheorie* (Köln, Germany: Pahl-Rugenstein Verlag, 1972).

Tesconi, Charles A. Jr. and Van Cleve Morris. *The Anti-Man Culture: Bureau-technocracy and the Schools* (Urbana: University of Illinois Press, 1972).

Torrance, John. *Estrangement, Alienation and Exploitation* (New York: Columbia University Press, 1977).

Van Doren, Mark. *Liberal Education* (Boston: Beacon, 1959).

Varner, Iris Ingrid. "The Educational Thought of Herbert Marcuse," (University of Oklahoma, Ph.D. dissertation, 1975).

Vedung, Evert. *Political Reasoning* (Beverly Hills, CA: Sage Publishing, 1982).

Weil, Simone. *Oppression and Liberty* (Amherst, MA: University of Massachusetts Press, 1973).

Weiss, Peter. *Äesthetik des Widerstands* (Frankfurt/M, Germany: Suhrkamp, 1975).

West, Cornel. *Race Matters* (Boston: Beacon, 1993).

Wiggershaus, Rolf. *Die Frankfurter Schule* (München, Germany: Deutscher Taschenbuch Verlag, 1988).

Woddis, Jack. *New Theories of Revolution: Frantz Fanon, Regis Debray, Herbert Marcuse* (New York: International Publishers, 1972).

Zis, Avner. *Foundations of Marxist Aesthetics* (Moscow: Progress, 1977).

Zwerling, L. Steven. *Second Best, The Crisis of the Community College* (New York: McGraw-Hill, 1976).

Name Index

Adorno, Theodor W., 7, 199
  all reification is a forgetting, 66
  critique of Heidegger and death, 120
  on form in art, 219
  surrenders cognitive competence to
    art (Habermas), 66
  Über allen Gipfeln, 219
Apollo, 129–30
Arato, Andrew, 29, 176
Ardebili, Morteza, 302n, 303n

Bahro, Rudolf, 3, 252–53
Barrett, William, 58, 110–11
Beckett, Samuel, 149
Benhabib, Seyla, 69
Bennett, William, 2, 190
Bloom, Allan, 2, 5–6, 190
Bollnow, Otto Friedrich, 185–86
Boyte, Harry C., 247–48
Brecht, Bertolt, 216–17, 235–36
Breines, Paul, 29, 176, 286n
Brodsky, David, 252–53, 257, 302–03nn
Bronfenbrenner, Urie, 159

Camus, Albert, 97
Cheney, Lynne, 190
Chomsky, Noam, 2

Davis, Angela, 15
Demmerling, Christoph,
  and Verdinglichung, 66
Demske, James M., 118n, 294n
Dilthey, Wilhelm, 7, 11–12, 28–31,
  42–46
  and aesthetics of history, 44
  as Prussian patriot, 43
  and educational philosophy, 43, 52
  and Geisteswissenschaften, 43, 49, 60,
    149
  and historicity, 45, 60
  and Lebensphilosophie, 44–46, 49,
    73, 186
Dionysus, 128–129
Douglass, Frederick, 254
D'Souza, Dinesh, 2
Dutschke, Rudi, 15

Ebert, Friedrich, 17
Eisler, Riane, 263

Fink, Eugen, 13
Franklin, Mitchell, 13, 69–71, 228
Freire, Paulo, 246–49
Freud, Sigmund, 6, 126, 128
  on high culture, 20

Subject Index